Sensory Penalities

EMERALD STUDIES IN CULTURE, CRIMINAL JUSTICE AND THE ARTS

Series Editors:

Yvonne Jewkes
University of Bath, UK

Travis Linnemann
Kansas State University, USA

Sarah Moore
University of Bath, UK

This series aims to take criminological inquiry in new and imaginative directions, by publishing books that represent all forms of criminal justice from an 'arts' or 'cultural' perspective, and that have something new to tell us about space, place and sensory experience as they relate to forms of justice. Building on emergent interest in the 'cultural', 'autoethnographic', 'emotional', 'visual', 'narrative' and 'sensory' in Criminology, books in the series will introduce readers to imaginative forms of inspiration that deepen our conceptual understanding of the lived experience of punishment and of the process of researching within the criminal justice system, as well as discussing the more well-rehearsed problems of cultural representations of justice.

Specifically, this series provides a platform for original research that explores the myriad ways in which architecture, design, aesthetics, hauntology, atmospheres, fine art, graffiti, visual broadcast media and many other 'cultural' perspectives are utilized as ways of seeing and understanding the enduring persistence of, and fascination with, the formal institutions of criminal justice and punishment.

Sensory Penalities: Exploring the Senses in Spaces of Punishment and Social Control

EDITED BY

KATE HERRITY
University of Cambridge, UK

BETHANY E. SCHMIDT
University of Cambridge, UK

AND

JASON WARR
De Montfort University, UK

emerald PUBLISHING

United Kingdom – North America – Japan – India – Malaysia – China

Emerald Publishing Limited
Emerald Publishing, Floor 5, Northspring, 21-23 Wellington Street, Leeds LS1 4DL.

First edition 2021

Selection and editorial matter © 2021 Kate Herrity, Bethany E. Schmidt, Jason Warr.
Individual chapters © their respective authors. Published under exclusive licence.

Reprints and permissions service
Contact: www.copyright.com

No part of this book may be reproduced, stored in a retrieval system, transmitted in any form or by any means electronic, mechanical, photocopying, recording or otherwise without either the prior written permission of the publisher or a licence permitting restricted copying issued in the UK by The Copyright Licensing Agency and in the USA by The Copyright Clearance Center. Any opinions expressed in the chapters are those of the authors. Whilst Emerald makes every effort to ensure the quality and accuracy of its content, Emerald makes no representation implied or otherwise, as to the chapters' suitability and application and disclaims any warranties, express or implied, to their use.

British Library Cataloguing in Publication Data
A catalogue record for this book is available from the British Library

ISBN: 978-1-83909-727-0 (Print)
ISBN: 978-1-83909-726-3 (Online)
ISBN: 978-1-83909-728-7 (Epub)
ISBN: 978-1-83909-729-4 (Paperback)

Printed and bound by CPI Group (UK) Ltd, Croydon, CR0 4YY

INVESTOR IN PEOPLE

Contents

About the Editors — vii

About the Authors — ix

Acknowledgements — xiii

Foreword
Alison Liebling — xv

Introduction: Welcome to the Sensorium
Kate Herrity, Bethany E. Schmidt and Jason Warr — xxi

Part I
Making Sense of the Sensory

Chapter 1   Hearing Order in Flesh and Blood: Sensemaking and Attunement in the Pub and the Prison
Kate Herrity — 3

Chapter 2   Fire! Fire! – The Prison Cell and the Thick Sensuality of Trappedness
Jason Warr — 19

Chapter 3   Sensing Supervision Through Stories and Songs
Jo Collinson Scott and Fergus McNeill — 35

Chapter 4   Touching Life, Death, and Dis/connection in a State Prison Infirmary
Daina Stanley — 53

Part II
Sensing the Field

Chapter 5   Sensing Transition: Exploring Prison Life in Post-Revolution Tunisia
Bethany E. Schmidt and Andrew M. Jefferson — 71

Chapter 6 Sensing Secrecy: Power, Violence and Its Concealment in Nicaraguan Prisons
Julienne Weegels 89

Chapter 7 The Embedded Researcher: Experiencing Life in a Probation Approved Premises
Carla Reeves 107

Chapter 8 Space, Surveillance, and Sound in Pre- and Post-Reform Prisons in the Dominican Republic
Jennifer Peirce 125

Part III
Subverting the Senses

Chapter 9 Sensing and Unease in Immigration Confinement: An Abolitionist's Perspective
Victoria Canning 143

Chapter 10 Rumbling Stomachs and Silent Crying: Mapping and Reflecting Emotion in the Sensory Landscape of the Courthouse
Lisa Flower 159

Part IV
Sensory Reflections

Chapter 11 Sensory Reflections on a Japanese Prison
Yvonne Jewkes and Alison Young 177

Chapter 12 The Everything Else
Amy B. Smoyer 195

Chapter 13 Ethiopian Notes
Ian O'Donnell 203

Chapter 14 The Street as an Affective Atmosphere
Alistair Fraser 217

Afterword: Sensing Carceral Worlds
Eamonn Carrabine 231

Index 239

About the Editors

Kate Herrity's doctoral research explored the significance of sound in a local men's prison using aural ethnography. She takes particular interest in researching at the edges both of criminology and epistemology, and curates www.sensorycriminology.com, a companion to this book. She is the Mellon-King's Cambridge Junior Research Fellow in Punishment (2020–2024).

Bethany E. Schmidt is a Lecturer in Penology at the Institute of Criminology's Prisons Research Centre at the University of Cambridge. Her main research interests lie at the intersection of democracy, citizenship, and punishment. She leads multiple international projects related to measuring the social, moral, and political climates of prisons.

Jason Warr is a Senior Lecturer in Criminology & Criminal Justice at De Montfort University. His research interests include prisons, punishment, criminological theory, sensory criminology, and the philosophy of science. His most recent book is *Forensic Psychologists: Prison, Power, and Vulnerability* (Emerald, 2020).

About the Authors

Victoria Canning is a Senior Lecturer in Criminology at the University of Bristol, Co-coordinator for the European Group for the Study of Deviance and Social Control, Associate Director at Border Criminologies at Oxford University, and Trustee at Statewatch. She is currently undertaking a British Academy project titled 'Unsilencing Sexualised Torture'.

Eamonn Carrabine is a Professor of Sociology at the University of Essex and the Editor-in-Chief of the *British Journal of Criminology*. He has published broadly in criminology and sociology and is currently researching a project on 'The Iconography of Punishment: From Renaissance to Modernity'.

Lisa Flower is a Lecturer and Researcher in Sociology and Criminology at Lund University. She has previously published a book – *Interactional Justice: The Role of Emotions in the Performance of Loyalty* – exploring the collective work involved in constructing criminal trials, and she is currently researching the impact of live blogs on open justice and legal professionals' work life.

Alistair Fraser is a Senior Lecturer in Criminology, and Director of the Scottish Centre for Crime and Justice Research, at the University of Glasgow. He is the author of *Urban Legends: Gang Identity in the Post-Industrial City* (OUP, 2015) and *Gangs & Crime: Critical Alternatives* (Sage, 2017).

Andrew M. Jefferson is a Senior Researcher at DIGNITY. His research focuses on prisons and prison reform in the Global South with a specific interest in countries undergoing transition and the relationship between confinement and subjectivity. Current research includes a project on legacies of detention in Myanmar (https://legacies-of-detention.org/).

Yvonne Jewkes is a Professor of Criminology at the University of Bath. She currently holds two ESRC research grants for projects on the rehabilitative prison and the persistence of the Victorian prison. Her main research interest is prison architecture and design, and she is a Founding Editor of the journal *Incarceration*.

Alison Liebling is a Professor of Criminology and Criminal Justice at the University of Cambridge and Director of the Institute of Criminology's Prisons Research Centre. Her books include *Prisons and Their Moral Performance*, *The*

Effects of Imprisonment, and *The Prison Officer*. She was awarded a Leverhulme Major Research Fellowship in 2020.

Fergus McNeill is a Professor of Criminology and Social Work at the University of Glasgow where he works in Sociology and in the Scottish Centre for Crime and Justice Research. His work explores institutions, cultures and practices of punishment, rehabilitation, and reintegration.

Ian O'Donnell is a Professor of Criminology at University College Dublin and an adjunct fellow of Linacre College, Oxford. His most recent books are *Justice, Mercy, and Caprice: Clemency and the Death Penalty in Ireland* (Oxford, 2017) and *Prisoners, Solitude, and Time* (Oxford, 2014).

Jennifer Peirce is a Doctoral Candidate in Criminal Justice (John Jay College and the Graduate Center, City University of New York) and a Pierre Elliott Trudeau Foundation Scholar. She works in research and policy with a focus on incarceration in Latin America, the Caribbean, the United States, and Canada.

Carla Reeves is an Acting Head of Department in Behavioural and Social Sciences, University of Huddersfield. Her research focuses on the lived experiences of, especially, people convicted of sex offences in criminal justice settings, as well as recently extending this to sexual age-play communities. She is particularly interested in the interplay between researcher and research.

Jo Collinson Scott is a Reader in Music at the University of the West of Scotland. She is currently Co-investigator on the ESRC-funded research project 'Distant Voices: Coming Home', exploring songwriting as/for/about 're'integration. Her main research focus is practice-led research in pop music, specifically focusing on exploring areas requiring urgent social change.

Amy B. Smoyer is an Associate Professor of Social Work at Southern Connecticut State University. Her programme of research examines women's lived experience of incarceration and the impact of this experience on health outcomes including HIV care and prevention, food justice, bladder health, housing stability, and psychosocial wellness (www.amysmoyer.com).

Daina Stanley is a Doctoral Candidate in Medical Anthropology at McMaster University. Her ethnographic research traces the end-of-life journeys of people in prison and the experiences of incarcerated peer caregivers. Her research is supported by the Wenner-Gren Foundation and the Social Sciences and Humanities Research Council of Canada.

Julienne Weegels is an Assistant Professor at the Centre for Latin American Research and Documentation (CEDLA), University of Amsterdam. She has conducted extensive research inside and around Nicaragua's prison system. Her research focuses on (former) prisoners' experiences of imprisonment and the state, violence, and the politics of (dis)order.

Alison Young is the Francine V. McNiff Professor of Criminology at the University of Melbourne. She is the author of *Street Art, Public City* (2014), *The Scene of Violence* (2010), and numerous articles on the intersection of law, crime, and culture. She is currently researching ghost criminology, crime scenes, and public memorials.

Acknowledgements

First, thank you to all of the contributors and to all we have encountered in the course of our research, whose generosity, trust and patience have lent so richly to our learning. It sometimes requires a staggering leap of faith to lend free reign to a project loosely defined, untried and innovative as it does to answer questions and queries the purpose of which is unclear. We would all be much poorer were it not for your courage and kindness.

Thank you to everyone who trusted us sufficiently to accompany us on this journey along the edges of what we think we know, and what we are accustomed to talking about. You have taught us many things about the academics and editors we would like to be. For this we are deeply grateful. This was an immensely enjoyable project which would have been otherwise were it not for each of you.

Thank you to Eamonn Carrabine for providing such a masterful Afterword and to Alison Liebling, not only for her powerfully moving Foreword but also for being a constructive ally in this project from its inception. Thanks also to Jules Willan, a top bird who is endlessly enthusiastic and encouraging. We also owe a debt of gratitude to our reviewers for their vigorous engagement with the initial proposal of this book. Our extended – if one-sided – conversations with you lent us focus and verve.

Lastly, a special acknowledgement from Kate …

And thanks to Bethany and Jason for their patience with me as I struggled to get things done in the wake of my Mum's unexpected death. My chapter here formed part of an ongoing discussion with her, begun in my thesis acknowledgements, which was painful to finish without her. These lessons in love and loss forge all of us too and have a place within these pages.

Foreword

Alison Liebling

> The air itself can become punitive ... can be an agent of slow violence. (Jewkes & Young, this volume)

Reading this creative and engaging book is like being taken on a sensory journey – through Tunisia, Nicaragua, the Dominican Republic, Denmark, Sweden, Japan, North America, Scotland and (less exotically for this reader, perhaps) England. We encounter many different kinds of prisons, asylum and deportation centres, a courtroom, a probation hostel and a city street, learning that violence, trauma and dignity 'exist and interact together' (Stanley, this volume) and that 'sensory knowledge has the capacity to unearth previously overlooked meanings and understandings' (Schmidt & Jefferson, this volume). This book is the first major publication in a broader project aimed at expanding our moral repertoires and theoretical resources via a more ready attunement to the senses in our work. The authors invite others to do what they are doing – sometimes for the first time – noticing the sounds, smells, feelings and sensations present in the places where we do fieldwork. The result is a remarkably moving, vivid and distinctly human collection of essays on experiences of the carceral.

The book's origins lie in friendships, intellectual encounters, a PhD or two, and a conference panel at the European Society of Criminology Conference in Sarajevo in 2018. This is the best kind of organically evolved rationale for bringing together a stimulating and well-organised collection of essays which, together, tell a new story, deeply. We inhabit and come to know our world, and the other people in it, in a body that feels, sees, hears, smells, can touch and be touched. Forgetting this, as Rowan Williams (2018) argues, is 'a philosophical mistake' (p. 67). Our bodies work intelligently, reading cues, interpreting tones and registering injustice (as I lightly argued in Liebling, 1999). The sensory and the moral work in tandem. What George Eliot calls 'the vibrations of fellow feeling' can help us to survive and grow (in prison, but also more broadly; see Liebling, 2020). Their absence or human vibrations of a different kind – 'tiny nervous blows that are truly the "ultimate unit of consciousness"' – can also create anguish, conflict and suffering' (Liebling, 2015; Raines, 2010, p. 186). That we 'vibrate', resonate and 'know bodily' (Williams, 2018) constitutes critical aspects of both our experience and our practical intelligence.

Each contribution in this volume has something significant and distinctive to offer. Herrity describes the fluctuating rhythms and sounds of prison life, the process of 'becoming sufficiently familiar with these rhythms to decipher

xvi Alison Liebling

and interpret them' and an exceptional officers' familiarity with 'the everyday tune that's normal for here', acquired through deep engagement over time (this volume). She shows how prisoners 'read the sound' of what is happening around them. Warr evokes the 'trappedness' and fear of being in a cell during a fire (or flood, or pandemic) – features of imprisonment we should not evade. 'Text ... flattens sensory experience', he argues, obscuring our understanding, limiting our dialogue and critique. We need 'vividness' to fully appreciate 'embodied captivity' (Warr, this volume).

In a beautiful series of passages by Stanley (truncated here), she describes her extensive encounter with a man who dies in a prison hospice:

> My initial encounter with Daniel in the prison yard would prove to be the first in an intense journey he would invite me to share, an expedition through the extremes of punishment in disciplinary segregation to the humanity enacted in prison hospice ... the *feel* of Daniel's life and death illuminating brutality and beauty, indignity and intimacy, in a contemporary prison medical unit ... what is framed as institutional care may take on the form of harm, thus illuminating 'repression and compassion [as] profoundly linked'. (Stanley, this volume)

Other chapters illustrate the value of 'moving with' our research participants across space and time (Weegels, this volume), within and beyond the prison, seeing how 'mind-body-and-environment' operate together, dynamically, almost rhythmically. The position of 'observant participator' helps to make more visible concealed dimensions of power in operation. Canning's account of 'being lost in the field' – emotionally and politically as well as geographically – is powerful and instructive as she describes personal encounters in Denmark's barely known 'triangle' of asylum, immigration and deportation centres.

An evocative chapter on a Japanese prison by Jewkes and Young raises the question of differences in our perceptions of, or susceptibility to, the atmospheric and affective dimensions of prisons. Reading it brought to my mind that remarkable scene in Rex Bloomstein's powerful (and deeply sensory) film, *KZ* (German shorthand for concentration camp) where a young schoolgirl faints. She is one of a party visiting Mauthausen in Austria as tourists. They are listening soberly to the deliberately brash young male tourist guide, shaven headed and dressed almost as an SS officer, describing the unimaginable details of the atrocities committed there. Her classmates are concerned and try to help. They more vaguely grasp the reasons for her collapse. Why her? Does she know something the others don't? Her body certainly does: it *caves in* to distress. The bleak and unavoidable message of humanity's cruelty to humanity is transmitted directly and starkly, via her body, outwards to all. She reappears later in the film, talking about the visit and what happened to her: 'I fainted ... I could imagine the suffering', she says. An older tour guide is destroyed by his work, and the memories evoked by it. He hears footsteps. He has bad dreams. He is 'obsessed by the place', possessed by it.

In their chapter, Jewkes and Young describe the 'visible and audible absence of the prisoners in most parts of the prison', explaining how

> absence-and-presence is evoked through a range of social, spatial and sensory practices which, in the case of the Japanese prison's atmosphere, reinforces an impression of human sequestration, withdrawal, reduction, diminishment and silencing.

What is not there (said, acknowledged) can haunt us as much as what is there. The absence of sound, if we notice it, can move us. In a discussion with Rex about *KZ*, which I found I had to watch again as I was reading this manuscript, we agreed that the austerity of his film technique is precisely what makes it so powerful. There is no music; there are no other effects; the scenes are direct, unvarnished, cruel. Until later, when the personal stories of the tour guides are introduced, and they become more human: their grandfathers may have committed war crimes. They wanted to make these atrocities imaginable. We talked about sound and the senses, about sparseness, absence and presence, whilst I was writing this foreword. Very few books make these kinds of conversations happen.

As well as getting to know the participants in each contribution viscerally, each chapter also carries glimpses of the personalities of its authors. I felt this most overtly when reading Ian O'Donnell's evocative and humble accounts of his encounters with local food, social rules and an iron roof in an Ethiopian prison (although a major disturbance in that prison after the fieldwork visits suggests that his description of its peacefulness may need revisiting). This intimacy with the authors is part of this book's appeal, but the real contribution is the way in which 'The Everything Else' (Smoyer, this volume) – sights, sounds, smells, sensations – normally omitted from research accounts, brings 'human syntax' to life.

This book constitutes an intellectual as well as methodological project, with much relevance beyond criminology. Even the references are more than usually, refreshingly, 'off' the beaten track'. The editors suggest that we are experiencing something of a 'sensory turn' in social research and theorising more generally, perhaps linked to the growing dissatisfactions of individualised conceptions of experience, and with inadequate forms of 'disembodied' knowledge, including concepts of freedom. Rowan Williams has captured this argument in his book, *Being Human*. Here he draws on (and simplifies) Iain McGilchrist's call for 'larger horizons':

> Iain McGilchrist's *The Master and his Emissary* offers an analysis of the history of Western culture in the last few centuries, based on the assumption that we are ... dangerously, misunderstanding the nature of our mental life in our current culture ... While it's clearly an oversimplification to think that the two hemispheres of the brain work in isolation ... the fact remains that the two hemispheres privilege certain kinds of thinking ... and mapping

of the world we're in. The left brain, which is generally the more analytic, pattern-making, problem-solving bit of the brain, is a crucial element in identifying what specific challenges face us and what specific responses are needed. It's reactive ... something that breaks down into smaller rather than expanding to larger patterns ... it's one of the things that makes us the competent agents we are, people who know how to do things with things ... The right brain, on the other hand, which is less associated with certain kinds of linguistic skills, builds larger models; it sees larger horizons, it makes connections that are not just argumentative or functional or practical. It scans the horizon, it risks putting phenomena together in what might be unexpected patterns ... the left brain is the 'emissary' in McGilchrist's terms: it does the routine work for the larger pattern-building enterprise of the right brain. When things are going badly wrong, the left brain ... takes over in ways that end up shrinking our horizons, reducing our capacity to formulate and understand the very problems that we're out to solve. (Williams, 2018, pp. 49–51)

McGilchrist argues that the left hemisphere has gradually 'colonised our experience', usurping the 'more contextual, humane, systemic, holistic but relatively tentative and inarticulate right hemisphere' (his book's argument is neatly summarised and discussed in Rowson & McGilhrist, 2013). Mary Midgley (2010) calls this 'left-hemisphere chauvinism'. The right hemisphere is, paradoxically, bigger and heavier in all social mammals; it sees more (Rowson & McGilhrist, 2013) and 'is truer to what is' (Rowson & McGilhrist, 2013, p. 28). To neglect it is culturally and morally stifling. Without it, things we human beings need (like mercy, touch, recognition) go missing in the world (Davis, 2017, p. 393; and all that has been written on the new penology, including Liebling, 2011). Midgley (2010) summarises McGilchrist's argument as follows:

> The encouragement of precise, categorical thinking at the expense of background vision and experience – an encouragement which, from Plato's time on, has flourished to such impressive effect in European thought – has now reached a point where it is seriously distorting both our lives and our thought. Our whole idea of what counts as scientific or professional has shifted towards literal precision – towards elevating quantity over quality and theory over experience – in a way that would have astonished even the 17th-century founders of modern science.

This is becoming a somewhat familiar critique, at least in some circles (George Eliot, my great guide, shares this 'refusal to adopt the quantitative view of human anguish', 2015, p. 299). I am very much on the side of integrated attention and thinking in our research lives, as well as in the world more generally: the kind of 'deep human regard' or 'ministry of presence' that ex-prison chaplain, David Beedon (2020), describes so powerfully in his work with imprisonment for public protection (IPP) prisoners. His account of 'somatic wisdom', or bodily sensations, in his own research is deeply insightful. Distressing interviews can also be, at one level, 'beautiful encounters' (p. 151) if we manage to connect, respond and even, for a moment, collude, or build, 'affective solidarity' (Collinson Scott & McNeill, this volume). Insight requires affective nuance, depth, perspective and engagement. Parts belong to a whole. Human beings must use all of their senses in order to make sense of, and navigate their way in, the universe.

We could stretch this argument further. Human beings must also use the senses to live morally or to work competently and compassionately in criminal justice professions (for examples of the opposite of these, see Reeves, this volume, and Flower, this volume). Zenon Bankowski (2013) argued that teaching lawyers artistic methods of movement (effectively, dance) developed their moral sensitivity (see Bankowski & Del Mar, 2013). Movement 'brings us down to earth', 'shows us that we are vulnerable beings', that our bodies are 'weak and finite'. 'The text' (here, the law) is never enough: imagination is required in any particular application of a rule, as everyday experience teaches us. Respect for persons, for example, when we negotiate space with someone else's space is, like so much of our moral life, 'embodied':

> Ethics and ideologies are inscribed on and through bodies. Ethical virtue will depend upon bodily dispositions. How can an act be charitable when it is done stiffly with an angry face? (Bankowski, 2013, paraphrasing Detmold, 1984)

The methodological and political are intertwined in the way we pay, or fail to pay, attention:

> Attention is a form of discernment; seeing what people are saying when they are hurt, seeing conditions of injustice … It is a way of 'reading others'. (Bankowski, 2013, p. 17, drawing on Simone Weil)

Time and patience are required (*attendre* to wait for, or expect) in order to read the world. Thought about this way, attention is an 'antidote to force' (Rozelle Stone & Davis, 2018). It is, almost, reverence.

As someone who has always 'thought with my body', who has advocated the use of emotions as data and who supports the development and practice of 'intelligent intuition', as well as deep human regard, I was already well disposed to this sensory project. Reading this book took me further. It helps us build a larger and more nuanced picture of what it is to live, struggle or die, in spaces of punishment and social control. It adds significantly to our collective struggle to engage, observe and know.

The overall project, to which this book belongs, includes a blog (*Sensory Criminology*) which makes it a living mission. I am delighted to recommend it, and I hope that it represents the signalling of a 'sensory revolution' in social and criminological research.

References

Bankowski, Z. (2013). The space to see: Law and the ethical imagination. In Z. Bankowski & M. Del Mar (Eds.), *The moral imagination and the legal life: Beyond text in legal education* (pp. 11–32). Surrey: Ashgate.

Bankowski, Z., Del Mar, M. & Maharg, P. (eds.) (2013). *The Arts and the Legal Academy: Beyond Text in Legal Education*. Abingdon: Routledge.

Beedon, D. (2020). *Hope deferred, humanity diminished: An ethnographic enquiry into the improvement of pastoral care offered to those serving an indeterminate sentence of imprisonment for public protection*. Unpublished Ph.D. thesis, Birmingham University.

Davis, P. (2017). *The transferred life of George Eliot*. Oxford: Oxford University Press.

Detmold, M.J. (1984). *The Unity of Law and Morality*. London: Routledge.

Eliot, G. (2015). 'Janet's repentance'. In T. A. Noble & J. Billington (Eds.), *Scenes of clerical life* (first published 1858). Oxford: Oxford World Classics.

Liebling, A. (1999). Doing prison research: Breaking the silence? *Theoretical Criminology*, *3*(2), 147–173.

Liebling, A. (2011). Perrie lecture: The cost to prison legitimacy of cuts. *Prison Service Journal*, *198*, 3–11.

Liebling, A. (2015). Appreciative inquiry, generative theory, and the 'failed state' prison. In J. Miller & W. Palacios (Eds.), *Advances in criminological theory* (pp. 251–270). Atlantic City, NJ: Routledge.

Liebling, A. (2020). Finding George Eliot in Prison: Reflections on its moral life. *George Eliot Review*, *51*, 80–88.

McGilchrist, I. (2010). *The master and his emissary: The divided brain and the making of the Western world*. New Haven, CT: Yale University Press.

Midgley, M. (2010). Review of the master and his emissary: The divided brain and the making of the Western world by Iain McGilchrist. *The Guardian Books*, January 2, 2010. Retrieved from www.guardian.co.uk/books/2010/jan/02/1 91

Raines, M. A. (2010). 'The utmost intricacies of the soul's pathways': The significance of syntax in George Eliot's Felix Holt. In D. L. Birch & M. Llewellyn (Eds.), *Conflict and difference in nineteenth-century literature* (pp. 186–200). Basingstoke: Palgrave Macmillan.

Rowson, J., & McGilchrist, I. (2013). *Divided brain, divided world: Why the best part of us struggles to be heard*. London: RSA.

Rozelle Stone, A. R., & Davis, B. P. (2018). *Simone Weil*. Stanford Encyclopedia of Philosophy. Stanford, CA: Stanford University.

Williams, R. (2018). *Being human: Bodies, minds, persons*. London: SPCK.

Introduction: Welcome to the Sensorium

Kate Herrity, Bethany E. Schmidt and Jason Warr

The aim of this book is to invigorate a conversation about the role of sensory experience in the production of knowledge. Despite its resolute interdisciplinarity, criminology has lagged behind other areas of the social sciences in taking the 'sensory' seriously as both a source of knowledge production and means of empirical investigation. Our sister disciplines, however, have embraced the instructive potentials of foregrounding the sensory in recent decades (see Cox, Irving, & Wright, 2016; Howes & Classen, 2014; Pink, 2015). It is not a nascent conversation, nor methodology, but one that has both heritage and legitimacy. Anthropology, in particular, has a well-established history of including an examination of sensory experience in ethnographic practice. Whilst ethnography has enjoyed a renaissance in criminology in recent years, this has not been accompanied by greater engagement with the potential of sensory experience as a source of insight. We contend that turning the criminological imagination (Young, 2011) towards those experiences – which occur beyond the criminological gaze – opens up both old and new realms of inquiry.

We wish to return to those first-order epistemological questions: How do we know? What is it that we are knowing? Serres (2008) argues that we are sensorial creatures who inhabit a world in which we are bombarded with sensory data. Researchers, as human beings, cannot divorce themselves from the sensescapes – physical spaces which impose and evince sensory experience (see Field, 2005) – they occupy and navigate. Nor can they evade the ways interpretation of that sensory data fundamentally shape our understanding of those spaces and of the meaning they hold for participants. We know the world first, not a priori; not from some system of logical reasoning but through our sensory interactions with the environment and with others (Serres, 2008; see also Gibson, 1966). This is where our first questions originate. Yet this understanding is often subjugated, by predominantly Western and andocentric forms of scientific idealism, which impose a visual reading of 'accepted' scientific methods (Classen, 1997). Rosenfeld (2011), discussing the historical importance of concepts of voice, the ear, and common sense (the mechanism by which it was thought we could regulate the morass of raw sensory input we are subject to), makes a similar point when she argues that this fundamentally Aristotelian (2012) perspective was, until recently, forgotten or subsumed by other traditions of science. Further, as Grosz (1993, p. 187) argues, the 'crisis of reason' – or fixation on rationality – has privileged the purely conceptual or mental over the corporeal:

it is a consequence of the inability of Western knowledges to conceive their own processes of (material) production, processes that simultaneously rely on and disavow the role of the body.

What does excavating beneath these layered assumptions of understanding to return to our first principles mean for criminological inquiry?

Foregrounding the sensory, by thinking about sounds, smells, taste, and touch, and utilising these sources of information as a mechanism for understanding, presents a new way of exploring phenomena which has long been the focus for criminological inquiry. This heightens awareness to a range of facets of experience – of crime, of punishment, of victimisation, of state power, of harm, of control – that we have not accounted for in our classical and foundational texts. The way that people physically and sensorially experience the realities with which we are concerned, and what such embodied experiences mean for those people, we believe, presents a significant gap in the literature. This represents an opportunity for us to explore anew, to revisit, to re-examine our assumptions about the criminological world. It also allows us to widen the scope of our investigations of phenomena, settings, and events; an opportunity to expand our collective criminological imagination.

The Background to this Collection

This book began life as a panel at the 2018 European Society of Criminology annual conference in Sarajevo. Inspired by the ethnographic work of Kate Herrity into the affects and meaning of sounds in prison (Herrity, 2015, 2019), the editors convened a panel entitled 'The Sensual Prison'. Our purpose was to explore wider sensory experiences of prison life and what such a focus could tell us about sociological and criminological thinking. In tandem, we wanted to expand beyond our Western-centric sensibilities into less represented sensory landscapes. All three of us are qualitative prison researchers, which has shaped the focus of this edited volume. This book's contributing authors and much of our attention remain anchored in sites of confinement and in the global north. However, we have aimed to reach across fields, global divides, and methodological practices. We hope this collection serves as a starting point, and with an invitation perhaps, for an answering volume that further explores the sensory in other contexts. The conference panel began a conversation amongst some of the contributors, particularly Fergus McNeill to whom we owe credit for this book's title, about the sensory nature of prisons, processes of social control, and how penality can be encoded into the senses evinced within spaces of punishment and other sites and forms of surveillance. From that conversation emerged the idea of *Sensory Penalities*.

The title itself is a respectful nod to Pat Carlen's (2008) seminal edited collection *Imaginary Penalities*. Various sociological and criminological thinkers sought to understand how overarching ideological, rhetorical, symbolic, and political conceptions of penal policy become constructed in the minds of those responsible for the operation of punitive edifices and thus embodied in penal governance. Likewise, the aim of this book is to refocus attention from our ocular-centric way of thinking, to capture the fuller contexts in which these ideologically, symbolically, socially, and politically informed structures of governance are embodied, manifested, and experienced. We aim to utilise the 'sensory' as a theoretical and analytical mechanism for our understanding and investigation of such edifices and practices. By so doing, we move closer to the way the world *is* experienced, not as discrete packages of information but as a constant deluge of lived-working-body and sensory input which we sift and prioritise to make manageable (Hockey & Allen-Collinson, 2009).

The use of this concept also echoes Garland and Young's (1983) *The Power to Punish*. Like them, we believe that in order to truly understand the construction, intent, purpose, practice, and experience of structures of penal governance, we must move beyond the traditional penological canon to find what lies beneath. Only then can we understand both their composition and impact. We also share their explicit emphasis on the sociological as well as their contention that to elevate one aspect of the expansive apparatus of punishment to the exclusion of others is to risk distorting analysis and to obscure the complex relationships between different parts of the penal whole. They eloquently argue that:

> The very contestability of social science suggests that its objects of knowledge are not simple reflections of naturally occurring events, but that social science creates its own objects by a process of theoretical and ... practical relevances and reflections. (Garland & Young, 1983, p. 2)

These conceptions provide our theoretical anchor. *Sensory Penalities*, therefore, has three interlocking themes. First, that the political, symbolic, and ideological are not only inherent to places and processes of punishment and social control but are encoded in the sensorial outputs and transmissions occurring within those places and processes. Second, that places and processes of punishment and social control are experienced sensorially by those subject to them, those who work within them, and those who are researching them. And third, that in order to fully understand and theorise about penalities, and places and processes of punishment and social control, we need to account for these multifarious sensorial experiences and their effects. We contend that penality has an inherent sensory component. Sound provides a means of demonstrating this. Listening to the prison environment makes certain operations of power audible, and therefore symbolic violence more tangible, in ways which are eluded by a preoccupation with what can be seen. Hearing the jangle of an officer's keys, for example, communicates different symbolic information to different parties within a penal setting. It can communicate the deprivations of liberty and autonomy, and of powerlessness, to a person locked within the prison, yet act as a comforting reminder of authority, and presence of colleagues and 'back-up', to a prison officer. The symbolic power of carcerality and indeed the wider facets of penality are here embedded within the aural experience of a jangling key chain (Herrity, 2019; see also Jewkes & Young, this volume, on the absence and presence of sound in prisons). Thus, by honing our sociological attention to the 'mundane, everyday sensory experience' (Rhys-Taylor, 2013, p. 394), we are able to move towards a more robust scholarship that operates within a greater 'democracy of the senses' (Berendt, 1992, p. 28; Rhys-Taylor, 2013, p. 394).

The extension of sensorial inquiry into the criminological sphere is informed and inspired by an established body of literature on the anthropology of the senses. According to Pink (2009, p. 15), this work is characterised by three main issues: it explores the question of the relationship between sensory perception and culture, it engages with questions concerning the status of vision and its relationship to the other senses, and it demands a form of reflexivity that goes beyond the interrogation of how culture is 'written' to examine the sites of embodied knowing. Low (2012, p. 271) further notes that 'sensory studies argue for the senses as social, revealing important insights pertaining to selfhood, culture, and social relations'. He also points out how sensory exploration confronts power imbalances in who produces knowledge and which knowledge is privileged:

> A common point of departure in sensory writings deals with the imperialism of sight and/or the Western pentad sensory model that is critiqued as both Eurocentric and limiting in exploring various other sensory orders across different societies and sensory hierarchies. (Low, 2018, n.p.)

These fundamental themes – power, representation, identity, social relations, culture, knowledge hierarchies – neatly map on to the intentions of *Sensory Penalities*, as well as other more recent movements in our discipline, like southern and global criminology (Carrington, Hogg, Scott, & Sozzo, 2018; Travers, 2017) and attention to criminological decolonisation (Blagg & Anthony, 2019; Moosavi, 2019). Our aim is to disrupt epistemological assumptions about how criminological knowledge is produced, to consider the implications which arise from this for how we understand processes and practices of research, and to examine how different modalities of sensory engagement (beyond the visual) interact with the way people experience, and make sense of, their environments (Pink, 2009, p. 16).

Sensing and Sensemaking

We recognise that the inclusion of the sensory into our research and analysis can represent a leap of the criminological and sociological imagination. In the development of this book, the editors faced difficulties in communicating the relevance, importance, and practice of including the sensory in accounts of the field. Part of the problem here, as highlighted by Cox et al. (2016) and Howes and Classen (2014), is that our language and disciplines have been constructed through very particular conceptions of the world in which the sensory has been relegated to an amorphous, intangible, and unmeasurable realm. But we do not experience the world singularly. Our impressions of the environments we inhabit are constructed from a panoply of senses that arrive, not discreetly packaged but all of a sudden and altogether (Butler, 2015;

Hockey & Allen-Collinson, 2009). This fits ill with a 'scientific' tradition that has attempted to divide, describe, analyse, classify – and, crucially, observe – the physical and social word into discernible and distinguishable packets of information. Difficulty and hesitance in attempting to decipher what we mean by 'instinct' in the field offers a prime example.

Efforts to render this aspect of 'knowing' more tangible amplify this point. 'Instinct' as a process of situated response and adaptation in the context of research lies somewhere between feeling – detached and differentiated from emotion, the interpretation of physical sensation – and 'sensemaking' – the act of making sense, incorporating both the situated nature of knowledge and its relation to bodily experience (de Rond, Holeman, & Howard-Grenville, 2019). Yet we hesitate to explicitly refer to this facet of knowledge because it is too indistinct, too imprecise, and too 'touchy feely' (see Paterson, 2009). This reluctance highlights two interconnected problems. First, the largely objectivist ontology and positivistic echoes of our discipline's past have imposed a lasting legacy on what is 'legitimate' scientific discussion. Instinct, with its relation to feelings, and sensemaking, is too 'soft' and vague to chime with this 'objectified' view. The second relates to the tangible and intangible nature of sensory data which informs our interactions with, and interpretations of, our environments (Mason & Davies, 2009). A link between the senses and instinct has been acknowledged as long ago as mid-nineteenth century (Bain, 1864). Whilst Bain explicitly focuses on the functions of mind and physiology, he notes that instinct and reflex are principally bodily reactions to sensory stimuli. What we think of, or refer to, as instinct is often the unconscious, or 'common sense' (Rosenfeld, 2011), processing of sensory data. Yet even in such an interdisciplinary field as ours, where old ontologies and epistemologies have been subjected to sustained critical revision since the 1970s, such discussions and inclusions invite hesitation. Why?

We are unused to utilising the language necessary for thorough sensory analysis and, as Carpenter and McLuhan (1960) note, lack the vocabulary for doing so. Our sensory experience is constructed from both discrete and overlapping sensory modalities (Kooley, 2002), which are frequently collapsed into a singular understanding, or interpretation, of our world. If we consider rain – interaction with rain involves touch, smell, sight, hearing, temperature, etc. – yet we reduce this into a singular message about the weather conditions. Criminology has neither been used to discussing these facets of experience in a way that 'sounds' suitably scientific nor assimilating this into our wider understanding of our discipline. One example of that is the initial hostile response that colleagues (two of whom are featured in this volume) received from reviewers over a paper which explored the notion of 'sensing prison environments' (Martin, Jefferson, & Bandyopadhyay, 2014). The reviews seemed to impose an intangibility to the discussion of 'sensing', which belied the rigorous empiricism that underpinned the work. Though rarely documented in formal ways, researchers often rely upon, and trust, their instincts in the field: we 'know' when something does not feel right and we can 'sense' a shift in mood or atmosphere. Liebling et al. (under review) describe how instinct played an imperative role in their team ethnography and their interaction with the field, which speaks to Cox's (2018, p. 225; see also Merleau-Ponty, 2012) assertion that sensory perception requires a process of active, intentional interpretation:

> Practiced intuition, grounded in expertise, played an important role in our research. Whilst social scientific methods provided a scaffold, judgement, feeling and instinct guided us through each decision, or each day. It is not always possible to distinguish between 'practical consciousness' (built up experiential knowledge) and good instincts, but a capacity to read a situation and know what it calls for, drawing on a wide range of information beyond 'scholarship', is essential … We know much of what we know (for example, in a prison, that a riot is brewing, that violence is in the air, or that someone is upset) non-cognitively. Paying attention to the moods and sensitivities of those around us, the unspoken sub-text, required keeping the pathway to our intuitions or gut instincts unblocked. Being both receptive *and* questioning and checking our readings against those of others in the team, produced better readings of complex situations than being certain, or slavishly following all the methodological rules.

Neglecting to acknowledge instincts, or be open to the senses, is born from an apprehension to incorporate the sensory in the manner in which we engage with the world and an insensitivity to our collective epistemological history. Embodied cognition, or the recognition of the body as a knowledge source, reflects 'the longstanding Cartesian mind-body dualism in Western culture that privileges thought over the supposedly separate and lower functions of the body' (Cox, 2018, p. 223). But, we do not think separately from the state of our body. What do we miss or overlook when we dismiss, ignore, or deny the senses? How do our researcher bodies perceive sensory stimuli related to pain, punishment, or deprivation? And how do the bodies of those inhabiting spaces of confinement or social control experience these environments? These questions are critical for considering how the sensory interacts with penality.

This brings us to reflexivity and positionality. Falling into observational description and the pitfalls of colonial anthropology, rather than applying robust critical analysis, are hazards in sensorially-informed criminological research when employing a Western-centric ocular lens. Having to look beyond surface-level explanations and descriptions of places and processes of punishment and social control, to how they are experienced and what that means for subjected individuals forces us deeper into analysis. It also demands a new or more attuned reflexivity. Customarily we do not account for our existence as physical entities when we research the places we do. However, we recognise that taking into account our positionality, and considering its impact on our research assumptions and the effect that may have on those with whom we conduct research, is an essential element of conducting qualitative research (Hopkins, 2007). We need to consider too what our sensory positionality is and the effects of that on our research (Pink,

Introduction: Welcome to the Sensorium xxvii

2015). For example, in Imai's (2010) ethnographic study conducted in the alleyways of Tokyo, she notes that whilst sharing food, the smells of the cooking and the taste of the food evoked very different sensations and memories for her than it did those with whom she was sharing the experience (see also O'Donnell, this volume). Their sensory experience was enshrouded in the particulars of their nostalgia and the two became combined to produce distinctly different experiences. However, it took some practice for her to begin to negotiate her own sensory positionality in such a way that it did not temper the experience of her respondents nor cloud her interpretation of their experiences. If we are to include the sensory in the exploration of the criminological, then we need to become much more practised in this process. This is especially true if we are to investigate the sensescapes of places and processes of punishment and social control where compounded vulnerabilities exist and are maintained.

A further point is raised by Imai's (2010) work: the relationship between sensory experience and memory. Herrity (2019) notes a collapse of time and traversing of space in the evocation of memory, which both amplifies and informs sensorial experience (see also Low, 2015). This requires us to move beyond a superficial understanding of subjective positionality in the interpretation of the sensory (like the variant understanding of the jangling key chain mentioned above) to a need to consider the role and interplay of prior history, memory, recall, and the sensorial present (Sparkes, 2009). In this regard, we cannot divorce our sensory experience from our memory, nor memory from our experience of the sensory (Seremetakis, 1994). Nevertheless, all those engaged in smelling a rose would accept that they are indeed smelling the same thing. Here we see an overlapping of seemingly competing ontologies, but ones that perhaps can be reconciled (Jackson, 2004), to some degree, by considering both these realist and constructivist positions. The traditional hard and fast disjunctions between these two positions or epistemologies are blurred by the consideration of, amongst other foci, the sensory (Cupchik, 2001). This has particular pertinence in the realm of penality. In Canning's chapter (this volume), she highlights how prior histories (of hers and her participants) and trauma of conflict shape the experiences of people held in an immigration detention centre that borders lands utilised for military exercises. The constructed and the real here overlap and inform one another. However, not only does that history fundamentally shape individual experience of immigration detention but also how past trauma is reawakened and re-experienced in the present each time they are subjected to the sounds of shells and mortar. That they are subjected to such re-awakenings tells us yet something else about the nature of the sensory and how it is utilised in places of punishment.

It is a contention of this book that sensory penalities – and more broadly a sensory criminology – take us beyond the phenomenological. Though the individuals present in that sensorial moment are experiencing the moment differently, they are all situated in the same space: the same feels, smells, sounds, tastes, and sights exist and are emitted in the same ways but are interpreted and perceived differently. A prison, for instance, communicates particular forms of penality through its sensory signifiers, but the interpretation of those experiences is as potentially varied as those who inhabit and work in those spaces. As Sykes (1958) notes, there are as many prisons as there are prisoners. However, if we are to have a sensory criminology, we must accommodate both of these convergent and divergent realities in order to account for the experience of penality and carceral life.

This phenomenological 'problem' is not a new one (Giorgi, 2006). The distinct challenges with phenomenology have been recounted in depth elsewhere (see Farber, 2017; Noë, 2007) and are beyond the scope of this Introduction. What we contend here is that a focus on the sensory can allow us to avoid some of the more pernicious ontological traps associated with phenomenological approaches. A focus on the sensory, as with a focus on the symbolic, invites a bridging between subjective and common experience. In this regard, we arrive at meaning, and interpret our realities, through social intersubjective processes (Prus, 1996). Attending to sensory aspects of social experience facilitates an explicit connection between the subjectivity and commonality of experience, traversing these boundaries to arrive at shared meaning and understanding. This is specifically important as part of the qualitative research process. Taking into account one's own sensory positionality, not just in design and analysis but in the field, makes a virtue of sensory subjectivity. Whilst it may not be transcended, it can be made explicit as a source of social learning. Sensory experience can be utilised as a means of inviting comparison with research participants – what am I hearing, what are you hearing, what am I smelling, this means X to me what does it mean for you? This enables the researcher to explore the means by which those sensory experiences acquire a social meaning. This turns positionality into a research tool and focuses us on the intersubjectivity of sensory experience as a means of uncovering both the subjective and shared experience of a particular sensescape. For instance, in the chapter by Schmidt and Jefferson (this volume), the overwhelming sensorium of extreme overcrowded conditions in a Tunisian prison could be elucidated only through the shared experience and intersubjective comparison that it allowed. What we see here is that sensory criminology, and a sensory epistemology more broadly, not only has the potential to collapse the distance between the subjectivities of individuals but also the now, as well as the pasts of those individuals.

A 'Sensory Turn' in Criminology?

Despite recognition that prisons 'are peculiar places from a sensory perspective, managing to deny and deprive while, sometimes simultaneously, overloading the senses' (Jewkes, 2014, p. 389), these sensorial accounts have not been well documented, or explored in depth, and even less so with other forms of social control or sites of confinement. The exception has been in the significant growth and interest in visual criminology, born out of cultural criminology, which situates crime and crime control in the context of cultural dynamics. Over a decade ago, Hayward (2009, p. 12) looked at 'mediascapes' and called for 'a new methodological orientation towards the visual that is capable of encompassing meaning, affect, situation, symbolic power and efficiency, and spectacle in the same "frame"'. Not long after, Carrabine (2012, p. 463) advocated for criminology 'to rethink its relations with the ascendant power of spectacle', in part because of the limitations of, and ethical questions around, visual representations of harm and crime. In more recent writings, visual criminologists have begun to consider the expansion of sensory engagement in sociological research by giving 'primacy to the embodied, haptic, sonic, spatial, temporal, visceral – modes of phenomenological immersion and immediacy' with accompanying 'methods that are in tune with the social world' (Brown & Carrabine, 2019, pp. 202–203).

Criminological scholarship related to the senses is now beginning to flourish, as researchers are attuning themselves to the sensorial features of detention, deprivation, control, and power, by incorporating new (or refined) methodological and theoretical approaches: Russell and Rae (2019) use 'earwitnessing' to explore how audible accounts of confinement shed light on the temporal and spatial aspects of carceral experiences; Cooper, Cook, and Bilby (2018) examine residents' sensory perceptions of neighbourhood brothels; Hemsworth (2016) considers the atmospheric, haptic, and emotive potential of sound in prisons; Millie (2019) investigates yarn bombing as 'a crime of the senses'; and Seal and O'Neill's *Imaginative Criminology* (2019) brings forms of sensory ethnography to the study of places of crime, justice, and punishment, to highlight a few. 'Sensory criminology' is starting to be mainstreamed with the help of McClanahan and South (2020, p. 3), who have provided a convincing argument for 'heightened criminological attention to the non-visual senses' and how these 'might uncover new sites and modes of knowledge and a more richly affective criminology'. It is on the heels of these pioneers that we present *Sensory Penalties*, a volume we hope will advance our thinking and understanding of how the sensory intersects with various forms of state and social control.

We have intentionally selected contributors who have an ethnographic sensibility. That is, researchers who have spent long periods of immersive presence in their respective fields. We sought to include authors of varying backgrounds, experience, and sites of research in order to maximise quality, range, and diversity. We encouraged contributions to sensorially provoke and evoke and creatively portray research and reflections that have typically been marginalised or left behind in fieldwork notes. We deliberately prohibited the use of visuals in the book, as an attempt to urge authors to find a 'language' and way of communicating that effectually described and represented their work and encounters. This is not, and has not, been a simple nor easy task. As noted above, the ontological and epistemological foundations of our discipline have, to some degree, militated against this process. Many of us have had to challenge and overcome not only our disciplinary training but also the limitations of the 'scientific' language we have been inculcated into using. Forging a path towards a new sensory epistemology in criminology has led to a degree of academic discomfort. A necessary discomfort and one that will hopefully reap rewards for those who come next – those who will help ground a sensory criminology into our shared criminological imagination.

As a new area of study within criminology, we believe it is necessary to frame our research in relevant and applicable ways that will be accessible to readers. Therefore, we have organised this book into four sections, each with a thematic focus, but all with a blend of methodological, empirical, and reflective components. In the first section, *Making Sense of the Sensory*, the authors consider and

xxx Kate Herrity et al.

contemplate creative (or less traditional) methodologies, including forms of data collection and interpretation, and engagement with participants and the field. In Kate Herrity's opening chapter, she explores the processes and practices of social control and order and how these are interwoven with the rhythms of life in the pub and the prison. The sensory experiences of these seemingly disparate spaces of pleasure and punishment, she argues, offer a means of understanding the maintenance of and disruption to orderly life. Jason Warr then presents a visceral account of how the concept of 'civic death' is encoded within the sensorial experience of being locked in a prison cell during a fire. He writes that the experience of enclosure, of trappedness, is a sensorial one in which the symbolic components of penality are communicated to the incarcerated. Next, Jo Collinson Scott and Fergus McNeill showcase their use of two novel methods for exploring and representing criminal justice imposed forms of supervision of people within the community. Framed with debates about 'imaginary penalties' and 'counter-visual criminology', they recount what an engagement between criminology, creative writing, and music can offer both academic and public understandings of supervision as a relatively invisible and inaudible form of punishment. Daina Stanley concludes this section by taking us to a maximum-security prison infirmary in the United States where her ethnographic work followed the journeys of imprisoned men at the end of life, and the prisoners who care for them. She critically reflects on her bodily engagement within this unique space, with a specific emphasis on how the role of her hands and touch intersected with the carceral 'deathscape'.

The second section focuses on empirical research experiences and findings, as they relate to *Sensing the Field*. Bethany Schmidt and Andrew Jefferson explore prison life in post-revolution Tunisia where stark, overcrowded conditions are juxtaposed with a reform agenda oriented towards the arts and creativity. They contemplate the contradictory tendency of prisons to be over- and under-stimulating, sensorially vibrant and sensorially oppressive. In Julienne Weegels' chapter, she argues that the management of (public) secrets is central to understanding the sensory qualities of the power that the hybrid Nicaraguan penal regime exerts. In particular, she notes how this regime is (re)produced precisely through an imposed and partial muting of the senses – the rendering unspeakable, un-seeable, and un-heard of the violence that is deployed to keep it in place. Carla Reeves' contribution expands the penality sphere by describing the research she carried out in a transitional housing unit for those on probation who were recently released from prison. She details how becoming embedded within the physicality of the research site allowed her to feel some of the same impacts of the constraints of the architecture and interpersonal power relations on her sense of being that the residents also experienced. In the last chapter of this section, Jennifer Peirce describes her study of pre- and post-reform prisons in the Dominican Republic, which highlights the distinct sensory manifestations between old and new spaces. She pays particular attention to the spatial, corporeal, and aural differences between the two prison designs and what this tells us about everyday order, power, and surveillance.

The third section, *Subverting the Senses*, challenges conventional notions of data and data collection by disrupting the sensory order and forms of sensemaking in and out of the field. Victoria Canning's chapter explores the role of activism in ethnography by focussing on the production of a confinement continuum through three key spaces in Denmark: an asylum centre, a deportation centre, and a closed immigration detention centre. In grappling with the contrast between seeking sanctuary and safety, and the limits of everyday freedom, this chapter addresses her own sensory unease in the very existence of such spaces. The last chapter in this section, from Lisa Flower, takes us into a Swedish courtroom. She demonstrates how the emotional landscape of the courthouse can be mapped out by paying attention to the sensual experiences that are shaped by the law's overarching emotional regime aimed at triumphing the absence of emotional involvement in judicial processes.

The final section, *Sensory Reflections*, is comprised of reflective pieces that explore the researcher's embodied and personal accounts of 'sensing' whilst in the field. Yvonne Jewkes and Alison Young present a sensorially attuned narrative located within a Japanese corrections facility. Their chapter draws out the many aesthetic and atmospheric similarities that Kyoto Prison shares with other prisons, whilst highlighting other aspects of its regime, operation, and daily life that are quite distinct from those found elsewhere. Amy Smoyer then shares 'the everything else' – a series of vignettes extracted from fieldwork notes that reflect the tensions between activist and researcher, the formal and informal, and the raw encounters experienced *in situ*. Ian O'Donnell's contribution relies exclusively on primary data generated by his eyes, ears, nose, mouth, and skin with a view to providing a thick description of a previously unexamined carceral world in Ethiopia. He argues that sensory experiences can be building blocks for shared understandings. Finally, Alistair Fraser explores 'the street' as an affective atmosphere. He contends that the street represents some of the most vital components of the criminological imagination – a site of danger and protection, crime and culture, art and politics – though has largely been represented as an inert backdrop. He aims to refocus the criminological gaze to the street itself; exploring the unique intersections of bodies and buildings, codes and regulations, movement and staticity, that together create a unique atmospheric dynamic.

This book is not designed to be an ethnographic 'how-to' in terms of researching places of punishment or processes of social control, though in charting sensory experiences whilst doing research we go some way to reducing the gap between textbook accounts and the reality of navigating 'the field'. There have been a number of recent texts focussing on this aspect of criminological research, most significantly Drake, Earle, and Sloan's (2015) *The Palgrave Handbook of Prison Ethnography*. Nor is this book designed to be a how-to-do sensory ethnography, as Pink's (2015) *Doing Sensory Ethnography* is a comprehensive dive into practice. This book is also not merely a reflective account of the immersive, embodied, and sensory experience of researchers in the field of prison studies. Rather, the collection is designed to offer an accessible entryway into exploring how penality is encoded in differing facets of sensory experience, what it means for knowledge production in penality more generally, and to take sensory data seriously. We want readers to come away from this book with an understanding of how paying attention to sensory modalities, or categories (Pink, 2015), can help us to explore the rather hidden and strange world of prisons, punishment, processes of control, and the concepts and ideologies on which they are built.

References

Aristotle. (2012). *De anima (on the soul)*. (Edited by M. Schiffman). Indianapolis, IN: Hackett Publishing Company.
Bain, A. (1864). *The senses and the intellect* (2nd ed.). London: Longman, Green, Longman, Roberts, and Green.
Berendt, J. E. (1992). *The third ear: On listening to the world*. New York, NY: Henry Holt.
Blagg, H., & Anthony, T. (2019). *Decolonising criminology: Imagining justice in a postcolonial world*. Basingstoke: Palgrave Macmillan.
Brown, M., & Carrabine, E. (2019). The critical foundations of visual criminology: The state, crisis, and the sensory. *Critical Criminology*, 27, 191–205.
Butler, J. (2015). *Senses of the subject*. New York, NY: Fordham University Press.
Carlen, P. (2008). Imaginary penalities and risk-crazed governance. In P. Carlen (Ed.), *Imaginary penalities* (pp. 1–25). Cullumpton: Willan Publishing.
Carpenter, E., & McLuhan, M. (1960). Acoustic space. In E. Carpenter & M. McLuhan (Eds.), *Explorations in communication: An anthology* (pp. 65–70). Boston, MA: Beacon Press.
Carrabine, E. (2012). Just images: Aesthetics, ethics and visual criminology. *British Journal of Criminology*, 52, 463–489.
Carrington, K., Hogg, R., Scott, J., & Sozzo, M. (Eds.). (2018). *The Palgrave handbook of criminology and the global south*. Cham: Palgrave Macmillan.
Classen, C. (1997). Engendering perceptions: Gender ideologies and sensory hierarchies in western history. *Body and Society*, 3(2), 1–19.
Cooper, E., Cook, I. R., & Bilby, C. (2018). Sex work, sensory urbanism and visual criminology: Exploring the role of the senses in shaping residential perceptions of brothels in Blackpool. *International Journal of Urban and Regional Research*, 42(3), 373–389.
Cox, A. M. (2018). Embodied knowledge and sensory information: Theoretical roots and inspirations. *Library Trends*, 66(3), 223–238.
Cox, R., Irving, A., & Wright, C. (2016). Introduction: The sense of the senses. In R. Cox, A. Irving, & C. Wright (Eds.), *Beyond text? Critical practices and sensory anthropology*. Manchester: Manchester University Press.
Cupchik, G. (2001). Constructivist realism: An ontology that encompasses positivist and constructivist approaches to the social sciences. *FQS: Forum Qualitative Social Research*, 2(1), Article 7.
de Rond, M., Holeman, I., & Howard-Grenville, J. (2019). Sensemaking from the body: An enactive ethnography of rowing the Amazon. *Academy of Management Journal*. doi:10.5465/amj.2017.1417
Drake, D. H., Earle, R., & Sloan, J. (Eds.). (2015). *The Palgrave handbook of prison ethnography*. Basingstoke: Palgrave Macmillan.
Farber, M. (2017). *The foundation of phenomenology; Edmund Husserl and the quest for a rigorous science of philosophy*. New York, NY: Routledge.
Field, S. (2005). Places sensed, senses placed: Toward a sensuous epistemology of environments. In D. Howes (Ed.), *Empire of the senses: The sensual cultural reader* (pp. 179–191). Oxford: Berg Publishers.
Garland, D., & Young, P. (1983). Towards a social analysis of penality. In D. Garland & P. Young (Eds.), *The power to punish: Contemporary penality and social analysis* (pp. 1–36). London: Heinemann Educational Books.

Gibson, J. J. (1966). *The senses considered as perceptual systems*. Boston, MA: Houghton Mifflin.
Giorgi, A. (2006). Difficulties encountered in the application of the phenomenological method in the social sciences. *Analise Psicologica, 3*(XXIV), 353–361.
Grosz, E. (1993). Bodies and Knowledges: Feminism and the Crisis of Reason. In, L. Alcoff and E. Potter (Eds.), *Feminist Epistemologies* (pp. 187–216). London: Routledge.
Hayward, K. (2009). Visual criminology: Cultural criminology-style. *Criminal Justice Matters, 78*(1), 12–14.
Hemsworth, K. (2016). 'Feeling the range': Emotional geographies of sound in prisons. *Emotion, Space and Society, 20*, 90–97.
Herrity, K. (2015). *Prison sound ecology: A research design*. Unpublished MSc dissertation, University of Oxford, Oxford.
Herrity, K. (2019). *Rhythms and routines: Sounding order in a local men's prison through aural ethnography*. Unpublished Ph.D. thesis, University of Leicester, Leicester.
Hockey, J., & Allen-Collinson, J. (2009). The sensorium at work: The sensory phenomenology of the working body. *The Sociological Review, 57*(2), 217–239.
Hopkins, P. E. (2007). Positionalities and knowledge: Negotiating ethics in practice. *An International E-Journal for Critical Geographies, 6*(3), 386–394.
Howes, D., & Classen, C. (2014). *Ways of sensing: Understanding the senses in society*. London: Routledge.
Imai, H. (2010). Sensing Tokyo's alleyways: Everyday life and sensory encounters in the alleyways of a city in transition. In D. Kalekin-Fishman & K. E. Y. Low (Eds.), *Everyday life in Asia: Social perspectives on the senses* (pp. 63–84). Farnham: Ashgate.
Jackson, P. T. (2004). Bridging the gap: Toward a realist-constructivist dialogue. *International Studies Review, 6*(2), 337–341.
Jewkes, Y. (2014). An introduction to 'Doing Prison Research Differently'. *Qualitative Inquiry, 20*(4), 387–391.
Keeley, B. L. (2002). Making sense of the senses: Individuating modalities in humans and other animals. *The Journal of Philosophy, 99*(1), 5–28.
Liebling, A., Schmidt, B. E., Beyens, K., Boone, M., Johnsen, B., Kox, M., Rokkan, T., & Vanhouche, A. S. (under review). Doing team ethnography in a transnational prison.
Low, K. E. Y. (2012). The social life of the senses: Charting directions. *Sociology Compass, 6*(3), 271–282.
Low, K. E. Y. (2015). The sensuous city: Sensory methodologies in urban ethnographic research. *Ethnography, 16*(3), 295–312.
Low, K. E. Y. (2018). Anthropology of the senses. *Oxford Bibliographies*. doi:10.1093/OBO/9780199766567-0192
Martin, L., Jefferson, A. M., & Bandyopadhyay, M. (2014). Sensing prison climates. *Focaal, 68*, 3–17.
Mason, J., & Davies, K. (2009). Coming to our senses? A critical approach to sensory methodology. *Qualitative Research, 9*(5), 587–603.
Merleau-Ponty, M. (2012). *Phenomenology of Perception*. London: Routledge.
McClanahan, B., & South, N. (2020). 'All knowledge begins with the senses': Towards a sensory criminology. *British Journal of Criminology, 60*, 3–23.
Millie, A. (2019). Crimes of the senses: Yarn bombing and aesthetic criminology. *British Journal of Criminology, 59*, 1269–1287.
Moosavi, L. (2019). A friendly critique of 'Asian criminology' and 'Southern criminology'. *British Journal of Criminology, 59*, 257–275.
Noë, A. (2007). The critique of pure phenomenology. *Phenomenology and the Cognitive Sciences, 6*(1–2), 231–245.
Paterson, M. (2009). Haptic geographies: Ethnography, haptic knowledges and sensuous dispositions. *Progress in Human Geography, 33*(6), 766–788.
Pink, S. (2009). *Doing sensory ethnography* (1st ed.). London: Sage Publications Ltd.

Pink, S. (2015). *Doing sensory ethnography* (2nd ed.). London: Sage Publications Ltd.
Prus, R. C. (1996). *Symbolic interaction and ethnographic research: Intersubjectivity and human lived experience*. Albany, NY: State University of New York Press.
Rhys-Taylor, A. (2013). The essences of multiculture: A sensory explorations of an inner-city street market. *Identities, 20*(4), 393–406.
Rosenfeld, S. (2011). On being heard: A case for paying attention to the historical ear. *The American Historical Review, 116*(2), 316–334.
Russell, E. K., & Rae, M. (2019). Indefinite stuckness: Listening in a time of hyper-incarceration and border entrapment. *Punishment & Society, 22*(3), 281–301. https://doi.org/10.1177/1462474519886546
Seal, L., & O'Neill, M. (2019). *Imaginative criminology: Of spaces past, present and future*. Bristol: Bristol University Press.
Seremetakis, C. N. (1994). The memory of the senses, part 1: Marks of the transitory. In C. N. Seremetakis (Ed.), *The senses still: Perception and memory as material culture in modernity* (pp. 1–18). Chicago, IL: University of Chicago Press.
Serres, M. (2008). *The five senses: A philosophy of mingled bodies*. (M. Sankley & P. Cowley, Trans.). London: Continuum International Publishing Group.
Sparkes, A. C. (2009). Ethnography and the senses: Challenges and possibilities. *Qualitative Research in Sport and Exercise, 1*(1), 21–35.
Sykes, G. M. (1958). *The society of captives: A study of a maximum security prison*. Princeton, NJ: Princeton University Press.
Travers, M. (2017). The idea of a southern criminology. *International Journal of Comparative and Applied Criminal Justice, 43*(1), 1–12.
Young, J. (2011). *Criminological imagination*. Cambridge: Polity Press.

Part I

Making Sense of the Sensory

Chapter 1

Hearing Order in Flesh and Blood: Sensemaking and Attunement in the Pub and the Prison

Kate Herrity

Processes and practices of social control and the order with which it is bound are woven into the rhythms of daily life in the pub and the prison. Exploring the sensory experiences of these seemingly disparate spaces of pleasure and punishment offers a means of understanding the maintenance of and disruption to orderly life. In the prison context, 'order' is defined as 'the degree to which the prison environment is structured, stable, predictable and acceptable' (Liebling & Arnold, 2004, p. 291). Orderly conduct in the liminal spaces of the night-time economy can be understood in similar terms, as the means by which predictable rhythms are (informally) maintained and re-established by those who occupy these spaces. I reflect on extensive experience working in pubs and bars and conducting research and volunteering in prisons as a means of sensitising the reader to the role of the sensory in understanding the fluctuating rhythms and processes of social organisation in the prison environment. 'Sensing' these spaces, I argue, is a process consisting of incremental stages of familiarity and proficiency. These stages can broadly be understood as sensemaking; acclimating and adapting to particular rules and rhythms of behaviour which have meaning in particular social contexts, and of attunement; becoming sufficiently familiar with these rhythms to decipher and interpret them. A sensory exploration of the management of social life within these spaces has utility for understanding order and its maintenance as well as social experience more broadly within places of punishment and social control.

I draw on organisational theory to construct a framework in which to capture something of the flesh and blood sociology Wacquant (2015) exhorts us to strive for:

> The reality and potency of carnal know how, the visceral, bottom up grasp of the social world – in the double sense of intellectual

understanding and dexterous handling – that we acquire by acting in and upon it. (p. 3)

My considerable experience in bar work provides a means of exploring the sensory, reflecting its sedimented nature, as Wacquant explains (2015), our interpretation of the sensorium which surrounds us is: 'cultivated and deployed over time through our engagement with the world, and … gradually deposited in our body as a layered product of our varied individual and collective histories' (p. 4). I begin by introducing the work and research backgrounds which inform this treatment of sensory knowledge and provide the means of illustrating the role of sensory experience in social life. I then reflect on the utility of particular qualities of sound as a tool in social research. I draw parallels between the sensory experience of pub environments and those of the prison as a means of exploring the research process as well as demonstrating the important distinction and relationship between sensemaking and attunement. I conclude by reflecting on what this tells us about the potential instructive value of more closely attending to, as well as accounting for, the sensory in social research in penal spaces and those of social control.

The Pub and the Prison

I first encountered the prison soundscape on a work-training visit to HMP Wandsworth as a library assistant. Deciphering what I was hearing as I stood in the central control point, listening to the swirling soundscape, and why it was significant, took a number of years of visits, volunteer work and research in prisons, as well as reflection on the broader context of experience I was drawing on; practices learned years previously when gauging the social climate in pubs and bars. I began working in these environments in 1995 at 18, in a variety of roles and as a manager and licensee between 1999 and 2003 in a local late-night bar. I have continued sporadically 'practising politics' working in the bar-trade (Joel, 1973). The finer points of bar work, as well as competence in performing of it, was a delicate social process. Practical tasks and working closely with others are relatively straightforward skills in this context. Sensemaking in this most particular of social spaces – deciphering shared social meanings – proved a more complex and delicate art. That this process of sensemaking was inextricably bound with sensory information and experience is implicit in the term but rendered explicit by retrospective examination (Weick, 1995). Building a methodology to explore the prison soundscape prompted additional exploration of the role of the sensory in mechanisms of making sense of social spaces. My doctoral research centred on an aural ethnography of a local men's prison where I spent nearly eight months exploring the role of sound in prison social life. At HMP Midtown, sound was a site of symbolic violence, barometer and mediator of the social climate and fundamental to temporal and spatial aspects of incarceration (Herrity, 2019).

Focussing on sound to explore prison life offered a means of harnessing its properties in the pursuit of understanding dimensions often overlooked or ill-defined. David Toop (2010) refers to sound as the 'temporal sense', emphasising the extent to which sound traverses boundaries of time and space, extending 'beyond touch and out of sight' (p. xv). This representation of sound echoes work in a diverse array of fields including literary criticism and philosophy, in which sound is understood as bridging multiple aspects of experience and imagination; social and personal, the past, present and future (e.g. Eliot, 1933; Ihde, 2007). Given the focus here is on the social utility of sound and its potential for enriching research, sound may be more accurately understood as auditory aspects of social experience. The decision for largely not referring to it in this way is both practical and aesthetic. Emphasising sound above other aspects of sensory experience is in no way an attempt to subvert or substitute one hierarchy of the senses (our current tendency to privilege the visual) for another. While I concentrate on sound, I do so with an implicit understanding that we do not sense our world in discrete sensory packages of information, but rather in a continual flood of stimuli which forms the stuff of our relations with other beings, our environments and ourselves (Ingold, 2000). Sound has particular pertinence for understanding places of punishment, in which inhabitants' sensory experience is in many ways prescribed by the constraints of circumstance and environment. In this respect, places of confinement can be thought of as pronounced acoustic communities; a group of people within a soundscape – comprised of both sounds and those who make and listen to them – for whom it has particular importance and meaning (Truax, 2001).

Prisons, of course, have little in common with pubs, the latter being places credited with a frequent over-abundance of sensory pleasure in contrast to the relative dearth of sensory stimuli – at least of the pleasant and enjoyable variety – which characterise the penal environment (Wener, 2012). The pub is a place in which usual social divisions may be partially suspended along with the complexities of power relations and restrictive systems of censure which sustain them. In contrast the prison is self-evidently a collection of spaces in which power is starkly apparent and brutally reinforced both within and beyond its walls. My purpose in drawing on sensory experience within these disparate spaces is not to suggest the two are immediately comparable but rather to explore similarities in the process of making sense of them. In so doing, I endeavour to explore the sensory within social practices of sensemaking and attunement and illustrate the distinction between sensemaking and attunement as a means of navigating and 'conducting' these spaces. Teasing out distinctions between sensemaking and attunement serve to demonstrate the role they play in honing the 'craft' of ethnographic practice to broaden our understanding of a fundamental aspect of penality and social control: order.

Making Sense of Sensemaking in the Pub

While in a pub waiting for my company to arrive, I took my place at the bar and reflected on the processes of interpreting the environment I was engaged in as I sat there:

> I take a seat at the bar. I know how a lone woman at a bar stool can be interpreted – but these are my spaces. I am at home here.

> Huddled male bodies gather around, nursing warm pints and sharing work-weary reflections. The smell of brick dust and excessive, lingering fabric conditioner released by the rustle of shell-suit fabric; the scent of a someone-at-home, signalling relative stability, safety. I contrast that with the memory of individuals who spent a great deal of time in pubs I worked in. The smell of bedsits – or their more modern and palatable, studio equivalent; cooking oil, stale fag smoke, neglect and simmering rage. Cranky in booze, volatile and bruised. Too many hours spent alone. I smell and listen to my surrounds and the chorus of individuals and groups who comprise it, measuring my spaces in delicately negotiated inches. I feel and listen to learn the environment, drawing on my intimate acquaintance with these processes to gauge the social climate, familiarising myself with the rhythms of the general hubbub as I settle in my seat, and into the social space in which it sits.

Making sense of social spaces in order to navigate their meaning can be understood as a process of sensemaking, albeit one in which the position of the sensemaker is relegated to one of relative passivity (Weick, 1995). Sensemaking is a rationalising process which guides identity and behaviour within a particular context and refers to the set of practices undertaken – largely unconsciously – to guide action and identity performance within places where people gather (Weick, Sutcliffe, & Obstfeld, 2005). While this process has much traction within organisational theory, these ideas are not restricted to private spaces, nor circumstances in which all present are gathered for a particular purpose in the sense suggested by 'organisations'. As has been documented within the medical profession, the sensory is interwoven with practices of sensemaking (e.g. Maslen, 2017). Our senses have a particular and pivotal role to play in these mechanisms, made explicit through their examination. Sound is a particularly accessible means of illustrating this. Auditory knowledge is embedded in medical practices, and in diagnostic processes – auscultation – sound plays a well-documented role, symbolised by the iconic stethoscope (e.g. Rice, 2010). Analogies between the human body and society are deeply entrenched and ubiquitous in social science, but the idea that similar principles can be applied in knowledge-gathering practices in both natural and social sciences is less so. As one accustomed to heightening my sensory awareness when entering new social spaces as a means of gauging potential for disruption, danger even, this operation is second nature. I retain the 'guvnor's' practice of identifying the greatest vantage point to occupy and experience discomfort unless my back is to the wall.

Social organisation conforms to discernible rhythms which have an audible component (Lefebvre, 2004). Applying this principle to familiar, personal routines articulates this point: the morning alarm, the spoon hitting the cereal bowl, train doors. Awareness of the array of roles sound occupies in social life places it at the heart of ways of making sense of our surroundings. The rhythmanalyst, Lefebvre (2004) asserts, must 'listen to the world, and above all to what are disdainfully called noises ... To murmurs ... silences' in order to tease out its social meanings (p. 19). If we accept that the rhythms of social life have an audible component – which is not to say sound provides the only means of exploring them – (e.g. Edensor & Larsen, 2018) – how then, is this technique of auditory sensitisation accomplished? Lefebvre (2004) offers further direction:

> Noise. Noises. Murmurs. When lives are lived and hence mixed together, they distinguish themselves badly from one another. Noise, chaotic, has no rhythm. However, the attentive ear begins to separate out, to distinguish the sources, to bring them back together by perceiving interactions ... A certain exteriority enables the analytic intellect to function. However, to grasp a rhythm it is necessary to let oneself go, give oneself over, abandon oneself to its duration. Like in music ... (p. 27)

In likening rhythmanalysis to the practice of listening to music, Lefebvre emphasises the familiarity of this enterprise as a facet of social behaviour. I would go further in borrowing from organisational theory to suggest this is part of a broader range of activities which comprise daily life, albeit largely unconsciously performed. When we encounter unfamiliar environments, we commonly engage in the processes of sensemaking; interpreting sensory information in order to decode what is going on; imagine entering a library for the first time, or a museum, a café, a karaoke bar. We encounter these situations so frequently that these practices are conducted unremarkably and, for the most part, without reflection. While arguably second nature, they are nevertheless fundamental to the way we understand and navigate embodied experience of space and place (Morris, 2020). Weick (1995) characterises these processes as largely retrospective, prompting reflection on past practice as a means of compiling cognitive maps with which to guide action. Sensemaking indicates a particular temporal and spatial orientation as a tentative newcomer, a process of acquiring sufficient understanding to move through social spaces. Assimilating this understanding as a means of navigating action requires not only a familiarity with but also an ability to interpret and respond to the meanings ascribed to particular sensory ecologies. Not only recognising but also interpreting, responding to and affecting the social climate are reliant on these sensemaking systems but are not confined to them. An attunement to what is being seen, smelled, heard, 'felt' rests on sense making but requires a social competence which puts these knowledges to work.

Within organisational literature there is much emphasis on the significance of interpreting 'cues' as a necessary step in the process of bending them to the task of forging understanding as a social actor. This process is more fully characterised as: perception, cognition, action and memory (Weick, 1995). Less focus is placed on the nature of those cues, how they are interpreted or what that process of familiarisation consists of, rather these mechanisms are taken-for-granted internal aspects of operations whose interest lies in their sociality. It is these mechanisms – and the role the sensory plays within them – with which I am concerned here. Sound can be understood as comprising a system of signification (Chion, 2010). An arrangement of social cues which can be learned, interpreted and, on occasion, manipulated. A soundscape can present a means of gauging the social climate, either as an observer or with a view to affecting it as a social actor. Social life is comprised of various parts – *lived lives mixed together interacting chaotically* (Lefebvre, 2004) – so too are interruptions to it's rhythms. Disruptions to the orderly ebb and flow of daily life, such as violence, also have sensory components (e.g. Spencer, 2014). Deciphering this sensory information requires an attunement to the ecology of the environment.

Ordering Attunement in the Bar

Bar staff are actors in the night-time economy, intimately involved with and on occasion implicated in the disorder and violence associated with this facet of social life (Tutenges, Bogkjaer, Witte, & Hesse, 2013). Pubs and bars are liminal spaces where the usual social conventions are suspended or overturned and the carnivalesque may be permitted (e.g. Bakhtin, 1984/1965; Fox, 2004). Places of leisure, in which people socialise, relax and unwind, and consume alcohol to varying degrees of excess. These aspects of pub life are characterised by a consensual cessation of formality, but nevertheless do not indicate an absence of rules. While distinctions of class and culture blur within these spaces, a complex structure of regulations and expectations pertain, the breach of which risk explosions of similarly informal mechanisms of social control: disruption, violence, constraint, ejection.

Attunement is a term used in fields as disparate as midwifery, performative ethnography, developmental psychology and organisation studies (Crowther, Smythe, & Spence, 2014; Fajen & Devaney, 2006; Willink & Shukri, 2018[1]). Its meanings are correspondingly fluid and ill-defined, though they share a focus on behaviour-shaping response to affective stimuli. These disparate treatments share an acknowledgement of the central role attunement plays in social life and the learning of it, though what part the sensory plays within this 'communicative musicality' remains less clear (Malloch, 1999; Powers & Trevarthen, 2009; Stern, Hofer, Haft, & Dore, 1985). While these uses and definitions necessarily vary, the wide range of disciplines drawing on it suggest its utility as an explanatory mechanism for understanding social behaviour. Attunement offers a means of considering how humans interpret, navigate and deploy their sensemaking: the way social actors 'feel', respond to and manipulate social settings. In accounting for these aspects of social behaviour, attunement comprises a framework for exploring the relationship between the sensory and emotion as guides for action. Attunement, then, can be understood as proficient orientation to the social environment enabled by sensemaking; as Wacquant (2015) terms it a 'social competency'. Whereas sensemaking draws on past social experience, competent attunement relies on familiarity with the rhythms of that particular environment. In this case, the particular pub and bar, each of which possess their own dynamics,

---

[1]With thanks to Adrian Marrison whom I met in HMP Durham's dojo where we stumbled into a conversation about research interests. I am immensely grateful to him for pointing me in the direction of organisational theory.

ebbs and flows. To draw on Lefebvre's analogy, learning the cacophonies and concertos of these spaces requires a patient acquaintance. To sing in time and tune you must first learn to hum along.

The significance of sound – and the senses more broadly – to understanding places of penality and social control is underscored by a number of recent contributions to 'acoustic jurisprudence'. Within this work, sound is understood as a specific dimension of legal experience; 'a necessary condition of the administration of justice and inalienable part of our legal worlds' (Parker, 2011, p. 962). Mulcahy (2019) develops this idea in specific relation to attunement practices within the courtroom, drawing on performing arts to articulate aspects of the courtroom frequently overlooked, or unheard, but which form important aspects of its rituals and routines. For Mulcahy, attunement is a practice of 'deep listening' and a means of recalibrating the courtroom audience. He draws on J. E. K. Parker's (2015) observation that identifying the theatrical elements of attunement requires a deep familiarity with legal oratory: its rhythms, cadences, effects, to reflect on the role of the senses and emotion in legal practices. This prompts comparison between the rhythms of social life in this most formal of spaces alongside others of interest to the criminologist. Comparing interpretations of rhythms in places of penality and social control are a valuable means of enhancing understanding of social life as it unfolds within these spaces. Examining those learning processes of attunement to the environment offers a means of better articulating practised techniques often relegated to instinct or intuition. Successfully attuning other social actors relies on shared meanings of symbolic signification – for example, imposing silence within a courtroom with a gavel or more complex direction such as emotion management (which Lisa Flower discusses elsewhere in this volume). I used the sensory as a means of interpreting and manipulating the social climate. The sensescape provided a means of gauging and a site for restoring order in the bar; manipulating sensory cues was a way of securing cooperation from revellers:

> A spikey atmosphere has its own rhythms (jerky, staccato?). Violence here can erupt as well as brew, ignited by the remnants of a boozy weekend, a line too many, fractious exchanges. A sharp, unprovoked attack, a glass, a dig at the back of an older man's head as he emerges from the toilet. Ugly, brutal, sudden and rippling.
>
> The assault, while sudden, is preceded by a discomforting jarring of rhythms, an unease. When it comes it is signalled by an increasing arrhythmia, discernible in sound and movement. We move in to rehearsed actions. I call for backup from upstairs, summoning doormen to help me escort offending and injured parties to safety, before launching in between to separate them. Bar staff remain in safety behind the bar as instructed, following practiced routines; music is turned off, lights turned up, transactions ceased – no one gets another drink until this is resolved. The rhythms of revelry are suspended, and customers dutifully part to give us space to work, the assailant is escorted out, the injured party tended to. And so the night resumes ...

This is one of many instances in which social life was sensorially interpreted and manipulated to reset order and control disruptive behaviour – most notably by limiting, preventing or ending violence[2] – within various pubs and bars I worked in. Disruption to order had sensory dimensions in these spaces, the handling of which required an extended process of sensemaking before confident interpretation and affect – attunement – could take place.

Attuning to the atmosphere and playing it as a means of re-establishing order reinforces the centrality of the sensory to understanding social worlds. If social worlds has a set of rhythms specific to particular spaces and activities conducted within them, it follows that disruptions to it – disorder – can also have sensorially discernible components. This has significance for how we understand social organisation more broadly but specifically for how order, and how it is 'worked at' can be understood in places and practices of punishment and social control (Sparks, Bottoms, & Hay, 1996).

Sensemaking at HMP Midtown

The process of sensorially orientating to the social environment is integral to uncovering some of its meanings, as well as how they are experienced by those operating within them. As with a piece of complicated text, these meanings are interdependent and negotiations of them contingent on shared understandings it takes time and care for the untuned ear to discern. Navigating the progression from theoretical research design to engaging in its practice similarly requires adjustment. How does one conduct an aural ethnography in a local men's prison in the absence of a clearly laid out blueprint to follow? I had used my master's research as an opportunity to pilot the study, developing a set of practices which aimed to assess the feasibility of a focus on sound ecology; the idea that sound presents a means of exploring processes of sensory meaning-making deriving from engagement between humans, their environment and one another (Ingold, 2000). Applying this method in the context of HMP Midtown involved a process of sensemaking in the first instance and drew on past experience of utilising sensory information to acclimatise to rhythms of social life in this particular setting:

> The first prisoner I interviewed, Stretch, halted the interview at one point: 'Never mind research and about being in and out of prisons. Tell me what's happening in this prison right now'. I responded with a rather sullen 'I can't'. 'I'll tell you now' he told me authoritatively, 'They're feeding dinner. They've got some of

---

[2]While violence is acknowledged as a routine aspect of life in spaces where people congregate to consume alcohol, emphasis is frequently – and understandably – on officially recorded instances and those that take place in open spaces, around closing time (e.g. Shepherd & Brickley, 1996). In many years of experience, the police were involved on a handful of occasions. Most violent incidents were managed informally, without outside involvement and resolved with minimum disruption to the evening.

the high fours out and some of the high threes, and they're feeding the low threes'. It is true that dinner service followed similar patterns, and there were a limited number of ways of ordering mealtimes. It was also true that I had no way of knowing [what I was listening to], at this point. Neither did I quite realise the pertinence of what he was telling me at the time. In later interviews my familiarity with the environment had shifted and I asked different questions of my interviewees when our conversation was interrupted by the strains of unusual activity outside. While talking to Robert I asked: 'that isn't trouble, but what is it?'. Someone has set off the fire extinguisher on the twos we discover when we emerge. (Herrity, 2019, p. 81)

While conducting interviews, I could not see but could hear and sometimes physically feel what was going on around the wing – banging gates, the rush of rubber soles on lino, all had particular sounds, vibrations, rhythms and, on occasion – for example, spice use, cell fires, dirty protests – smells. When around the prison, I took time familiarising myself with its sensescapes, standing in corners where my vision was obscured and, increasingly, asking questions of members of the community – what was that I could hear? What was I smelling? Experience in the bar increased my confidence that these were questions pertinent to understanding prison life, though I had a way to go to make the nature of this pertinence clear.

De Rond, Holeman and Howard-Grenville (2019) persuasively document the role of embodied experience in sensemaking, demonstrating how it 'is forged from, and into, corporeal experience' (p. 1963). They emphasise the significance of who is involved in these sensemaking processes, drawing on Wacquant's (2015) call for a 'Sociology of flesh and blood' in doing so. Stretch echoed this approach to decoding his environment, inviting me to listen more deeply and engage more fully until I could begin to answer his questions: what was I hearing? What was I feeling? The exchange between Stretch and I invited further collaborative interrogation of the environment, diminishing the distance between our respective positions (Herrity, 2020). As noted by De Rond et al. (2019) as 'sensemaker', I drew on my position as both attentive outsider and one accustomed to interpreting the 'feel' or 'mood' of a group as a means of gauging safety. My ability to interpret the social ebbs and flows of the prison was a slow process of inhabiting the space and adapting to its rhythms and routines but one informed by sedimented experience.

I entered the prison by tentative degree. Association initially sounded like a bustling chaos of too many men, in too small a space, with too diverse a range of purposes to discern. It took time and a little patience before my *attentive* ear began to perceive distinctions between the hustle and bustle of daily lives conducted around the wing. It took time and care too before I could 'distinguish the sources, to bring them back together by perceiving interactions' (Lefebvre, 2004). Making sense of the cacophonous clamour of daily life at HMP Midtown required a careful, attentive interrogation, as directed by Stretch, before

I could begin to make sense of, and then move towards familiarity with, its component parts. The hustle and bustle of life at Midtown was comprised not only of a diverse array of human beings, with various roles and activities to perform, and their relationship with one another, but rather the complex interplay of people and place through the warp and weft of time which comprised the fabric of their existence. Bars, gates, keys, radios, all had meanings derived from associations with the various social actors within the spaces of the prison, the time in which they sounded and their respective contributions to the sensory ecology of the place (Ingold, 2000). The jingle of approaching keys at association time could mean unlock to a prisoner, in the early hours an unexpected ghosting,[3] bad news or for an officer a facet of identity performance or the reassuring presence of a colleague. Proceeding to a position from which to perform some degree of social auscultation relied on drawing from this bank of embodied knowledge. De Rond et al. (2019) suggest the role of the senses in sensemaking is a rather fruitless field of enquiry, eschewing the sensory for embodied knowledge. Partial immersion in the sensory landscape demonstrates, rather, that the sensory constitutes a means of exploring and articulating this understanding. Attending to the sensory experience of place offers a means of overcoming the dualism between mind and body, of coming closer to understanding how Midtown was experienced, was 'felt', both physically and emotionally, by those within it, and in so doing the ways in which the array of interactions between people and place maintained, for the most part, an orderly rhythm.

Acknowledging the potential of auscultation in particular, and the value of sensory knowledge more broadly to enhance our understanding, prompts analogy between the rhythms of daily life, the social body, and those of the organism: its organs, breath, pulse. Reflecting on auscultation in this way in turn leads to consideration of the role the sensory plays in social life beyond that of research practice. Gradual sensemaking in the prison decoded various aspects of daily life at Midtown. Increased darting to and fro between huddles of men indicated the purpose and place of individuals on the prison social totem pole as well as the amount of illicit activity on the wing. Disembodied, too-loud music was a sonic harbinger of a fractious day with tensions ratcheting. Walking on to the wing a little later, the eased tension in the aftermath of a potting was made tangible by the steady rhythm, the ease of movement among officers as well as the attendant ripening odours and remnants on grimy, increasingly tacky floors. Attuning to daily life at HMP Midtown involved attunement also, to its actors, and an increasing sensitivity to their delicate navigations of the intensely changeable microclimate of their social world.

'Everyday' Attunement

As time went on at HMP Midtown, and members of its community became more accustomed to my presence, prisoners and officers would increasingly ask how it

---

[3]'Ghosting' refers to movement around the prison system without the prior agreement, and sometimes without prior knowledge, of the prisoner being moved.

'sounded today' by way of greeting. Rather than asking for a literal reflection on how my eardrums were holding up, this was commonly understood as a proxy for what kind of day it was. I was to learn that 'quiet' was never an acceptable response: the prison equivalent of invoking the portentous Scottish play, though the chiding was delivered with considerably better humour. Rather, in deference to my particular point of interest, the social vocabulary for detailing the 'feel' of the day expanded to accommodate me, echoing a rich bank of sensory metaphor relating to the social climate (Cacciari, 2008). A 'bad' day had a 'feel' to it, a 'spikiness' or 'bubbliness', descriptions familiar from time spent in other prisons, summoning a sense of unpredictability and unease. Something was in the air, though the nature of that something was not always immediately clear, as Senior Officer Rose explained

> Somethings gonna go. Don't know what it is, it'll probably be somebody's gonna come out and batter somebody else, something like that. But you can sense it's gonna happen but you just don't know what it is. And then it happens ...

A 'good day' in Midtown, as at other prisons, was rather more difficult to capture, reflecting both its fragile, changeable state (Herrity, 2019; Liebling, Price, & Shefer, 2010; Sparks et al., 1996) and its position as a point of departure. Commonly, in prisons literature, it is the absence of order which forms both the stimulus for and the focal point of inquiry. In the daily life of HMP Midtown, however, it was familiarity with 'the everyday tune that's normal for here' (Derek, Senior Officer) that formed the vital point of reference. Advancing beyond sensemaking to the point of attunement enabled a greater sensitivity to aspects of prison life that might otherwise remain unarticulated. Not only was I engaged in practices of sensitising to the sensory ecology of Midtown, but I did so alongside its more established inhabitants. In the acoustic community of Midtown, attending to the climate as a means of gauging the degree of order was central to safety and self-preservation. If attunement enabled an increased awareness of the vagaries of prison life for this researcher, it was an indispensable tool in the repertoire of order maintenance for those relying on its rhythms for survival.

In such an environment, it is every bit as important to distinguish between incidents requiring the telltale shout: 'staff' and stampede of rubber soles on walkways and lino and those which do not.[4] Other components of the prison soundscape sounded similar to 'trouble' or disorder until familiarity enabled easy discernment: voices raised in the service of being heard over the clamour and din, shouting across space as a means of saving time, or the range of random sounds which characterise the prison soundscape; occasional shrieking, tuneless singing, whooping, animal noises, banging. I observed this adept attunement in members

---

[4]The size of Midtown meant the alarm was rarely raised for incidents on the wing, which seemed to increase the ability to identify their source.

of the Midtown community long before I had acquired the ability to recognise the distinction myself:

> Using sound as method involved subjecting myself to the same process of understanding as I sought to discern in the field. On a number of occasions quite early on, I heard what I assumed was violence erupting. As I looked around I noticed no one else was responding to it. Everyday rhythms continued on. What was everyone else hearing that I was not? Or, conversely, what was the quality of this sound that allowed others to differentiate between this and something they needed to respond to which eluded me? I returned to this question repeatedly, receiving a number of different answers. Prisoners would shrug, 'you just know', staff would mysteriously refer to experience and familiarity: 'you learn' or offer vague speculation in an attempt to satisfy me; 'something about the tone' 'it's how long it goes on for', 'it's what goes on around it'. I would interrupt conversations, my head going up like a meercat. 'What?' the prisoner/s I was chatting to would ask. 'Oh, thought it was trouble' I would answer, until I reached a point where I too recognised the difference. I still do not know what it is, but I understand that acclimation to the environment is partially rooted in attuning to its soundscape. (Herrity, 2019, p. 216)

When concluding the project, I identified my inability to describe exactly what the distinction between trouble and not-trouble was as a failure of my approach, a deficiency of method. Upon reflection, it might more accurately be understood as intrinsic to it. Undergoing this process of attunement as an inhabitant of the environment – albeit only as a temporary visitor and resolute outsider – necessarily involved participation in it. In this sense, I was failing to acknowledge another distinction, that of 'social competency – as opposed to empirical saturation' (Wacquant, 2015, p. 1). Focussing on the sensory allowed for a more explicit articulation, as well as scrutiny, of this social process. This focus also revealed the degree to which sensory information is central to experience of place, from which a researcher – certainly one seeking to embed themselves within it – is no more immune than any other social actor. In articulating the pivotal role sensory engagement plays in understanding, we carve out additional space to harness the potentials of the sensory for explicating how individuals construct embodied and emotional senses of place (Morris, 2020).

When interviewing Derek, a senior officer, in the course of my research, he described the significance of sound to his working life as a process of familiarising himself with the 'the everyday tune that's normal for here' (Herrity, 2019, p. 172). Derek, who had worked within the prison service for several decades, maintained that both different prisons and the spaces within them had sensorially distinct and recognisable rhythms, tunes, which formed a focus for assessing and monitoring safety. Sensory information provided the cues to learning the 'everyday tune' as well as surveilling deviations from it. Derek explained the ways in which familiarity with, and interpretation of, sensory information formed a vital, though under-articulated, part of the officer's skill set:

> They'll know. But if you try to explain it to 'em they'll be like you whacky ... what you talking about, tunes 'n noises? What you talking about? But people won't understand, but that's how it is. That's how we react. Yeah, tuning stuff with your eyes and you hear things. That's what it is. So when you go to a particular department ... seg, or the first night centre, or education or one of the workshops, or the gym ... you'd know that tune. And if something's out of sync you'll know. Speak to the PI'[5]s, if you spoke to the PI's and asked them what do you listen out for here when you know something's wrong? If someone, what's the difference between someone dropping a weight, and someone throwing a weight down. They'll know the difference but they won't know they know. They'll subconsciously know it. That's why I say it's kind of like a Derren Brown thing ... (Derek, Senior Officer)

Contrary to Derek's anticipated dismissal of these insights as 'whacky', he persuasively explains the centrality of familiarity with the sensory to the business of navigating social life within prison spaces. Derek's assertion that interpreting the environment is key to identifying when 'something is wrong' echoes Martin, Jefferson and Bandyophadhyay's (2014) assertion that 'climate' is both a key component of penal environments and central to interrogating how they are experienced, as well as how they are survived. While Derek is speaking across, and within prisons in England and Wales, Martin et al. (2014) suggest that the salience of gauging climate holds across continents, encompassing concerns both universal and particular to those who live and work in prisons, as well as those who seek to understand them. So what is meant by this rather vague term? While it has a pleasing elasticity which lends itself to a range of metaphorical devices – hot, cold, close, light, for example – this unsatisfying imprecision inhibits shared understanding. Martin et al. (2014) provide a useful definition: prison climates are comprised of 'entanglements of relations, practices and dynamics' (p. 3). The prison climate, then, can be understood as the social condition created by the collective, comprised of various interactions, rituals and routines within its spaces. The sensory, in providing a mechanism by which the 'climate' can be assessed and experienced by those within its perimeters, offers a means to understand prevailing conditions. Sensory aspects of the environment – the way it sounds, smells, 'feels' – act as a barometer with which to measure it.

The climate of a prison society is intimately bound with its survivability. Recognition that relationships between people and the environment are fundamental to safety is well established in prisons research. The frequent focus on creating a safer, better working environment emphasises the centrality of these concerns to

---

[5] PI = physical instructors. Always found in short shorts regardless of the weather.

living and working in secure settings (e.g. Tonkin et al., 2012). An instrumental focus on the conditions of an 'ecology of survival' can distract from its substance, as Toch (1992) notes:

> The link between persons and environments holds a position in the social sciences similar to that of virtue in society. We love to preach and teach it, but we often ignore it in practice. (p. 1)

While order is a complicated and perpetually unfinished business, its manifestations in daily life when extricated from power and authority are, partially at least, sensorially discernible. An orderly day that runs on predictable rhythms and routines comprises the 'everyday tune that's normal for here'. As Derek attests, interpreting sensory cues offers a means of identifying deviation from the 'everyday tune' by indicating 'something's wrong'. Associations between sensory knowledge of his environment and practices of order maintenance are made explicit in Derek's account of his experience as a member of the Midtown community. Elsewhere he refers to himself as a 'conductor' successfully managing movement at mealtimes around the wings, so attuned to its rhythms he is able to sustain and manipulate them. Privileging the sensory completes the circle between climate, order and survivability. The senses provide a means of making daily rhythms tangible, of sensemaking, while attuning to them illuminates aspects of daily life in places of penality and social control which otherwise elude us.

Sensemaking and Attunement in Flesh and Blood

Attending to the social rhythms of pubs and bars comprised a frame of reference from which to embark on processes of sensemaking in prisons. Drawing on this process as a means of making sense of the soundscape at HMP Midtown allowed for a heightened sensibility to often overlooked aspects of social experience. Only in the course of excavating the basis for this understanding do the layers of experience which inform it become apparent. The researcher is as sedimented, skilled and situated as those we seek to understand (Wacquant, 2015).

Foregrounding the sensory enriches understanding of the multiplicities of carceral experience, and the order which lends it form and meaning. Sound, as is the case for the sensory more broadly, is less bounded by time and space; is felt and lived in prison, as in other spheres of social life, both here and there. Sensemaking is a process that holds the potential for disrupting hierarchies of knowledge by drawing on this bottom-up, lived experience which brings us closer to how social worlds are 'felt' by those who inhabit them. Research practices in which these grounded skills are developed and reflected upon draw not only on those 'sedimented layers of knowledge and experience' of the researcher but also of those other social actors within the spaces we inhabit (Wacquant, 2015). Foregrounding the sensory renders embodied practices of sensemaking in places of penality and social control tangible. It adds texture and nuance to distinctions between those orientations in time and space required of the novice sensemaker, and the social competence, and reorientation to the-now as it unfolds, demanded by attunement. The process of interrogating these practices enables deeper scrutiny of how we operate in the field and in so doing better sensitises us to social practices bound up with attuning to order and those imperatives of safety and survival with which it is entangled. Not only do these practices go further towards diminishing distance in time, space and understanding between ourselves and those who live and work in the fields of our enquiry but also between that age-old dualism of mind and body, between how we feel and how we know. Focusing on the sensory holds the promise of better representing the vagaries and vitality of human life within these penal spaces and brings us closer to capturing our fellow humans, as Wacquant (2015, p. 1) entreats, as the 'sensate, suffering, skilled, sedimented and situated' creatures we are.

References

Bakhtin, M. (1984/1965). *Rabelais and his world*. (Trans. H. Iswolsky). Bloomington, IN: Indiana University Press.
Cacciari, C. (2008). Crossing the senses in metaphorical language. In R. W. Gibbs (Ed.), *The Cambridge handbook on metaphor and thought* (pp. 425–443). Cambridge: Cambridge University Press.
Chion, M. (2010). *Sound: An acoulogical treatise*. (Trans. J. A. Steintrager). London: Duke University Press.
Crowther, S., Smythe, L., & Spence, D. (2014). Mood and birth experience. *Women and Birth*, *27*(1), 21–25.
De Rond, M., Holeman, I., & Howard-Grenville, J. (2019). Sensemaking from the body: An enactive ethnography of rowing on the amazon. *Academy of Management Journal*, *62*(6), 1966–1981.
Edensor, T., & Larsen, J. (2018). Rhythmanlysing marathon running: 'A drama of rhythms'. *Environment and Planning A: Economy and Space*, *50*(3), 730–746.
Eliot, T. S. (1933). *The use of poetry and the use of criticism*. London: Faber and Faber.
Fajen, B. R., & Devaney, M. C. (2006). Learning to control collisions: The role of perceptual attunement and action boundaries. *Journal of Experimental Psychology*, *32*(2), 300–313.
Fox, K. (2004). *Watching the English: The hidden rules of English behaviour*. London: Hodder and Stoughton.
Herrity, K. (2019). *Rhythms and routines: Sounding order and survival in a local men's prison using aural ethnography*. Unpublished Ph.D. thesis. University of Leicester, Leicester.
Herrity, K. (2020). 'Some people can't hear, so they have to feel': Exploring sensory experience and collapsing distance in prisons research. *ECAN Bulletin, January, 2020*(43), 26–31.
Ihde, D. (2007). *Listening and voice. Phenomenologies of sound* (2nd ed.). Albany, NY: State University of New York.
Ingold, T. (2000). *The perception of the environment: Essays on livelihood, dwelling and skill*. London: Routledge.
Joel, B. (1973). *Piano man*. New York, NY: Columbia Records.
Lefebvre, H. (2004). *Rhythmanalysis: Space, time and everyday life*. London: Continuum.
Liebling, A., assisted by Arnold, H. (2004). *Prisons and their moral performance: A study of values, quality, and prison life*. Oxford: Oxford University Press.
Liebling, A., Price, D., & Shefer, G. (2010). *The prison officer*. London: Routledge.

Malloch, S. (1999). Mothers and infants and communicative musicality. *Musicae Scientae*, *3*(1), 29–57.
Martin, T. M., Jefferson, A. M., & Bandyophadhyay, M. (2014). Sensing prison climates: Governance, survival and transition. *Focaal*, *68*, 3–17.
Maslen, S. (2017). *Layers of sense: The sensory work of diagnostic sensemaking in digital health*. Digital Health. Retrieved from https://www.ncbi.nlm.nih.gov/pmc/articles/PMC6001234/
Morris, N. (2020). Teaching sensory geographies in practice: Transforming students' awareness and understanding through playful experimentation. *Journal of Geography in Higher Education*. https://doi.org/10.1080/03098265.2020.1771685
Mulcahy, S. (2019). Silence and attunement in legal performance. *Canadian Journal of Law and Society/Revue Canadienne Droit et Societe*, *34*(2), 191–207.
Parker, J. (2011). The soundscape of justice. *Griffith Law Review*, *20*(4), 962–993.
Parker, J. E. K. (2015). *Acoustic jurisprudence: Listening to the trial of Simon Bikindi*. Oxford: Oxford University Press.
Powers, N., & Trevarthen, C. (2009). Voices of shared emotion and meaning: Young infants and their mothers in Scotland and Japan. In S. Malloch & C. Trevarthen (Eds.), *Communicative musicality: Exploring the basis of human companionship* (pp. 209–240). Oxford: Oxford University Press.
Rice, T. (2010). Learning to listen: Auscultation and the transmission of auditory knowledge. *Journal of the Royal Anthropological Institute*, *16*(1), 41–61.
Shepherd, J., & Brickley, M. (1996). The relationship between alcohol intoxication, stressors and injury in urban violence. *British Journal of Criminology*, *36*(4), 546–566.
Sparks, R., Bottoms, T., & Hay, W. (1996). *Prisons and the problem of order*. Oxford: Clarendon.
Spencer, D. C. (2014). Sensing violence: An ethnography of mixed martial arts. *Ethnography*, *15*(2), 232–254.
Stern, D. N., Hofer, L., Haft, W., & Dore, J. (1985). Affective attunement: The sharing of feeling states between mother and infant by means of inter-modal fluency. In T. M. Field & N. A. Fox (Eds.), *Social perception in infants* (pp. 249–268). Norwood, NJ: Ablex Publishing.
Tonkin, M., Howells, K., Ferguson, E., Clark, A., Newberry, M., & Schalast, N. (2012). Lost in translation? Psychometric properties and construct validity of the English Essen Climate Evaluation Schema (EssenCES) social climate questionnaire. *Psychological Assessment*, *24*, 573–580.
Toop, D. (2010). *Sinister resonance: The mediumship of the listener*. London: Continuum.
Toch, H. (1992). *Living in prison: the ecology of survival*. Washington DC: American psychological association.
Truax, B. (2001). *Acoustic communication*. Stamford, CT: Ablex Publishing.
Tutenges, S., Bogkjaer, T., Witte, M., & Hesse, M. (2005). Drunken environments: A survey of bartenders working in pubs, bars and nightclubs. *International Journal of Environmental Research and Public Health*, *10*, 4896–4906.
Wacquant, L. (2015). For a sociology of flesh and blood. *Qualitative Sociology*, *38*(1), 1–11.
Weick, K. E. (1995). *Sensemaking in organisations*. London: Sage.
Weick, K. E., Sutcliffe, K. M., & Obstfeld, D. (2005). Organizing and the process of sensemaking. *Organization Science*, *16*(4), 409–421.
Wener, R. (2012). *The environmental psychology of prisons and jails: Creating humane spaces in secure settings*. Cambridge: Cambridge University Press.
Willink, K. T., & Shukri, S. T. (2018). Performative interviewing: Affective attunement and reflective affective analysis in interviewing. *Text and Performance Quarterly*, *38*(4), 187–207.

Chapter 2

Fire! Fire! – The Prison Cell and the Thick Sensuality of Trappedness

Jason Warr

Something woke me up. What is it? Is it that cunt upstairs again with his music? No. Smoke? Yes, shit, smoke. Fuck it, ignore it … Did I leave the fag burning in the ashtray? No, you threw it in the bin. Shit, is the bin on fire? Those were my thoughts. That's what dragged me from the hazy depths of sleep and drove me out of the cot, to turn the light on, check the bin. Flick the switch. Realise the cell is thick with smoke. What the f …?! Its disorientating. Cough. I crash from the murky fog of disturbed sleep to full awareness. Quick, get the window open, cough, relief from cool air. Short lived. It sucks the smoke through the cell. Heart beats fast. Coldness in the gut. Cough.

I can hear shouts, angry, short, loud. 'What's going on?' 'Has the fraggle set himself on fire again?' 'Which cell is it?', 'Oi, what's going on?'. The voices multiply as more and more of the lads suss on to what is going on. Cough. Someone starts banging on their door bang, bang, Bang, BANG, BAAAAANG. Cough. Others pick up on it. More voices, hassled, but calm, authoritative 'Cut it out lads, we're dealing with it'. The banging stops, the jokes start. There's mention of Barbeque for breakfast. Cough.

Suddenly, everything changes. The atmosphere changes. The smoke is thicker, blacker, noxious. It tastes sour and scorches the throat. The sounds are more panicked. Jokes stop. Pulse races. Coldness in gut moves, worms, snakes its way downwards. Bladder is full of ice. Need to piss. Cough. See ghostly flickers at the window. Hints of amber against the ebon night. Realise the fire is in cell below. Its escaped. Jumped. Flickers getting higher. Can see

---

Sensory Penalties: Exploring the Senses in Spaces of Punishment and Social Control, 19–33
Copyright © 2021 Jason Warr. Published under exclusive licence by Emerald Publishing Limited
All rights of reproduction in any form reserved
doi:10.1108/978-1-83909-726-320210003

the orangey yellow now, not just shadow. The Balrog! Start to feel the heat. This is what they call 'thermal change', didn't know that at the time. A somewhat neutral term to describe when the heat from a fire begins to change the heat in the wider environment. Eyes are stinging. Heart thumping out of control. Throat burning. Nose raw. Panic. Need to get out. Need to get away. Search the small cramped 8x8 cell for a way out. There is no way out. The walls seem real all of a sudden. Inescapable. Solid. Impenetrable. My cell becomes alien. No longer a retreat. Something else … makes me feel small, vulnerable. Powerless.

Can't see the other side of the cell smoke is so thick. Can hear them below shouting. 'Get the fuck out'. 'Shut it. Move. Get him to the fucking block'. 'Right inundate'. 'Is the fire brigade on the way'. More. I can't hear. Cough. I can't get out. There's no way out. Bang. Bang. BANG. I kick the door. 'Guv, Guv! GUV! GUUUUV!' I can barely think. Torrents of ice in my guts. I'm shaking. I can't think. I need to get out. I need to get the fuck out. The walls are closing in like a trash compactor. Squeezing the space. The world shrinks. I need to get the fuck out of this cell.

'What do you want?'
'Guv, [cough] you need to let me out, I can't breathe [cough]'.
My throat, raw, scratched, singed, can barely make the words. Pain. Hope.
'No'.
'Guv???' Cough. COUGH.
'No. I'll come and see you when its sorted. If need be, we'll get you to the doctor in the morning, alright? Now get your head down'.
'… but Guv??'

He's gone. He left me here. I'm alone. Powerless.

Without power. Unable to do anything. No choices. No alternatives. Can do fuck all. For the first time in years my situation becomes stark. This is what prison is. Trapped. Locked-in. No escape. The feeling is thick, viscous, pressurised. The walls, the locked door, the bars on the window, I can feel them without touch, without seeing.

I can hear screaming, shouting, banging. It's me. I am screaming. Shouting. Banging. Cough, cough, cough. I get down on the floor. Wet towel over head. Try to breathe. Cough. Cough. It hits me. I'm going to die here. I can't get out. There is no way out. I'm in a sealed box. This cell is a trap. A death trap. I'm trapped. I'm fucking trapped.

In his classic book, *The Five Senses: A Philosophy of Mingled Bodies* (2008), Michel Serres highlights the visceral and sensorially overwhelming experience of being trapped in a fire while upon a naval vessel. He describes how, being trapped in with the fire, he becomes immutably aware of himself as a being of senses. The heat, the feel, the movement of the ship, the pain, the Hellishly vivid sight of flames and smoke, the noise of the terrifying rumbling thunder as the fire progresses, the taste and sting of the smoke. This sensory overload conspires to render every sense of the body a mingled mass of communication that swamps his consciousness and renders him a reactionary, primal, being. From this beginning, he contends that we as humans are sensory creatures that first and foremost experience the world through our embodied perceptions. The sifting and rationalising of this sensorium, or 'sensescape' (Field, 2005), comes later in our cognitive processes (see Fuster, 2003). He argues that we know the world first not a priori (through deduction and reason) but through our sensorial experience. The senses provide our antecedent perception from which our consequent emotion and later understanding arises. We sense first, then we feel, then we rationalise, then we understand, and only from there can we communicate. This is then how we know. Not, you would have thought, a particularly contentious epistemological conceptualisation. However, it is a sequence with an implied hierarchy that has plagued both philosophy and the social sciences throughout the last century.

Given the focus of this chapter, the work of Serres has particular import. However, the core contribution he has for this chapter, and perhaps this book, is that he argues that in order to truly understand the experiences of humans, as sensory entities, we need to understand how humans experience their realities sensorially. While in many ways a phenomenological account he nevertheless argues that this premise, privileging the sensorial, takes the understanding of human and social life beyond the subjectivity problems that traditionally beset phenomenologies of perception (Merleau-Ponty, 2012). This chapter then is concerned with exploring incarceration as a sensorial experience while trying to avoid the problems of phenomenology, and like Serres, I will focus on how the sensory overload of being locked-in during an extreme event tells us something fundamental about what it means to experience not only imprisonment but also punishment at the hands of the state. As such, this chapter had two distinct challenges: first, to explore what 'trappedness', the physical sensation of being trapped, and the resultant fear response that this can generate, tells us about imprisonment and penality? The second was how best to communicate and discuss this sense of 'trappedness' and the consequent thick sensuality of that sensation, given that it lies so far beyond our normal range of experience? I will start with the second of these two challenges.

Something Woke Me Up. What is it?

Geertz (1994), in his classic work on 'thick description', argues that in order to communicate the lived experience of those we encounter in our fieldwork we must attempt to capture the richness of their cultural and social experiences. However, when it comes to communicating the lived experience of the varying sensescapes which underpin those cultural and social experiences, there is a particular problem. This problem is one of language and its relationship to textual formats (see Clifford, 1986). This is a twofold problem: first, English is particularly limiting in capturing and communicating the complexities and nuances of our sensory lives (Majid & Levinson, 2011). Our language, which can be beautiful in its evocation of emotion, is, oddly, just ill-equipped to capture the overlapping and intermingled nature of sensory experience. It tends to impose a discreteness that is not reflective of our actual experience and sometimes the words we have at our disposal are just inadequate.[1] Second, text, which has become the dominant (visual) format of communication,[2] flattens sensory experience by omitting all the non-linguistic signifiers and elicitors (tone, pitch, pacing, volume, inflection, sound effects, body movement/language, etc.) that occur in the natural communication of sensory experience (Cox, Irving, & Wright, 2016). These two interrelated problems have haunted scientific thought and method in the West, from the Enlightenment onwards. The visual is the only sense to have emerged triumphant from this history as science has, at best, minimised and, at worst, omitted all but the visual from our scientific accounts (see Classen, 1997; Howes & Classen, 2014). This visual dominance has, they argue, shaped the objectification of human experience in such ways that our primary methods of investigation, and corresponding communication, have become predicated upon, and grounded in, the observable. What can be measured, quantified, catalogued, shown. They, like Serres, conclude that this ocular-fetish and scriptural flatness, even in traditional qualitative approaches, robs our accounts of society of an experiential richness that actually obfuscates our understanding of it.

Attempts at overcoming this qualitative flatness, in order to create a form of *Verstehen*[3] for the reader (Simmel, 1905), have often resulted in phenomenological accounts of the social world. Utilising the epistemological logics of the likes of Edmund Husserl (2001) and Maurice Merleau-Ponty (2012) who were, in the first half of the twentieth century, attempting to counter the extant cold analytics of pure reason and structural accounts of social life. The phenomenon of phenomenology grew apace in the twentieth century as more and more approaches were developed and utilised. However, there is little orthodoxy about phenomenological approaches or methods. What is agreed is that the phenomenological turn attempted to ground our understanding of human and social life not in

---

[1] Try to accurately and fully explain the sensation of eating a slice of lemon.

[2] Image has in the twentieth century began to rival the text as the dominant visual form of communication (GIFs epitomise this), but the image, while imbued with elicitorial symbolic content which evoke or provoke the senses, is still poor at elucidating those senses.

[3] Thank you to Rod Earle who pointed out that this concept (one of an empathetic understanding towards the foci of study) is an example of the limited scope of English I mentioned above. There is no direct translation in English and as such is not a sentiment that occurs easily in our vocabulary. Of course, this does not mean that English speakers do not feel this empathy for nor utilise it.

objective facts but in the experiential realities of people, the mental states that perception evinces, and the richness of these subjectivities. However, this approach to social enquiry soon ran into an intractable philosophical problem: Is it possible to reconcile individual subjectivities (given that they are incomparable) in order to affirm a collective reality (Giorgi, 2006)? This is a question that has, despite much debate and rancour, been left largely unanswered in the West.[4] A fact that Achille Mbembe, in his book *Critique of Black Reason* (2017), highlights as being a central flaw in Western metaphysical and analytical traditions. These traditions, he argues, impose self-reflective logics that blind academics and researchers to non-colonial ways of thinking and understanding. Such limitations, including a blindness to the viscerality of lived experience, necessarily limit the way in which the social world can be described/discussed. Sensory anthropology has, to some extent, circumvented this problem by not being concerned with extrapolating from individual experiences of the sensorium to determine a collective sense reality. Rather they are concerned with examining how the understanding of the sensorium informs (and is informed by) the cultural and social meaning making of groups of individuals (Howes & Classen, 2014). In this way, rather than trying to make some 'objective' ontological claim about sensescapes, they explore the commonalities of interpretation of those sensescapes in order to understand how the sensory informs the socio-cultural realities of the members of the group.

I Crash from the Murky Fog of Disturbed Sleep to Full Awareness

Of course, one area of our practice in the social sciences, and ethnographic approaches in particular, which does involve consideration of some of these issues and questions is the processes of reflexivity. Much of the discussion of reflexivity is couched in terms of ethics and ethical reflection (see Guillemin & Gillam, 2004). However, as Dean (2017) notes, it is more concerned with accounting for how our humanness affects our research and attempting to reconcile the dual tensions of positionality and subjectivity. He goes on to argue that the effective researcher is one who considers the manner in which their individual characteristics (race, gender, ethnicity, class, economic status, habitus, and disposition) coupled with their 'position' in the field (role, purpose, focus, seniority, power, etc.) impact on both themselves and the research questions they pose, the manner in which they conduct their research, on the data they can gather, and how they then interpret that data (see also Davies, 1998). The purpose here is one of examining the assumptions which underpin and then affect what we do. It is an accounting of ourselves as much as the research we conduct. However, as discussed in the introduction of this volume, this reflexive practice often excludes the most primary parts of ourselves as researchers. Reflexive practice is ideally suited to the examination of the sensorial. Yet we tend not to examine how our

---

[4]For a similar discussion of how this and other Western centric problems have beset psychological studies of perceptions, see Howes and Classesn (2014).

subjective experience of a sensorium affects the manner in which we research it. Furthermore, even if we do consider this aspect of ourselves and our research, those considerations rarely make it out of the field notes and onto the academic page. Yet it is as important to consider these elements as it is class, race, gender, and power.

Regardless of these ontological, epistemological, and reflexive intricacies there is a further problem: how do we, in a flattened, textual, scientific account communicate effectively the sensory, or in this case, the intense sensorial experience of living through a fire in a prison, to our readers? This is, after all, a sensory experience that is alien to most? Taking a leaf from Serres (2008) and Sparkes (2009), the answer is to be found in the conventions and mechanisms of storytelling. More specifically, evocation. The literary form, and its ability to capture the prosody of natural communication, is ideally suited to communicating complex sensory experience as it is necessarily evocative in nature. The mechanism of evocation is designed to transport the reader into the experience being described, and in so doing, both communicate the vividness of that experience and mitigate the flatness of the language being utilised. So, when I needed to evoke for my readers both the overwhelming sensorium of the fire, the viscerality of being 'locked in', and a sense of Verstehen towards the central character, literary forms come to the rescue. By highlighting the characters' experience with 'Eyes are stinging. Heart thumping out of control. Throat burning. Nose raw. Panic. Need to get out. Need to get away', I am able to take the reader inside that experience and create the necessary empathy for someone subjected to it.

This is not as uncommon as we might think within academic texts. Leavy (2013) points out that there is a long tradition in qualitative research of writers adopting certain narrative conventions (bibliographic detail, thick and rich description, verbatim quotes, metaphor, simile, vignettes, etc.) in order to communicate either complexity or vividness. All, she argues, are attempts at countering the limitations of the textual form as we attempt to bring our research worlds to life. Nevertheless, she argues that it can be desirable, or even necessary, to go beyond the adoption of some literary forms to utilising the full range of narrative conventions. This is especially true, as Bochner and Ellis (2016) note, when trying to communicate very complex, rare, or little understood lived experiences. In such cases, there is a need to use the varying conventions of literature to evoke or create an imaginarium in which the reader can experience the previously unexperienced.

This is why I started with a vignette. This descriptive snapshot is designed (hopefully) to evoke the experience of a fire in prison. I wanted to communicate the varied sensory overload of the experience by evoking all nine senses. Vision (sight), audition (hearing), gustation (taste), olfaction (smell), taction (touch), thermoception (heat/cold), nociception (pain), equilibrioception (balance, gravity), proprioception (bodily position) (Macpherson, 2011) as are all relevant. To create a sufficiently vivid imaginarium for the reader to enter, the full gamut of these sensations needed to be evoked in order to come close to communicating the viscerality of living through a fire in prison. All were needed to also communicate a further sense, one particular to the carceral lifeworld, a sense that, at present, does not have a name. As such, and for the purposes of this chapter, I define this sense as captiception[5] – the sense or perception of being trapped, of being unable to escape. This was important as the accumulation of those other senses combined to create a new sensory experience that is almost uniquely context specific. The vignette was the most efficacious way of communicating this sensory overload and trapped reality.

The vignette itself is an amalgamation of 12 different accounts told to me during fieldwork conducted in four very different prisons in England and Wales.[6] I have conjoined these accounts with my own experiences of fires while being 'banged-up'. During 12 years of continual custody between 1992 and 2004, I experienced being trapped within a cell while a fire raged beneath or around me three times in two different prisons. The overwhelming sense of trappedness, abandonment, and fear that I personally experienced, and had assumed was fairly unique to my own subjectivity, was then, much to my surprise, echoed in every single one the accounts given to me by these 12 men. The experience nearly always progressed in the exact same way from waking or becoming aware of the fire, to panic, to a realisation of helplessness, and then the building of fear as one is unable to effect any escape or reprieve from the approaching fire, to a sense of abandonment, to an overload of sensory input, to a hyperawareness of the physicality of their cell and their place within it, to a hollow realisation of themselves as an unimportant, disposable, thing. I have tried to capture the basic essence of all these accounts here and combine them into a coherent and singular vignette that can bring this alive for the reader.

The Walls Seem Real All of a Sudden

To return to the first challenge, what does this 'trappedness', this 'captiception', the physical sensation of being trapped, and the resultant fear response that this can generate, tells us about imprisonment and penality? 'Penality' has come to be understood as not just the juridical/punitive justifications of punishment but also the matrices of rhetorics, logics, policies, institutions, discourses, symbols, rituals, techniques, practices, and purposes that define punishment in late-modern society (see Carlen, 2008; Garland & Young, 1983). However, as Herrity (2019) notes in her exploration of sound in prison, the symbolism of penal power is not just communicated through operational and discursive means but also the very sounds of the prison (jangling keys, slamming doors, alarms, bells, tannoys, etc.). Each of these inescapable sounds communicate, and reinforce, to people in prison their status and experience as 'prisoners'. Informed by this seminal work, it is my

---

[5]This is a term, which I acknowledge is both very clumsy and ugly, coined for the purpose of this chapter as, at present, no better term exists. The word itself derives from the Latin captum (captured or trapped) and utilises the suffix -ception to denote the sense of.

[6]These include a large Category B local prison, a long-term young offender institute, a special function prison in the south east, and a Category C Training prison for long termers in the North Midlands.

contention here that just as social, political, economic, and punitive influences are embedded within penal practice, they are too encoded into the sensorium of the penal institutions wherein they are enacted. Within the captiception of not being able to 'get out', of the feeling that 'There is no way out', and the embodied trappedness of being in a 'sealed box' lies encoded the very nature of what a prison is. Therefore, moving beyond the traditional justificatory, penological, and discursive explanations of prison and punishment to exploring the sensorial and embodied experience of incarceration reveals new and important considerations about the nature, practice, and purpose of imprisonment.

The notion of captiception, or embodied captivity, in prison settings is both incredibly mundane, obvious, and tragically important. In 2005, hundreds of prisoners were abandoned by correctional staff inside Orleans Parish Prison for four days as the flood waters and mud from Hurricane Katrina swamped the prison. Trapped, locked-in, they suffered some of the worst effects of the hurricane and were left severely traumatised (ACLU, 2006). On St Valentine's Day 2012, 358 prisoners died in fires in Honduras after prison staff had evacuated the prison leaving 800+ prisoners trapped, screaming, to face the fires, and death, alone (Navarro, 2012). These are extreme, but historically recurrent, events. The reality of the prison is that individuals can be trapped within, where in extreme but quotidian circumstances, their lack of autonomy and power becomes a stark and potentially fatal experience. In England and Wales, fires in prison are a daily occurrence. Between 2012 and 2016, there was a 61% increase in Emergency Fire Services attending prisons, 83% of these callouts involved a fire. In the last three years, there have been 6,118 recorded fires in the 118 prisons of England and Wales (Ministry of Justice, 2019). This equates to multiple fires every single day in the prisons of England and Wales and thus an experience that a significant number of the men, women, and children in custody are forced to endure. Yet this issue, how it is experienced, what the effects of this are, and what it can tell us about policies and practices of punishment have yet to be explored in the relevant prisons literature.

Part of the problem here is the ocular-centric nature of prison research. Herrity (2019) argues that the visual paradigm that has dominated prison sociology and studies of penality has limited much of the extant research to that which can be seen and observed. As researchers, and (quasi)ethnographers, we tend to operate in those areas of the prison which we can observe what is happening. We take note of that which takes place in plain sight and this informs our research about the social worlds within. There are clear and reasonable reasons (security for instance) that limit where we can operate as researchers within the prison. However, this has traditionally constrained, and imposed certain forms of assumption upon, our research foci and questions. As noted above, this is not solely a problem in prison and penality research but rather one that has emerged from the development of social scientific thought and practice in Western societies since the Enlightment (Classen, 1997). However, in terms of the carceral world, as Herrity (forthcoming) points out, the vast majority of prison life is lived behind the door, in cell, locked-in, beyond the gaze of the researcher. In England and Wales specifically, it is now not unusual for prisoners to remain in their cells for 20+ hours a day. Yet much of our research, whether it be on geographies, the nature of totalities, the experience of sentences, family life, pains, order/disorder, violence, sociality, etc., within prison fails to capture this reality. This aspect of prison life, which I argue is fundamental to a carceral life, just does not have a great deal of exposure in the contemporary prison literature. As a consequence, the embodied sensory dimensions of imprisonment, and thus what it means for the state to incarcerate one of its citizens (or those considered alien others (see Bosworth, 2011)), is missing from our understanding of what prison is, how it is experienced, and what it does.

I'm Alone. Powerless.

Sykes in his classic text *The Society of Captives* (1958) explains that there are a number of 'deprivations' which mark out the experience of incarceration. These are the classic 'pains of imprisonment'. Of course, as Sykes notes, there are as many accounts of prison as there are prisoners (p. 63). Nevertheless, he was interested in marking out those deprivations which are common to all and which define the nature of incarceration. As such, he defined these 'frustrations' as the deprivations of liberty, autonomy, goods and services, heterosexual/social relationships, and security. However, for all the sophistication and long-term impact of his account, it is a somewhat hollow rendering of the prison experience. He talks of isolation and rejection (deprivation of liberty, p. 65) and states that it is a painful loss of emotional lives, relationships, and the imposition of loneliness and boredom. Likewise, the deprivation of autonomy is described as profoundly painful as the prisoner is reduced to the '… weak, helpless, dependent status of childhood': a state from which the prisoner cannot escape. On the deprivation of security, he states that the close proximity of other prisoners who can pose both a physical and an existential threat is '… anxiety-provoking even for the hardened recidivist …' (p. 77). However, these accounts tell us little about what it is like to actually experience the deprivation of liberty, autonomy, and security. The qualia[7] (those accessible phenomenal aspects of our internal mental lives) are distinctly missing from this classic account of what it means to be incarcerated.

This deprivation model has been expanded by a number of scholars (for instance, see Crewe, 2009; Johnson & Toch, 1982; Warr, 2016). In each of these instances what we see is an extension of the deprivation model, with the introduction of new 'pains', in order to explain the nature of prison and how it relates to the systems of penality which underpin and inform practices of punishment. Often empirical examples are provided to take us beyond the abstraction of the theoretical model in order to show us what the effects of those experiences are. In

---

[7]I know this term is problematic in terms of the philosophy of mind (especially mind/body dualism). Nevertheless, suits the purposes of this chapter in describing those mental elements of experience with which we, as qualitative and ethnographic researchers, attempt to capture and communicate. For a good description of this problem, see Crane (2000).

some of the very best texts, there is even some attempt at providing an account of the experience itself (for an exemplar, see Crewe, 2009). However, many of these accounts focus upon the social world of the prison, or the manner in which the imposed penalty shapes a prisoner's carceral habitus (Caputo-Levine, 2013; Schept, 2013), and thus do not quite manage to communicate the impact of this on the internal lifeworlds of those they encounter. The qualia of embodied captivity, and any form of sensory penalty, remain a frustratingly ephemeral aspect of these foundational, vigorously theoretical, and empirically grounded accounts.

While not in the tradition of penological texts, the 'captive narratives' literature (for instance, see Pearce, 1947; Strong, 2018), which explores the captivity experiences of Native Americans at the hands of colonial powers, comes close to communicating these experiences. Often told in 'Saga' type formats, they explore the personal and subjective nature of being 'captive' while simultaneously exploring what this tells of colonial power and imposition. Yet this literature, coming from a very different tradition, tells us little about contemporary incarceration and penality. Texts from former prisoners do slightly better in this regard. Of particular note here is Erwin James' *A Life Inside* (2003) and Victor Hassine's *Life Without Parole* (1996). In both of these explorations of life in prison, they speak eloquently about their subjective experiences of sounds, noises, tastes, and the feelings of being 'inside'. Nevertheless, even these autobiographical musings, though coming the closest to addressing the feeling that comes with a near complete removal of liberty, agency/autonomy, and security, do not quite communicate the wider implications of what it means for this to be imposed.

I'm in a Sealed Box. This Cell is a Trap

To once more return to Serres (2008), he notes that the story that he tells of being trapped in with the fire tells us not only fundamental things about human experience and how to communicate it but also of serving aboard the naval vessel. It reveals essential elements of what the ship is, how it is constructed, what it does, how it is operated, and, importantly, how these structural factors become imposed upon and thus experienced by those subject to them. This is my fundamental argument – the vignette above, and the sense of trappedness it reveals, tells us essential elements of what the prison is, how it is constructed, what it does, how it is operated, and what it is like to experience it. It reveals to us that the deprivation of liberty is not just a removal from community but also a complete and totally immersive sense of embodied captivity. The individual here who is seeing the '*ghostly flickers at the window*', the '*Hints of amber against the ebon night*', is forced into the visceral experience by their very loss of liberty. Correspondingly, this deprivation is encoded within those evoked sensations. This is what the prison is and what it is designed to do. It reveals that the deprivation of autonomy is not just related to constrained choice and agency but the rendering of utter helplessness. The person within the cell has no power to mitigate that sense of embodied captivity even in a circumstance that could prove fatal to them. There is a complete lack of agency revealed in this story, the fate and life of the individual is in the hands of someone else ('*Guv, Guv! GUV!*'). Again, this is what the prison is designed to do, and it is constructed and operated in such a way as to reinforce this loss of autonomy. Lastly, that the character feels like they are '*going to die here*' because they '*can't get out*' it reveals that the deprivation of security is not just related to the presence of threat from others but also a potentially fatal threat from the very institution itself. This is the essential nature of the prison and how it becomes imposed upon the 'prisoner'. The conjunction of these deprivations reveals the utter abjection of the prisoner status. An abjection that an exploration of the sensorial nature of incarceration allows us to capture in more detail than in traditional accounts.

This is What Prison is

However, the story allows us to go beyond deepening our understanding of the deprivation model to explore some of the wider themes of penality. For instance, that a person in prison can be subjected to such an extreme sensorial experience tells us something significant about the practical, operational, and corporeal implications of a 'prisoner's' civil death. Civil death (or *civiliter mortis*) has, in the late twentieth century, mostly been related to the disenfranchisement of prisoners from the democratic process (for instance, see Behan, 2015; Chin, 2012; Manza & Uggen, 2004). Much of the discussion has focussed on the minutia of the legal standing of denying people in prison their voting rights and the implications of this for successful resettlement. Yet the issue of civil death goes beyond this superficial legal conundrum to the symbolic status of the prisoner as a non-citizen and what this symbolic status means for how that person can and is treated within carceral settings (see Easton, 2018). Price (2015) extends the notion of civil death to one of 'social death' as he argues that it is not just the civic life of prisoners that is mortified but all aspects of their social self (legal, civic, moral, etc.). The person who was is no more. What is left is a 'prisoner' who has forfeited not only their civic rights but so too any moral consideration. The act of incarceration (including pre-conviction) establishes a symbolic status, whereby the person is diminished in the eyes of society and law. This is evident in the story above if we examine the response of the officer in this narrative.

It may seem that the officer here is somewhat callous in their response to the prisoner and in the denial of providing relief. However, the officer here is operating under a strict set of guidelines (Prison Service Instructions (PSI) 11/2015 Fire Safety in Prisons; Prison Service Order (PSO) 3803 Fire Safety) from which they cannot deviate (see NOMS, 2015). The actions of the officer here adhere to the correct procedure for dealing with cell fires of a night. They may not be representative of how that officer feels when confronted with the reality of an out of control cell fire but they are representative of how they must act. That set of guidelines, then, provides evidence of the diminished civic status of prisoners. Before exploring that in further detail, it is important to note that at night, the wing officer on duty will not have cell keys and thus cannot unlock a cell. Even if they did have a set of keys on the wing, they would not be allowed to unlock the cell if they are on their own. Both the PSI and PSO mentioned above set out the requirements for staff responding to in-cell fires. To cover the full requirements would be to exhaust this chapter however the basic process is that once the fire is discovered and reported, orderly officer called (and equipment/cell and inundation keys brought) to the wing, fire safety equipment donned in a safe area, and an attempt is made to inundate the in-cell fire (an attempt to supress the fire and the occupant of the cell by using a fire hose) then and only then is an attempt made to communicate with the cell occupant. If the person is compliant, they will attempt to remove them from the cell while inundating the fire but only if there are more than two staff (not including orderly officer) present. At night, they cannot open the cell door unless multiple staff are in attendance. Given that the prison runs only a skeleton crew of a night-time, this can often be a problem. If the person in the cell is not compliant or non-communicative, any attempt to remove them from the fire will only occur at the point that it is safe to do so.[8] All of that takes time. Dealing with the vicarious impacts of a fire (how others suffer the consequences of smoke, thermal change, etc.) is given little consideration, and unless in extreme circumstances requiring a general evacuation, those individuals will be left to cope alone. That is policy.

The correct procedure here traps those in prison into experiencing fire in the way set out in the vignette; *'This is what prison is. Trapped. Locked-in. No escape. The feeling is thick, viscous, pressurised'*. The prison and its rules of operation force those locked into their cells to experience this thick sensuality of trappedness and fear. *'The walls, the locked door, the bars on the window, I can feel them without touch ...'* This is the punishment that lies within the punishment of imprisonment. Having such sensory experiences imposed reinforces every single symbolic communication of their 'prisoner' status to those trapped individuals. They are subject, helpless, dependent, and, perhaps, even worthless. This imposition of trappedness is by design and intent rather than just being some form of 'institutional thoughtlessness' (Crawley, 2005). The symbolic nature of the prisoner status is encoded within and imparted to the individual by the constructed sensorium of the prison. That these impositional sensations are then fundamental aspects of the prison as an institution tells us what the carceral institution is designed to do. It is designed to immolate the 'offending' individual's moral and civic self, by subjecting them to a totally immersive sense of embodied captivity, in order to inflict some external juridical/disciplinary end (Foucault, 1979, 1994).

Conclusion

This chapter has sought to explore two interrelated issues: first, can the use of story format communicate the deep sensorial nature of incarceration; and, second,

---

[8]This is the process for dealing with an in-cell fire. If the fire jumps in magnitude to become a general fire, then the process of evacuation will be triggered. All prisons must have evacuation plans but these must adhere to the processes set out in the orders/instructions detailed here and present problems at night, as an operational centre needs to be established and external emergency prison staff called in from home in order to facilitate any evacuation.

what, if anything, can an exploration of the sensorial nature of incarceration tell us about the wider themes of penality. Whether I have been successful in either of these endeavours is for the reader to judge. However, I would contend that the vignette works in a way to invoke a form of *Verstehen* in the reader that a more traditional approach would not. The narrative format is specifically designed to evince the type of empathy response needed and desired for an outsider to understand the deep sensorial nature of incarceration. I would also contend that an exploration of the penal sensorium does in deed tell us something fundamental about the processes of deprivation that people in prison are subjected to and of the civic death which they experience. This further informs us about the nature and purpose of these institutions. Simply put the purposes, functions, ethos, practices, symbol interactions of penality are very much encoded into all the inescapable and subliminal sensory elements of the prison.

So, where does this leave us? I think this leaves us in quite an exciting place for research into prisons, penality, processes of social control, and criminology. What would taking into account the penal sensorium tell us about classic concepts and foundational research in our field? Perhaps an exploration of the sensorial nature of Melossi and Pavarini's (1981) political economy of the prison in terms of its reinforcement of labour ideations (prison/factory)? Or a revisiting of what it means for an institution to be 'total' (Goffman, 1961)? Or perhaps how *Papa's discipline* is imposed upon women in prison (Carlen, 1982)? Or perhaps … the list is endless. The advent of a sensory criminology means that many of our traditional perspectives and assumptions can be revisited, re-explored, re-learned. I believe that we can renew our discipline and explore these penal worlds anew with different senses and, by the use of sensorially informed techniques, begin to impart our knowledge more successfully to the public and wider society.

References

ACLU. (2006). *Abandoned & abused: Orleans Parish prisoners in the wake of hurricane Katrina*. American Civil Liberties Union. Retrieved from https://www.aclu.org/files/pdfs/prison/oppreport20060809.pdf

Behan, C. (2015). *Punishment, prisoners and the franchise. Howard league what is justice?* Working Papers, 20/2015. The Howard League, London.

Bochner, A., & Ellis, C. (2016). *Evocative autoethnography: Writing lives and telling stories*. New York, NY: Routledge.

Bosworth, M. (2011). Deportation, detention, and foreign national prisoners in England and Wales. *Citizenship Studies*, *15*(5), 583–595.

Caputo-Levine, D. D. (2013). The yard face: The contributions of inmate interpersonal violence to the carceral habitus. *Ethnography*, *14*(2), 165–185.

Carlen, P. (1982). Papa's discipline: An analysis of disciplinary modes in the Scottish women's prison. *Sociological Review*, *30*(1), 97–124.

Carlen, P. (2008). Imaginary penalities and risk-crazed governance. In P. Carlen (Ed.), *Imaginary penalities* (pp. 1–25). Cullumpton: Willan Publishing.

Chin, G. J. (2012). The new civil death: Rethinking punishment in the era of mass conviction. *University of Pennsylvania Law Review*, *160*(6), 1789–1834.

Classen, C. (1997). Engendering perceptions: Gender ideologies and sensory hierarchies in Western history. *Body and Society, 3*(2), 1–19.

Clifford, J. (1986). Introduction: Partial truths. In J. Clifford & G. E. Marcus (Eds.), *Writing culture: The poetics and politics of ethnography* (pp. 1–26). Berkeley, CA: University of California Press.

Cox, R., Irving, A., & Wright, C. (2016). Introduction: The sense of the senses. In R. Cox, A. Irving, & C. Wright (Eds.), *Beyond text? Critical practices and sensory anthropology*. Manchester: Manchester University Press.

Crane, T. (2000). The origins of qualia. In T. Crane & S. Patterson (Eds.), *The history of the mind-body problem* (pp. 169–194). London: Routledge.

Crawley, E. (2005). Institutional thoughtlessness in prisons and its impacts on the day-to-day prison lives of elderly men. *Journal of Contemporary Criminal Justice, 21*(4), 350–363.

Crewe, B. (2009). *The prisoner society: Power, adaptation and social life in an English prison*. Oxford: Oxford University Press.

Davies, C. A. (1998). Reflexive Ethnography: *A Guide to Researching Selves and Others*. London: Routledge.

Dean, J. (2017). *Doing reflexivity: An introduction*. Bristol: Policy Press.

Easton, S. (2018). *The politics of the prison and the prisoner: Zoon politikon*. London: Routledge.

Field, S. (2005). Places sensed, senses placed: Toward a sensuous epistemology of environments. In D. Howes (Ed.), *Empire of the senses: The sensual cultural reader* (pp. 179–191). Oxford: Berg Publishers.

Foucault, M. (1979). *Discipline and punish: The birth of the prison*. (A. Sheridan, Trans.). London: Allen Lane.

Foucault, M. (1994). Truth and juridical forms. In J. D. Faubion (Ed.), *Michel Foucault: Power – Essential works of Foucault 1954–1984* (Vol. 3, pp. 1–89). London: Penguin Books.

Fuster, J. M. (2003). *Cortex and mind: Unifying cognition*. New York, NY: Oxford University Press.

Garland, D., & Young, P. (1983). Towards a social analysis of penality. In D. Garland & P. Young (Eds.), *The power to punish: Contemporary penality and social analysis* (pp. 1–36). London: Heinemann Educational Books.

Geertz, C. (1994). Thick description: Towards an interpretive theory of culture. In M. Martin & L. C. McIntyre (Eds.), *Readings in the philosophy of social science* (pp. 213–232). Cambridge, MA: MIT Press.

Giorgi, A. (2006). Difficulties encountered in the application of the phenomenological method in the social sciences. *Analise Psicologica, 3*(XXIV), 353–361.

Goffman, E. (1961). *Asylums: Essays on the social situation of mental patients and other inmates*. New York, NY: Anchor Books: Doubleday & Co.

Guillemin, M., & Gillam, L. (2004). Ethics, reflexivity, and 'ethically important moments' in research. *Qualitative Inquiry, 10*(2), 261–280.

Hassine, V. (1996). *Life without parole: Living and dying in prison today*. New York, NY: Oxford University Press.

Herrity, K. (2019). *Rhythms and routines: Sounding order in a local men's prison through aural ethnography*. Unpublished Ph.D. thesis. University of Leicester, Leicester.

Herrity, K. (forthcoming). Hearing behind the door: The cell as a portal to prison life. In V. Knight & J. Turner (Eds.), *The prison cell: Embodied and everyday spaces of incarceration*. London: Palgrave Macmillan.

Howes, D., & Classen, C. (2014). *Ways of sensing: Understanding the senses in society*. London: Routledge.

Husserl, E. (2001). *The shorter logical investigations*. (J. N. Findlay, Trans., 1970). Introduced by D. Moran (2001). London: Routledge.

James, E. (2003). *A life inside: A prisoner's notebook*. London: Atlantic Books.
Johnson, R., & Toch, H. (1982). *The pains of imprisonment*. Beverly Hills, CA: Sage.
Leavy, P. (2013). *Fiction as research practice: Short stories, novellas, and novels*. New York, NY: Routledge.
Macpherson, F. (2011). Individuating the senses. In F. Macpherson (Ed.), *The senses: Classic and contemporary perspectives* (pp. 3–46). Oxford: Oxford University Press.
Majid, A., & Levinson, S. C. (2011). The senses in language and culture. *The Senses and Society*, 6(1), 5–18.
Manza, J., & Uggen, C. (2004). Punishment and democracy: Disenfranchisement of nonincarcerated felons in the United States. *Perspectives on Politics*, 2(3), 491–505.
Mbembe, A. (2017). *Critique of black reason*. Johannesburg: Wits University Press.
Melossi, D., & Pavarini, M. (1981). *The prison factory: Origins of the penitentiary system*. (G. Cousin, Trans.). London: Palgrave.
Merleau-Ponty, M. (2012). *Phenomenology of perception*. (D. A. Landes, Trans.). London: Routledge.
Ministry of Justice. (2019). *Prisons: Fires – Response to parliamentary question posed by Richard Burgon MP*. UK Parliament. Retrieved from https://beta.parliament.uk/questions/bnWgIDQz
Navarro, M. (2012). *Honduras prison fire kills more than 350 inmates*. Reuters. Retrieved from https://www.reuters.com/article/us-honduras-jail-fire/honduras-prison-fire-kills-more-than-350-inmates-idUSTRE81E0OK20120215
NOMS. (2015). *Prison Service Instructions (PSI 11/2015): Fire safety in prison establishments*. National Offender Management Service. Ministry of Justice.
Pearce, R. (1947). The significances of the captivity narrative. *American Literature*, 19(1), 1–20.
Price, J. M. (2015). *Prison and social death*. New Brunswick, NJ: Rutgers University Press.
Schept, J. (2013). 'A Lockdown facility ... with the feel of a small, private college': Liberal politics, jail expansion and the carceral habitus. *Theoretical Criminology*, 17(1), 71–88.
Serres, M. (2008). *The five senses: A philosophy of mingled bodies*. (M. Sankley & P. Cowley, Trans.). London: Continuum International Publishing Group.
Simmel, G. (1905). *Die probleme der Gechichtsphilosophie. Eine erkentnistheoretische Studie*. Leipzig: Verlag von Dunker und Humboldt.
Sparkes, A. C. (2009). Ethnography and the senses: Challenges and possibilities. *Qualitative Research in Sport and Exercise*, 1(1), 21–35.
Strong, P. T. (2018). *Captive selves, captivating others: The politics and poetics of colonial American captivity narratives*. New York, NY: Routledge.
Sykes, G. M. (1958). *The society of captives: A study of a maximum security prison*. Princeton, NJ: Princeton University Press.
Warr, J. (2016). The Prisoner: Inside and Out. In Y. Jewkes, B. Crewe and J. Bennett (eds), *Handbook on Prisons* (2nd ed., pp. 586–604). London: Routledge.

Chapter 3

Sensing Supervision Through Stories and Songs

Jo Collinson Scott and Fergus McNeill

Introduction

In this chapter, we take the opportunity to reflect upon our recent collaboration in relation to Fergus' book *Pervasive Punishment: Making Sense of Mass Supervision* (McNeill, 2018). The book's central argument is that supervisory forms of punishment (e.g. probation, parole, community service and electronic monitoring) have become very much more pervasive in late-modern societies and, importantly, that they have become more pervasive in the lives of those subject to them. Yet these forms of punishment remain largely invisible and inaudible to such an extent that public and political debate about the emergence of 'mass supervision' is seriously undermined. We cannot meaningfully debate the justice or injustice of forms of punishment that which we cannot imagine, and most of us lack the resources to imagine supervision (see McNeill, 2018, chapter 1). Here, we focus specifically on how paying more careful and more creative attention to the sensory might help address this problem.

In so doing, we are informed by our separate and shared experiences of using creative methods to engage the senses in ways which are relatively novel, at least in criminology. By working with research participants to represent their experiences in visual and auditory forms, creative approaches can help to share the work of representation and to refuse or resist, to some extent, the conventional researcher's analytical privilege in making sense of human experience (Liebling, McNeill, & Schmidt, 2017). They may allow a potential means of expression that overcomes 'hermeneutical injustice'; meaning the injustice attendant on our inability to engage with a lived experience because of a paucity of shared resources for expressing, hearing and understanding it (Fricker, 2007).

Just as creative methods can allow participants space to explore and represent their own experiences and concerns, they also generate artefacts (e.g. pictures and songs) that leave space for their audience to engage with and be affected by the context of their creator's experience. In an environment of supervision's invisibility and inaudibility, we argue that this affective engagement is crucial to making the experience of supervision more 'feel-able' and more imaginable, thus enabling public dialogue about it. Perhaps more ambitiously, we hope that,

> in this process, the creator may cease to be a 'moral stranger' (Loewy, 1997). As we become better morally acquainted through these forms of representation, indifference to one another's fate, or even the hostility reserved for outsiders, is perhaps undermined (Bauman, 2016). (McNeill, 2018, p. 148)

As we argue below, the object here is less to elicit sympathy or even empathy and more to encourage what Claire Hemmings (2012) calls 'affective solidarity'.

That said, it is important to heed significant cautions around the oversimplification of these relationships, particularly with relation to music (e.g. Clarke, DeNora, & Vuoskoski, 2015; Kramer, 2001, 2003). For example, Hesmondhalgh (2013) discusses the potential for popular music to distinguish or alienate people as much as to bring them together, given that music does not 'float free of the profound problems we face in our inner lives and in our attempts to live together' (p. 171).

Nonetheless, even bearing these challenges in mind, we suggest that creative approaches to criminology are necessary not just to the *descriptive* project of sensory penalties that is the main focus of this book but also in engaging with *prescriptive* questions about criminology's public and political role (Loader & Sparks, 2010).

The writing of *Pervasive Punishment* surfaced many of these questions for Fergus. To him, it seemed that a conventional academic book might not provide its readers with the resources required to enable affective engagement with supervision, far less to encourage any affective solidarity with people under supervision and their supervisors. For that reason, he decided to write a short story – a work of sociological fiction, informed by research and scholarship, both creative and conventional – intended to bring to life the book's key themes. Later in the process, he invited the first author to use her 'research-led-practice' expertise to create an EP of songs that would offer an additional, complementary form of inquiry into these themes.

In the remainder of this chapter, we provide an account of the processes through which we produced the short story and the EP, focussing on the role of the sensory both in their creation and, we hope, in helping them fulfil their purposes. In the first section, Fergus discusses 'The Invisible Collar' and, in the second, Jo discusses 'System Hold'.[1] In the conclusion, we offer some brief reflections on the process.

---

[1] The full text of the story can be accessed here: https://www.pervasivepunishment.com/2019/11/18/invisible-collar/. The EP can be found here: https://jomango.bandcamp.com/album/system-hold.

A Sensory Story About Supervision

Fergus McNeill

Beginnings. My partner is a primary (or elementary) schoolteacher, with limited interest in criminal justice and, therefore, in most of what I have written before. When I started writing *Pervasive Punishment*, I asked her if she was going to read it. She replied with a question of her own: 'Are you going to make it interesting?' That led on to an important conversation about what makes books interesting to read. As an avid reader of fiction (including crime fiction), she enjoys engaging plots but, more importantly, she needs to feel something for and come to care about a book's leading character/s. So, I decided to shed my academic (and personal) inhibitions and write her a story, or at least the beginning of one. I spent several hours of a long train journey drafting the few hundred words that comprised the first draft of the first episode of 'The Invisible Collar'. The final version is reproduced here:

> Waiting
>
> Joe sat on the bench in the waiting room. Looking down, he noticed that the bench was screwed to the floor. Not even the furniture here was free. Perspex screens and locked doors separated him and the others waiting from those for whom they waited; the veils between the untrustworthy and those to whom they were entrusted.
>
> Joe absent-mindedly read the graffiti carved into the bench; testimonies of resistance that made the place feel even more desperate.
>
> Joe scanned the postered walls, shouting their messages in pastel shades and bold print. Problems with drugs? Problems with alcohol? Problems with anger? Stay calm. Apparently help was at hand. But meanwhile remember that abusive language and aggressive behaviour will not be tolerated. Not in this room that itself felt like an installation of abuse and aggression. To Joe it said: 'You are pathetic, desperate or dangerous. You are not to be trusted. You must wait'.
>
> He fidgeted and returned his eyes to the floor, downcast by the weight of the room's assault, avoiding contact, avoiding hassle, staying as unknown as possible in this shame pit. Better to be out of place here than to belong. This was no place to make connections.
>
> Joe wondered what she would be like – Pauline – the unknown woman who now held the keys to his freedom. Her word had become his law: This was an order after all. He was to be the

rule-keeper, she the ruler – cruel, capricious or kind. She might hold the leash lightly or she might drag him to heel. Instinctively, he lifted his hand to his neck, but no one can loosen an invisible collar. At least it was not a noose. Joe swallowed uncomfortably, noticing the dryness of his mouth and the churning in his gut. He was not condemned to hang. He was condemned to be left hanging.

Joe wondered what Pauline would be like.

When I asked my partner to read the first draft of this opening episode, her response was positive. These few short paragraphs had succeeded at least in stimulating an interest in the two characters and in the relationship that might develop between them. So, I continued with the creative experiment.

Having established a project blog (www.pervasivepunishment.com), I developed the practice of sharing draft episodes of the story as they were written, noticing that these often elicited more comment (via social media) than other posts. Admittedly, much of this interest came from other academics (staff and students) and from criminal justice practitioners, sometimes comparing what was depicted with their own experiences. But it did seem that the story was working broadly as I hoped: it was sparking and interacting with people's imaginations and generating dialogue. At the book's launch (which involved me reading 'An Invisible Collar' from the story and Jo and friends performing the songs from 'System Hold'[2]), and on numerous other occasions since when I have shared episodes of the story, similar reactions to and engagements with the story have been apparent. For present purposes though, the key questions concern how exactly these engagements were enabled, and what role the sensory played in these processes.

Senses and Settings. Although I have drawn on people, places, experiences and academic literature in writing the story, I did not set it consciously in any specific jurisdiction or at any precise moment in time. The institutional form of supervision that it depicts is perhaps closest to the current situation in Community Rehabilitation Companies in England and Wales (Burke, Collett, & McNeill, 2018). Indeed, some English managers and practitioners have identified painfully closely with some aspects of the story. If there is a temporal setting, it is the near future.

Perhaps somewhat artificially, the story's plot evolves in parallel with the pre-existing structure of the academic analysis of 'mass supervision' offered in the book. In all but the final chapter of *Pervasive Punishment*, the fictional episode precedes – and sets the scene for – the academic writing and is then referred to within it. With hindsight, those references back to the fiction might be understood as attempts to keep the sensory and affective connection between the reader and the book alive, even as the style of writing shifts in form.

---

[2]A short film of the launch can be found here: https://www.youtube.com/watch?v=PaMwzRNyo1E.

But even if the analytical structure of the academic argument framed the evolution of the story's plot across each episode, my writing was also anchored in specific places and then developed through an encounter between characters. Most often, when I started writing each episode, I didn't know what was going to happen. In this sense, the plot was produced by the interactions between settings and characters. Thus, for example, in episode V, all that I did was arrange a home visit by Pauline to Joe's flat. Here is how I described that setting:

> While Joe re-boiled the kettle, Pauline studied their surroundings. Joe's place was not, she imagined, a deliberate effort at Scandinavian minimalism taken to extremes; more likely, it revealed that lack of self-care that often accompanies depression. The living room in his one-bedroom apartment boasted only a large bean-bag, an easy chair (bottom of the range Ikea) and a small coffee table. An old TV sat on the floor in a corner. The un-curtained window looked out over the courtyard of what was a converted 1920s fire station. She'd seen much worse places, but she couldn't imagine Joe's kids being keen on sleepovers, unless they shared their dad's newfound ascetic tastes.

The flat that I describe here is a version of one that I once lived in; and in my mind's eye, I pictured it as it was at the point of moving in; empty. All of us can probably recall being in a new 'home' that is not yet home, and the discomfiting sense of unarticulated nervousness about whether and when a new place will come to *feel* like home. Until then, it is a liminal space. In Joe's case perhaps, that liminality seems to be indefinite – he has not *settled* – and this triggers a concern for Pauline about his mental health and social isolation. While the dialogue in the episode explains and extends that mood, the descriptive writing sets the physical and the affective scene.

The sensory potency of describing settings in the story is also apparent in episode 1 above. Again, that setting was a mixture of the real and the imagined. When writing it, I was recalling the waiting area of the social work office where I first worked. My first memory of that waiting room is vivid because I sat there waiting to meet the Area Manager who had the power to decide whether or not to take me on, and whether or not to allow me to work in criminal justice. Almost 28 years later, I can still recall the bespoke carpentry of the varnished plywood bench; it was hard and uncomfortable and it looked cheap. But while those qualities seemed to devalue and demean those who would have to sit there (much longer and many times more often than me), nervously waiting, I also noticed that the carpenter had carefully counter-sunk the screws in brass ring fittings, presumably so that they wouldn't snag people's clothing. That juxtaposition stayed with me. I can also still feel, as a sensory memory, the worrying weight of twin doors on heavy springs that swung back violently on their hinges; I can see the wire-mesh glass on the reception window, and the forbidding receptionist behind it, whose demeanour suggested that any inquiry would be an irritation.

Not all of these sensory memories feature in the fiction, but they informed its writing nonetheless. But while my own memories – of working as a criminal justice social workers and of visiting countless offices both as a practitioner and as a researcher – informed the writing, the fiction was also directly informed by more recent empirical research. In particular, I drew on visual representations of probation work (including probation offices) provided by practitioners in the 'Picturing Probation' project (Worrall, Carr, & Robinson, 2017) and the typically more abstract photographs representing supervision taken by supervisees in the 'Supervisible' project (Fitzgibbon, Graebsch, & McNeill, 2017; see also McNeill, 2019); some of these photographs accompany episodes of the story in the book.

Perhaps the most influential of these representations is a photograph taken by a young man serving a community sentence in Scotland; one of the participants in the 'Supervisible' project. He explained his picture to a group of other participants in these terms:

> … my first picture is just a picture of the beach, going up to the beach right there. A woman walking her dog. For me it kind of relates prison and probation and stuff. Whereas it's the kind of relationship is one's the boss. One's the obedient one: the dog. *[Murmurs of agreement from the group]*. It depends how you're treated. The dog looked happy on a walk, obviously treated well, that's the first one.

Clearly, this image is one of constraints. Again, it invites a sensory or affective reaction by offering a seemingly brutal and visceral visual metaphor, implying dehumanisation. I read his description and immediately imagine myself as the dog; I feel the collar and the pull of the lead. Yet, as the quote suggests, 'Messiah 10' offers a more nuanced reading, suggesting that the extent of dehumanisation depends on *how* he is constrained, not simply on the *fact* of his being constrained. Indirectly perhaps, he invites us to ask what kind of treatment might make penal constraint more or less endurable. In writing the last two paragraphs of the first episode above, these are the question that I wanted the reader to begin to consider. How tight or loose is the invisible collar of the story's title? How is the lead being held and with what consequences?

Feeling (for) Characters. Readers of the project blog, reviewing drafts of the early episodes, asked me about the story's central character, Joe, and why I chose to centre the story on such an apparently atypical supervisee. Joe is middle-aged and middle-class and has few previous convictions. A more statistically representative character might have been, for example, a relatively young, poor man with a substance use problem and a significant history of offending.

While I could have written the story around such a supervisee, I felt uncomfortable about doing so. For reasons similar to those that Jo articulates in more detail below, I feared it would lack authenticity and might come across as patronising or even stigmatising in some way. I thought that I would create a more convincing or believable character if I could relate to him; indeed, if, in other circumstances, I might have been him or might yet become him. In one sense then, Joe is a middle-aged, middle-class man because I am. This helped me imagine feeling some of what he is feeling – and of course that also made easier by putting him in places of which I retained sensory memories.

But I realise that this approach also has some disadvantages. In particular, it produced an atypical story of supervision and one that reflects my position and my partialities – and some of my privilege. That said, necessarily, any character that I created would reflect my situation and my limitations – and any single story of supervision is necessarily bound to be partial. In the end, I decided that the story needed depth rather than breadth, authenticity rather than representativeness.

Pauline is a composite of many social workers and probation officers that I have met during both my practice and research careers. Her fictional boss, Norm, characterises her as a 'lifer'; a reference to work on the occupational identities of English probation workers by Mawby and Worrall (2014). 'Lifers' are career probation officers who see their work as a vocation. More generally, my portrayal of Pauline's position and disposition tries to convey the sort of tormented habitus generated by a changing criminal justice field (as suggested, e.g., by McNeill, Burns, Halliday, Hutton, & Tata, 2009 and Deering, 2011). Her name is also significant. Like many probation workers (and like her near-namesake the Apostle Paul), Pauline might say: 'I have become all things to all people so that by all possible means I might save some' (1 Corinthians 9: 22). Although I offer no physical description of her in the story (nor of any other characters), in describing her habitus and hexis – and how she carries and expresses herself differently in the company of Norm, as opposed to Joe – again I was recalling memories of specific former colleagues.

Sensing Endings. The way that the story sits in the book's final chapter is a little different. Here, I settled on writing two episodes that offered different possible endings. Chapter 7 opens with a dystopian ending (episode VIIa) and ends with a utopian alternative (episode VIIb). Episode VIIa may read as being a little more like science fiction than the rest of the story, but all of the technology that it introduces either exists or is imaginable. For example, probation reporting booths already exist (as an alternative to or supplement for 'human' supervision) and I have myself been at a meeting where Dutch technologists discussing their efforts to design a Virtual Reality headset that allows for its wearer to be 'counselled' by a future self, though I should stress that my dystopian imagining of 'Future Joe' is not what they had in mind. Transdermal devices that test the wearer's sweat for evidence of alcohol use also exist and are in operation in some justice systems.[3]

In the imagining of this dystopian future then, the sensory plays a key part. But now it is not just Joe who is doing the sensing; it is also the technological surveillance to which he is subject that is sensing him: his handprint, his retina, his pulse, his sweat. The invisible collar with which the story started has taken a new form here; one that now surrounds him, as is evoked in this brief description of the reporting booth:

> Forty minutes later, Joe was glad to find a reporting booth empty at the probation office. It looked like a cross between an arcade

---

[3]See: https://www.youtube.com/watch?v=KYHRvhE_hqE.

game, a confessional and an upright coffin. He took a deep breath and sat inside, pulling the black curtain across …

After describing Joe's encounter with his virtual supervisor and with an avatar of his reformed and successful future self, the story goes on: 'Outside, Joe steadied himself on the railing, taking in as much air as he could'. I notice only now that what I have imagined and described here employs new metaphors of burial, submersion and suffocation, even as it returns to and sustains the opening episode's differently depicted struggle for breath. It's hard to imagine a more elemental or sensory metaphor than that.

By contrast, episode VIIb is told from the perspective of the reformed managerialist Norm (Pauline's boss). This ending represents the more hopeful sort of 'adjacent possible' referred to by Loader and Sparks' (2012) in their discussion of Roberto Unger's work. It feels nearby, to me at least, in so much as I have given evidence at Parliamentary Committees (in Scotland) alongside people with convictions whose experience and expertise appeared to be recognised and respected at least by the parliamentarians involved. In the story's final paragraph, I write:

The gang of four met at the coffee stall in the train station. Even Pauline was on time. They greeted one another as old friends, collected their orders and, as was their habit, made for the front carriage. They knew they were going to be in a hurry when they arrived in the capital. They had already come a long way together in a short time, but there was a lot of work still to be done.

Again, here I am invoking sensory memories of travelling through Glasgow's Queen Street station on route to the capital. In stark contrast with Joe's isolation, submersion and suffocation in the static, upright coffin of the reporting booth, the 'happy ending' invokes both a sense of purpose, membership of a community and forward momentum.

Offering these two endings seemed a helpful way of inviting the reader to think about what kinds of choices might propel us away from one future and towards the other. Thus, the conventional academic part of *Pervasive Punishment's* final chapter is sandwiched between these two possible worlds, hoping to help steer us onto what I argue is the better path.

Perhaps that last admission raises the obvious question of whether what I have written in the story is an example of instrumentalising my own creativity in pursuit of propaganda. It is obviously the case that I wrote the story with a purpose and even a message in mind, though I would argue that my intention was simply to help readers imagine and think about supervision (and especially *being* supervised), rather than to persuade them (or even trick them) into a particular position on it.

In discussing the limits of our solidarity in and with one another's suffering, John Updike, the US writer, once wrote that 'the space of indifference is where we breathe'. Like much fictional writing perhaps, 'The Invisible Collar' clearly aims to shrink this 'space of indifference'. Since it draws upon accounts of the sensory experiences of the suffocating effects both of supervision and (in a different way) of managerialism, interwoven with my own memories, it might even evoke a sensory reaction in the reader. Maybe, at certain points in reading the story, they will at least catch their breath or swallow hard. But while story aims to enable an affective engagement with supervision, it doesn't seek to evoke any specific reaction, and it doesn't tell the reader what to *think*. It aims to inform and enable deeper dialogue about these questions; not to make an argument about them. It does try to insist upon taking punishment more seriously precisely by engaging with its sensory and affective dimensions. To confront and explore these experiences and feelings – or at least to find ways to come a little closer to them – is surely necessary if we are to think more clearly and carefully about supervision in particular and about punishment in general.

Sounding Supervision

Jo Collinson Scott

Before reading more about the writing of the songs on the 'System Hold' EP (released by 'Jo Mango and Friends' (2018) on Olive Grove Records), we encourage you to listen to them, either via your choice of streaming service or on Bandcamp.[4]

Purpose. When Fergus first approached me with the idea that his book might have an EP of tracks to accompany it (as it did chapters of a short story), we reflected together on what the nature of those tracks might be, how they might be created and for what purpose. We considered that songs could be co-created with those who had lived experience of supervision and use songwriting to explore this directly. However, we decided that this process had already been undertaken very skilfully in a recent project called 'Seen and Heard' (linked to the 'Picturing Probation' and 'Supervisible' projects mentioned above), and that an EP of those songs was already available and was discussed in *Pervasive Punishment*.[5] We also agreed that it would be good to add to the rich variety of forms of exploration of the research questions the book addresses by presenting music that reflected not primarily on direct lived experience of supervision, but on the wider understandings of pervasive punishment as discussed in the book. This opened out the potential for the EP to reflect on the broader structures and concepts surrounding pervasive punishment, and the societal impact of mass supervision, as well as to ask what it sounds like, feels like or means for people to be supervised.

Mark Pevely suggests that popular music can be helpful in reimagining futures in three main ways. First, as communication (music as a means of mediating issues); second, as art (as 'creative, aesthetic, symbolic and affective' expression of meanings related to the subject); and third, as advocacy (an attempt to 'inform,

---

[4] The 'System Hold' EP can be found on Spotify: https://open.spotify.com/album/7B 0kZTRqaolYU6lxf3dSSe?si=1dTO5we6Su2_thlm18qYSA, or on Bandcamp: https://jomango.bandcamp.com/album/system-hold.

[5] The 'Seen and Heard' EP can be found here: https://voxliminis.bandcamp.com/album/seen-and-heard-ep.

inspire and persuade audiences') (Pedelty, 2012, p. 7). Green and Street (2018) similarly distinguish between the 'prefigurative' (expressive) and the 'pragmatic' (instrumental) approach to the use of music in activism. The pragmatic or advocating approach, if treated as the sole focus, can result in boring art lacking in quality – propaganda, as Fergus discusses above – and as Pedelty notes, 'music is about affect rather than effect' (p. 203). Consequently, we decided that prefigurative, communicative or expressive aims should constitute our focus. Thus, the EP was developed in order to attempt to 'sound' some of the affective aspects of mass supervision.

As the reader may have surmised, and as the editors of this volume argue, there is often an 'ocular-centrism': an over-emphasis on seeing when it comes to knowledge (e.g. in the name of the fields of 'visual sociology' or 'visual criminology'). This is the case with the naming of 'supervision' itself – with its focus on being seen. Because the ways that we talk about punishment are a crucial part of penal imaginaries, this means that music – as a way of hearing differently – is also a particularly fresh way of helping us to imagine differently.

Speaking Nearby. In the process of developing the EP tracks along these lines, and after its release, I have reflected frequently on issues of authenticity. This is a consideration that is seen as particularly relevant to creative endeavours such as short-story writing, and even more so in relation to popular music, especially in genres where songs tend to be performed by the individuals who wrote them (Moore, 2002, 2012). I have no direct experience with being supervised or with supervising (as Fergus does) and I did not directly carry out research with those who do for this project. This will raise questions about what grounds I have to address these experiences.

As a professional songwriter who frequently writes for other performers, I have skills and experience in imagining and then representing creatively the experiences of others, in order to fashion believable perspectives and strong sensory and affective connections for a listener. While recognising this, however, it is important to consider whose experiences it would be appropriate or inappropriate for this to encompass and from which perspectives. Although some academic writers have begun to engage with the importance of incorporating similar considerations of positionality, authenticity and representation into their work (as represented, for example, in recent debates about feminist ethnography (Skeggs, 2001)), there is an extra and more complex imperative in this regard in a songwriting(-as-research) context, where the songwriter-performer's own personal identity and perspective would generally be presumed to have a dominant role[6] and where emotional content is mobilised. This can be helpful in avoiding the challenge Tim Ingold (2011) describes for anthropological work that

> remains yoked to an academic model of knowledge production, according to which observation is not so much a way of knowing

---

[6]The question of who a listener perceives they are listening to when they appreciate the performance of a song is a complex one, which is explored most comprehensively by Allan Moore in his book *Song Means* (2012).

> what is going on in the world as a source of raw material for subsequent processing into authoritative accounts that claim to reveal the truth behind the illusion of appearances. (p. 15)

There is no historic assumption among listeners that songs are such authoritative accounts, more than that they will make us feel something. However, critiques around ventriloquising or appropriating the stories of others remain valid concerns given that songs have text-based content as well as musical/sound-based components.

The work of postcolonial feminist theories can be helpful in exploring these issues and suggesting ways forward. In particular, we can consider the idea of 'speaking nearby' as proposed by Trinh T. Minh-ha (Chen, 1992) with relation to the work on 'System Hold'. As Rutten, van Dienderen and Soetaert (2013) contend, 'since one cannot speak *about* or *for* the other in an unproblematic way, it might be better to aim to "speak nearby", without ignoring these unequal relations' (p. 470). According to Schneider (2013), in artistic work this requires a recognition of one's own position, of 'dialogical inequality' and an 'uneven hermeneutic field' (p. 525) and then an honouring of difference. What Trinh T. Minh-ha describes of the practice of speaking *nearby* is what I would aim for in any of my creative work that engages with experiences that are not (and particularly those that could not be) mine:

> In other words a speaking that does not objectify, does not point to an object as if it is distant from the speaking subject or absent from the speaking place. A speaking that reflects on itself and can come very close to a subject without, however, seeing or claiming it. A speaking in brief, whose closures are only moments of transition opening up to other possible moments of transition – these are forms of indirectness well understood by anyone in tune with poetic language. Every element constructed in a film refers to the world around it, while having at the same time a life of its own. And this life is precisely what is lacking when one uses word, image or sound just as an instrument of thought. To say therefore that one prefers not to speak about but rather to speak nearby, is a great challenge. (Chen, 1992, p. 87)

There are indeed great challenges in this approach, not least with relation to the creation of popular music. To listen to the experience of supervision in ways that are not complicit with systems of domination may, as Wood (2001) describes it, 'require more than ... critics are willing or able to give, on terms and with results that will not satisfy' (p. 430). It also involves honouring difference, which would require resisting what Murray (2018) calls, 'constructing a homogenizing gaze, appealing to a "global" form of emotion' (p. 91). This is particularly challenging with relation to the practice of songwriting in popular music, because many of the attendant skills in this field relate to the creation of material that has appeal to a wide audience and engages their emotional responses. The challenge here – and part of the research process in developing the material for the 'System Hold' EP – was to engage a wide audience without generating stereotypes or appealing to standard emotive tropes. Sometimes this aim works against the idea of generating empathy, which Clare Hemmings (2012) has argued can lead to 'sentimental attachment to the other rather than a genuine engagement with her concerns' (p. 152). She would advise an aiming for 'affective solidarity' – including rage, frustration and the desire for connection – rather than mobilising empathy or sympathy alone (Hemmings, 2012, p. 48, as cited in Murray, 2018, p. 99).

Although there will certainly have been areas where I have failed in this endeavour, it is important to me to try to 'speak nearby' (or perhaps in conjunction, to 'sound nearby') to the experience of mass supervision where I can. This is in order to contribute to the making audible of important problems, not to point at the problem as if it is 'over there' with those who experience its results, nor to simplify it to the point that anyone could identify with it from any position, but to complexify it into reality, to unflatten images that have been flattened (or undeaden sound that has been deadened), to identify my complicity in the problem, to point to my interconnectedness to it, and to instigate dialogue about potential change.

Songs of Depth, Weight, Tightness and Suspension. In exploring the areas where 'affective solidarity' might be built via musical or lyrical means, I found some of the most resonant concepts that were explored in *Pervasive Punishment* to be those described by Ben Crewe as the 'pains of imprisonment' and then extended by Fergus to help us understand the pains of supervision. These are detailed under the categories of 'Depth', 'Weight' and 'Tightness' (Crewe, 2011). After talking to Fergus about those as exploratory headings for the work, we added 'Suspension' to this list as an important addition.

Depth, weight, tightness and suspension are all terms that are very evocative in a musical sense as they relate to timbre, time, style and performative gesture among other things. It was under these headings that I began to coalesce and develop sensory ideas relating to the themes explored in the book and the characters in the story – this was a combination of the development of these concepts into representative sounds, and an exploration of their affective dimensions as might be performed in song. My collaborators and I did not set out to represent or 'communicate' these concepts, but rather it was the case that beginning to explore these terms and their creative resonances in a sensory way foregrounded other key concepts and related practices including identity, the pains of *self*-supervising and the representation of failure.

Depth. As we began exploring the idea of 'depth' with relation to the creation of song, the most productive sensory avenue emerged around the idea of identity – given that identity might be seen as one's understanding of the constituents of the full depths of self. The experience of the 'Malopticon' of supervision (which, as Fergus argues, sees the person badly, sees them as bad and projects their 'badness' (McNeill, 2018)) seems to be the imposition of the understanding of a crime being at the core of a person's identity via their constant visibility as an offender and/or a risk of future offending. It therefore requires the constant monitoring and questioning of aspects of the self that should usually go unnoticed (like impulses, needs, desires or physical actions). The lyrical content of the song therefore asks the listener quite directly, to consider how far down into their concepts of themselves their mistakes and failings might go – the use of second person perspective directly challenges the listener and, as such, makes *them* a subject of the song. In this position, the narrator of the song holds no unambiguous direct claim to personal experience except the ability to ask critical questions, while still allowing for emotional engagement. The perspectival engagement in this song therefore seeks to challenge the listener to engage in 'othering' the 'self', where a first-person perspective, in inviting direct empathy, might have encouraged a 'selving' of the 'other' (Foster, 1992, p. 304, cited in Rutten et al., 2013, p. 462).

In attempting to sound something nearby to this experience, I drew upon the experience of 'semantic satiation'; for example, the loss of recognition or 'making strange' of an everyday word that can happen when it is repeated too frequently. I drew upon this (relatively) common sensory experience as a means to attempt to sound something nearby to the loss of identity that can happen when repeatedly asked to state one's name for purposes of tracking, monitoring, labelling or proving oneself.

In exploring the vocabulary of depth, I discovered that the 'shackle' was a term for what used to be a common measurement of depth of water. This semantic connection between depth, imprisonment and, more recently, electronic monitoring (Kilgore, 2017) was creatively exciting and following it led to a fruitful avenue of development of lyrical images, including thinking about mining practices.

Exploring these more oblique angles on 'depth', I found there was resonance with some affective memories of my own, which came from the part of my formative years spent in an area of Yorkshire that was built upon former coal mines. As a small child, I vividly remember waking up one day to find that several houses in my street had collapsed overnight into large sinkholes in the ground. This, we were told, was caused by sudden subsistence into old mine shafts that were improperly supported to sustain housing developments on the ground above. I remember so clearly the feeling of horror at the thought of deep, gaping holes beneath the seeming security of the pavement of my home street. And the emotional impact of being able to look straight into my neighbours' houses and see their bath, for instance, teetering on the edge of an abyss, or their sofa perched facing directly out into the street through the hole where their house frontage used to be. The lives of these people became 'supervisible' to me through the form of the literal depth of past mistakes and their traumatic re-emergence. I chose to explore this image in 'Depth', as an emotive and intriguing way of surfacing feelings of invasion of privacy, constant visibility, the threat of something from deep in the past that could open up at any moment, the fear of never having a home (or identity) on solid foundations and the questioning of the potential depth of cracks or weaknesses in these.

Weight. In discussing the characters in 'The Invisible Collar' with novelist Martin Cathcart Frödén (co-writer of 'Tightness' along with Lucy Cathcart Frödén), we began to wonder about Joe being listed as supervisee number 59. If that was the case, then who were the other 58? This was part of the process of complexifying the idea of the generation of a single-voiced narrative and began to widen our focus to include the characters only implied in the story (or obliquely mentioned). 'Weight', therefore, is written from the perspective of a loved one of someone under supervision. Developed in collaboration with artist A. Wesley Chung, the narrator of the song – much like the narrator of Dolly Parton's song 'Jolene' (1974) – sees their 'stranger' (parole/probation officer) as a threat to her way of life, and a threat that is at a complete remove from anything she can control or interact with. She feels the need to plead with them for leniency and empathy. The quiet C-section with the sudden dropout of the busy, multilayered arrangement of the chorus, draws the ear. In this moment, emphasis is placed on the lyrical focus of 'you', as the singer sings:

> You write my life
> You sign your name
> You cut him out the final frame
> You write my daughter calling out his name

This creates a very direct form of engagement of the listener and serves at this moment to place them in the position of the 'stranger'. This positioning serves to pose the question – how do I 'write the life' of others? How do I 'sign my name' on them? How do I contribute to a system that is over-zealous to remove the loved ones, fathers and mothers, of other members of our wider community and with what effect?

Tightness. Related to the experience of the problematising of identity under supervision is the pain of *self*-supervision or the attempt to internalise sets of external rules and ways of seeing oneself so as to fashion a new identity. The idea of wrestling with a potentially alien-seeming set of instructions to normalise and internalise them in generating a new future self was the underlying idea that was explored in the track titled 'Tightness'. We wanted, in part, for this track to exemplify that constant friction. To generate such an embodiment, my co-writer Lucy Cathcart Frödén suggested that we might construct something like a lipogram, where a writer systematically omits a certain common letter from their writing. In this case, we decided to omit everything other than every fourth word from passages of Fergus' story, a chapter of this book, and Ben Crewe's writing on his definition of 'tightness' in the context of imprisonment. The result of this process sounded very much like the speech of someone who was trying to understand the rules of the English language in order to describe aspects of supervision but didn't have a natural grasp of how language worked. We then developed the idea of the narrator of the story as being a camera in a probation/parole office waiting room, describing its socially deficient understandings of what it views. In this sense, 'Tightness' is narrated by the 'robot Pauline' of the future, prefigured by Fergus in the dystopian alternate ending of 'The Invisible Collar'.

Developing the song this way generated some very powerful results for us. First, taking only every fourth word of a piece of writing makes a barely comprehensible, let alone comprehensive impression of its subject. The narrative thus constructed demonstrates very viscerally how half-hour snippets of someone's life in a probation interview cannot possibly lead to an acceptable level of understanding of their identity and humanity. The melody that was constructed around the lyrics in this track is largely pentatonic (the use of only five notes in contrast to the usual seven-note scale), which also works to make audible the feeling of removal of aspects (or tones) of normal experience. Using this approach also resulted in lyrical ambiguities that meant the perspective of this song with relation to the listener is not particularly clear. This opened up the possibility that the perspective of the narration could also more broadly encompass publics who are themselves doing the work of monitoring within the same system as they are monitored. Indeed, the refrain 'also of we that system holds' invites the question as to who else is held by this system and how.

Suspension. The final song on the EP was developed most clearly out of the premise of the imagined sound of suspension. In constructing the original harmonic accompaniment on piano, I began working with literal harmonic suspensions. A suspension in this context is a note of one chord that is held over when the harmony underneath shifts to a new chord. The 'suspended' note hangs over the new chord where it wouldn't usually belong and this gives the listener a feeling of tension – their ear naturally would like the note in question to 'resolve' by moving on (the way the rest of the notes in the chord have) to the expected chord note.

Lyrically, the track works by the evocation of the sounds of suspended things. The words developed from exploring the content of an urban myth that asserts that if you use a stethoscope to listen to one of the main cables of a suspension bridge, you can hear the strings inside snapping, one by one. This may only be the case over a very long period of time (i.e. longer than one could remain listening with a stethoscope); however, this image led to the underlying sensory impression in the lyrics of the song, which is the evocation of things that seem static, unmoving or calm, but that underneath or inside are full of unbearable tension and frantic motion. The attempt to speak (or sound) nearby to this experience challenges the surface notion that supervision is an 'easier' form of punishment to endure than others, which is based in what is visible on the surface of the experience, rather than what might be heard through deep listening.

Sounding Failure. There is no more space to describe in any detail the specific ways in which the tracks on the EP explore the audibility of these subjects. But it might be good before we finish to discuss something more with relation to the specific sound of the EP and how this was developed. In exploring what sounds might best be employed to expand understandings of mass supervision, I struck upon the area of 'glitch' music. 'Glitch' is a genre of music associated with a popular production trend of the 1990s, in which musical failure is foregrounded and celebrated as an aesthetic ideal. Glitch is the word used to describe a small hitch of some kind in the playback or recording of sound. A key example of this might be the sound that is made when a CD skips while playing, or that a speaker makes when a mobile phone is held near it while transmitting signal. There are numerous means by which digital glitches are made too, including malfunctions in music production software that generate unwanted noise. Glitch music celebrates these noises to such an extent that they become ubiquitous to the sound of the genre. In this sense, glitch can be seen to be a form of redemption of the failure of the system within which it is created (Bates, 2004; Hainge, 2007; Hofer, 2006; Sangild, 2004).

'Swift and Certain Sanction' is how the response to failure is described in the dystopian future that provides one ending of the 'The Invisible Collar'. And yet, in the creative process, failure is often one of the most potent sites of potential for breakthrough and advancement. As such, an intersection of the glitch genre with music such as my own seems a productive (and somewhat subversive) place to begin an aural exploration of such a system. As one of the key names in the burgeoning of the folktronica movement in the UK, the producer here (Adem Ilhan) has been well placed to help explore the combination of my signature alt-folk sound with aspects of glitch and electronic music in order to make these concepts more audible. This has involved exploring, among other things: slightly nudging keyboard tracks out of sync with each other, enhancing and playing with the sound that splicing two vocal takes together makes (a sound that is normally smoothed out with production software), reincorporating the noise of recording back into the tracks and celebrating skipping and jolting of all kinds by employing these rhythmically.

Conclusion

In reviewing this chapter, it seems to us that – both in methodological and in ethical terms – the struggle for affective solidarity and sensory engagement in these creative representations is particularly important and telling. That struggle was different for each of us because we were differently positioned in relation to our works of imagination and to the characters and situations represented within them. From her perspective as an artist and researcher without personal experience of penal supervision, Jo follows Trinh T. Minh-ha's (in Chen, 1992) injunction to avoid the objectification and appropriation of other's experiences and positions by seeking instead to 'speak nearby'. But this is a profoundly challenging practice; one that resists simplifying and fixing meanings and that refuses definitive interpretations of the human and social experience that it tries to approach, explore and express. 'Speaking nearby' aims for proximity and connection and, ethically, at the very least, it seeks the possibility of the 'affective solidarity' that Jo also discusses rather than 'mere' empathy or sympathy.

It is important to highlight that these questions of authenticity and representation are brought to the fore in creative practices perhaps more so than in most accounts of the use of more conventional research methods. Of course, both ethnographers and historians – as storytellers – have often reflected about (and been questioned about) the extent to which the accounts that they construct constitute fictions, albeit fictions assembled (like 'The Invisible Collar') from 'realities'. Yet, even within ethnography, as in criminology more broadly, perhaps there has been less discussion of the 'epistemic privilege' (Liebling et al., 2017) that is claimed in asserting the right (and even the duty) to interpret other peoples' discourses, practices and experiences.

We suspect that criminology in general – and the project of developing 'sensory penalties' in particular – has much to gain from exploring and applying the insights of artists and arts-based researchers to its various modes of inquiry, interpretation and representation. For our part, we would suggest that thinking about whether and when we speak *for*, speak *with*, speak *to*, or speak *nearby*, and about whether and when we work against 'the space of indifference' and for affective solidarity, should be a necessary and urgent aspect of our practice.

Perhaps at the conjunctions between sensory, creative and public criminologies, we can find better ways to seek and sustain that affective solidarity. A first, sensory step in that process must be to develop and attune our attentiveness to what we (and others) can hear, smell, taste, touch and see when we experience or explore or express or seek to change and challenge aspects of penality. We hope that our reflections in this chapter and our own practices can help in this regard.

References

Bates, E. (2004). Glitches, bugs and hisses: The degeneration of musical recordings and the contemporary musical work. In C. Washburn & M. Derno (Eds.), *Bad music: The music we love to hate* (pp. 275–293). London: Routledge.
Bauman, Z. (2016). *Strangers at our door*. Cambridge: Polity Press.
Burke, L., Collett, S., & McNeill, F. (2018). *Reimagining rehabilitation: Beyond the individual*. Abingdon: Routledge.
Chen, N. (1992). 'Speaking Nearby': A conversation with Trinh T. Minh-ha. *Visual Anthropology Review*, 8(1), 82–91.
Clarke, E., DeNora, T., & Vuoskoski, J. (2015). Music, empathy and cultural understanding. *Physics of Life Reviews*, 15, 61–88.
Crewe, B. (2011). Depth, weight, tightness: Revisiting the pains of imprisonment. *Punishment and Society*, 13(5), 509–529.
Deering, J. (2011). *Probation practice and the new penology: Practitioner reflections*. Farnham: Ashgate.
Fitzgibbon, W., Graebsch, C., & McNeill, F. (2017). Pervasive punishment: Experiencing supervision. In E. Carrabine & M. Brown (Eds.), *The Routledge international handbook of visual criminology* (pp. 305–319). London: Routledge.
Fricker, M. (2007). *Epistemic injustice: Power and the ethics of knowing*. Oxford: Oxford University Press.
Green, A., & Street, J. (2018). Music and activism: From prefigurative to pragmatic politics. In G. Miekle (Ed.), *The Routledge companion to media and activism* (pp. 171–178). London: Routledge.
Hainge, G. (2007). Of glitch and men: The place of the human in the successful integration of failure and noise in the digital realm. *Communication Theory*, 17, 26–42.
Hemmings, C. (2012). Affective solidarity: Feminist reflexivity and political transformation. *Feminist Theory*, 13(2), 147–161.
Hesmondhalgh, D. (2013). *Why music matters*. Chichester: Wiley Blackwell.
Hofer, S. (2006). I am they: technological mediation, shifting conceptions of identity and techno music. *Convergence: The International Journal of Research Into New Media Technologies*, 12(3), 307–324.
Ingold, T. (2011). *Being alive: Essays on movement, knowledge and description*. London: Routledge.
Jo Mango & Friends (2018). *System Hold [CD/Digital EP]*. Glasgow: Olive Grove Records.
Kilgore, J. (2017). 'You're still in jail': How electronic monitoring is a shackle on the movement for decarceration. *Truthout*, October 22. Retrieved from https://truthout.org/articles/you-re-still-in-jail-how-electronic-monitoring-is-a-shackle-on-the-movement-for-decarceration/. Accessed on May 7, 2020.
Kramer, L. (2001). The mysteries of animation: History, analysis and musical subjectivity. *Music Analysis*, 20(2), 153–178.

Kramer, L. (2003). *Franz Schubert. Sexuality, subjectivity, song.* Cambridge: Cambridge University Press.
Liebling, A., McNeill, F., & Schmidt, B. E. (2017). Criminological engagements. In A. Liebling, S. Maruna, & L. McAra (Eds.), *The Oxford handbook of criminology* (6th ed.). Oxford: Oxford University Press.
Loader, I., & Sparks, R. (2010). *Public criminology?* London: Routledge.
Loader, I., & Sparks, R. (2012). Beyond lamentation: Towards a democratic egalitarian politics of crime and justice. In T. Newburn & J. Peay (Eds.), *Policing: Politics, culture and control* (pp. 11–42). Oxford: Hart.
Loewy, E. H. (1997). *Moral strangers, moral acquaintance, and moral friends. Connectedness and its conditions.* Albany, NY: State University of New York Press.
Mawby, R., & Worrall, A. (2014). *Doing probation work: Identity in a criminal justice occupation.* London: Routledge.
McNeill, F. (2018). *Pervasive punishment: Making sense of mass supervision.* Bingley: Emerald Publishing.
McNeill, F. (2019). Mass supervision, misrecognition and the Malopticon. *Punishment and Society, 21*(2), 207–230.
McNeill, F., Burns, N., Halliday, S., Hutton, N., & Tata, C. (2009). Risk, responsibility and reconfiguration: Penal adaptation and misadaptation. *Punishment and Society, 11*(4), 419–442.
Moore, A. (2002). Authenticity as authentication. *Popular Music, 13*(2), 209–223.
Moore, A. (2012). *Song means: Analysing and interpreting recorded popular song.* London: Routledge.
Murray, R. (2018). Speaking about or speaking nearby? Documentary practice and female authorship in the films of Kim Longinotto. In B. Ulfsdotter & A. B. Rogers (Eds.), *Female authorship and the documentary image* (pp. 90–106). Edinburgh: Edinburgh University Press.
Parton, D. (1974). Jolene. [Recorded by Dolly Parton]. *Jolene.* RCA Victor.
Pedelty, M. (2012). *Ecomusicology: Rock, folk, and the environment.* Philadelphia, PA: Temple University Press.
Rutten, K., van Dienderen, A., & Soetaert, R. (2013). Revisiting the ethnographic turn in contemporary art. *Critical Arts, 27*(5), 459–473.
Sangild, T. (2004). Glitch – The beauty of malfunction. In. C. Washburn & M. Derno (Eds.), *Bad music: The music we love to hate* (pp. 257–274). London: Routledge.
Schneider, A. (2013). Contested grounds: Fieldwork collaborations with artists in Corrientes, Argentina. *Critical Arts, 27*(5), 511–530.
Skeggs, B. (2001). Feminist ethnography. In P. Atkinson, A. Coffey, S. Delamont, J. Lofland, & L. Lofland (Eds.), *Handbook of ethnography* (pp. 426–442). London: Sage.
Wood, C. (2001). Authorizing gender and development: 'Third world women', native informants, and speaking nearby. *Nepantla: Views from the South, 2*(3), 429–447.
Worrall, A., Carr, N., & Robinson, G. (2017). Opening a window on probation cultures: A photographic imagination. In E. Carrabine & M. Brown (Eds.), *The Routledge international handbook of visual criminology* (pp. 268–279). London: Routledge.

Chapter 4

Touching Life, Death, and Dis/connection in a State Prison Infirmary

Daina Stanley

I encountered Daniel[1] at a men's state prison tucked away on the rocky Maine coast.[2] It was late summer; I sat in the prison infirmary yard with several of the men currently housed in the acute-care medical unit for a myriad of health issues. Surrounded by 20-foot cement walls and an open ceiling of sky, we soaked up the sun as it beat down on us. In a world of grey stone and uniform blues, an uncharacteristic pop of colour caught my eye; an assaulting orange jumpsuit overwhelmed the thin frame of the man who lingered in the open doorway. For weeks I had wondered who was confined to the dark shadows of the infirmary's cell no. 5. I carefully looked over its occupant. In his first visit to the 'outside', the man in orange continued to stand silently several feet away, squinting as though blinded by the sunshine. His hair was long and dishevelled, hiding a handsome but drawn face. Gingerly holding a plastic meal tray, he approached the group and, without speaking, took a seat beside me at the wooden picnic table – the only piece of furniture in the yard. He popped the opaque lid off the meal tray. Using a plastic fork, he poked through his 'veggie' tray, picking up an unwieldy mass of over-processed cheese. Tossing it back into the tray, he looked over to me. 'Hi, I'm Daniel', he said and lifted his hand in a small wave. As we began to make the small talk of strangers, I found myself transfixed by the shimmer of his greasy hair under the summer sun. An airy current brushed across us; the scent of unwashed human flesh filled my nostrils, the potent odour of punishment mingling with the refreshing coastal air. The brightness of the yard faded further as my gaze fixed on his hands, dried, cracked, and faintly yellow. Daniel snapped

---

[1]Pseudonyms and nicknames may be used to protect the identities of participants. Some participants are identified by name at their request.
[2]In order to protect the identity of participants, the time period of data collection is not disclosed. Fieldwork took place over two years, including 14 consecutive months of participant observation in several state prisons.

the cover back onto the meal tray. 'Well, see you around', he said, shrugging his shoulders. I watched as he disappeared back into the dim depths of the infirmary. *SLAM! Click.* The sounds of Daniel being closed into the margins by heavy steel that sealed him away from us.

Introduction

> And so sensuous scholarship is ultimately a mixing of head and heart. It is an opening of one's being to the world – a welcoming. Such embodied hospitality is the secret of the great scholars, painters, poets, and filmmakers whose images and words resensualize us. (Stoller, 1997, p. xviii)

The United States has the highest rate of incarceration in the world (Fazel & Baillargeon, 2011), a direct consequence of 'tough on crime' policies which have led to longer average prison sentences (Caverley, 2006; Hoffman & Dickinson, 2011) and a significant increase in the number of individuals serving life sentences without the possibility of parole (Nellis, 2010). While levels of incarceration in the United States have stabilised, the punitive criminal justice agenda that unfolded over the last four decades has led to perilous consequences, including an epidemic of deaths in American prisons.

Each year, thousands of imprisoned persons die from 'natural' causes (Hoffman & Dickinson, 2011). Prisoners[3] are more likely to experience illness (Maruschak & Berzofsky, 2015) and 'early' death (Kouyoumdjian, Evgeny, Borschmann, Kinner, & McConnon, 2017; Venters, 2019; Williams, 2007), as they are more prone to chronic health conditions and infectious diseases, which have a higher prevalence in incarcerated than non-incarcerated communities (Mumola, 2007; Plugge, Elwood Martin, & Hayton, 2014). This is the result of substance use history, poverty, and inadequate access to healthcare services, both before and during incarceration (Hoffman & Dickinson, 2011; Williams, Goodwin, Baillargeon, Ahalt, & Walter, 2012). Studies also indicate that unhealthy lifestyles and poor access to health care may speed the ageing process, and research suggests that the psychological and biological health status of an 'older' prisoner may be more similar to that of someone who is 10–15 years older in the outside community (Aday, 2003; Maschi, Viola, & Sun, 2013). This has contributed, in part, to a rapidly rising number of older persons in prison and is further compounded by changing population demographics (i.e. the baby boomer cohort) (Bedard, Metzger, & Williams, 2016; Caverley, 2006), as well as an increase in later-in-life convictions for historical sex offences. The number of adults aged 55 years and older incarcerated in a US state prison increased from 3% in 1993 to 10% by 2013, and the median age of incarcerated adults rose from 30 to 36 years old

---

[3]This decision to use the term 'prisoner' was determined in an advisory meeting with interlocutors.

(Carson & Sabol, 2016). Given the rise in the number of older persons in prison, the complex health profiles of prisoners, and generally poor access to appropriate care, it is not surprising that the number of people dying in custody is also rising.

This chapter is based on my larger doctoral study examining the end of life journeys of incarcerated men, as well as the experiences of the prisoners who care for them. In this piece of 'sensory scholarship' (Stoller, 1997),[4] I draw on 'sensory data and impressions to make sense' of the penal worlds in which I found myself (Atkinson, Delamont, & Housley, 2008, p. 179). In what follows, I present an intentionally thickly descriptive (Geertz, 1973) account of my experiences as a subjective sensory explorer engaged 'bodily in and with' (Blake, 2011, p. 3) Daniel's end of life in the prison infirmary. This is a heartfelt and humble attempt to contribute to 'thickly-textured studies' (Howes, 2010) in the emerging field of sensory penology. As the other works in this collection illuminate, and as anthropologist Paul Stoller (1989) compellingly pens,

> [C]onsidering the senses of taste, smell, and hearing as much as privileged sight will not only make ethnography more vivid and more accessible, but will render our accounts of others more faithful to the realities of the field. (p. 9)

Thus, I dig deep into the depths of my field notes and research diaries to explore my sensorial experiences as an ethnographer immersed in the world of prison deathscapes.

First, I will share a brief description of my methodological journey into the medical spaces of contemporary prisons. I then return to Daniel, an interlocutor whose end of life I followed over several months. I introduce the sensorium of disciplinary segregation to present a densely descriptive account of the sights and imagined sensations of punishment. This section is short, abrupt, and may leave the reader reaching for more. My hands then take hold as I share a thickly textured description of the intimate sensorium of Daniel's prison hospice cell. The two sections hold a mirror to the dissonant sensations of life, death, and dis/connection experienced in the rooms of the prison infirmary. Together they shed light on the contingency of relations and personhood, and paradoxically, the humanity and dignity that sensory recognition makes possible amidst a harsh penal regime. I conclude this chapter by reflecting on the ways in which engaging my sensorial subjectivity and particularly touch as a medium of inquiry (Blake, 2011) reconstituted my ethnographic practice.

Researching Dying and End-of-Life Care in Prison

Over the course of two years, I spent thousands of hours in state prisons in Maine. My research journey began a year before I met Daniel, on a phone call with the

---

[4]'Sensuous scholarship' was invoked by Paul Stoller (1997) to denote the centrality of the ethnographer's embodied experience in their ethnographic work.

director of a state prison hospice programme, Kandyce. After speaking for about an hour, Kandyce asked if I would like to attend a hospice event to be held at the prison in a few weeks time. Unfortunately, the event was not approved. Instead, Kandyce invited me to join her in an educational class she held once a week with prison hospice volunteers. I jumped at the opportunity and, several weeks later, I pulled open the door to Maine State Prison – a maximum to medium security prison for men – for the first time. I conducted regular pre-field visits to foster relationships and build trust with my interlocutors and to learn more about the institution in which I hoped to conduct my study. Six months after my first steps behind barbed wire, I packed my car and made the 13-hour drive from the bustle of my lakeside Canadian city to a charming seaside town in Maine, moving in with Kandyce in order to immerse myself in the world of prison hospice.

US prisons and jails have often been described as relatively impenetrable and marked by opacity (Fassin, 2017; Venters, 2019). However, after months of pre-fieldwork, and with the support of Kandyce and a progressive prison warden, I encountered comparatively few administrative hurdles – the Department of Corrections (DOC) was surprisingly open to having an ethnographer infiltrate its walls. A research schedule and research activities were negotiated in collaboration with prison administration. I participated in a weeklong training session for non-correctional staff and was provided with an ID badge that would allow me to pass through the secured doors of various state facilities. Site access initially involved unescorted daily immersion in the prison medical unit during the hours of 7 a.m. to 6 p.m. but evolved into 24-hour access, the result of an unanticipated suggestion made by a long-time administrator who felt open access would be necessary for me to more fully 'capture' the experience of peer-based end-of-life care, and especially the hospice vigil. I was thus given the rare opportunity for an outsider to enter some of the most impenetrable corners of the penal world. The ability to come and go, and to spend extensive periods of time in the field, allowed me to study the everyday life of the prison and its care spaces, in a fluid and unstructured manner that mirrored the unpredictability and uncertainty of life and death. I observed various custodial settings, including close custody and medium custody housing units, administrative segregation, and educational classes, but largely focussed my time in prison medical spaces, including acute-care clinics, a long-term-assisted living unit, and the prison infirmary where I first encountered Daniel. In addition to observation, I conducted unstructured interviews with prisoners in these various housing units, peer caregivers, correctional security and medical staff, as well as palliative and hospice care experts. This methodological account is, admittedly, overly simplistic, and fieldwork was not without myriad and complex challenges. However, the description of the prison ethnographer's 'dance' (Jefferson & Schmidt, 2019) would fill these pages – and more – and is thus left to be told in the pages of another piece.[5]

---

[5] See Stanley (2018, May; 2020).

Serving Empty Time in Cell No. 5

> Death in all its guises stalks the wings of our prisons. (Steve, n.d., 'Life After Death')

As summer turned to fall, I would only share one more moment in the yard with Daniel, when he would join us, once more, at the communal picnic table outside. In earlier weeks, Daniel had been suspected of attempting to bring contraband into the facility, 'They said I tried to get an Apple watch in here', he explained. This infraction, of which prison security determined he was 'guilty', had resulted in 'D-time' – disciplinary time for an infraction. Daniel's precarious health status meant he could not serve his time in the prison's dedicated D-time pod. Therefore, he was dressed in disciplinary oranges to distinguish him from the light blues and greys of regular prison-wear and moved to the infirmary's small segregation unit. Involuntarily removed from the textures and 'rhythms of life' (Haney, 2003), Daniel was confined 23–24 hours a day to cell no. 5 and monitored under the intrusive lens of a security camera, a technological extension of the 'all-seeing institutional eye' (Crewe, Warr, Bennett, & Smith, 2014, p. 58).[6]

The segregation cell was smaller than the four other cells in the prison's infirmary and the cell appeared to be an environment of marked deprivation. Unlike the other medical cells in this space, there was no window; cell no. 5 was devoid of any sunlight or view of the outdoors, denying Daniel any access to the 'natural world' outside (Wener, 2012, p. 321).[7] The cell was also strikingly barren. The only furniture, a standard steel toilet, sink, and dated hospital bed. The cell was noticeably absent of sound; no chattering television voices, staticky local news stations, or thump of music that bumped from the CD players in other cells, giving me the sense Daniel had little 'acoustic agency' (Rice, 2016; Waller, 2018).[8]

During these long weeks, I observed as Daniel served empty time, each passing day a near mirror of the one before (Wahidin, 2006). The rest of the infirmary buzzed with life, yet a heavy haze seemed to hang over cell no. 5. In 'routine acts of humanity the incarcerated show towards one another' (Venters, 2019, p. 6), his infirmary counterparts and peer caregivers called greetings to Daniel through

---

[6] In the time period in which I conducted my research and in the time since, the Maine Department of Corrections has undergone a number of administrative changes. These have resulted in reforms to practices of segregation.

[7] See Wener (2012) for a discussion about some of the health risks associated with poor, or no access to, lighting, windows, and nature views.

[8] The sounds of prisons, such as music, provide a rich site of analysis for understanding the social and political worlds of prison(er)s; see Rice (2016), Waller (2018), and Herrity (2018, 2020). Waller (2018) suggests music's 'sanctioned role in the day-to-day running' of the prison is to ensure well-being and compliance. The institution may confiscate technological possessions under certain conditions. In Daniel's case, such technologies were confiscated or not permitted as part of his D-time conditions, thereby becoming 'mechanisms of carceral control' (Waller, 2018, pp. 277–278).

the steel blockade, filled the small infirmary bookcase with new books for him – Daniel was a voracious reader – and shared messages from 'population'. I made daily visits to his darkened cell but my interactions with him were restricted to a small wave and an empathetic smile. I longed to linger at his cell and share in dialogue, but with strict policies and rules that mediated our interactions, I often passed by feeling helpless and complicit in his punishment. The invisible bands in my stomach knotted tighter and tighter as I imagined the 'weight' of isolation baring down upon him (Crewe, Liebling, & Hulley, 2014; King & McDermott, 1995). The stale air of the cell seemed to grow more potent, the cinder block walls heavier, each time I laid eyes on Daniel's still body, as he lay beneath the thin white hospital blanket. At times, Daniel would be staring blankly at the cell door, and, upon seeing me, he would slowly raise a hand in recognition; other times I would see only a still figure curled inwards facing the white cinderblock wall, withdrawn within the confines of his isolation.

There was something so completely unsettling about an ill man locked away in a tiny cement room, severed from the sensations and relations of everyday life.[9] Daniel's disciplinary status was eventually lifted and he was permitted by prison authorities to move freely throughout the infirmary during regular recreation time or meals. However, he continued to spend most of his days occupying the fringes of the infirmary, in cell no. 5.

***

On a cool day, as summer moved into fall, I heard the low rumble of a cell door rolling open. Flip flops slowly scuffling across the linoleum floor cut through the unusual quiet of the infirmary. I raised my head from my notebook and was surprised to see Daniel outside the shadows of his cell. He appeared unsteady. With small, methodical slides, he shuffled fragile feet to the nurses' desk only a few steps away, and slumped over it, setting his hands on its laminate top. His body shook. Afraid his legs were about to crumple beneath him, I reached my arm out to steady him. He lifted his head slowly and his eyes met mine; I was jolted by the deep yellow that now tinted the whites of his eyes. Mary, the nurse on duty, rushed over to us and took hold of Daniel's other elbow. His head fell forward as he leaned further over the desk in an effort to steady himself. The sound of the nurse asking Daniel if he was okay seemed to echo from far away as I caught sight of small red circles that stained his worn white t-shirt. Haunted by my previous work in infectious diseases, my stomach wrenched as I realised what the blood spotting his shirt might mean. Mary helped Daniel back to his cell. When she returned, she rounded the desk and motioned for me to join her. In a whispered voice, I shared my concerns with her and she confided that she too

---

[9]A number of studies highlight the detrimental impacts of isolation on the health and well-being of individuals; see Charleroy and Marland (2016); Cloud, Drucker, Browne, & Parsons (2015); and Guenther (2013), for example. Social deprivation through the inability to establish or maintain human connections 'may be the most damaging consequence of prison isolation' (Wener, 2012, p. 321) and can have detrimental effects on the health and well-being of prisoners (Cohen, 1998; Toch, 1992).

worried about Daniel's well-being; he had been refusing his antiretroviral treatment for some time.

Shortly thereafter, amidst his declining health, Daniel was shackled and sent to a hospital located beyond the walls of the prison. Several days later, doctors indicated that life-sustaining treatment was no longer a viable option and Daniel was transferred back to the infirmary to spend his final days in the care of fellow prisoners who were trained and state certified, through a peer-based prison hospice programme, to provide hospice and palliative care.[10] Upon his return to the prison's infirmary, and after undergoing the humiliation of the policy-mandated strip search, Daniel was assigned a new cell, the 'terminal cell'. Both prison administration and medical administration had determined that he would be placed on hospice vigil and would be provided comfort care. The hospice programme had a carefully crafted vigil rotation that ensured two peer caregivers were with Daniel at all times until he died. The caregivers expressed feeling a stake in Daniel's dignity at the end of his life; at the core of their work, a peer caregiver explained, is to 'validate the worth of [a patient's] humanity' and to ensure they are provided the 'dignity that they deserve'. In marked contrast to earlier weeks that were characterised by strictly enforced boundaries and isolation, Daniel's life at the end would be marked by the human connection, that he had been previously denied. In the weeks that would come, I would observe Daniel at the centre of a network of caring relations (Kleinman, 2012; Taylor, 2008).

Warm(ing) Hands and Hearts in the Prison 'Death Room'

> [T]he same environmental conditions that shape the land also leave their mark on the skin. This is a distinctive feature of the skin for, while we may perceive aspects of the environment with all of our sensory organs, only the skin can manifest the marks of what it has perceived. The skin may be dried by the sun and roughened by the wind; it bears the scars and bruises of its scrapes and bumps and the imprint of what has pressed into its soft surface, it becomes warm through perceiving warmth and cold through experiencing coldness (Howes, 2005, p. 33)

As I pulled into the prison parking lot on Daniel's first day back from the hospital, I was eager to make my way through the five steel doors and two metal detectors that separated us. After passing through the various barriers, I opened the infirmary door using my DOC-issued pass and greeted the officer sitting at the

---

[10]Peer caregivers participated in an extensive 150-hour training facilitated by the Maine Hospice Council and the Centre for End-of-Life Care. Forty hours of this included Personal Support Specialist (PSS) training. Upon successful completion, peer caregivers received state certification as a PSS. For a discussion about the peer-based hospice programme, see Stanley (2020).

small black desk. A few more steps and I rounded the long nurses' desk, crossing over the yellow tape used to demarcate 'staff only zones'. I set down my clear plastic lunch kit, given to me by the medical service provider contracted by the DOC, and removed my wool jacket. I approached Daniel's new cell with trepidation – I had not witnessed death or dying before. Unlike his previous cell on the margins of the infirmary, the 'death room', as many referred to it, was located in the centre. The cell contained a window and private shower, a television mounted on the wall, as well as a state-of-the-art medical bed.

I could hear the vibrant thump of '90s pop music playing as I neared the open metal door and made eye contact with Pépé, a senior prison hospice volunteer. Before I could ask if I could enter, Pépé waved his thin arm, motioning for me to join them in Daniel's new cell. As I entered, Pépé approached Daniel's bedside. 'Daina's here', he enthusiastically informed Daniel. Slowly, Daniel turned his head to look at me. His dark eyes, set into a face sunken by long illness, brightened with recognition and he reached out to me. I eased towards Daniel, Pépé nodding his approval and took a seat beside the bed, which hummed mechanically. I reached my hand out to meet his open palm. Daniel suddenly exclaimed in horror, 'You're so cold!' His other hand crossed his body in an unconscious reaction and encased my frosty fingers. The heat from his fever warmed my cold hands.

As I recall Daniel slipping in and out of consciousness, the heavy medications coursing through his body, the words of French philosopher Michel Serres (2008) echo, 'I embrace you: here and now our contingency creates nuance on nuance, mixture on mixture' (p. 28). As my hand warmed in Daniel's, I was struck by the significant shift in our relations from distant observation to intimate encounter, the tactile granting sensory recognition, and the mutuality of a relationship uncomplicated by consciousness and future expectations (Buber, 1970).[11] Where raised hands once met stale air, they now enfolded human flesh.

***

On a snowy December night, five weeks after this visit to Daniel, Kandyce and I prepared to leave the nearby minimum-security prison after our bi-weekly hospice class. An officer approached me. 'You received a call from up the Hill', he said.[12]

---

[11] The work of philosopher Martin Buber (1970) offers a way of understanding the relational processes and states that unfolded in the prison. Buber understood the *I* and *Thou* relationship as characterized by presence and mutuality, through which both participants in the relationship become wholly human. Buber (1970) writes, 'It is in encounter that the creation reveals its formhood; it does not pour itself into the senses that are waiting but deigns to meet those that are reaching out' (p. 77).

[12] The maximum-medium security prison, where the infirmary was located, was located on a slight hill a few minutes from the minimum-security facility.

Having just left the prison a few hours before, I was surprised to hear the prison had called for me. We hurriedly made our way into the blustery cold and back up to the Hill. Adrenaline coursed through my body as we walked down the stale bleak white hallway that would take us to the medical clinic door – our passage to the infirmary.

With the prisoners locked into their cells for the night and most staff home for the evening, the eerie silence of the night was cut only by the sharp squeaks of my wet winter boots on the linoleum floor. I shivered; the chill of the air recalled the cruel purpose of the corridor: to bring people into the depths of locked doors. I sped up my steps, anxious to be in the more comfortable warmth of the hospice. Reaching the door, I quickly connected my ID badge to the security censor. The slider rumbled back allowing us to pass through.

We exchanged a few words of appreciation with the night shift officer, thanking him for his kind gesture of calling down the Hill. 'Of course, of course', he said nodding as we moved with intention towards Daniel's cell. The sounds of our booted footsteps alerted ears trained to pick up even the most silent of sounds, a developed sonic sensitivity key in a place where 'much can be heard that is not seen' (Rice, 2016, p. 111), and Pépé emerged from the unlocked cell. 'We called ya!' he announced, ushering us into the darkened room. There had been a notable change in Daniel's breathing – a sign to a seasoned hospice volunteer that death would be arriving soon. Upon entering the hospice sensorium, my ears were met with the familiar sounds of the monitors and IV pump beeping away and the hum of the hospital bed. Daniel's favourite dance music played from the CD player, the scratched CD skipping every so often. I had grown accustomed to the rhythms of the prison hospice cell over the past few weeks and I felt the tension ease from my body. I was surprised when I saw Daniel's brother, who was also incarcerated in the prison, in the cell with the volunteers. It was unusual for him to be permitted here at this time of night and I was grateful for the kindness of the staff and administration in accommodating this final interaction.

Writing about the moments of Daniel's nearing death, the memories that return equally vividly are the moments of both levity and care that characterise the ways peer hospice care affirms the patient's existence. In the preceding weeks, Daniel's brother and peer caregivers had shared with me their favourite stories and memories of the gentle yet witty man whose impending death brought us together. We had shared many gleeful laughs as Daniel 'vogued', wriggling in his bed to pop music, which had become as much part of the hospice sensorium as the vibrating of the medical bed. On one night, Daniel insisted on standing, a peer caregiver on each side holding him steady, and began to shake his hips from side to side, his mouth curling into a cheeky smile as all of us laughed and danced alongside him. Other days, I observed intently as the volunteers carried out acts of care that might in any other setting be regarded as 'simple': they carefully wiped chocolate pudding from his chin; tenderly massaged cream onto his dry feet; and showed his brother how to sponge Daniel's mouth. Other times, we sat in silent presence, words seeming to lose meaning as the physiological process of death brutalised Daniel's body

(Tornøe, Danbolt, Kvigne, & Sørlie, 2014), giving comforting hands when the pain he was feeling was too great (Blake, 2011; Classen, 2005; Peloquin, 1989).[13]

As my eyes adjusted to the greyness of the cell, I laid my hand on Daniel's arm to let him know I was present. My ears pricked at the sounds of a crackling deep within Daniel's chest. The 'death rattle'. His chest racked up and down, every breath seemed to be a painful struggle. I moved my hand to his concave shoulder. My hand moved up and down, in sync with his laboured breaths, feeling every crackle, pop, and gurgle and every heavy *thumph* of his beating heart. I stayed like this for a moment, feeling the sensations of his dying body and intensely connected to the man whose bodily tempo let me know the end was near.[14]

After several hours, Daniel's breathing had not changed. With his feet still warm and free of the small purple pools indicative of mottling, Kandyce and I decided to make a quick trip back home – I had been at the prisons since dawn and it was nearing midnight.

***

We arrived back in the infirmary in the early morning hours. Daniel's brother remained by his side, with two peer caregivers – Agelu and C.R. – who were assigned to the overnight vigil shift. Kandyce and I joined them at Daniel's bedside, the five of us encircling him. I sat in silence at the foot of the bed beside C.R., who was also experiencing a hospice death for his first time. I listened intently to Daniel's breathing, each breath fewer and further between. Daniel's brother quietly stepped out of the room. Kandyce and Agelu stood at Daniel's bedside. I sensed a natural intimacy as Agelu tenderly stroked Daniel's head with large hands that had experienced nearly a decade of death as a peer caregiver. An electric calm, an impenetrable tranquillity came over the cell. With ears that I had learned to open in new ways, I caught Agelu's whispered words: 'Enjoy the journey'. As the moon glistened through the small window, Daniel's chest rose in a large breath. Froze. And then fell for the last time. An indescribable burst of energy shot through my body and C.R. exploded up from his chair beside me, breaking through the peacefulness that had filled the room only moments before. Streams of heavy tears began to pour from his eyes as he rushed out of the cell. 'I hadn't felt my heart my whole life, my life was on stagnant water and that night the stagnant water was removed; there was a thump and it's been thumping ever since,' he would later tell me.

---

[13]In the instance of hospice vigil, interpersonal touch is permitted as a gesture of comfort. Tornøe et al. (2014) suggest that compassion and consolation may be 'communicated through a caring touch [of] gentle hand[s]' (p. 3).

[14]Buber's (1970) *I and Thou* resonates; Buber understood human existence as fundamentally interpersonal with persons engaged in shifting relationships. There are two relations, according to Buber. The *I–It*, from which objects are more distantly encountered as something to be experienced or known. The *I–Thou* relationship extends beyond experience to unconscious encounter whereby being is not consciously mediated, a more 'pure' relationship and mutual intimacy.

I moved to stand at Daniel's bedside. C.R. rejoined us; Agelu, C.R. Kandyce and I enfolding Daniel. I fought the embodied impulse to reach over to C.R. and rest my hand on his arm in a simple empathetic gesture of comfort, yet which remained beyond the bounds of acceptability in the prison. This 'necessary suppression' (Herrity, 2020) was part of the careful craft of the ethnographer, a precarious balancing act, even in the intimacy and immediacy of human death. Daniel's brother returned to the room, took a step and then stopped. His eyes moved from Daniel's still body to meet mine. Without speaking, but keeping my gaze connected to his, I gave a slow nod to confirm what he was silently asking, speaking not in sound, but in silence. Suddenly an officer entered the cell. With 'time of death' confirmed, it was time to leave the cell, and Daniel. The cell was secured, the tiny tray slot opened to offer a small rectangular view into the death room, and Daniel's body laid alone in wait for the prison's investigator.

Conclusion

> Visiting with prison hospice volunteers and correctional staff has reminded me of William Golding's classic novel, *Lord of the Flies* ... Penitentiaries are islands within our society, yet prison hospices are the opposite of Golding's chaotic island. (Byock, 2002, pp. 112–113)

> The boundaries of his world are drawn by his bodily experiences to which visits of the dead belong quite 'naturally'. Any assumption that the non-sensible exists must strike him as non-sense. (Buber, 1970, p. 71)

My initial encounter with Daniel in the prison yard would prove to be the first in an intense journey he would invite me to share, an expedition through the extremes of punishment in disciplinary segregation to the humanity enacted in prison hospice. In allowing me to bear witness to this journey, and through our sensory encounters, a dissonance emerged, felt most acutely through prison policies that mediated the tactile boundaries of dis/connections. Howes (2005) suggests that 'While knowledge of the world may be said to come from many bodily channels, the sense of touch is a particularly diffuse and varied source of information' (p. 28). I came to cultivate an understanding of penal life and death in new and intimate ways. More precisely, the *feel* of Daniel's life and death illuminating brutality and beauty, indignity and intimacy, in a contemporary prison medical unit.

Daniel's D-time placement in the prison infirmary was rooted in the custodial need to care for his chronic illness. However, in doing so, Daniel was subjected to additional layers of punishment such as shackles (Granse, 2003) and strip searches.[15] Further, there was an institutional ambivalence and indifference to his well-being, with care not extending beyond medical treatment of his existing health condition.

---

[15] See 'The Power of Touch' (Warr, 2020).

As I have discussed elsewhere (see Stanley, 2018, 2020), what is framed as institutional 'care' may take on the form of harm, thus illuminating 'repression and compassion [as] profoundly linked' (Fassin, 2005, p. 381; see also Ticktin, 2006). In prison, there is a fundamental tension as violence and dignity exist and interact together. Though Daniel was provided with the crucial medical treatment needed to sustain his physical life, he was intentionally deprived of the 'everyday' textures of the prison sensorial and the 'bodily presence of others' (Guenther, 2013).

In *Solitary Confinement: Social Death and Its Afterlives*, Lisa Guenther (2013) explains, '[T]here is something about the absence of regular bodily contact with others, the absence of even the *possibility* of touching or being touched, that threatens to unhinge the subject' (p. xiii, emphasis original). Thus, cauterising Daniel from social relations and tactile sensations was a callous denial of his personhood and humanity, possibly a 'death-in-life' (Guenther, 2013), or social death experience (Cohen & Taylor, 1972). As former prisoner Five Omar Mualimm-ak shares of his time in isolation,

> There was no touch … The very essence of life, I came to learn during those seemingly endless days, is human contact, and the affirmation of existence that comes with it. Losing that contact, you lost your sense of identity. You become nothing. (Quoted in Venters, 2019, pp. 77–78)

Therefore, disciplinary policies and practices impose limits to tactile engagements, impeding possibilities of sensory recognition and damaging the personhood of prisoners. Under the harsh penal regime, the approach of physical death was the twisted catalyst needed to move Daniel into a zone in which the reconstitution of relational personhood could become a glimmering possibility.

As Blake, drawing on the work of Peloquin (1989) contends, 'touch can diminish the distance between people and can [thus] be used to engage our awareness of ourselves and others and the connection between us' (p. 3). The shared sensation of touch, of human connection, was my real entry point into Daniel's end-of-life experience, the point at which he truly invited me into his life and to become an engaged participant in his final curtain call. In doing so, my distant relationship with Daniel moved from the *It* of detached experience and monologue, to the reciprocal encounter of *Thou*. The mutuality and dialogue of our tactile encounters pushed my understandings of the relational possibilities of prison ethnography into new realms. As a participant observer in this peculiar prison deathscape in which any form of intimacy challenged prison expectations for relationality, boundaries were breached and closeness attained with interlocutors. Blake (2011, p. 1) expresses a similar experience, writing:

> Although I was familiar with and in favour of calls for a subjective and bodily awareness in the field, I found myself ill-prepared for the large role that touch would come to play in my interactions with the children in the ward and how this would affect me … I became aware that I had in fact been holding onto a perception of myself as the detached observer and I became aware of this in the moment it became impossible to retain such a perception.

Annette Leibing and Athena McLean (2007) suggest that pushing against the borders of the generally perceivable and observable is crucial to not only illuminate new knowledge and understandings, but 'because the shadow might directly trouble or "overshadow" what lies in the light' (pp. 1–2). Sensorial scholarship thus provides a way of conceptualising and symbolising relations, around which prisoners live their lives, die their deaths, and structure their realities.

As a prison hospice volunteer once shared,

> When you learn to be truly present for someone in their last days of this life, you unlock a part of yourself, a part of the universe that was completely and utterly unknown to you previous to that moment.

Day after day, as I set my cold hand in Daniel's feverish palms, I felt the physical manifestation of the deep emotional bond between the participant observer and her 'subject'. When I walked out of the heavy prison doors on that fateful December day, the volunteer's words resonated deeply with me. Perhaps the most important sensemaking imparted to me through my sensorial engagement was what it truly means to be *present* as a prison ethnographer.

Acknowledgements

I would like to acknowledge Bethany, Jason, and Kate for giving me the opportunity to delve into areas of my research that otherwise may have remained hidden, as well as for their careful and thoughtful reading of an earlier version of this chapter. I am also grateful to Kathryn Goldfarb, Ellen Badone, and Katrina Lamont for their thoughtful and incisive comments. I would also like to acknowledge the Maine Department of Corrections for their support of my study. My deepest gratitude to Daniel, the prison hospice volunteers, Kandyce, and the Maine Hospice Council and Centre for End of Life Care. The study was supported by the University of Colorado at Boulder through a Visiting Research Scholar appointment, the Wenner-Gren Foundation for Anthropological Research, the Social Sciences and Humanities Research Council, and the School of Graduate Studies and Department of Anthropology at McMaster University.

References

Aday, R. H. (2003). *Aging prisoners: Crisis in American corrections*. Westport, CT: Praeger.
Atkinson, P., Delamont, S., & Housley, W. (Eds.). (2008). *The contours of culture: Complex ethnography and the ethnography of complexity*. Lanham, MD: AltaMira Press.
Bedard, R., Metzger, L., & Williams, B. (2016). Ageing prisoners: An introduction to geriatric health-care challenges in correctional facilities. *International Review of the Red Cross*, *98*(903), 917–939.
Blake, R. (2011). Ethnographies of touch and touching ethnographies: Some prospects for touch in anthropological enquiries. *Anthropology Matters*, *13*(1), 1–12.

Buber, M. (1970). *I and thou* (W. Kaufmann, Trans.). New York, NY: Touchstone/Simon & Schuster.
Byock, I. (2002). Dying well in corrections: Why should we care? *Journal of Correctional Health Care, 9*(2), 107–117.
Carson, E. A., & Sabol, W. J. (2016). *Aging of the state prison population, 1993–2013* (Bureau of Justice Statistics, Special Report). New York, NY: U.S. Department of Justice.
Caverley, S. (2006). Older mentally ill inmates: A descriptive study. *Journal of Correctional Health Care, 12*(4), 262–268.
Charleroy, M., & Marland, H. (2016). Prisoners of solitude: Bringing history to bear on prison health policy. *Endeavour, 40*(3), 141–147.
Classen, C. (Ed.). (2005). *The book of touch.* Oxford: Berg Publishers.
Cloud, D., Drucker, E., Browne, A., & Parsons, J. (2015). Public health and solitary confinement in the United States. *American Journal of Public Health, 105*(1), 18–26.
Cohen, F. (1998). *The mentally disordered inmate and the law.* Kingston, NJ: Civic Research Institute.
Cohen, S., & Taylor, L. (1972). *Psychological survival: The experience of long-term imprisonment.* Hammondsworth: Penguin.
Crewe, B., Liebling, A., & Hulley, S. (2014). Heavy–light, absent–present: Rethinking the 'weight' of imprisonment. *British Journal of Sociology, 65*(3), 387–410.
Crewe, B., Warr, J., Bennett, P., & Smith, A. (2014). The emotional geography of prison life. *Theoretical Criminology, 18*(1), 56–74.
Fassin, D. (2005). Compassion and repression: The moral economy of immigration policies in France. *Cultural Anthropology, 20*(3), 362–387.
Fassin, D. (2017). *Prison worlds: An ethnography of the carceral condition.* Cambridge: Polity Press.
Fazel, S., & Baillargeon, J. (2011). The health of prisoners. *The Lancet, 377*(9769), 956–965.
Geertz, C. (1973). *Thick description: Toward and interpretive theory of culture.* New York, NY: Basic Books, Inc.
Granse, B. (2003). Why should we even care? Hospice social work practice in a prison setting. *Smith College Studies in Social Work: End-of-Life Care, 73*(3), 359–376.
Guenther, L. (2013). *Solitary confinement: Social death and its afterlives.* Minneapolis, MN: University of Minnesota Press.
Haney, C. (2003). Mental health issues in long-term solitary and 'Supermax' confinement. *Crime & Delinquency, 49*(1), 124–156.
Herrity, K. (2018). Music and identity in prison: Music as a technology of the self. *Prison Service Journal, 239.* Retrieved from http://search.proquest.com/docview/2120899006/
Herrity, K. (2020, February 3) Close, closer. Blog post. Retrieved from https://sensorycriminology.com/2020/02/03/close-closer/
Hoffman, H. C., & Dickinson, G. E. (2011). Characteristics of prison hospice programs in the United States. *American Journal of Hospice and Palliative Medicine, 28*(4), 245–252.
Howes, D. (2005). Skinscapes: Embodiment, culture, and environment. In C. Classen (Ed.), *The book of touch* (pp. 27–39). Oxford: Berg.
Howes, D. (2010). Response to Sarah Pink: The future of sensory anthropology. *Social Anthropology, 18*(3), 333–336.
Jefferson, A. M., & Schmidt, B. E. (2019). Concealment and revelation as bureaucratic and ethnographic practice: Lessons from Tunisian prisons. *Critique of Anthropology, 39*(2), 155–171.
King, R. D., & McDermott, K. (1995). *The state of our prisons.* Oxford: Clarendon Press.
Kleinman, A. (2012). Caregiving as moral experience. *The Lancet, 380*(9853), 1550–1551.

Kouyoumdjian, F. G., Evgeny, A. M., Borschmann, R., Kinner, S. A., & McConnon, A. (2017). Do people who experience incarceration age more quickly? Exploratory analyses using retrospective cohort data on mortality from Ontario, Canada. *PLoS ONE*, *12*(4), e0175837.

Leibing, A., & McLean, A. (2007). 'Learn to value your shadow!' An introduction to the margins of fieldwork. In A. McLean & A. Leibing (Eds.), *The shadow side of fieldwork: Exploring the blurred borders between ethnography and life* (pp. 1–28). Malden: Blackwell Publishing.

Maruschak, L. M., & Berzofsky, M. (2015). Medical problems of state and federal prisoners and jail inmates, 2011–2014. U.S. Department of Justice, Office of Justice Programs, Bureau of Justice Studies. Retrieved from https://www.bjs.gov/content/pub/pdf/mpsfpji1112.pdf

Maschi, T., Viola, D., & Sun, F. (2013). The high cost of the international aging prisoner crisis: Well-being as the common denominator for action. *The Gerontologist*, *53*(4), 543–554.

Mumola, C. J. (2007). Medical causes of death in state prisons, 2001–2004 (BJS Publication No. NCJ 216340). Washington, DC: U.S. Bureau of Justice Statistics.

Nellis, A. (2010). Throwing away the key: The expansion of life without parole sentences in the United States. *Federal Sentencing Reporter*, *23*, 27–32.

Peloquin, S. (1989). Helping through touch: The embodiment of caring. *Journal of Religion and Health*, *28*(4), 299–322.

Plugge, E., Elwood Martin, R., & Hayton, P. (2014). Noncommunicable diseases and prisoners. In S. Enggist, L. Møller, G. Galea, & C. Udesen (Eds.), *Prisoners and health* (pp. 81–86). Copenhagen: World Health Organization Regional Office for Europe.

Rice, T. (2016). Sounds inside: Prison, prisoners and acoustical agency. *Sound Studies: Special Issue: Sonic Skills in Cultural Contexts: Theories, Practices and Materialities of Listening*, *2*(1), 6–20.

Serres, M. (2008). *The five senses: A philosophy of mingles bodies*. London: Bloomsbury Revelations.

Stanley, D. (2018, May 9). Discussion about what constitutes ethical and responsible research in prisons [Presentation] International Correctional Research Symposium, Prague, Czech Republic. Retrieved from https://icpa.org/library/crs2018-discussion-about-what-constitutes-ethical-and-responsible-research-in-prison-settings/

Stanley, D. (2020). *Caring in custody: Subjectivity and personhood in a men's prison hospice*. Unpublished Ph.D. thesis, McMaster University, Hamilton, ON.

Steve. (n.d.). Life after death. *Blog post*. Retrieved from https://www.compen.crim.cam.ac.uk/Blog/blog-pages-full-versions/life-after-death

Stoller, P. (1989). *The taste of ethnographic things: The senses in anthropology*. Philadelphia, PA: University of Pennsylvania Press.

Stoller, P. (1997). *Sensuous scholarship*. Philadelphia, PA: University of Pennsylvania Press.

Taylor, J. (2008). On recognition, caring, and dementia. *Medical Anthropology Quarterly*, *22*, 313–335.

Ticktin, M. (2006). Where ethics and politics meet: The violence of humanitarianism in France. *American Ethnologist*, *33*(1), 33–49.

Toch, H. (1992). *Mosaic of despair: Human breakdown in prison*. Washington, DC: American Psychological Association.

Tornøe, K. A., Danbolt, L. J., Kvigne, K., & Sørlie, V. (2014). The power of consoling presence – hospice nurses' lived experience with spiritual and existential care for the dying. *BMC nursing*, *13*, 25.

Venters, H. (2019). *Life and death in Rikers Island*. Baltimore, MD: Johns Hopkins University Press.

Wahidin, A. (2006). Time and the prison experience. *Sociological Research Online*, *11*(1). doi:10.5153/sro.1245

Waller, C. (2018). 'Darker than the Dungeon': Music, ambivalence, and the carceral subject. *International Journal for the Semiotics of Law, 31*(2), 275–299.
Warr, J. (2020, June 1). *The power of touch.* Blog post. Retrieved from https://sensorycriminology.com
Wener, R. (2012). Correctional environments. In *The Oxford handbook of environmental and conservation psychology.* https://doi.org/10.1093/oxfordhb/9780199733026.013.0017
Williams, B. A., Goodwin, J. S., Baillargeon, J., Ahalt, C., & Walter, L. C. (2012). Addressing the aging crisis in U.S. criminal justice health care. *Journal of American Geriatric Society, 60*, 1150–1156.
Williams, N. (2007). Prison health and the health of the public: Ties that bind. *Journal of Correctional Health Care, 13*(2), 80–92.

Part II

Sensing the Field

Chapter 5

Sensing Transition: Exploring Prison Life in Post-Revolution Tunisia

Bethany E. Schmidt and Andrew M. Jefferson

Introduction: 'Seeing is Believing, But Feeling is the Truth'

We begin with two encounters from our fieldwork in Tunisia:

(i) On a hot day during Ramadan in June 2015, we interviewed four former prisoners in Tunis. They had all been incarcerated under the ousted regime, before the 2011 revolution. Although we did not (explicitly) ask about their experiences of torture in detention, each shared their story of abuse, in different ways. It was, like Das (1996, p. 68) observes, as though their words just had to come out. But words were not the only means through which they expressed suffering. Their pain and grief were also articulated through the body. As they recounted the violence they had endured, they pointed to scars, commenting on how each had been imprinted. One former prisoner, a man, shared his story but also asked for one of his scars to be touched. He said, 'If you can touch it, it is real' – as though just *seeing* was not enough to bear witness and validate his experiences; we must *touch*, he implied, in order to confirm the authenticity of the violence. Our bodies – his and ours – then, became haptic[1] instruments enabling a 'grasp' of his embodied experience (Crang, 2003, p. 499).

(ii) In March 2016, we met with the then Director of Prisons. At this time, we had been to Tunisia on several occasions and had conducted fieldwork in two prisons. The purpose of this meeting was to debrief on our research to date and discuss how to move forward. He expressed interest in understanding how overcrowding impacts on daily life in prisons, for both staff and prisoners. He was frustrated with policy-makers whom, he felt, were unable to comprehend

---

[1]We employ Rodaway's (1994, p. 42) conception of 'haptic', which refers to 'touch as an active sense which is integrally involved with the locomotive ability of the body and specifically focuses upon the role of touch in the perception of space and relationships to place'.

the intensity of overpopulation, despite years of growing and vocalised concern internally, and from human rights organisations and other watchdog groups. He shared with us a desire 'to make a test with policy-makers – make them stand in a hot, crowded Tunisian bus for 15, 30, 45 minutes and then write about how that felt'. He wanted to simulate the forced intimacy of an overcrowded cell[2] – 'smell what people had for lunch ... be in proximity to other people's sweat and breath' – and recreate the discomfort and unease of the situation. This, he thought, would make them internalise, via sensorial exposure, the corporeal experience of overcrowding.

These encounters represent some features of the Tunisian state in transition: individuals struggling to come to terms with the recent and brutal past; a prison service's recognition of 'what is' versus 'what we aspire to be'; and the discord that comes from ongoing suffering, change, and democratic expectations. They also draw attention to the importance of bodily imprints and emplaced sensations (which Howes, 2005, p. 7, defines as 'the sensuous interrelationship of body–mind–environment') and remind us of the double meaning of *sensing* and *feeling*. Feeling can be associated with the physical experience of touching or being touched, but feelings are also the term we give to experiences of emotion or affect. We *sense* with our bodies but we also *make sense* of our worlds cognitively. This is not to argue for a mind–body dualism. Quite the contrary. What we seek to affirm is akin to Crouch's (2001, p. 62) assertion that the *feeling of being* can be practised as a *feeling of doing*, a means of grasping the world and making sense of what it feels like, the *feel* at once physical *and* in a process of *sensemaking*. This form of embodied practice, or 'emplaced participation', has epistemological and methodological implications. It requires a reflexive attunement to our own bodily responses within different spatial and cultural contexts, as well as an awareness of the sensual geographies of the people and places we study (see also Herrity, this volume). We agree with Pink (2009, p. 72) that:

> Learning to sense and make meanings as others do thus involves us not simply observing what they do, but learning how to use all our senses and to participate in their worlds, on the terms of their embodied understandings.

These orientations – towards an emplaced and embodied sensorial practice – we contend, enable us to better explore and contemplate the changing nature of prison life in Tunisia, and prisons more generally. Like Rodaway (1994, p. 4), we regard the senses integratively in order to critically consider how we think about and document the physical, social, cultural, and aesthetic dimensions of prison life.

---

[2] We use the terms 'dormitory' and 'cell' interchangeably. It should be noted, though, that custodial arrangements in Tunisian prisons are almost exclusively in dorms, which are intended to hold more than one person.

Sensing prison climates in a time of significant change, is, as Anderson (2009, p. 77) notes, interesting and worthy of study 'because it holds a series of opposites – presence and absence, materiality and ideality, definite and indefinite, singularity and generality – in a relation of tension'. These conflicting yet interrelated dualities present an intriguing heuristic space for analytical exploration. By seeking out contradictions, we allow for multiple, and possibly competing experiences to emerge. The senses do not always work together or convey the same message, as Howes (2010, p. 335) reminds us, which is why the blurring of sensory boundaries and perceptions provide a novel way to probe these special betwixt and between spaces (Graham, 2017, p. 133).

Our effort to sense, and make sense of, transitioning prisons in Tunisia highlights the sensorial dissonance produced within the prison's landscape – the tensions between old and new, reform ideals and reality, and what the sensual experiences in these mutable spaces *feel* like. We examine the tendency for prisons to be contradictory, as sites that are intensely corporeal, 'depriving and numbing the senses, and, paradoxically, heightening them' (Griffiths, 2014, p. 227). Our aim is to empirically explore what McClanahan and South (2020, p. 9) hypothesise: 'For criminology, the significance and power of the senses is particularly obvious when they are considered in terms of their removal, loss, degradation or ... their weaponization', as well as their possible enhancement or intensification (i.e. sensory overload or amplification). We further contemplate how sensorial accounts of spaces and places of punishment (and transition) get us closer to answering some of the questions posed by Liebling (2011, p. 532): What constitutes 'inhuman and degrading treatment', as experienced by the prisoner? What is 'prison pain'? Or 'cruelty'? And what does this terminology *mean* when we consider conventional forms of assessing 'standards of decency'? Equally, what is the meaning and importance of the senses and their role in coping and survival within prisons?

The remainder of this chapter is structured as follows. First, we describe post-revolution prisons in Tunisia and the research conducted. Next, we discuss a shifting carceral landscape that includes legacies of the revolution, current practice, and reform efforts that promote 'human rights' and arts-based 'rehabilitation'. Alongside this, we reflect upon our sensory engagement with the field, and how our (foreign) bodies navigated spatial and sensorial geographies. Lastly, we consider the sensual pains of living in severely overcrowded spaces and the implications for definitions of inhumane treatment. This is juxtaposed with the 'new' reform world and the spectrum of sensorial ecologies we encountered. We conclude with some final reflections on how sensory accounts of the prisoner, prison officer, and the researcher mediate experiences of prison harm, power, and punishment and illustrate the utility of an approach that is deliberately attuned to sensoriality.

Prisons in Post-Revolution Tunisia

Prior to the Arab Spring, detention in police stations and prisons in Tunisia was synonymous with torture and abusive practices. Political 'opponents' were targeted, as were their family, friends, and neighbours. Imprisonment, then, was largely for containment and the suppression of dissidence (see Ghachem, 2018; McCarthy, 2018). Following its revolution in 2011, the country has been transitioning to the region's only democracy with aims to stabilise and legitimise social and political institutions. This has included reform efforts within the criminal justice system, which is reshaping itself to be more closely aligned to the international standards expected from a democratic state.

However, Tunisian prisons continue to raise concerns among human rights monitoring groups, in part due to persistent and severe overcrowding (OHCHR, 2014). At the time of our research, some men's prisons were operating at over 200% of their intended capacity. In practice, this means that prisoners often sleep 2–3 to a mattress, under bunk beds (the 'trunk'), in aisle ways (the 'highway'), on storage shelves, or in toilet areas. Many are confined to a single room with dozens of others for 23 or more hours a day, and with little access to fresh air, sunlight, exercise, or showers. These are, generally, inert environments – bodies and time move slowly, air is thick and stagnant, movements are restricted due to lack of space, and there are few distractions or activities. While kinetically under-stimulating, these spaces are sensorially over-stimulating. They contain layers of rich sensory textures: the smells of homemade meals; kaleidoscopic colours from bedding, clothing, and textiles brought in by families; handicrafts and photos hung from every available surface; prison cats and birds flitting about meowing and chirping; and a cacophony of sounds produced by many bodies in a small space (from heavy breathing to quiet prayers to snoring or singing or laughter or quarrels). These dormitories are both deeply human (corporeal, affective, pulsating) and inhumane (claustrophobic, congested, extreme).

Most of the country's 27 prisons were originally constructed for industrial or agricultural use and later converted into detention facilities. Consequently, many establishments suffer from compromised infrastructure. In recent years though, several purpose-built prisons have been erected and several more are being upgraded and refurbished. All four of the prisons in our study were in some kind of structural transition. The most striking of these were in the prisons of Mornag, where an entirely new prison was being built onto the side of the existing one, and in Sfax, where the inside of the prison was an active construction site with heavy equipment occupying the central courtyard, forcing prisoners and staff (and us) to dash past excavators, bull dozers, holes, exposed pipes, and various bits of construction materials. Sfax was especially noteworthy in that it was the prison system's reform aims presented in architectural and spatial form. This was the 'modern' Tunisian prison evolving. Dorms were to have enough space to allow for tables to be set up so that prisoners could eat together and play games, without having to conduct all activities in bed (eating, sleeping, socialising, and reading).[3] The new built prisons and those being refurbished to reflect the post-revolution

---

[3]This was the desired practice and ideal outcome – that is, one man per bed with more available and flexible space for movement and activities. However, prisons are at the behest of the judiciary and cannot refuse prisoners. Thus, prison officials have no power to control overpopulation.

prison reform agenda were, to varying extents, incorporating the arts, creativity, and 'cultural citizenship' into the aesthetics and regime. These new spaces were decorated in colourful murals and prisoner artwork, theatre spaces were created, prisons were participating in the annual Carthage Film Festival, craftsman workshops on jewellery making, pottery, and weaving were on offer, courses in other arts-based activities were increasing, and local musicians and singers were coming in to perform at special events.

Our fieldwork in Tunisia[4] was wholly dependent on translation and required a recalibration of – and attunement to – our senses. In this environment, exploring the 'feeling of doing' through embodied fieldwork practice was necessary. Anything written (like signs or paperwork) or spoken was inaccessible to us, unless translated by one of our research assistants. We came to recognise that our tendency to privilege visuality (the gaze) was limiting within this context. In addition, our inability to communicate casually and spontaneously created some awkwardness, particularly when sensitive topics arose. Interpretation made it difficult for us to maintain control of conversations, which was especially acute when pain was discussed. When violence or torture was spoken about, for instance, we were sometimes incapable of adequately sensing the depth of pain in others, due to the limits of language. On occasion, participants – perhaps sensing how pain gets muddled in translation – would transcend these limitations by communicating in alternative ways. One prisoner, when describing how isolated he felt in prison, grabbed Bethany's hand and would squeeze it rhythmically, as if creating a percussive cue for when the conversation, or his emotions, intensified. In Longhurst, Ho, and Johnston's (2008, p. 208) terms, bodies were producing knowledge and 'being and knowing' were not easily separated.

The encounters presented above provide some initial insight into how sensuous dispositions interacted, and were exhibited and interpreted, within the Tunisian prison field. They also support Stoller's (2004, p. 820) claim that cross-cultural 'complexities require a more sensuous approach to ethnography, an approach in which local epistemologies and sensory regimes are more fully explored'. We discuss this in more detail next.

Sensing Prisons in Transition

The notion of 'transition' is multifaceted. Prisons are constantly in flux, always both 'persisting and mutating'. Prisons undergoing reform, though, suggest a deliberate, intentional strategy to direct change in a particular direction (Martin, Jefferson, & Bandyopadhyay, 2014, p. 12). In Tunisia, there was a spectrum of change, at once deliberately focussed (through reform efforts) and organically

---

[4]From 2015 to 2018, we conducted four periods of intensive fieldwork in four prisons. Interviews, meetings, and activities with other criminal justice stakeholders (former prisoners, prison authorities, activists, non-governmental organisations (NGOs)) were also carried out. We worked with two local research assistants who acted as both apprentice fieldworkers and (cultural and linguistic) interpreters.

occurring. Prisons were reflecting shifts in wider society, which occasionally produced friction, and some moral discord, in daily operational practice. One example of this came from the changing composition of the prisoner population. Following three high-profile attacks in 2015, the number of individuals being charged with or convicted of terrorist offences was increasing, and the death penalty had been reinstated for terror-related crimes (Tamburini, 2018). So, while the authorities aimed to develop prisons that emphasised human rights and rehabilitation, this new and growing prisoner group (a) generated angst, fear, and distrust among staff, and (b) was often subject to intensified surveillance and suspicion, and excluded from rehabilitative activities. Such shifts posed complicated questions for prisons and prison personnel about punishment, justice, humanity, worthiness, and the use of authority.

The Arab Spring uprisings and resultant democratic revolution in Tunisia acted as a point of reference for staff and prisoners to discuss the changing nature of prisons, and their society more generally. It was often the physical structures around us that led to these discussions. Deep scars in the architectural tissue of many prisons remained – remnants of the revolution and the upheaval surrounding it. These scars held serious emotional and sensorial power (Mihai, 2018). For staff, trauma and anxiety were still live issues ('what if it happens again?'; 'I will never get those images out of my head'). They described how the days and weeks of disturbances in 2010–2011 resulted in destruction, deaths, fear, and uncertainty (it was 'like in war'). In two prisons, which experienced substantial damage and revolt, staff were keen to show us memorials that were constructed to honour the staff who were harmed or killed, and the physical reminders still visible. In Mornag prison, one officer guided us around a closed-off section of the prison that was being renovated. On the outside wall were pockmarks from helicopter gunfire, as the National Guard had attempted to 'scare' prisoners back into the prison to prevent escapes. In another part of the prison, scorched walls from fires set in the courtyard by prisoners were now part of the landscape, passed daily by prisoners and staff. In Sfax prison, we encountered a still intact, but closed-off, burnt out dorm. It was an officer who suggested we 'witness' it. As we stood outside the dorm, he recounted his experience of working in prison during the revolution, and the impact of this on him still. Our fieldwork notes reflect the intensity of this moment:

> The burnt out cell is in the fourth pavilion. The door cannot be opened because the key has gone missing, but the flap can be. Taking a closer look in through the little barred window is amazing – the sight and smell of it is overwhelming. This could have happened a week ago – seems after the revolution the door was closed and hasn't been touched since. It smells of fire and charring. It took my breath away ... The desperation and confusion and anger and terror and excitement that must have been felt during that period is almost too much to comprehend. This is powerful ... The officer struggles to tell the whole story. He chokes up. Doesn't want to cry. He turns away from me to hide his face. (BES fieldwork notes, 010618)

In Borj Erroumi, a staff member Andrew spoke with described what happened in this prison, with the use of photos, perhaps as visual 'evidence' of just how scary and chaotic this time was:

> It was like a dream ... we touched the death and we lived the death ... we had lived with prisoners for a long time and all of a sudden they're against you as the enemy.

The legacies of the revolution persisted, as did the visceral memories that had been imprinted onto the minds and bodies of those who lived through it. For many prisoners who were incarcerated during the uprising, the architectural scars represented something fundamentally different: the reclamation of power, the undoing of authority, a collective and social fight for freedom and dignity, and a call for justice. For other prisoners, however, their trauma and anxiety was just as palpable as that of staff. They too were nervous that 'it could happen again': 'they [the authorities] beat us, they trapped us – we were fighting for our lives'; 'we were abandoned and starving ... locked in with fires and the wounded' (see also Warr, this volume). Even several years after the revolution, at the time of our research, the senses connected to this event were still corporeally alive (Stevenson, 2014).

We did not seek out 'the sensory' – in either our fieldworker experience or in that of our participants. But confronting, noting, and feeling the sensorial aspects of prison life here was inescapable. Some sensual features struck us quickly, like the use and role of touch, as well as sensory stimuli related to home (in particular, food and smells, which are discussed below). Physical affection was pronounced, especially among men. This was surprising to us, particularly within the context of prison. Prison governors and officers would often kiss, embrace, and place their arms around male prisoners. It was usually a form of recognition, familiarity, and connection – they came from the same community, or their families knew each other. Prisoners, too, would walk with arms linked or with arms around each other as they paced in circles in the outside courtyards. This kind of (voluntary) intimacy was common practice and imitated ordinary social life in the country. It was intriguing to us that these men, who spent most of their days subjected to forced intimacy and in constant proximity to others' bodies, chose to remain physically close in 'their' time outside of the dorms. This was, it seemed, an important exercise in bodily autonomy (or, in Berlin's (1969, p. 131) words, the embodied practice of 'positive liberty': deciding, not being decided for).

We participated in these displays of affection as well (despite our own bodily discomfort). When entering or exiting meetings, for example – kissing each cheek, hugging, and holding hands for a longer period than we are accustomed. Touch and other forms of haptic expression were also apparent in the language and descriptions of events or practices. In Manouba prison, Bethany became a participant in the prison bakery as one of the instructors grabbed her by the hips to demonstrate the right motion for rolling dough. She then cupped Bethany's hands to 'show' her how best to perform the task and said, 'If your hands do not understand, your mind will never understand' (reminiscent of Merleau-Ponty's, 1962, p. 144, 'knowledge of the hands'). These physical encounters were the same when the instructor worked with prisoners. While an initial affront to our Western-sense of spatial boundaries, we found it somewhat refreshing to witness so much 'normalised' contact in prison. But there were ways in which touch was punitively inflicted or controlled as well. Touch of any kind was not permitted during standard weekly visits with family, as prisoners and their loved ones were separated by a partition wall.[5] In the women's prison, affection was closely policed and scrutinised because sexual relations between prisoners was a punishable offence, often resulting in solitary confinement. We also observed everyday or 'mundane' violence (Jefferson, 2005, p. 489), like when officers would lightly kick or slap prisoners to stay in line during counts. And as we discuss later, overcrowding appeared to us as a form of weaponised touch through forced intimacy and invasive proximity.

Haptic expressions were another way that, linguistically, the privileging of senses other than sight were communicated. When a prisoner was asked about whether the revolution had changed prison life (he had been incarcerated before and after), he replied 'does this *feel* like democracy?', suggesting that the texture and atmosphere of his carceral experience was embodied in a way that was separate from the material or optic evaluation of his surroundings. This is in contrast to prisoners in the UK, for instance, who often say things like 'does this *look* like rehabilitation?'

Food, Smell, and the Re-creation of Home

Prison life in Tunisia revolved around food. Families were able to bring food baskets ('el koffa') for their family member up to three times a week. The large baskets were packed with plastic containers filled with home-cooked traditional meals, along with bottles of olive oil, peeled fruits, hardboiled eggs, fish, and other culinary treats. Meals were often still hot upon arrival at the prison, despite the hours-long journey and wait many families endured. Food equated to power, in many respects. For prisoners, food was currency that could buy a better bed or sleeping placement within the dorm, be traded for other goods or services, and it was a symbol of status. For staff, the value of prisoner food was understood and, as such, operated as a means for maintaining order and discipline (see also Valentine & Longstaff, 1998) – the most common punishment was the withholding of baskets for one or more weeks. Prisoners would then be dependent on prison food (described as 'one pot slop') or the generosity of others with baskets.

We got to know Tunisian prisons and Tunisian life by watching the food baskets being delivered and subsequently searched. Our research assistants would point out to us regional differences in how the food was prepared – variations in ingredients, spicing, or presentation provided geographic clues as to where the family came from. The practice of searching the baskets varied from prison to

---

[5] See also Booth's (2020) questioning of the control of tactility in prisons and whether it is possible for people separated by imprisonment to stay in touch by *actually* staying in touch.

prison, though there were standard guidelines from headquarters posted. Some rules were adhered to more than others, and some prisons imposed further restrictions (though they all told us that 'the rules are the rules' and 'we follow the guidelines exactly'). In one establishment, there was an ethos of respect and preservation – do as little harm to the food as possible, despite having to cut open peppers or roasted chicken when searching for contraband. As one officer noted, when carefully slicing open a whole fish: 'This is love. This food is their home. We try not to disrupt that'. In this prison, they also made efforts to get the baskets to their respective prisoners as fast as possible so that the warmth would be retained. In another prison, the searching process was a display of overt power and often, punitiveness (Godderis, 2006). Here, little care was taken when slicing open food and, with regularity, the destruction of the food's integrity was intentional. When one basket came in – for a prisoner convicted of a terrorist offence – the officer deliberately rejected food (that was technically allowed) and mangled what was left. Baskets in this prison would sit for hours before being delivered.

The homemade meals brought in by families functioned as a meaningful way for prisoners to emulate the sensory features of home (Law, 2001). Upon receiving their baskets, prisoners would often open each lid, close their eyes, and slowly take in whatever that container held. These rituals evoked memories of family, holidays, celebrations, and time spent with loved ones (see also Sutton, 2010). We observed the same with clothing baskets. Men would often plunge their faces into the freshly laundered items and stay in that position for long periods. It was not until we asked that this act became clear – 'it smells like home'. Extra laundry soap would be used in order to intensify the scent. Some men opted to keep their fresh laundry unused for as long as possible just to keep the scent preserved.

Reform, the Arts, and Sensing Change

After the revolution, the reform efforts which integrated arts and creativity began to flourish in prisons. We found a variety of activities being developed and implemented. These ranged from various art classes to more immersive forms of engagement (e.g. dance, yoga, theatre, and music). This mirrored a social movement in wider Tunisian society where freedom of expression and creative arts were being revitalised after decades of censorship and suppression (Shilton, 2013). The vision coming from prison headquarters tethered together ideas of rehabilitative reform (via positive and constructive purposeful activity) with the notion of 'cultural citizenship'. Tunisia's Director of Prisons, when making a public statement regarding the expansion of the Carthage Film Festival into prisons, said: 'The deprivation of liberty doesn't mean prisoners should lose all of their cultural rights ... cultural creativity tends to inculcate values of tolerance'.[6] Cultural exposure and engagement, then, was seen to be a form of civic rehabilitation. We had the pleasure of partaking in the Film Festival in the women's prison. We also participated in a theatre workshop in Borj Erroumi prison.

---

[6]Elyes Zalleg, statement from 31 October 2018.

A distinct feature of both of these experiences was the kinaesthetics associated with them, especially in the latter, and how this contrasted with the inertness and lethargy of dorm life. Prisoner bodies moved in ways we had not seen before: they were alive, energetic, excited, dynamic, and responsive. When the film viewing was being set up, loud pop music played as staff and prisoners lined up chairs, decorated, and prepared snacks. The women laughed, sang, and danced in this (temporary) free space. In the theatre workshop, physicality was a core part of the training. 'Getting in touch' with, and attuning oneself to the body were integral to many of the exercises. These were intended to build trust within the group of a dozen male prisoners and to challenge their senses as they got to know their own bodies and others as well. In one exercise, the men stood in two parallel rows facing each other with their arms crossed with those in front of them. One prisoner was to then, with a running start, leap into this bed of arms. Prisoners had their own styles – some skipped or twirled, others twisted as they jumped. One exuberant prisoner leapt so far that he flew over the bed of arms and crashed into the floor. Everyone laughed and the workshop continued. The next day we met this prisoner again, who had just come from a visit with his mother. He was anxious and worried. His crash from the day before had caused a grim black eye, which his mother was convinced had been inflicted by staff. She was distraught and thought her son was lying to cover up for the authorities. At the time we saw him, he was looking for a trusted member of staff to explain to her that it was indeed from an accidental fall during the workshop. We found this to be a notable occurrence of bodies being misinterpreted from the friction produced in the nexus between a history (and expectation) of brutality and a reforming model of custody.

Creating more porous prisons was a deliberate post-revolution strategy intended to demonstrate a willingness to be more transparent. This was also expected to increase 'rehabilitative' efforts and activities. Throughout the year, family dinners were held, usually on holidays and other days of celebration (like breaking the Ramadan fast together with iftar feasts). These took place in decorated outdoor spaces around the prison where prisoners and their loved ones could embrace, remain close, eat, and share in culturally and socially important rituals. However, as is often the case, only a small proportion of prisoners were able to participate in these activities. In some prisons, we saw the same handful of prisoners engaged in all of the 'best' events or workshops. For those who remained in the cells without access to these activities, an additional layer of sensory deprivation was experienced. For these prisoners, they could often smell the food from the celebratory feasts and hear the music and chatter from the attendees. But they did so at a distance and from behind dormitory walls.

Just below the surface of these liberal, 'old penology' ('transformative') reform efforts was an emerging 'new penology' discourse around classification and standardisation aimed at creating greater efficiency in the management of prisons and prisoners (Feeley & Simon, 1992). There were long-term plans to discontinue food and clothing baskets and replace them with standard prison-issued meals and provisions. In essence, all 'basic need' items would be supplied in-house, which would allow better control over security (e.g. the prevention of contraband being smuggled in via the baskets) and bodies (the creation of uniformity through the restriction of autonomy). This process of technocratic rationalisation was already appearing in some places. In one of the new units that modelled 'the ideal' reform prison, prisoners were required to wear solid green uniforms, volumetric control measures[7] had been imposed, and prison-issued bedding was used. This military barrack-style unit (clean, ordered, beds made) was 'human rights compliant' and was thus the pride of the authorities. While 'humane' by most measures, the unit was also sterile and anonymous: a non-space that removed the personal and the sensory (see also Jewkes, 2018, p. 328). In this regard, the old cells – crowded marketplaces filled with bodies, textiles, colours, sentimental objects, home-cooked food (and distinctly Tunisian) – were 'anthropological places' that enabled some retention of the self (Augé, 1995) and allowed for 'sensory anchors' related to home that offered some comfort (Bailliard, 2015, p. 6). But, as we discuss next, the sensuous geographies of the overpopulated dormitories were also rich and complex in ways that were often experienced as stifling and dehumanising.

The Sensual Pains of Overpopulation

The, at times, sensorial and corporeal 'freedom' experienced in the new prison spaces and arts-based activities was in stark contrast to life in the densely populated dormitories. Being in these areas made us uncomfortable. They were overwhelming and claustrophobic, and we were often overcome with our sensory experience. When occupied, there was no capacity for maintaining personal space. We found the dorms to be oppressive and 'thick' – atmospherically (compacted, stale air), in affect (visceral and charged, with fluctuating intensities), and climatically (heavy dormancy). There were conflicting sensations as well. The cells were full of life yet lacking liveliness, both under- and over-stimulating (sluggish and slow, yet pulsating and sensorially saturated), and dull but still vibrant. Prisoners frequently described the 'feeling of being' here in analogies, with many hinting at a distortion or dissociation in 'bodily being' from living in such congestion. The men used phrases like 'a piece of melting wax', 'a lump of clay', 'molten lava', and 'a puddle' that swells or recedes, depending on spatial capacity. These seemed to speak not only to a feeling of passive (or resigned?) pliability in terms of bodily autonomy to others[8] ('there is no "my" space') but also to a cognitive numbness that was employed to cope with the environment, circumstances, or from deep tedium. One man compared his experience (and body) to an anchor:

> I was dropped here, so I stay here. Sometimes the captain [officers or other prisoners] needs me to move, so I do … I don't even think anymore – I just do what my body needs me to do in this space.

---

[7]This refers to the regulation of the volume or amount of property each prisoner is allowed to possess. In this unit, each man was designated a narrow locker for clothing and belongings.

[8]For example, when sharing a single mattress with 2–3 others, often the men would have to move together in unison (like rolling from one side to another) to prevent someone from falling out of bed.

This appeared to be a deliberate, possibly necessary, separation (or blunting) between the mind and body, sensing and feeling.[9] Like Guenther (2013, p. 127), we question the effects of this kind of hypercrowded, 'intensive confinement' experience and its assault on, or violation of, a person's ontology.

Overcrowding is one of the, if not the, most cited problems of prisons in the Global South. It is often represented in terms of percentages, rates, and square meters, remarkably disconnected from the living human beings crammed into limited spaces, sharing beds, showers, drinking water, toilets, and each other's everyday bodily presence. Terms such as 'prison congestion' or 'occupancy levels' seem to reveal an institutional bias when thinking about the issue. It is as though the lived experience of overcrowding is almost ungraspable. Sensing excess intimacy demands an ethnographic sensibility; an attunement to what surely must matter intensely to prisoners. But the lived experience of overcrowding is difficult to fathom, its cost difficult to evaluate accurately (see also Haney, 1997, pp. 532–533). Overcrowding, we believe, cannot be understood only as a quantitative category. It is not about percentages or about exceeding capacity but bodies in close proximity, living, breathing, infectious, aching, sick, damaged, and sensorially extreme.

There is a substantial body of literature on the pains of sensory deprivation in prison, specifically focussed on the experience (and effects) of solitary confinement. According to empirical and phenomenological analysis, isolation is deeply problematic and deeply dehumanising. It can have devastating costs (Guenther, 2013; Haney, 2018; Reiter & Koenig, 2015; Shalev, 2009; Smith, 2006). But what about conditions of overcrowding? What about too much proximity, too much embodied human contact, too much human presence? Where Guenther (2013, p. xi) asks, 'Who are we, such that we can be unhinged from ourselves by being separated from others?', our questions are who do we become when any sense of autonomy is drastically compromised and intimacy is forced and excessive? What kind of 'abjection, despair and impoverishment' (Povinelli, 2008, p. 511) is produced by overpopulated dormitory cells? Might too many people in too little space also somehow, even paradoxically, index 'the impersonality of sheer being' (Guenther, 2013, p. 213)?

One of the prisoners we spoke with likened his experience of living in an overcrowded cell to 'life in a fripé', referring to the piles of clothing for sale commonly found in North African street markets. He explained that he was 'like one of those pieces of clothing': crumpled, discarded, drowning within a mass. Using his body when he spoke, he communicated the heaviness or 'weight' of living in crowded conditions by pressing down on his shoulders and simulated suffocation. The lack of being seen or recognised as an individual within a 'sea' or

---

[9]This is not to suggest that all prisoners were 'docile' bodies easily moved or manipulated, compliant or submissive. Tensions ran high, fights (verbal and physical) were frequent, drugs were available, rules were broken, contraband flowed, men were hunger striking in protest, and so on. Prisoners navigated, and coped with, this landscape in countless ways.

'pile' of people was repeatedly mentioned by prisoners when discussing life in the dense cells: 'they [officers] don't see us as individuals, they just see a blur of a hundred faces'. It seemed to us that prisoners were describing the experience of being 'depersonalised persons' (Dayan, 2011, p. 32) – social or legal outcasts 'drained of self-identity, forever anomalous, condemned as extraneous to civil society, excluded from belonging'.

We encountered other variations of 'depersonalised' practices and experiences in dorm life. We often witnessed prisoner counts. This entailed prisoners filing out of dormitories only to line up in the corridor outside to then file back in. We were continually taken aback to see how many men emerged from a single cell. In one prison, we observed a peculiar corporeal exercise we later referred to as 'the zombie walk':

> We stopped our walk up the corridor to observe [prisoners] coming out of the cell and turning right, walking a few meters before turning into the area [exercise yard] They came out sullen, squinting, eyes to the ground raising their right hands horizontally towards their temple though rarely reaching that far. It was a 'salute' we heard, designed to instill discipline (or at least remind people who is in charge), marking through bodily practice the power differentials of the institution. Every man did it per automatic as they crossed the threshold of the cell door; an embodied acknowledgement that there is a relation of dominance at play. But it was done in such a slovenly fashion that they resembled zombies carrying a deformed arm bent and half raised, suspended indifferently and unnaturally around chin height. It mirrored a little the slightly twisted gait of the men cuffed right wrist to right wrist emerging from the [prison] van.[10] Both created a sub-human appearance. (AMJ fieldwork notes, 310618)

How to define inhumane treatment is usually considered to be the domain of the courts. The scene described above significantly reorients us from the courtroom or legal rulings (realm of law) to the corridor (realm of everyday control and regulation). In the light of the zombie walk, we would consider inhuman or degrading treatment as present when circumstances cause people to no longer *look* fully human. This form of 'bodily deadness' (Meiring, 2016, p. 2) is also depicted in Dayan's (2011, pp. 21–22) metaphor for depersonalised entities as 'zombies': the dead-alive flesh and bones that survive as the remnant of loss and

---

[10]Prison transport vans were another site of overcrowding. Vans that were meant to hold 8–10 men (4–5 sat on parallel benches) often carried double that or more (some men would have to sit on the floor, stand hunched over, or sit on laps). To minimise the risk of escape, prisoners were handcuffed to each other – left wrist to left wrist (or right to right). This made movements awkward and stilted, and the prospect of running nearly impossible.

dispossession – 'the zombie represents the self undone'. We see documentation of something hinting at this in a recent human rights report (OHCHR, 2014, p. 17) on prisons in Tunisia as well, where the word 'slackening' is used to describe the physical and psychological impact of overcrowding, suggesting a 'loosening' between the body and the psyche (echoing Toch's, 1985, p. 71, 'stultifying quiescence').

Our concern with the issue of privacy was challenged by prisoners' accounts of living in severely overcrowded cells, which focussed on the relentless surveillance from the in-cell leaders ('kabrans'); the lack of dignity, and indecency, from such conditions; and the medical and physiological issues that arose from these environments (like skin infections, the 'prison bugs', difficulty breathing, anxiety, etc.). Many reported that 'it is not a privacy issue' because 'Tunisians are social – we always live with a lot of people' (meaning, extended families often share a household). Many also joked that 'the whole of Tunisia is overcrowded!', referring to overstuffed public transportation, streets, markets, and the number of cars. 'Privacy', then, was not the issue. What the men were describing were the detrimental effects of forced intimacy, invasive proximity, and radical exposure.

The only time 'privacy' was mentioned was in reference to a specific practice in the cells whereby the men draped cloths or towels over their faces as a way of 'escaping' (escaping the gaze of others, or escaping in their mind). We were at first startled by this practice: men dotted around a dorm with their entire heads covered, not moving but not sleeping, looking like faceless statues (and non-human). This is a form of 'draga' or a 'curtain that hides reality' – a curtain to conceal things and to create a physical and symbolic space of 'privacy'.[11] Draga enabled prisoners to escape the forced exposure (Schwartz, 1972, p. 230) of dormitory overcrowding and to 'buffer unwanted interaction' (Clements, 1979, p. 222; see also Dirsuweit, 1999, p. 76). Draga also created a 'space' for prisoners to 'indulge in private fantasies' (Cohen & Taylor, 1972, p. 80). When asked what the men do or think when they had a draga cloth over their heads, they described forms of escapism to produce alternative sensoryscapes: 'I dream with my senses'; 'I create new smells and sounds. It is a beautiful escape'; and 'Close your eyes and focus your ears. Hear what you want to hear - the birds, the wind, the trees ... we are transported'. 'Coping' through sensory escapism seemed a distinctive feature of managing life in an overcrowded cell. In Borj Erroumi, a prison with a large population of long-term and lifer prisoners, keeping small birds as pets was a

---

[11]In the past, draga was a curtain used on bottom bunks – sheets or blankets were hung in order to encapsulate the bed. Its purpose was for any number of reasons: to hide taboo things, like sexual encounters between prisoners, the consumption of drugs, to exchange forbidden or contraband items with others, or, more simply, to create a private space. Because cells are so densely populated now, it is rare for prisoners to have a single bed to themselves. Thus, this adapted form of draga – a towel or shirt draped over the head and face – seems to serve the same purpose as a way to create a 'private' space. Many thanks to Yasmin Haloui for her translation help regarding this topic.

lifeline. Prisoners built makeshift cages out of materials found around their cells, typically from broken bits of plastic containers woven together with unravelled sweaters. These cages were then hung on the walls of the dorms in between and above the bunk beds. Walking into these cells was deafening for us, but the incessant chirping of dozens of birds had become pleasant and muted white noise to the prisoners. For some, they would attempt to isolate the noise of the birds when in draga: 'I just tune out the rest and only listen to mine [my bird] – it's like being in a park or forest; very peaceful'.

For these men, draga produced a 'territory of the self', a material and imaginative space not susceptible to regulation by the regime or other prisoners (Sibley & van Hoven, 2009, pp. 199, 202). But we also wondered whether this 'solution' signalled withdrawal, apathy, or self-insulation? Guenther (2013, p. 241), discussing the work of Merleau-Ponty, writes:

> the body is both *in* space and *of* it ... But it also is the site of lived experience; I feel things not just in my body but as a body.

Was draga a necessary means to manage such intense intercorporeality, where the mass fusing of bodies makes one indistinguishable from another? How else might a person situate and differentiate their embodied being when little to no separation between their body and multiple others is available?

In his review of the psychological and environmental effects of overcrowding, Clements (1979, p. 217) concluded that it 'brings out the worst in both individuals and systems'. His review highlighted some fundamental and problematic aspects of living in density, like the increase of stress from an inability to control one's privacy, personal space, and unwanted social interaction (Clements, 1979, p. 220). He also questioned the phenomenological consequences of 'forced idleness' (which he distinguishes from freely chosen non-productivity; Clements, 1979, p. 222). This, in tandem with involuntary intimacy, invasive proximity, and the materialisation of bodily deadness, seems, to us, to be quite profound forms of sensory degradation and sentient suffering. We juxtapose this against a prison reform agenda underpinned with the notion that engagement with cultural creativity and the arts has the ability to 'inculcate values of tolerance'. But what might overcrowding inculcate? What is communicated – and embodied – when prisoners are made to feel like, and exist as, 'a blur'? How can we adequately comprehend the impact of prolonged, unrelenting sensory intensity from 'living in a pile of bodies'? If 'radical isolation' and 'mind-killing solitude' are an affront to dignity (Dayan, 2011, p. 85), what might radical exposure, social density, and sensorial overload do to one's sense of self, being, and personhood?

Concluding Reflections

The aim of this chapter was twofold. First, we sought to examine how sensory accounts of prison life interact with, and mediate, experiences of harm, power, punishment, and survival. In the post-revolution context of Tunisia, we found a series of sensory paradoxes produced during a time of significant change:

spaces and practices that were over- and under-stimulating, sensorially liberating and sensorially oppressive; tensions between reform ideals and a reality tinged with brutal legacies; and various forms of corporeal deprivation and intensification that have implications for how we think about and document inhuman and degrading treatment. We also highlighted how the sensory can be weaponised, like through the desecration of food, from forced intimacy in overpopulated dorms, or via other modes of haptic regulation or infliction. Sensing, and making sense of, prison life in transition entailed everyday embodied experiences – of touching and feeling, violence and abuse, sensation and emotion – alongside a cognisance of the physicality of the body (Paterson, 2009, p. 766), both of the researcher and those we engaged with in the field.

Our second, and related, aim was to demonstrate the utility of an embodied approach that is deliberately calibrated to sensoriality. Emplaced participation required a reflexive attunement to our own bodies within different spatial and cultural landscapes, as well as an awareness of the sensual ecologies of the people and places we study. For researchers who are already inclined toward ethnographic methods, this is not necessarily new territory. But, reflecting upon the sensory, *sensing* and *feeling* it in the field, and finding the language to write about it, may be. Embodied immersion attentive to the senses to learn to 'know as others know' (Pink, 2009, p. 70), we argue, is a useful practice for exploring dimensions of the lived experience not well articulated or represented within criminology. Multi-sensorial dimensions of penality open up new avenues for insights and the expression of embodiment. From 'the smell of love' in the form of home-cooked meals we observed in Tunisian prisons to the 'scent of terror' associated with torture and death at the hands of the state (Rainsford, 2020), the sensoryscapes of power, punishment, and control are worthy of further study.

Our exploration into the sensory lifeworlds of Tunisian prisons, we hope, will contribute to the growing body of sensuous scholarship. It is our contention that sensory knowledge has the capacity to unearth previously overlooked meanings and understandings. In Tunisia, we were able to get closer to grasping the significance of deeply imprinted institutional memories formed from collective trauma during the uprisings, as well as the sensual pains and survival strategies of those living in extreme conditions of confinement. Using sensuous ethnography to bear witness to the fascinating intricacies of the human condition, Stoller (2004, pp. 831–832) asserts, can produce knowledge that allows us 'to think new thoughts or feel new feelings' vital to making sense of the carceral experience.

References

Anderson, B. (2009). Affective atmospheres. *Emotion, Space and Society*, *2*(2), 77–81.
Augé, M. (1995). *Non-places: Introduction to an anthropology of supermodernity*. London: Verso.
Bailliard, A. L. (2015). Habits of the sensory system and mental health: Understanding sensory dissonance. *American Journal of Occupational Therapy*, *69*(4), 1–8.

Berlin, I. (1969). Two concepts of liberty (1958, Clarendon Press). Reprinted in: I. Berlin, *Four essays on liberty* (pp. 118–172). Oxford: Oxford University Press.
Booth, N. (2020). Staying in touch. *Blog post from February 3*. Retrieved from https://sensorycriminology.com/2020/02/03/staying-in-touch/
Clements, C. B. (1979). Crowded prisons: A review of psychological and environmental effects. *Law and Human Behavior, 3*(3), 217–225.
Cohen, S., & Taylor, L. (1972). *Psychological survival: The experience of long-term imprisonment*. Harmondsworth: Penguin.
Crang, M. (2003). Qualitative methods: Touchy, feely, look-see? *Progress in Human Geography, 274*, 494–504.
Crouch, D. (2001). Spatialities and the feeling of doing. *Social & Cultural Geography, 2*(1), 61–75.
Das, V. (1996). Language and body: Transactions in the construction of pain. *Daedalus, 125*(1), 67–91.
Dayan, C. (2011). *The law is a white dog: How legal rituals make and unmake persons*. Princeton, NJ: Princeton University Press.
Dirsuweit, T. (1999). Carceral spaces in South Africa: a case study of institutional power, sexuality and transgression in a women's prison. *Geoforum, 30*, 71–83.
Feeley, M. M., & Simon, J. (1992). The new penology: Notes on the emerging strategy of corrections and its implications. *Criminology, 30*(4), 449–474.
Ghachem, B. (2018). The resurgence of prison memory in post-revolutionary Tunisia testimonies between truth and memory. *Journal of North African Studies, 23*(1–2), 246–258.
Godderis, R. (2006). Food for thought: An analysis of power and identity in prison food narratives. *Berkeley Journal of Sociology, 50*, 61–75.
Graham, E.-J. (2017). Babes in arms? Sensory dissonance and the ambiguities of votive objects. In E. Betts (Ed.), *Senses of the empire: Multisensory approaches to Roman culture*. Abingdon: Routledge.
Griffiths, A. (2014). Sensory media: The world without and the world within. In C. Classen (Ed.), *A cultural history of the senses in the age of empire*. London: Bloomsbury.
Guenther, L. (2013). *Solitary confinement: Social death and its afterlives*. Minneapolis, MN: University of Minnesota Press.
Haney, C. (1997). Psychology and the limits to prison pain: Confronting the coming crisis in eighth amendment law. *Psychology, Public Policy, and Law, 3*(4), 499–588.
Haney, C. (2018). The psychological effects of solitary confinement: A systematic critique. *Crime and Justice, 47*, 365–416.
Howes, D. (2005). Introduction. In D. Howes (Ed.), *Empire of the senses: The sensory culture reader* (pp. 1–17). Oxford: Berg.
Howes, D. (2010). The future of sensory anthropology/the anthropology of the senses: Response to Sarah Pink. *Social Anthropology, 18*(3), 331–340.
Jefferson, A. M. (2005). Reforming Nigerian prisons: Rehabilitating a 'deviant' state. *British Journal of Criminology, 45*, 487–503.
Jewkes, Y. (2018). Just design: Healthy prisons and the architecture of hope. *Australian & New Zealand Journal of Criminology, 51*(3), 319–338.
Law, L. (2001). Home cooking: Filipino women and geographies of the sense in Hong Kong. *Cultural Geographies, 8*(3), 264–283.
Liebling, A. (2011). Moral performance, inhuman and degrading treatment and prison pain. *Punishment & Society, 13*(5), 530–550.
Longhurst, R., Ho, E., & Johnston, L. (2008). Using 'the body' as an 'instrument of research': Kimch'i and pavlova. *Area, 40*(2), 208–217.
Martin, T. M., Jefferson, A. M., & Bandyopadhyay, M. (2014). Sensing prison climates: Governance, survival, and transition. *Focaal, 68*, 3–17.

McCarthy, R. (2018). *Inside Tunisia's al-Nahda: Between politics and preaching*. Cambridge: Cambridge University Press.

McClanahan, B., & South, N. (2020). 'All knowledge begins with the senses': Towards a sensory criminology. *British Journal of Criminology, 60*, 3–23.

Meiring, J. (2016). How does justice smell? Reflections on space and place, justice and the body. *HTS Teologiese Studies/Theological Studies, 72*(1), 1–7.

Merleau-Ponty, M. (1962). *Phenomenology of perception*. London: Routledge.

Mihai, M. (2018). Architectural transitional justice? Political renewal within the scars of a violent past. *International Journal of Transitional Justice, 12*, 515–536.

Office of the United Nations High Commissioner for Human Rights, Tunisia Office (OHCHR). (2014). *Prisons in Tunisia: International standards versus reality*. Geneva: OHCHR.

Paterson, M. (2009). Haptic geographies: Ethnography, haptic knowledges and sensuous dispositions. *Progress in Human Geography, 33*(6), 766–788.

Pink, S. (2009). *Doing sensory ethnography*. London: Sage.

Povinelli, E. A. (2008). The child in the broom closet: States of killing and letting die. *South Atlantic Quarterly, 107*(3), 509–530.

Rainsford, S. (2020). 'Scent of terror' created in protest against Moscow perfume store'. *BBC News* – published February 27. Retrieved from https://www.bbc.co.uk/news/av/world-europe-51647596/scent-of-terror-created-in-protest-against-moscow-perfume-store?fbclid=IwAR3JQhSJiR8KGviBvW0by43CsWlIgqnhFZMT5BYnmzIwkCFmTyhX3SrPba8

Reiter, K., & Koenig, A. (Eds.). (2015). *Extreme punishment: Comparative studies in detention, incarceration and solitary confinement*. Basingstoke: Palgrave Macmillan.

Rodaway, P. (1994). *Sensuous geographies: Body, sense and place*. London: Routledge.

Schwartz, B. (1972). Deprivation of privacy as a functional prerequisite: The case of the prison. *Journal of Criminal Law, Criminology and Police Science, 63*(2), 229–239.

Shalev, S. (2009). *Supermax: Controlling risk through solitary confinement*. Cullompton: Willan.

Shilton, S. (2013). Art and the 'Arab Spring': Aesthetics of revolution in contemporary Tunisia. *French Cultural Studies, 24*(1), 129–145.

Sibley, D., & van Hoven, B. (2009). The contamination of personal space: Boundary construction in a prison environment. *Area, 41*(2), 198–206.

Smith, P. S. (2006). The effects of solitary confinement on prison inmates: A brief history and review of the literature. *Crime and Justice, 34*(1), 441–528.

Stevenson, A. (2014). We came here to remember: Using participatory sensory ethnography to explore memory as emplaced, embodied practice. *Qualitative Research in Psychology, 11*, 335–349.

Stoller, P. (2004). Sensuous ethnography, African persuasions, and social knowledge. *Qualitative Inquiry, 10*(6), 817–935.

Sutton, D. E. (2010). Food and the senses. *Annual Review of Anthropology, 39*, 209–223.

Tamburini, F. (2018). Anti-terrorism laws in the Maghreb countries: The mirror of a democratic transition that never was. *Journal of Asian and African Studies, 53*(8), 1235–1250.

Toch, H. (1985). Warehouses for people? *Annals of the American Academy of Political and Social Science, 478*(1), 58–72.

Valentine, G., & Longstaff, B. (1998). Doing porridge: Food and social relations in a male prison. *Journal of Material Culture, 3*(2), 131–152.

Chapter 6

Sensing Secrecy: Power, Violence and Its Concealment in Nicaraguan Prisons

Julienne Weegels

Secrecy magnifies reality. (Georg Simmel)

'In prison you gotta understand that you're blind, deaf, and mute, that you don't see or hear anything even if it happened right in front of you', Javi stressed.[1] The violent punishment that the breaking of prison secrets entailed still reverberated in Javi's words and body, even after having put an ocean between himself and Nicaragua. As we talked about those parts of prison life that were generally rendered unspeakable – the beatings by both prisoners and authorities, the corruption, the indoor drug trade – his verbal repetition of this rule pointed out how he had learned to carefully mute his senses, to un-see, un-hear and un-speak, in order to survive the eight and a half years he spent inside.

Building in this chapter on recent work around concealment and ethnographic practice in spaces of (supposed) state control (e.g. Jefferson, 2015; Jefferson & Schmidt, 2019; Martin, 2015), as well as on an embodied and sensorial understanding of knowledge production (Ingold, 2000; Pink, 2009; Wacquant, 2004), I argue that the management of (public) secrets is central to understanding the sensory qualities of the power that the hybrid Nicaraguan penal regime exerts. In particular, this regime is (re)produced precisely through an imposed and partial muting of the senses – the rendering unspeakable, un-seeable and un-heard of the violence that is deployed to keep it in place. This implies that particular bodies implement and suffer this violence, which is meant to be *felt*, but not discussed. In other words, in Nicaraguan prisons punishment is irrevocably impinged on and enacted through the body (by way of neglect, overcrowding, and outright physical violence), while these expressions of penal power are simultaneously actively

---

[1] All names used are pseudonyms. Exact research locations are omitted for safety reasons.

Sensory Penalities: Exploring the Senses in Spaces of Punishment and Social Control, 89–105
Copyright © 2021 Julienne Weegels. Published under exclusive licence by Emerald Publishing Limited
All rights of reproduction in any form reserved
doi:10.1108/978-1-83909-726-320210007

concealed. As such, learning how to sense, navigate and enforce secrecy is pivotal for surviving prison.

Prisons and Secrecy

The interdependence of prison order on secrecy is not unique to Nicaragua: as 'peculiar' bureaucratic institutions, prisons across the world tend to invest heavily in keeping their inner workings secret (e.g. Cohen & Taylor, 1978; Jefferson & Schmidt, 2019; Martin, 2015). Yet many of the secrets they seek to keep take on the form of *public secrets*. Public secrets are secrets that are in fact 'shared and known, but unspoken' (Taussig, 1999, p. 50). Often, they are hinted at through a veil of unspeakable confirmation and 'acts of unknowing', including omission, caution, warning, indirection and silence (Penglase, 2014; Taussig, 1999). Like the warning articulated by Javi, the politics surrounding public secrets regulate prison's broader penal–sensorial realm. Incorporated in this warming is the cardinal 'no-snitching' command that, like in many other prison systems, mediates the everyday politics of concealment (and revelation) and punishes knowing or talking *too much*. Importantly, not only prisoners but also authorities enforce this command. In this way, public secrecy manifests not only as a politics of concealment but also as a governance strategy that obfuscates the violence and collusion involved in prison governance by rendering these issues both shared and known but unspeakable.

Over the seven-year period that I conducted ethnographic research[2] with prisoners and former prisoners amid an increasingly closed-off and politicised institutional landscape, I not only met many more prisoners like Javi but also learned from them how, when and where to 'do' being blind, deaf and mute myself. Wandering ever deeper into the life world of the prison(er), in a process of *moving with* my research collaborators across the power field that is Nicaragua's prison system, I came to understand how penal power is exerted both over and through the sensory realm. This was not so much as violence was made directly sense-able to me, but rather as it was muted and rendered unspeakable in particular ways. Given the no-snitching command and the politicised climate of concealment, I found that knowing, talking and snitching existed along a locally articulated

---

[2]My research took place between 2009 and 2016 with prisoners of a Regional Penitentiary System (SPR, 2009–2013) and a City Police Jail (CPJ, 2015–2016), who participated in a theatre-in-prison programme that me and my husband, a Nicaraguan theatre artist, set up. The programme at the SPR consisted of between 8- and 23-long-sentenced prisoners, convicted to sentences of 5–30 years (which is the maximum sentence), largely for violent and/or economic crimes. The programme at the CPJ consisted of 13 short-sentenced prisoners, convicted to sentences of one to five years, largely for drug-related and/or economic crimes. My research also included former prisoners of those two sites and of the capital city penitentiary La Modelo. It was conducted in six more or less yearly periods of three to eight months each, totalling 31 months, followed by periods of follow-up interviews as some of my research collaborators left prison.

continuum of secrecy that ranged from careful concealment to purposeful revelation.[3] On the ground, this continuum was constantly (re)negotiated as prisoners and authorities engaged in interaction with one another and with prison 'outsiders', who are involved in prison's everyday life to different degrees (family visits, programme facilitators, press, religious groups, researchers like myself, etc.). Hence, even though Javi repeated the prison code of silence before we discussed a heavily guarded public secret – that of the indoor drug trade – he did in effect *talk* to me, though it was not until after he left prison. Many prisoners and former prisoners thus negotiated and renegotiated their relation to the continuum of secrecy depending on when, where and with whom they spoke.

Becoming gradually immersed in the prison environment as the co-founder of a theatre-in-prison programme with a strongly physical approach,[4] all the while conducting research with the prisoner-actors in this largely unsupervised and highly collective setting, also opened me up to the realm of the embodied and unspoken. In this way, I began to *sense* prison life and the power, violence and secrecy enveloping it alongside the prisoners. Rather than 'discovering' what prison(er) 'secrets' were by *asking* and obtaining a verbal response, by *moving with* my research collaborators they were invoked in a sense of understanding what is going on, of *knowing*, not speaking – knowing *not* to speak – but finding one's knowledge confirmed on instances where (parts of) the public secret are revealed.

Sensing Prison Secrets: An Embodied Approach

Like most other social scientists, prison researchers tend to embark on their research from a positivist epistemological premise, built on the notion that people 'possess' knowledge about their environments that can be readily and rationally transferred to the researcher, who can 'collect' this knowledge and process it as data or information. What such a positivist premise pushes us towards, however, is the placing of 'rational knowing' above tacit, embodied, sensory, sentient, or other forms of knowledge and knowledge production, which makes much of what is conferred to us 'unusable'. This epistemological tension has been debated at length, as ethnographers noted that a disembodied focus on the (often narrow) arena of the rational and explicit will not do if what we are attempting to understand and convey is how others relate to and give meaning to the world around them (e.g. Ingold, 2000, 2011; Marchand, 2010; Pink, 2009, 2011; Wacquant, 2004). As my research centred precisely on the ways in which (formerly) incarcerated men socially navigated and experienced the prison system, I was pulled towards an epistemological stance that acknowledges 'knowledge-making [as] a

---

[3]In their consideration of concealment and revelation for bureaucratic and ethnographic practice, Jefferson and Schmidt (2019) speak of 'deliberate display' and 'defensive concealment'.

[4]Part of the reason why the theatre-in-prison programme came to be largely focused on physical theatre was that in this way the prisoners could express feelings and experiences that would otherwise fall into the continuum of secrecy.

dynamic process arising directly from the indissoluble relations that exist between minds, bodies, and environment' (Marchand, 2010, p. 2). Borrowing from Henrik Vigh (2009), who conceptualised social navigation as 'moving within a moving environment' (p. 425), this means that I recognised my research collaborators as agents who (re)produce knowledge of their (power-infused) environments *as they move through them*. This *moving* across the power field is situated, sensory and relational and can tell us a lot about prison life. Attempting to understand my research collaborators' navigational trajectories, I thus situated myself as both an apprentice of the research environment *and* as a subject on that power field, too.

In the prison context, an apprenticeship in the classic sense (e.g. Wacquant, 2004) is, however, not so straightforward. Even if I could attempt to 'become' a physical theatre performer through the theatre-in-prison programme, and even as I did acquire particular physical skills from my research collaborators (like prisoner sign language), I could never *become a prisoner*. Instead, I sought to situate myself as *close* as possible to them, and as *long* as I could in their environments (Hamm & Ferrell, 1998, p. 270; Gaborit, 2019). In this way, my 'apprenticeship' meant learning to navigate the prison environment both with and alongside them – learning to move, like they did, within a constantly moving environment, and through this embodied state of *moving with*, 'become knowledgeable' of the parameters, rules and movement of the power field itself (Ingold, 2010, p. 121; Vigh, 2009). In this way, Vigh's conceptualisation of social navigation proved not only analytically but also methodologically useful to me, especially to grapple with structure as more than simply its reduction to a set of (fixed) external constraints, but rather as a constantly evolving power field *across* which we move in divergent vertical and horizontal trajectories.

Moving with my research collaborators across prison's power-infused spaces implied both getting to know and acknowledging our different positions on that field, including the ways in which I had at once more *and* less room to manoeuvre than they did. In this sense, it is pivotal that the prisoners I worked with did not conform a unison group: outside the theatre space some were perceived as cell block leaders, some were prisoner council members, others were relegated to the lower echelons of the prisoner hierarchy, and yet others attempted to extract themselves from this hierarchy altogether (see also Weegels, 2017, 2019b). In a prolonged attempt to narrow the multiple perceived distances (gendered, social and power-infused) between us, both within and around the theatre space, I sought a corporeal and emotional attunement to their movement and rhythm(s). I did this beyond sporting a purposely less feminine and more urban 'prison attire' (sweat pants, sneakers, black tank top), to learning to feel 'off-days', shift posture and adapt my movement with them across the prison environment and beyond it.

In doing so, I struck evolving balances along the line of the possible and the appropriate from the position of an 'observant participator' rather than a participant observer. Most of this *moving with* included attuning to simple gestures and actions, like touching the prison floor, sharing non-workshop time, walks and food and learning by trial and error how to interact with (former) prisoners and authorities in different capacities. Most importantly, it included moving with my research collaborators across space and time, in the sense of accompanying them over (lengthy) periods in the field and into their post-release lives, as well as across different (trans)carceral spaces (inside prison, on stage and into the digital realm). It also meant fulfilling expectations towards the authorities – an issue to which I return later. Beyond physically learning to acquire particular skills then, through this embodied approach I gradually became knowledgeable of the prison's power field. Taking the prisoners' and my own navigational trajectory through the prison world seriously, the moral economy of violence and the politics of concealment surrounding it became apparent, as well as how I had become partial to them.

(Un)Muting

> Passing through those gates after bag-check for the first time, with the camera rolled in a t-shirt in my hands, I tried to be as cool as possible, like I'd seen it all before, like I was not taking it all in – eagerly, nervously, with big gulps at a time as the gate closed and we followed [the guard] into the main building.[5] The prisoners all seemed to be looking, staring, with prying eyes, looking at the strange new people who had just passed through their gate. They put their fingers through the chain-linked fence still separating us from them in the courtyard; as we entered the corridor they stopped to look, a lost '*adiós*' sounded, followed by an air-kiss. I waited nervously on the wet concrete of the visit hall, and then all twenty-seven adolescents swarmed around us.[6] I tried to look up, to face them. Mick [the theatre facilitator] immediately got started, but for me there was so much of the unknown, of the uncertain [...] I instinctively cast my eyes to the ground. I noticed all the cracks in the concrete floors and walkways then, the puddles of water on them, and the stiff, trampled stubs of grass outside, sticking stubbornly out of the grayish yellow dirt. My gaze followed the uncovered water drainage system running right under the chain-linked fence and the concrete wall beyond it – to freedom. I wished to be there. I wondered how many new eyes noticed the same things when they first came in. How many of them did not look up? I sat down on a bench, fiddling with the camera. It had been my decision to come here, *be here*, they had not really had the same choice.

---

[5] Field notes, SPR, 2009.
[6] Our first theatre workshop at the SPR was with a large group of adolescent prisoners. Unfortunately, they had their privileges revoked that same week due to a fight on their wing. After that we were requested to work with a group of adult men, who would become my main group of research collaborators at the SPR.

When I first set foot in the regional penitentiary (SPR), I was overwhelmed by all the impressions. On the one hand, there was the prison's physical installations: the relatively low walls dotted with barbed wire and watchtowers with AK-47 toting guards, the inner chain-linked fence leading to the dusty courtyard, the grungy barrack-style one-storey building with its fish-grate corridor and cells, its peeling paint and stale smell, its barrenness. Each section was divided from the next by a metal bar divider, locked with bolts in the absence of an electronic surveillance system. I'd later find you could look directly into the dormitories from the metal bar doors that lead to the cell blocks. Walking behind the unarmed guard then, the only one in the corridor, who opened and locked every divider up to the visit hall, I noticed dozens of prisoners watched us. Though I grew up looking at a classic cupola-panopticon from my bedroom window, I had never been *inside* a prison and never actually *saw* the prisoners. As I sat down on that bench, seeking to find a way to present myself while grappling with all of the impressions, a young prisoner with a tattooed teardrop below his eye sat down next to me. Without hesitation he asked me for my earrings. Touching my ears I realised I had forgotten to take them off, and stammered they were dear to me (they weren't really, but what would happen if I gave them up?). More than the prison's run-down appearance, what made my first impression so lasting was the prisoners' overwhelming physical presence.

This directly obliged me to acknowledge my own physical presence – an issue that sparked some initial unease in me. Here I was: a 21-year-old female student from Europe, and this was *not* the street, proving my previous experience of limited use. Yes, I was there accompanied by my husband (a then 26-year-old Nicaraguan theatre artist), who was facilitating the theatre training, but what would I be *doing*? The narrative approach I had included in my research methodology suddenly made little sense. Relieved to slide into the focus of a specific activity (taking pictures) when Mick called for the start of the workshop, I noticed my attention shifted to the prisoners as objects rather than subjects, toning down my sense of insecurity, until I learned the unwritten rules of prison interaction.

Over the course of the following weeks, as we began working with what would become our steady prison theatre group, the prison and its routine became familiar. The atmosphere on the courtyard became readable rather than tense; it became easier to mute the bustle, and I began to recognise the prisoner's postures and faces. Similarly, we became a fixture in the prison environment. I began to find comfort in the courtyard dust stuck to my sneakers after class on the bus ride back to the city – in the physical tiredness of my body after breaking a sweat with the guys, still feeling the rough concrete under my hands. When I visited alone, I noticed how the theatre group members sought to make me feel physically safe, by walking towards me as I crossed the yard or standing close by as we waited amid a large group to enter the class hall.

During the workshops, I gradually switched note-making and picture-taking for participating in the discussions and some of the physical theatre training exercises. In physical theatre, at risk of sounding redundant, physical interaction is key: *touch* becomes one of the primary senses deployed to construct movements and scenes. However, both in prison and society at large, there are numerous unstated rules that regulate and limit the degree to which people can touch one another. These rules are highly gendered: in order to present as a *manly* man inside prison, it is pivotal to demonstrate a readiness to violently react to the undesired proximity (especially the feminising threat) of other men.[7] This includes standing and defending one's ground, cultivating a physical presence that exudes confidence (or dominance) and rejecting most forms of touching one another. Yet as an essential part of the training for and performance of the plays that they created together with Mick, the physical theatre space became one where the prisoner-actors were encouraged to push their physical boundaries and bend these rules.

This meant that there was room for them to physically interact with one another and us – making it possible to both touch and *be touched*. This process entailed a sensory renegotiation of the rules that regulated the ways in which prisoners could touch one another and train their bodies. Building on known bodily registers that allowed for exception, like (break)dance, acrobatics and trust exercises (e.g. falling into one another or being thrown up in the air and caught by the group), the rules that regulated the physical interactions between *prisoners* were relaxed as those between *actors* were introduced. Here, proximity communicated trust rather than threat. As the prisoner-actors invested themselves in the theatre practice, it thus began to provide them with a sensory idiom through which they could express feelings and conditions that were shrouded in secrecy or not readily verbally conveyable, like the strain of overcrowding:

> During the theatre training today the prisoner-actors crammed together and piled on top of one another to indicate the overcrowded conditions.[8] 'Closer, closer!' Mick said, and they would huddle together even tighter for the opening scene of the play. [...] Smiling at the end of practice, sweaty and out of breath, they agreed that in prison your body is taken to all kinds of extremes, and it makes sense to show that to the audience.

The participants in the prison theatre programme often described prison as a 'cemetery of the living' (Manuel, SPR, 2009), a place 'where I was dead' (Javi, former SPR, 2016) or where 'it feels like my body no longer belongs to me' (Araña, City Police Jail (CPJ), 2015). Inside the CPJ, where the second prison theatre group we set up spent their time, they were forced to live (quite literally) on top of one another. Held in 20-square-meter cells in one of the country's warmest cities with as many as 40 prisoners to a cell, they slept in layers of bunks and hammocks hanging over mattresses on the ground, their belongings stashed in plastic bags knotted to the metal bars or the grille ceiling. There, they learned carefully *not* to touch one another. 'Touch a guy's hammock and you're in for a beating'

---

[7] I have discussed these gendered dynamics at length elsewhere (see Weegels, 2014, 2019b).
[8] Field notes, CPJ, 2015.

Bobby explained,[9] indicating that fellow prisoner's (sleeping) bodies, space and belongings are literally not to be touched. Only friends shared their spaces and thus the prerogative to touch one another and their belongings – this had already been evident at the SPR, where during the most boundary-pushing exercises, the prisoner-actors paired up with their closest friends. After all, entrusting someone with control over your body by opening up to someone's (potentially menacing) touch was not taken lightly. Moreover, as the prisoner-actors moved in and out of the theatre space, they wanted to leave no doubts as to the nature of their physical interaction.[10]

This sensory restriction of touch – or rather, the governance of *touching* – feeds directly into the prison's local economy of violence. In fact, besides the no-snitching command, the other two cardinal prisoner rules pertain to regulating (undesired) touching: no stealing and respect those higher up. In other words, do not touch somebody's belongings and do not touch their position. These are entangled: in Nicaraguan prisons, one's sleeping space indicates one's position on the prisoner hierarchy (the better the bunk the higher up, the closer the mattress on the floor is to the toilet, the lower down) – if either are touched, let alone one's *body*, the response is violence. Fights and stabbings were common. '*Es el encierro* (it's being locked up), confinement makes you fight about everything', Marlon explained.[11] Inside, prisoners engaged in acts of violence (but also solidarity) to govern their spaces and prison's indoor markets. But the authorities hold a stake in these too.

Violence, Power and Secrecy

What is commonly known as the prisoner 'law' (referred to at the CPJ as *la ley de la gallada*, the law of the roosters) consists largely of the three above-mentioned commands: no snitching, no stealing and respect those higher up. This code regulates what prisoners are to see, hear, touch and speak of. It also regulates which prisoners may be victimised and on what grounds. Importantly, this means that prisoner survival does not necessarily entail avoiding violence altogether, but enduring it in the right way and resorting to it at the right time. Survival, or adaptation, was thus held to be about *endurance*[12] and learning one's 'place' – *when* to dominate and when to submit, *how* to ascend up the hierarchy and how to keep good relations with one's fellow prisoners as well as the authorities in the process.

When I followed up with Javi after he was released, we ended up engaging in a series of lengthy conversations about many aspects of prison life that had been largely off limits when he was still in the theatre programme at the SPR.

---

[9]Bobby, former La Modelo, 2015.
[10]Again, this has to do with gendered cultural conceptions of touch and sexuality (Weegels, 2014).
[11]Marlon, CPJ, 2015.
[12]*Aguantar* being the Spanish verb used (transl.: endure, bear, put up with, stomach, suffer, ride out).

We mutually agreed on the topics of these conversations to supplement my knowledge of what transpired in the SPR's cells in order to be able to understand fully what was going on and eventually compare its internal order to that of the CPJ. However, when the topic of the indoor drug trade came up Javi dropped off the radar. After about a month's absence he resurfaced. Though he had noted before that he was planning on writing his own book about his prison experience, he assured me that if those plans came to fruition he would omit *any* reference to the drug trade – 'it's too dangerous', he stated. Whether out of fear or loyalty to those still inside, prisoners and authorities alike, he made no illusions as to the dangers of revelation. 'In prison you gotta understand you're blind, deaf, and mute, that you don't see or hear anything even if it happened right in front of you', he warned. This warning was meaningful. Even though Javi was no longer inside prison, his repetition of the code of silence highlighted its continued governance over his words and senses. Yet he underlined the importance of the topic 'for your book', specifically in relation to the (power) 'relations within the cell blocks'. Though he proceeded to elaborate extensively on the intricacies of the trade at the SPR, he did so without any reference to his own position within or vis-á-vis the trade. When I asked him about this he underlined:

> *Yo vivía mi tabo yo solo* (I did my time by myself).[13] I didn't say anything to anyone. Not to the guards, not to my visitors, and not to my friends. Because you know that *you* can keep information, but you don't know if the other person might be loose-lipped. *Y la guardia es maldita* (and the guards are two-faced). They can tell *el mero* (the boss or leader of the trade), in exchange for some money, who told them – who snitched. They stabbed people all the time [at the SPR].

Even though Javi had witnessed the ins and outs of the trade then, he had been actively invested in un-seeing, un-hearing and not speaking of any of it. He knew the potential physical repercussions and he knew his place. Highlighting the double position of the authorities towards the trade (at once colluding and disorganising) as well as the violence involved in subordinating, sanctioning or scaring fellow prisoners out of stepping out of line, his account furthermore demonstrated that physical violence is deployed to enforce 'the rules'. Both prisoners and authorities are invested in this:

> 'There's two ways in which the authorities receive you at the penitentiary', Javi explained on a different occasion.[14] 'The first is that they don't beat you, they just shave your head, give you a number and take your picture. Second is that they beat and kick the shit

---

[13] Javi, former SPR, 2016, private conversation.
[14] Javi, former SPR, 2016, private conversation (other than the previous).

out of you and throw you cuffed into the *calabozo*.[15] They do this most of all with the dangerous guys, or those coming in on long sentences, so they understand that *the officers are in charge of the prisoners* and not the other way around'.

Though authority use of violence may seem volatile or marginal compared to the violence exerted by the prisoner hierarchy, both feed into the governance arrangements in place. In fact, the authorities largely depend on the prisoners' capacity and structures to self-govern their cells – hence their need to clarify that despite what prisoners may encounter in their cells, *they* are in charge. I have argued elsewhere that prisoner governance practices are incorporated in the prison's governance structure to such an extent we can speak of a co-governance system that girds both the legal and extralegal spheres of prison life (Weegels, 2018b, 2019a). Herein, authorities largely deploy violence against prisoners to maintain the power balance in their favour.[16] As such, officer-on-prisoner violence is fundamental for demonstrating *who is in charge*, rather than 'merely' for adjudicating disciplinary punishment (even if it usually disguises itself as such). In effect, it evidences the authorities' power to punish beyond the constraint of the law and impinges on prisoners a particular penal–sensorial regime. Consider the following incident:

> In a video clip sent to the newspaper *Hoy*,[17] filmed in La Modelo by a prisoner with his cell phone, we can see how eight prisoners have been taken to stand against the wall outside their cell, presumably so their cell can be searched. There, the penitentiary officers, who outnumber the prisoners, order them to strip naked and face the wall with their hands on their heads.
>
> One of the officers proceeds to beat all of the (naked) prisoners – judging from the dry whipping sound probably with a stick or a doubled belt – while the other officers stand grouped around the prisoners.
>
> The prisoner who is filming the scene with his phone across the hallway repeatedly states 'See, *see* what they do to us, this is so you can see, you *hear* that [the whipping]? They're beating them up, see? Look, so you see that we prisoners don't *tell* lies'.

---

[15]*Calabozos* are small, one- or two-person isolation cells where prisoners are kept when they are sanctioned by the authorities. Usually more prisoners occupy the cells than the number they are built to keep, and they are barely allowed to leave the cell for sun-time.

[16]See Crewe (2009) and Sykes (2007 [1958]) on the notion of power balance or equilibrium in prison.

[17]'*Reos denuncian abusos en Penitenciario Nacional La Modelo*' [prisoners denounce abuses in La Modelo National Penitentiary], retrieved from https://www.youtube.com/watch?v=jdQL2K1_tIQ (last viewed 9 November 2019).

The recording pushes the public to unmute their senses: to *see* and *listen* not just to what prisoners have to *say* but also to what they are *witnessing* as an audience to this video. For prisoners, authority extralegal use of force is a type of power that is enacted directly on their bodies – that they are made to *feel* and endure but cannot speak of without being doubted. The phrase 'see that we prisoners don't tell lies' points to the extension of this power in muting prisoners' voices in the discursive realm. There, the authorities have a hegemonic advantage and prisoners are readily portrayed as lying delinquents.[18]

While the abuse of authority – ranging from corruption, to beatings and even the obscuring of prisoner deaths[19] – is systemic in the exercise of penal power in Nicaragua, what is at stake in *concealing* it is not the perceived legitimacy of a particular violent 'incident', but the discursive legitimacy of Nicaragua's entire re-educational prison model. Pivotal here is that penal re-education is presented not just as a penal ideology but also as a political project born of the Sandinista revolution. To keep it in place, authority abuses and their collusion in prison's illicit economies must remain concealed so that the integrity and efficacy of the prison system *as a revolutionary state project* are not called into question. This brings me to my final considerations on the entanglement of power and secrecy in Nicaragua's penal–sensorial realm, and my own involvement in this.

Keeping Secrets

Arguably, those who manage to set foot in Nicaragua's prison system are exposed and drawn to participate in its undercurrent of public secrecy by default. Over the past decade, with the implementation of a series of laws and regulations that pushed the centralisation and political (re)alignment of the institutions of crime control with the Sandinista state, this has become ever more evident.[20] In fact,

---

[18] I have explored this in depth in an analysis of prisoner performances of resistance (Weegels, 2019a).

[19] The number of reports of human rights violations at the hands of state authorities has increased over the past decade (much before the 2018 anti-government protests started), and human rights organisations have accused the Ministry of Governance of purposely obscuring prisoner deaths occurring due to the lack of medical attention, torture and suicide, at the rate of one death per month (e.g. '*Un reo muere cada mes en las cárceles de Nicaragua, según procurador de DDHH* [One prisoner dies every month in Nicaraguan prisons, according to human rights procurer],' El Nuevo Diario, 26 February 2015). Following the 2018 anti-government protests and the political imprisonment of hundreds of protesters, critique of the prison system has swollen and numerous accounts of abuse have surfaced (e.g. GIEI, 2018).

[20] Daniel Ortega, leader of the Sandinista party since 1984, was re-elected president in 2006 and has not left the office since. In the meantime, non-government aligned press and human rights organisations have been banned from inspecting prisons, while the prison population steadily tripled (from approximately 6,000 prisoners in 2005 to over 18,000 prisoners in 2018) and reports of human rights violations became ever more daunting. In 2011, a new penal jurisdictional law was implemented, which curtailed

access itself is governed through the logics of concealment. In order to prevent public scrutiny of the deteriorated and overcrowded conditions, by and large only those who can prove their political affiliation or alignment with the governing party are entrusted with access. Their presupposed commitment to the Sandinista 'revolutionary state-building project' is held to guarantee their capacity to mute their senses to the benefit of the state. That is, to participate in the continuum of secrecy. As such, the possibility of seeing, hearing, touching and being in the prison environment is from the outset restricted to three groups of people: state authorities, those on the receiving end of state power (i.e. prisoners and their families), and outsiders able to produce such proof – as we did.

At first, I was not fully aware of the degree to which my own access had been subject to political scrutiny and allowed through connections to the party-state. Initially, I was drawn to the supposed humanist and re-educational foundation of the prison system. Yet at every level I found mechanisms in place to obstruct and conceal what is happening – to progressively mute one's sensory and perceptive abilities. Eventually, given the far-reaching institutional and political changes that took place over the course of my research, my research itself became a muted endeavour as it became partially undisclosed to the authorities. Without underestimating the ethical dimensions of this gradual shift,[21] I initially believed that a degree of unspoken 'distance' from the authorities was necessary to ensure the safety of both my research collaborators and myself vis-à-vis the Sandinista state and its extralegal expressions of power. The multiplicity of roles I assumed (as workshop assistant and facilitator, coordinator of the theatre-in-prison programme and co-organiser of an officially government-aligned prisoner rights and anti-discrimination project and campaign) nevertheless had me managing ever more relations with them. While my increasing engagement with the authorities made me more knowledgeable of the politics of concealment that they engaged in vis-à-vis the outside world, my own 'secret-keeping' also opened me up as an interlocutor for prisoners on subjects that they concealed and introduced me to the complexities of secret-keeping.

Importantly, I found that a different idiom pertained to public secrets kept by prisoners and authorities. Whereas the secrets that authorities kept were considered to be political armament and never conferred to me directly (i.e. by the authorities themselves), the prisoners seemed to make a distinction between two types of 'insider knowledge'. On the one hand was knowledge of prisoner

---

the discretionary power of prison wardens and relocated this with the General Direction of the National Prison System, the courts and the Ministry of Governance. At the same time, the president extended the terms of judges and police commissioners politically aligned with his political project. In 2014, the police law was reformed, moving the institution even closer to the executive (from their position under the Ministry of Governance to directly under the mandate of the president). Finally, the brutal repression of massive anti-government protests in 2018 by a combination of (riot) police and pro-government para-police groups undeniably evidenced the extensive hybridisation of the Nicaraguan (penal) state (e.g. Weegels, 2018c).

[21] I have reflected on these extensively elsewhere (see Weegels, 2018b).

hidden (illegal or illicit) activities, considered knowledge usable against them. On the other hand was knowledge about the authorities and their abuses of power. This was considered knowledge usable against the system. Usually, revelation of aspects of the latter preceded disclosure of the former. A politics of 'siding' is involved in this as well. When one 'knows' and loyalty is silence, this loyalty can be both felt by the other 'side' and tested by either. Once one can be trusted to be on, in my case, 'the prisoners' side', more of what that side keeps hidden may be revealed and slippage becomes more heavily policed. Immersed in evolving relations of loyalty to both the prisoner-actors and the authorities, I became aware of the extent to which life in prison is not only subject to a politics of concealment, but that secrecy and power are intimately related to one another and to prison governance. As Elias Canetti (1984) pointed out, 'secrecy lies at the very core of power' (p. 290). Yet, as Foucault (1990) later noted, this is 'not only because power imposes secrecy on those whom it dominates, but because it is perhaps just as indispensable to the latter' (p. 86). Let me provide a final example.

On one of the many days I spent at the community centre, where 30 prisoners of the CPJ were bussed to every day to participate in the different programmes at the centre, including the prison theatre programme, I screened a documentary about Tupac Shakur's life as a gangster rapper. As usual, I sat in the back of the room to be able to note the prisoners' reactions, interested to see at what point the movie might resonate with them and provoke reactions that could later serve a group discussion. Yet it was not the movie that proved to be a turning point that afternoon; it was the secrets that one of my research collaborators confided in me during the screening. Pulling up a white plastic chair next to mine, Araña told me in a soft voice about his prior involvement in the prison drug trade. Confiding in me the basis of his leadership conveyed trust, but in terms of the no-snitching code also demanded loyalty. The dynamics that governed his secrets, the process of concealment they set in motion and the powers and violence they involved – both directly and indirectly – were precisely of the nature that I had learned to leave untouched. It affirmed the undercurrent of violence and corruption I had gotten to know through numerous unfinished hints: 'it's just the way things work', 'they wanna block the sun with a finger', 'the system only benefits the system …' With this, all the previous bits and pieces I had heard and observed, but learned to turn away from, began to fall into place and beg attention. In the process, these secrets irreversibly 'magnified' my sense of reality (to speak with Georg Simmel), as I began seeing and hearing what I had learned to ignore. About a week earlier, Mick told me that officer Danilo had proposed to him to 'collect data' on the prisoner-actors, meaning on their illegal activities and particularly the flow of drugs into prison. Mick had declined, but the pressure was on.

> Chatting and listening to music, I decided to tell Araña about my worries.[22] It's lunchtime and we're breaking from practice. We're sitting on the concrete benches across the entrance to the community centre. Other CPJ-prisoners participating in the community

---

[22]Reconstructed from field notes, CPJ community centre, 2015.

centre program and the Juvenile Affairs-captain are sitting two tables over. Araña doesn't pay my worries much mind. Instead, he begins to talk in a regular tone of voice about some of his experiences trafficking drugs on the streets before he was imprisoned. Instantly, I feel my body tense and my ears peak to notice if either the prisoners or the captain two tables over may be eavesdropping. Have they stopped their own conversations? Is anyone watching us? Since Araña told me how the indoor trade works, the way in which other, older prisoners act around him has begun to stand out to me. But so has the presence of a supposedly former antinarcotics officer – I'll call him 'Danilo' – who recently joined the police's Juvenile Affairs team. From the corner of my eye, I see Danilo and another officer come out of the building. I quietly 'tell' Araña we can change the subject by signaling the entrance (which is behind him) with my eyes. Yet without hesitation he continues his story in the same tone of voice, his posture exuding a confidence that tells me that *even if* they could hear him, his fellow prisoners would never rat on him, and the police are either in on it or oblivious.

Finding myself incapable of muting the effects and seemingly endless possibilities of Nicaragua's hybrid penal power, I began to realise that the intimate knowledge of the prison system's inner workings that I acquired by moving with my research collaborators across its politicised power field had become explosive. The threat of discovery was daunting. In a sordid attempt to un-see and un-hear what I knew, I burned the physical copy of my notes on Araña's prior involvement in the indoor drug trade. But that did not make the pressure of the secrets I kept go away. After all, those concerned not only whatever Danilo may have been after but also my research at large. I realised that I already knew *too much* and that any form of revelation would be met by the silencing powers of the state. Beginning to step away from the prison environment and the muting power of its penal–sensorial regime, this particular secret would mark the start of a reverse process of revelation.

The body that would suffer the consequences of the authorities' doubts as to my commitment to secrecy was, however, not mine, but Mick's. Compelling me to silence prior to the 2017 municipal elections, by physically drawing us into the penal–sensorial regime imposed on those who dare break the continuum of secrecy – that is, by way of violence – the police tried to prevent the revelation of what they thought I knew about the drug trade, the CPJ and its corruption. Though this event reverberated beyond what I can neatly describe here, its threat 'worked' as it pushed me to place my doctoral thesis under embargo. Their secrets were safe, at least for a moment, as half a year later the authorities would find themselves amid massive anti-government protests. Contrary to before, the more violence they deployed to quell them, the louder the revelation of all they sought to conceal for so long resounded. Yes, the violence was unbearable – more than 300 protesters were shot dead – and yes, the state subsequently deployed its full hybrid carceral apparatus to force people back into silence (over 900 people were imprisoned and many more beaten and tortured), but by way of its own reaction the state revealed its most nefarious workings. Now, no matter how hard it tries, those can no longer be unseen, un-heard and kept secret.

Conclusion

In this chapter, I have argued that the management of (public) secrets is central to understanding the sensorial and penal qualities of the power that Nicaragua's hybrid carceral state exerts. By moving with my research collaborators I found that the entanglement of power and secrecy articulated in Nicaragua's prison system constitutes a particular penal–sensorial regime. In particular, this regime is (re)produced through an imposed and partial muting of the senses – the rendering unspeakable, un-seeable and un-heard of the violence that is deployed to keep it in place. Taking an embodied approach to prison life, I committed to my research and its collaborators beyond 'data collection' purposes – and was pushed to ask and answer different *kinds* of questions, as well as to reflect constantly on the research process. Did this sensing and *moving with* 'bias' my research 'findings'? Yes, and it may indeed preclude reproducibility and neutrality. But if we are truly interested in the social navigation of the prison environment, and the ways in which power relations are produced and negotiated throughout it, then do these supposed limits not outweigh the gains that an embodied approach to prison ethnography can bring to the criminological field?

In their audacious *Ethnography at the Edge*, criminologists Mark Hamm and Jeff Ferrell (1998) advised to

> situate yourselves as close as you can to the perpetrators of crime and deviance, to the victims, to the agents of social control; put yourselves, as best you can and for as long as you can, inside their lives. (p. 270)

'You won't experience it nicely', they warned,

> and if the danger and hurt become too much, be glad of it – because as near as you will ever get, you have found your way inside the humanity of crime and deviance. (Hamm & Ferrell, 1998)

While being 'glad' of the danger and hurt involved in closely experiencing the prison world is challenging, I must agree that placing ourselves in our research collaborators' lives and, if possible, *moving with* them, allows for a holistic and embedded sensorial understanding of the prison worlds we engage with. Taking seriously their navigational trajectories, and considering especially the penal–sensorial qualities of secrecy and violence – the muting it implies – brings us to an understanding of the power and the prison environment beyond the rational. Yet significant challenges exist in moving with prisoners and former prisoners across the system's power field, especially where secrecy is a potent organiser of the prison experience. After all, if we get too close, we may be exposed to the silencing capacities of secrecy, too.

References

Adloff, F., Gerund, K., & Kaldewey, D. (Eds.). (2015). *Revealing tacit knowledge: Embodiment and explication*. Bielefeld: Transcript Verlag.
Canetti, E. (1984/1962). *Crowds and power*. New York, NY: Farrar, Straus and Giroux.
Cohen, S., & Taylor, L. (1978). *Prison secrets*. London: Radical Alternatives to Prison.
Crewe, B. (2009). *The prisoner society: Power, adaptation, and social life in an English prison*. Oxford: Oxford University Press.
Foucault, M. (1990/1978). *The history of sexuality. Volume I: An introduction*. New York, NY: Random House, Inc.
GIEI. (2018). Nicaragua: Report on the violent events that took place between April 18th and May 31st, 2018. Retrieved from https://gieinicaragua.org/#section04
Gaborit, L. V. (2019). Looking through the prison gate: access in the field of ethnography. *Cadernos Pagu*, 55, e195505. https://www.scielo.br/pdf/cpa/n55/en_1809-4449-cpa-55-e195505.pdf
Hamm, M. S., & Ferrell, J. (1998). Confessions of danger and humanity. In J. Ferrell & M. S. Hamm (Eds.), *Ethnography at the edge: Crime, deviance, and field research* (pp. 254–272). Boston, MA: Northeastern University Press.
Ingold, T. (2000). *The perception of the environment: Essays on livelihood, dwelling and skill*. New York, NY: Routledge.
Ingold, T. (2010). Footprints through the weather-world: Walking, breathing, knowing. *Journal of the Royal Anthropological Institute*, 16, 121–139.
Ingold, T. (2011). *Being Alive: Essays on movement, knowledge and description*. New York, NY: Routledge.
Jefferson, A. (2015). Performing ethnography: infiltrating prison spaces. In D. Drake, R. Earle, & J. Sloan (Eds.), *The Palgrave handbook of prison ethnography* (pp. 169–186). Basingstoke: Palgrave Macmillan.
Jefferson, A., & Schmidt, B. E. (2019). Concealment and revelation as bureaucratic and ethnographic practice: Lessons from Tunisian prisons. *Critique of Anthropology*, 39(2), 155–171.
Marchand, T. (2010). Making knowledge: Explorations of the indissoluble relation between minds, bodies, and environment. *Journal of the Royal Anthropological Institute*, 16, 1–21.
Martin, T. M. (2015). Accessing and witnessing prison practice in Uganda. In D. Drake, R. Earle, & J. Sloan (Eds.), *The Palgrave handbook of prison ethnography* (pp. 424–441). Basingstoke: Palgrave Macmillan.
Penglase, B. (2014). *Living with insecurity in a Brazilian Favela: Urban violence and daily life*. New Brunswick, NJ: Rutgers University Press.
Pink, S. (2009). *Doing sensory ethnography*. London: Sage.
Pink, S. (2011). Multimodality, multisensoriality and ethnographic knowing: Social semiotics and the phenomenology of perception. *Qualitative Research*, 11(3), 261–276.
Sykes, G. (2007 [1958]). *The society of captives: A study of a maximum security prison*. Princeton, NJ: Princeton University Press.
Taussig, M. (1999). *Defacement: Public secrecy and the labor of the negative*. Stanford, CA: Stanford University Press.

Vigh, H. (2009). Motion squared: A second look at the concept of social navigation. *Anthropological Theory*, 9(4), 419–438.
Wacquant, L. (2004). *Body & soul: Notebooks of an apprentice boxer*. Oxford: Oxford University Press.
Weegels, J. (2014). The prisoner's body: Violence, desire and masculinities in a Nicaraguan prison theatre group. In G. Frerks, A. Ypeij, & R. S. König (Eds.), *Gender and conflict: Embodiments, discourses and symbolic practices* (pp. 151–173). Farham: Ashgate.
Weegels, J. (2017). Prisoner self-governance and survival in a Nicaraguan City Police Jail. *Prison Service Journal*, 229, 15–18.
Weegels, J. (2018b). *Performing prison: Power, agency and co-governance in Nicaraguan prisons*. Unpublished Ph.D. thesis, University of Amsterdam, Amsterdam.
Weegels, J. (2018c). Inside out: Confinement, revolt, and repression in Nicaragua. *PoLAR APLA Speaking Justice to Power Series*. Retrieved from https://politicalandlegalanthro.org/2018/10/03/inside-out-confinement-revolt-and repression-in-nicaragua/
Weegels, J. (2019a). Prison riots, creative violence and the (re)articulations of co-governance in Nicaragua. *International Criminal Justice Review*. doi:10.1177/1057567719849485
Weegels, J. (2019b). Undoing the 'cemetery of the living': Performing change, embodying resistance through prison theater in Nicaragua. *Revista Crítica de Ciencias Sociais*, 120, 137–160.

Chapter 7

The Embedded Researcher: Experiencing Life in a Probation Approved Premises

Carla Reeves

Introduction: The Importance of Sensory Analytical Reflection

Primary themes in reflexive accounts of fieldwork have arisen around accessing fieldwork sites, negotiating gatekeepers, the balance between insider and outsider positionality and the covert and overt nature of researcher status and research focus (cf. Crossley, Arthur, & McNess, 2016; Delamont, 2016; Liong, 2015; Lyle, 2018; Reeves, 2010; Worley, Barura Worley, & Wood, 2016). Within these accounts, there is often an implicit recognition that researchers are enmeshed within the place and interpersonal relationships of the research site: a recognition that is gathering pace, particularly by social geographers and anthropologists but also by ethnographers in other fields, including criminology and penology (cf. Bloch, 2016; Bucerius & Urbanik, 2018; Crewe & Ievins, 2015; Hoolachan, 2015). Despite this, reflexivity in fieldwork remains under-published, and those that are largely prioritise considerations of the emotional, ethical and practical challenges faced by the researcher and the research, as well as impacts on the research participants. These types of account, while often very useful and informative, tend to isolate the researcher and consider them as separate to the research site and/or people, even while acknowledging the possible impacts they may have simply because they are present.

This presence of the researcher in the site or community hints at the importance of the researcher just 'being', and all the attendant meaning that someone being present in a place has: their social and personal connections to others; their relationship to institutional rules, regulations and values; their hearing of the noises of the place, smelling the scents and seeing the sights. In short, how researchers experience the 'feeling' and 'knowing' of the place. As Mason and Davies (2009) argue, these tangible and intangible sensory experiences shape the researcher's understanding of the place and community being studied. Pink (2008) describes this deep form of reflexive analysis in terms of the embodied experience of doing place-making through ethnographic research. Thus, it is not only important but also essential to consider the embodied experience of researchers in the field to fully appreciate the totality of the data captured. As Hurdley and Dicks (2011) state:

> What participants say and do needs to be interpreted alongside the material and sensorial *settings* in which they say and do it, and which play an active role in the shaping of emergent situations and encounters. (p. 278, emphasis in original)

In reflecting on my sensory experience of doing ethnographic research in a probation-approved hostel within this chapter, it is highlighted that recognising, acknowledging and analysing researchers as being embodied within the research site or community is highly valuable to the quality and depth of the data analysis and interpretations. This appreciation of embodiment in the place of the fieldwork site specifically, and the interactions there within, can be referred to as researcher emplacement (Pink, 2008): in essence, not only an appreciation of researcher *being* or *presence* but also an understanding of our *being in place*. With place understood in a Lefebvrean sense as more than a structural physical space in which things are located or happen, but rather loaded in values, meaning and significance which are shaped by, and in turn shape, the daily social relations and interactions occurring in that place. To understand place, therefore, a researcher needs to understand how a place is socially produced through the 'appropriation' of space and the meanings and rhythms of use within daily life (Stanek, 2011).

Thus, being able to appreciate the sense of place for participants requires us, as researchers, to fully consider our own sensory experiences of being in that place, including the physical spatial nature of the place, understandings of history and tradition, emotional attachments, social group belongings and identities. As Meiring (2016) states in his study of the 'smell of justice' related to space and place:

> So how does justice smell, and specifically spatial justice? I am not quite sure, but I do sense that it is not only about the smelling of justice, but also the tasting of it, the feelings of it, the speaking of it, the hearing of it, the whole bodily experiencing of justice in a certain place. (p. 6)

Places, thus, become sensory experiential spaces, which people (researchers and participants) co-create over time through interactive place-making (Pink, 2008), and which we feel a sense of relationship to, because those spaces come to have meaning and identity in themselves – becoming *places* (cf. Avey, Avolio, Crossley, & Luthans, 2009; Devine-Wright, 2009; Dixon & Durrheim, 2000; Reeves, 2016).

Exploring the Sensory Criminal Justice Experience: The Research Study

Of particular concern for the analysis of myself as an embodied researcher is how these sensory experiences come together to form a holistic emotional experience of the place and how this can assist in better appreciating the meanings and lives of people in the setting under study (Longhurst, Ho, & Johnston, 2008). To illustrate my argument, in this chapter I explore how I subjectively experienced doing ethnographic fieldwork in a Probation approved premises (referred to informally as a probation hostel) over 21 months, setting my experiences in the context of previous sensory reflections on ethnographies.

Located in a primarily rural region of England and Wales, the hostel formed a single case study exploring the lived experiences of people convicted of sexual offences from their entrance into the hostel after release from prison, to their subsequent exit into the community. In this fieldwork site, I engaged in participant observation and semi-formalised interviews with mainly adult male residents convicted of a sexual offence and staff. Access included the staff offices, resident living and recreational areas and outdoor spaces.[1] In these fieldwork reflections, I consider how I became embedded within the physicality and sensorality of the research site; feeling some of the same impacts of the constraints of the architecture and interpersonal power relations on my sense of being that the residents and staff also revealed. As a result, I had emotional reactions to the sense of place that meant I was able to not only understand my participants' accounts or behaviours in the abstract (as an onlooker) but also empathically as one who feels some of the same impacts of place and space as they do. I know that saying I was able to empathically relate (albeit only partially) to the experience of people convicted of a sexual offence is very contentious (writing as a female with no convictions), but this sharing of the experience of place was able to bridge some of those distances between us, allowing for a deeper understanding of life for them, which enabled me to talk about this with them in ways that reflected a shared experience, despite our vastly different social positions, status and envisioned futures. Thus, sensory reflective analysis sensitised me to the emotional realities of hostel life and working that I would otherwise have understood in a much more superficial way. In the following discussions, I consider my experiences as an embedded researcher in terms of the physical building and the social interactions within the hostel under study, bringing out the understanding and appreciations that such a sensory analytical approach afforded me.

---

[1] Please note that quotes are from contemporaneous field notes of observations and interviews, but I have removed names and identifying features to protect the anonymity of participants.

The Physicality of the Hostel: The Sensory Experience of Space

At first approach, the architecture and setting of the hostel was that of a large Victorian home with pleasant gardens, standing alone on the semi-rural outskirts of a small cathedral city. On one side next to a middle-class suburban village and on the other side an industrial retail estate; both of which hostel residents were banned from entering without approved employment. It took around 20–30 minutes to walk to the edge of the city shopping centre, but there was also a direct bus route, passing by a housing estate notorious for both high crime rates and high populations of people with convictions (again, residents were banned from entering this estate). This geographic location as a sort of isolated space, enclosed by areas that were not permitted, only allowing for access routes away and bypassing these no-go spaces, resulted in a strong sense of insular separation and dislocation. This was emphasised by the limited cross section of the population that residents routinely came across unless entering the shopping area, as life in the hostel afforded access to a limited range of other adults only. As in prison, the deprivations of carceral life continued to some extent through the limited access and engagement with services, goods and social relationships (Sykes, 1958). Life in the hostel was, thus, insular time lived separately and differently than that outside, with different rhythms and interactions. This reflected the hostel's penal institutional status as both carceral and community, intended as it was, as a staging post in moving people from imprisonment into community resettlement. This within, but also without, physical liminality of the hostel setting therefore symbolised its carceral setting as being closely situated to, but also completely cut off from, local communities.

The hostel building itself was set back and side-on from the road in fenced, wrap-around mature gardens with car parking area, small pond and greenhouses and a computer room that was kept locked outside of class times. The hostel had one main front door into the foyer area, both overseen by the staff office which overlooked the car park and entrance into the hostel grounds. The only other egress was via patio doors from one of the resident lounges into the garden, but these were locked and unlocked by staff and did not have unobserved or unobstructed access to the road away from the hostel. The grounds were not only fenced but also bordered by tall tightly planted coniferous trees. The enclosed nature of the gardens, as well as the monitored, restricted access controlled by staff, reinforced the hostel not only as penal but also as secluded, isolated and insular, separated from normal, outside life. On first entrance, this closed feel, which mirrored the internal regulatory regime, did not necessarily engender a sense of being trapped within its confines but could also be regarded as peaceful, quiet and, for some, protective.

> When I first went into town [...] it was hard. [...] There was so many people, walking in all directions. You get used to walking in one direction; following people in front of you. I just stopped by the clock in the middle of town and wanted to cry. I felt all panicky. I was scared. (Resident in interview)

Interestingly, this inward insularity was also felt by staff, although of course they could leave the hostel at the end of their shift. Nevertheless, it shaped and coloured their view of working life:

> There is one member of staff that I do not like working with, I know others don't too.
> *CR: Is that just the same as in other jobs though?*
> I think that it is worse here because you are in such a closed environment. (Staff member in interview)

I found this inward-looking feel strangely at odds with the aim of the hostel as ostensibly forward- and outward-looking, supporting people newly released from prison towards resettlement in the community.

The initial external impression of the building as an isolated, but nevertheless, ordinary residential house was challenged only by limited outward signs of difference, such as the number of cars in the car parking area and rather unobtrusive official sign by the gated entrance. However, on walking into the foyer, this homely impression was overturned by the interior architecture and décor. This was immediately recognisable as institutional due to the colour schemes (magnolia and a pale green reminiscent of council buildings and hospitals across the country), faint smell of cleaning fluid, the fire doors and official signage and general shabby condition of the place coupled with the lack of personal furnishings and accoutrements.

Inside, the hostel was over two floors. The upper floor accommodated the residents' rooms and personal washing facilities. The lower floor was the living floor where residents were required to spend the day when in the hostel and where staff had offices and administrative space. The staff offices were locked from residents except for confidential meetings. These offices comprised the main general staff administration office which overlooked the entrance foyer, car park and pond, and this office also included the hatch through which residents requested things; the probation office in which confidential and quiet work could be undertaken during the day; the staff bedroom and facilities for the 'sleeping' overnight shift that assisted the 'waking' overnight shift; the medication room, where the medicines cabinet and files were kept, and medications issued twice daily; and the kitchen. The resident areas included foyer space, games room, dining room, laundry room, the 'smoking' lounge and 'non-smoking' lounge (though since the Health Act 2006 implemented the smoking ban in 2007, it was no longer permitted to smoke in the hostel at all). The non-smoking lounge was also a staff meeting room, and the dual purpose of this room was immediately evident when comparing the sensory differences between the two lounges. The smoking lounge was dishevelled even when tidy as a result of the tired and worn furniture. Chairs were orientated towards the TV, and it was always dark as windows were kept closed, and the curtains drawn to simultaneously accord what privacy could be attained, as well as maximising the space for use as a makeshift cinema. Despite the ban on smoking, this was routinely breeched and evidence was discernible in the faint smells, burn marks on some surfaces and impromptu ashtrays fashioned from saucers and cups: smoking of any substance not generally being a priority for staff. Residents compared it unfavourably with the non-smoking lounge, which was alone in being a resident-accessible area that was bright and airy, having many windows, refreshed and newer paintwork and furniture. The main smells here were air-freshener and the scents of the garden from open windows. Older residents were more likely to use the latter space and the TV was less of a central feature, being used more as a space for conversation. The worn feel was prevalent throughout the hostel in resident areas and considered indicative of resident social status within the hostel:

> Examples of this are the toilets which are not kept in a good condition, they are always dirty and often do not have toilet roll in them. (Resident in interview)

However, unbeknown to residents, it was the same throughout the staff areas that were not used routinely for visitors too.

As may be understood from this description, the architectural structure of the lower floor was rather confusing and complex for such a small space, serving to disorientate those unfamiliar with the hostel and so create unease in the first instance, dominated as it was by the corridors that led around and through the lower floor. As Hurdley's (2010a) ethnography of corridors in an institution (in that case, a university) exemplifies: corridors can have multiple uses and meanings, being ways to connect or disconnect other spaces, boundaries against or to openings as well as being places in themselves. As she and Armstrong (2018) noted, corridors are part of the controlling design of the place in which movement is curtailed and organised. In the hostel, they were closed, contained spaces which, due to the high number of turns and doors blocking the way, had little natural light or actual room within them. People did not linger in corridors; they were not places for chance meetings and conversations, nor to read notices or signs, but rather conduits to traverse to get to the next place. As Armstrong (2018) further explores, corridors simultaneously exemplify the mobility of the place, as well as the nature of the hostel as a place of waiting (for the next room, for a staff member, to be relocated in the community). However, as in her conceptual consideration of corridors in the context of the doing of disciplinary power, corridors can be understand as highly controlled places, not only in terms of movement of people (permitting movement around the spaces in particular ways and structures) but also in respect to how that movement occurs, using examples of painted walkway lines and visibility screens. Nevertheless, she also recognises that corridors may be understood and experienced as outside of the social norms of the place: a sort of spatial outlaw. In the hostel, this sense of corridors being closed, private spaces, often outside of the behavioural controls exerted via the disciplinary 'gaze' (Foucault, 1977), and so spaces where residents and staff may be violently accosted unseen by others meant that they were not spaces in which to delay. The place-meaning of corridors in this broader hostel context was, thus, that they were potentially dangerous, relatively unobserved areas in which residents could take advantage of this relative freedom from view to engage in aggressive or otherwise criminal behaviour, if the opportunity arose; a particular concern for staff or vulnerable residents fearing the aggression of other residents. This apparent freedom of the place was, therefore, in tension with the sense of possible danger that resulted in people using the corridors as conduits only. That the corridors were so enclosed and winding through the hostel spaces further added to this sense that the place was not 'free' but constraining, controlling and repressive: a physical representation of the feeling of the place that generally prevailed throughout the hostel.

On entry, I had expected initial formative sensory cues to the institutional penal nature of the place but was not prepared for how unavoidable this sense was, and the extent to which this context could not be forgotten or hidden, and remained explicit throughout my time in the hostel. It felt like a place of work, even for those not working there, especially as these physical environmental cues combined with the temporal rhythm of the working day and week, in which most staff came into work based around the normal 9–5, Monday to Friday patterns (with the exception of the evening and weekend more limited staff cover). This enabled me to appreciate how residents were constantly reminded that they were in an official institution of correction and (to some extent) punishment. This appreciation of the institutional feel of the place allowed me to better understand how residents felt being accommodated in the hostel. Despite the efforts to ensure residents had access to activities and leisure pursuits, residents did not relax into the hostel – it never became 'home' or homely, even for those who were there for longer than my data collection period.

This was symbolically reinforced each morning when residents were woken at 7 a.m. to undertake their chores and all the communal areas were cleaned and tidied: wiping away the evidence of individualism and personality daily. Falk, Wijk, Lars-Olaf, and Falk's (2012) exploration of how to create a sense of home in residential care somewhat parallels the need for the hostel to create (and be) a home for the residents, albeit involuntarily and (normally) temporarily, while also being part of a broader organisational and institutional structure. In trying to create a place of home (encapsulating the cultural and emotional attachments and meaning attendant within the word 'home'), Falk et al. discovered residents needed to 'nest': they needed to be able to personalise their environment so that it both reflected and reinforced their individual self-identity, as well as engage in an agentic daily routine. In undertaking enforced, defined daily chores in living areas which returned them to clean, sanitised rooms, without evidence of the individuals using them daily, this expression of self-identity and attachment was, thus, also removed. Of course, the sense of place was not removed: the meaning that place had within the broader context of hostel life and residents' social groupings, but the *individual* residents were not reflected in those spaces or places.

However, attachment to the residential care home in Falk et al.'s (2012) work was mostly a result of the use of the private space rather than the communal, in that, not only did residents have their own personal accoutrements (photographs, pictures, ornaments and so on) in their rooms but also were able to choose how to arrange these and look after them. In the hostel, this was just not possible.

Few hostel residents had a private space (most shared a room) and those that did could not lock them to protect belongings:

> Wants all residents to have single rooms (he shares with one other person). This is so that he can protect his belongings (has had some stuff stolen in the past), and so that he can have some privacy. Says that he has no privacy in the hostel at all, 'when you are upset you want to be able to be on your own' – can't do that here. (Notes from resident in interview)

Even fewer residents were permitted, owned or could afford personal belongings beyond the necessities of clothes, personal hygiene items, limited technological and leisure equipment (if they could, they had a mobile phone and game station to stave off boredom). Most residents lost their possessions through their imprisonment, with the remainder placing items in storage or with family, if they kept any at all. Thus, personal items just were not present in the hostel. Furthermore, this sense of the bedroom as belonging to that of the person residing in it was disrupted through the frequent and unannounced room searches that staff undertook, demonstrating in a physical way the institutional ownership of that space. Sometimes this was framed in respect to tensions between resident and staff social divisions and respect for rights:

> Privacy is not respected because staff (including female staff) will walk into residents' rooms (even if locked) without knocking – can be asleep or getting dressed. They will walk through the showers without warning and the toilets do not have locks on them. (Resident in interview)

This meant that rooms mostly had the stark, sterile feel of a cell. Consequently, the symbolism of the room also echoed that of the prison cell, with which the residents were, of course, familiar: that of waiting ... waiting to move on from the hostel and re-commence normal life in the community (Armstrong, 2018).

The Production of Place: The Sensory Experience of Social Interactions

The hostel was also a place in which the sense that the unexpected should be expected was never far from the fore. This seemed to mainly result from the turnover of residents. Although some, especially older residents convicted of sexual offences, tended to stay in the hostel for long periods of time (over a year), others, often younger residents, were more likely to be moved on within a few months or even weeks. These moments of resident compositional change were moments of disruption in the otherwise mundane and routine 'sameness' of daily life in the hostel. As Armstrong (2018) notes regarding prison life, while there is flux and activity constantly within the hostel as residents and staff leave and enter during the pattern of the working day and week (in relation to curfew and office hours, rehabilitative programmes or employment, as well as residents moving on and in to the hostel), nevertheless, the repetitive and unvarying rhythms of this activity result in a static and unchanging feel to hostel life. This is exacerbated by the waiting that Armstrong explains characterises much of carceral life. This waiting was a significant source of resident dissatisfaction as many had imagined leaving prison to actually feel like a release, only to be moved immediately into another form of penal institutional living with its own challenges:

> People just don't realise how hard it can be coming out. […] They don't prepare you for any of it. Not how you will feel. On the first day you are just so happy to be out, you are euphoric and you don't notice anything around you, it's after that. (Resident in interview)

Hostel living, however, lacks a clear and defined end (or even a defined process through which to work to achieve that end):

> He is angry and resentful that he is still here [some months later] although he was told he should move on in a couple of weeks. (Notes from resident in interview)

Despite this, new residents were rarely regarded as a welcome break in the routine. Rather, they could upset the established group dynamics and heighten tensions between resident networks as they renegotiated new social divisions and got a 'feel' for the new resident, their place in the hostel, attitude and behaviour towards others. New residents could disrupt fragile balances between resident social groupings, be they built on alliances or carefully studied avoidances, and potentially could lead to physical assaults. For example, one new resident who claimed to have been convicted of attempted murder (actually threats to kill) made those residents convicted of sexual offences '"apprehensive and uneasy", and at least one [resident], is spending more time in his room' (field notes, 6-03). Although, as noted, residents' rooms were not always the safe spaces that, outside of such penal institutions, people normally experience:

> Shares a room – at first with [resident name] – did not like this, and it has now been changed, hated sharing because he did not trust [resident name] – says he would not go to sleep until he had. (Notes from resident in interview)

Staff also felt this sense of apprehension generally pervading the hostel environment:

> This place is like a time-bomb, a sleeping time-bomb. You never know what's going to happen next. (Staff member, field notes 7-04)

As a visitor with access to staff spaces, I felt I had an easy refuge, enabling me to feel comfortable and confident within the hostel, but also I was aware that there were no panic buttons in the communal areas, nor did I, like staff, have a personal panic alarm. Consequently, I was better able to appreciate how some staff felt about their work with residents as situated within the context of the hostel and appreciate the significance of their efforts to either stay safe or exert their dominance or control over residents. For the most part, informal and interpersonal strategies of control were based on routine interactions in spaces where staff and residents were required to interact, such as at the administrative office hatch, medication distribution and the kitchen during meal times. They included, for example, making residents wait for half an hour before responding to requests, whether they were busy or not.

> There was a couple of times there though that they [staff] were a bit controlling with giving the medication, they'd make them wait. And they'd [residents] be getting agitated saying they need it; they need it. [staff said] 'well, we're fucking busy' you know. And that, I used to think, how much of that is control again, and how much is genuinely being rushed off your feet? It doesn't take you a minute, does it, to give a drug, sign for it, whatever. (Staff member in interview)

These exercises of power and powerlessness were often enacted by staff utilising the architecture to emphasise and exert penal structures in place. For example, normally residents would make a request (for an appointment, for more milk, for equipment from the games cupboard) through knocking at the administrative office hatch, an officer on duty going and opening the window hatch and hearing the request and then responding. However, I routinely noted that when this happened many staff heard the request and said they would respond in a while, shut the window on the resident and sat down and recommenced their conversation with fellow staff. On asking why they did this even when they were not busy, they said it was to make sure the resident knew who was in control. This evidently shaped relations between residents and staff, who saw this as symbolising their position within the penal, disciplinary structures of the hostel, with residents' position as lacking in agency or control in comparison to staff authority:

> [staff] are not bad – it's just that when you ask for help they tell you to wait, but when they want something doing it has to be done straight away. (Resident in interview)

Similarly, appointments tended to be scheduled at the convenience of staff, which impacted in how residents could use both their time and space by leaving the hostel outside of curfew hours (normally 12 midday to 7 p.m.). This non-curfew time was conceptualised as the residents' time, when they could be free from the hostel confines and, thus, the penal restrictions upon them:

> Many other hostels let people out earlier [from curfew hours]. Then we have to have appointments with people and they are

> arranged at their [hostel staff] convenience, which is always after 12 in our own time. And if we don't turn up we get a warning. We have to get back for meetings that are in the middle of the afternoon, or sometimes we don't know when they are coming and have to stay in to wait for them. We had more freedom in prison.
> (Resident in interview)

This ability to shut out the resident, deny access and enforce waiting on them reflected the structural power positions inherent within the status of the staff. Enforced waiting is here a symbolic function of both punishment through the legitimate use of authority by staff and the penal purpose of the hostel. However, this powerplay through enforced waiting was also exerted by residents against staff, though this time regarded as illegitimate. For example, each meal and medication time was a half-hour window when residents came to receive food or medications. Most would attend within the first 10 minutes, but there were a few residents who deliberately always attended in the last few minutes of the window of time, requiring staff to remain in that room, waiting to serve them for that period of time. Staff found this extremely frustrating and were angry about this agency being removed from them, however briefly, leading to some staff responding in kind:

> He relates how [name of a resident] used to control little things in the hostel so that he was gaining power in small ways over the staff. When meds are given out the staff member puts the correct medication for each person into a small cup which is emptied into the hand of the resident. Normally people would hold out their hand cupped ready to take the pills but [resident] holds out his hand straight so that the staff member cannot just empty the cup into his hand. After a couple of seconds or so he cups it, but in this way he is controlling the behaviour of the staff for that time, even if it is in a minor way. [Name of staff member] says that it took the staff 'ages' to see what was going on and after then they tried to make sure that they were aware of what he was doing and took back control by holding back his medication until after he had signed the book and then going to pour his meds into his hand whether it was cupped or not. He had to react to the staff then.
> (Field notes 9-04)

Thus, at least for some residents and staff, a battleground of minute power-plays shaped the social interactions between them. Residents regarded these as petty displays of power, serving to highlight their low status, but I could appreciate for staff that, although not clearly verbalised, these were strategies that helped them maintain their sense of social status and authority. Of course, on an individual basis residents and staff sometimes had positive and constructive working relationships, but the 'them and us' social group divisions were clear and maintained through such interactions, as well as the architectural power structures, in which staff had keys and private spaces, and residents did not.

As a result of reflecting on the importance of how having such access may change how a person may use and experience the place of the hostel, after approximately six months of fieldwork, I chose to forgo my staff keys to try and ensure residents did not perceive me as closer to a staff identity and status. Consequently, I started to become much more aware of how residents felt living in the communal environment of the hostel, and particularly their sense of not being able to escape from the feeling of being watched, assessed and judged. This led one resident to exasperatedly comment that 'being at the hostel is like living in a goldfish bowl' (field notes 5-04). Again, *being present* in the hostel and using the full range of my sensory experience to interpret observations meant that I could appreciate the meaning and impact this constant sense of being under surveillance had on the lives of the residents. In this instance, as Goffman (1991) explains, places which are comparatively 'free' from the gaze of the institution (staff and CCTV) were highly valued places towards which residents gravitated to enable themselves to feel distanced from the institution of the hostel (Cohen & Taylor, 1992). Due to the resident composition in which older residents convicted of sexual offences against children dominated numerically and were long-term residents, they were able to carve out territories and occupy free spaces in the hostel and defend them through their sheer presence and repelling stigma as known sexual abusers. In the hostel, free spaces were mainly focussed around the polytunnels, being at the back of the garden, out of view of the main staff offices, not covered by CCTV, and hidden from view when inside them (and sheltered from the elements which frequently kept others out of the garden). Thus, being in the polytunnels had meaning for the inhabitants beyond the functionality of shelter and seedlings, but as liminal places which were somehow in-between the penal structures and constraints of the hostel and the (almost mythical) freedom of the 'outside' community. This meaning of place and routine appropriation by this stigmatised resident group, irrespective of whether they liked gardening or not, consequently, changed the use of the space[2] and rippled through the hostel in terms of impacting on the rehabilitative journeys of other residents, and the spaces they used and occupied in the hostel:

> [Resident with convictions for physical violence] talking about liking gardening in prison. I asked [do you want to] keep it up in here: 'no not here, I'd have to go down the bottom of the garden with the sex offenders'. (Field notes 5-04)

Being able to have a sensory appreciation of how such places are experienced helped me better understand the nature of life and the importance of residents' choices about where and how they lived their life in the hostel. What I found more challenging, however, was that despite experiencing the hostel as an oppressive and controlling penal environment, some residents nevertheless preferred hostel

---

[2]For more discussion on grouping and the use of space in the hostel, see Reeves (2013b,).

life to what they perceived as the alternative: living alone in the community under the stigmatising shadow of their convictions. Again, considering how the place felt and was experienced helped me better appreciate this. These residents tended to be older with convictions for sexual offences against children. They were the most likely to have age-related health issues, lost contact with peers and family as a result of their offending and lengthy prison sentences. They were also the most likely to be isolated in the community as they were past retirement age and therefore had no push to education, employment or training: they faced a future of hiding their past and living alone. In the hostel, however, this was different. Their offences were broadly (if not specifically) known by staff and residents alike, and because of the nature of Probation Approved Premises work, hostel life formed a type of supported living for these residents.

Despite their frustrations and dissatisfactions with the formal structures and rules of the hostel and their licence conditions, many of these residents expressed their desire to stay in the hostel due to the protections it offered them. This was also observable in watching their daily habits and use of hostel space; they were the least likely to choose to leave the hostel during the day (outside of curfew hours; often citing that they were 'scared of being attacked' (field notes 8-04)), the least likely to be pushing staff on working towards a release date and the least likely to be coming to staff to request things. They were the most evidently embedded within the hostel; observable through their established routines and apparent contentment with the rhythms and restrictions of hostel living. They largely did not seek to test these boundaries, staying well within the hostel rules, such as not using the full curfew time permissible, rarely being discovered with contraband (such as drugs, alcohol or offence-related prohibited materials). These residents appeared to continue life in the hostel much as they had left it in prison: quietly, compliantly and without explicit resistance to the regulatory, temporal and spatial structures of penal life. This meant that many of the residents in this category became well grounded in the hostel place, but this 'rootedness' was a cause for staff concern:

> He feels very settled here now. Too settled, he's not looking to move himself now; he's stopped trying. (Staff member, in interview)

It also caused tensions between staff and residents on occasion, as evidenced by staff anger and resentment towards one older resident who informally led on the gardening and took self-responsibility for maintaining the grounds. For many months, he gained praise for this work, but his behaviour eventually became regarded as inappropriate for a resident, being too proprietary, resulting in other residents reporting 'that when they first came to the hostel they thought that [the resident] was a staff member because he treats the garden as his own' (field notes 9-04). Eventually, when he started growing seedlings and giving them away, staff became resentful that he should feel he had the right to do this without their permission: 'he thinks he's quasi-staff now' (RSO staff member, field notes 8-04). Thus, these social interactions verbalise and make observable what the internal architecture and furnishings symbolise: the power structures in place and the social position and status of the residents subjected to institutional control.

Leaving the Hostel: Sensory Experiences of Time in Place

In undertaking the process of leaving the hostel, I tried to talk to all remaining staff and residents who were involved in the fieldwork to explain this process, and how I could be reached if they had any questions or wanted to see the results of the research. It was at this point, in particular, that I realised while many residents were indifferent to my presence (or lack of it), some residents did not truly understand my role, or the research, despite my efforts to explain, and had viewed me not only as a researcher but also as something of a friend. They were confused (and a little hurt at times) that finishing fieldwork meant I would not (and could not as I did not have permission) visit them. Their position as a node within a penal network dominated by professional social relationships dependent on their conviction status was thrown into stark relief. The true isolation and loneliness of many residents was evident, despite their apparent unending routines of appointments, programmes and social interactions within the hostel. Similar to the dual experience of being resident in a hostel as both movement (the constant doing of chores, meetings, staff shift changes and so on) and static (waiting for change, a risk assessment, a visit, to leave), so many residents' social experiences were both filled with connections and simultaneously empty of meaningful personal relationships. Seeing behind these penal-based distanciated relationships further highlighted why so many of the older residents with sexual offence convictions were fearful of leaving the hostel, and consequently leaving these social structures and relationships[3] they were dependent on, while still resenting as enforced. Thus, for me, leaving became an emotional and ethical process more than a practical one, and one which I tried to take as much care to explain as I could and, within the relatively short time frame of a month, decreased my presence to ease out of residents' lives.[4]

For many residents, this sense of the static was compounded by the indefinite nature of their residence requirement, as well as the lack of clear progression and exit routes. This sense of not progressing, but also not knowing when things may change, and uncertainty over how to affect it, relates to what Crewe (2011), when discussing prison life, called 'tightness'. Tightness generates feelings of anxiety and concern and relates to the power relations in the hostel (in that residents had little or no formal power and decision-making potential around their release). Different individuals had to overcome different barriers to not only work towards demonstrating their reduction in riskiness but also establish a safe and secure place to go in the community. For many of the residents with sexual offence convictions even when a release looked possible, it was overturned when a risk assessment of accommodation was undertaken (and rejected); often multiple times. As so many residents were older, this was exacerbated by their health and support needs. On occasion, even end of licence did not result in release with two residents

---

[3]It must be remembered that social relationships between residents were not permitted after leaving the hostel and were regarded as indicative of risk of reoffending and in some cases may breach licence conditions. Reeves (2013a).
[4]For more on leaving the research site, see Reeves (2010).

during my time in the hostel having to sign voluntary agreements to stay as there was no where appropriate for them to go in the community.[5]

Concluding Thoughts

It was after leaving the hostel that I really had time to reflect and appreciate how the embodied and embedded experience of doing research enabled me to better understand the experience of the place and community I was studying. Had I this appreciation for the sensory (and made the time to more explicitly draw out and analyse the sensory experience of place) as the fieldwork was progressing, perhaps new insights may have been uncovered and informed my observations and subsequent findings. Nevertheless, as I became enmeshed in data analysis considering my sensory experience, I further came to appreciate how my full embeddedness, utilising the totality of my senses in the hostel, facilitated my critical reflection on how and why I interpreted the data in particular ways (which evolved through and after the fieldwork phase of the study). For example, I chose a primary theoretical framework which meshed Foucauldian power discourses with Goffman's exploration of interpersonal resistance. This choice was not only a direct consequence of what I was hearing and seeing from observing and talking to residents and staff within the institution but also a consequence of the *physical feel of the place*: a feeling that is the culmination of the totality of sensory experience of consciously *being* in the place. This highlights how, by using the body as a research tool (as Longhurst et al., 2008, put it), we are enabled to appreciate how place and participants are intertwined and relate to each other: in short, how people live their lives in a place.

In this example of analysing the sensory experience of researching a particular type of criminal justice institution, namely the probation hostel, we are able to better address the main aim of the research being undertaken: to explore what life is like for those with sexual offence convictions moving through hostel residence from prison release to re-entering the community. Without such analysis, the experience can only partially be understood, and this allows for a fuller and more rounded appreciation of their emplaced experiences of daily life. The appreciation of how both the apparent mutually exclusive experiential dichotomies of staticness and change, isolation and social connection, are nevertheless simultaneously powerful lived realities for residents (particularly those convicted of sexual offences) could not have been uncovered or understood. Nor could the understanding of how the physicality of the hostel structure leads to emotional responses based on a sense of institutionalised closeness, tightness and watchfulness, as well as vulnerability that pushes both residents and staff into particular behaviours and patterns of being within that place. Thus, to understand life and

---

[5]Please note that although residents with sexual offence convictions may have come to the end of their licence in the community period, they were still subject to the sex offender register, and as such, their residence in the community was still subject to risk assessment and approval.

how it is lived in the hostel, as with any place, it is necessary to consider how people use their senses and make sense of the place.

These are not issues understood by most, if any, people when considering place or space, abstracted as it is from the forefront of conscious experience, and so could not be discussed in interview. Nor are they observable phenomena that can be truly appreciated via the fundamentals of the various forms of participant observation, as commonly regarded as central to the ethnographic tradition. But add to the mix a sensory analysis of the place and how, as a situated person experiencing the hostel through not only talking to, and watching the people in that place, an additional layer of understanding may be appreciated.

References

Armstrong, S. (2018). The cell and the corridor: Imprisonment as waiting, and waiting as mobile. *Time and Societ*, *27*(2), 133–154.

Avey, J. B., Avolio, B. J., Crossley, C. D., & Luthans, F. (2009). Psychological ownership: Theoretical extensions, measurement and relation to work outcomes. *Journal of Organizational Behavior*, *30*, 173–191.

Bloch, S. (2016). Place-based elicitation: Interviewing Graffitti writers and the scene of the crime. *Journal of Contemporary Ethnography*, *47*(2), 171–198.

Bucerius, S. M., & Urbanik, M. (2018). When crime is a 'young man's game' and the ethnographer is a woman: Gendered researcher experiences in two different contexts. *Journal of Contemporary Ethnography*, *48*(4), 451–481.

Cohen, S., & Taylor, L. (1992). *Escape attempts: The theory and practice of resistance to everyday life* (2nd ed.). London: Routledge.

Crewe, B. (2011). Depth, weight and tightness: Revisiting the pains of imprisonment. *Punishment and Society*, *1*(5), 509–529.

Crewe, B., & Ievins, A. (2015). Closeness, distance and honesty in prison ethnography. In D. H. Drake, R. Earle, & J. Sloan (Eds.), *The Palgrave handbook of prison ethnography* (pp. 124–142). Houndmills: Palgrave Macmillan.

Crossley, M., Arthur, L., & McNess, E. (Eds.). (2016). *Revisiting insider-outsider research in comparative and international education*. Oxford: Symposium Books.

Delamont, S. (2016). *Fieldwork in educational settings: Methods, pitfalls and perspectives* (3rd ed.). London: Routledge.

Devine-Wright, P. (2009). Rethinking NIMBYism: The role of place attachment and place identity in explaining place-protective action. *Journal of Community & Applied Social Psychology*, *19*, 426–441.

Dixon, J., & Durrheim, K. (2000). Displacing place-identity: A discursive approach to locating self and other. *British Journal of Social Psychology*, *39*, 27–44.

Falk, H., Wijk, H., Lars-Olaf, P., & Falk, K. (2012). A sense of home in residential care. *Theoretical Studies*, *27*(4), 999–1009.

Foucault, M. (1977). *Discipline and punish: The birth of the prison*. London: Penguin.

Goffman, E. (1991). *Asylums: Essays in the social situation of mental patients and other inmates*. London: Penguin.

Hoolachan, J. E. (2015). Ethnography and homelessness research. *International Journal of Housing Policy*, *16*(1), 31–49.

Hurdley, R. (2010a). The power of corridors: Connecting doors, mobilising materials, plotting openness. *The Sociological Review*, *58*(1), 45–64.

Hurdley, R., & Dicks, B. (2011). In-between practice: Working in the 'thirdspace' of sensory and multimodal methodology. *Qualitative Research, 11*(3), 277–292.

Liong, M. (2015). In the shadow of deception: Ethical dilemma, positionality, and reflexivity in ethnographic fieldwork. *Qualitative Research Journal, 15*(1), 61–73.

Longhurst, R., Ho, E., & Johnston, L. (2008). Using 'the body' as an 'instrument of research': Kimch'i and pavlova. *Area, 40*(2), 208–217.

Lyle, E. (Ed.). (2018). *The negotiated self: Employing reflexive inquiry to explore teacher identity*. Boston, MA: Brill.

Mason, J., & Davies, K. (2009). Coming to our senses: A critical approach to sensory methodology. *Qualitative Research, 9*(5), 587–603.

Pink, S. (2008). An urban tour: The sensory sociality of ethnographic place-making. *Ethnography, 9*(2), 175–196.

Reeves, C. (2010). A difficult negotiation: Fieldwork relations with gatekeepers. *Qualitative Research, 10*(3), 315–331.

Reeves, C. (2013a). How multi-agency are multi-agency risk assessment committees? *Probation Journal, 60*(1), 40–55.

Reeves, C. (2013b). 'The others': Sex offenders' social identities in probation approved premises. *Howard Journal of Criminal Justice, 52*(4), 383–398.

Reeves, C. (2016). The meaning of place and space in a probation approved premises. *Howard Journal of Crime and Justice, 55*(1–2), 151–167.

Stanek, L. (2011). *Henri Lefebvre on space: Architecture, urban research and the production of theory*. London: University of Minnesota Press.

Sykes, G. (1958). *The society of captives: A study of a maximum security prison*. Princeton, NJ: Princeton University Press.

Worley, R. M., Barura Worley, V., & Wood, B. A. (2016). There were ethical dilemmas all day long: Harrowing tales of ethnographic researchers in criminology and criminal justice. *Criminal Justice Studies: A Critical Journal of Crime, Law and Society, 29*(4), 289–308.

Chapter 8

Space, Surveillance, and Sound in Pre- and Post-Reform Prisons in the Dominican Republic

Jennifer Peirce

Descriptions of the crisis in Latin American prisons almost always emphasise deplorable physical conditions, overcrowding, and violence (Bergman, 2018; Carranza, 2012; Fonseca, 2018). Many countries have turned to high-tech supermax-style facilities as a solution (Dardel & Söderström, 2018). The Dominican Republic's 'New Prison Management Model', developed in 2003, is unusual in its emphasis on human rights, including the UN Mandela Rules. The premise is that decent buildings with extensive staff and work programmes generate transformative experiences for incarcerated people. However, people incarcerated inside both old and new prisons express mixed views about their conditions and experiences – and some of these run counter to conventional wisdom about physical environments and other sensory aspects of prison life.

This chapter explores the sensory experience of life in new and old Dominican prisons, based on what incarcerated people and staff express, as well as my experiences as a researcher. Three dimensions of sensory experiences in Dominican prisons are most prominent: physical space, sense of monitoring and surveillance, and sound. I explore differences in these sensory dimensions between 'old' and 'new' prisons, as well as between facilities of the same type. Furthermore, some of the sensory experiences of prison life were taken for granted by participants but were striking to me as an outsider from North America: verbal and physical interactions that are friendly and warm, unregulated movement within facility areas, and ubiquitous religious events. I argue that incarcerated people emphasise that autonomy and some kind of 'normalcy' in daily life matter most, and that they often find this in material conditions that appear, on first glance, to be harsher.

Research Methods

To build this project, I approached the Dominican authorities for permission to undertake the overall project and to visit facilities. The headquarters leadership (both old and new model) were quite receptive and readily signed on.[1] My impression is that this was because they wanted external recognition of what they view as a successful reform, and the prestige of an American university also helped. After doing exploratory visits and interviews in 2016–2017, I developed a survey for incarcerated people, based on the concepts of the *Measuring the Quality of Prison Life* (MQPL) framework (Liebling, 2004; Liebling, Hulley, & Crewe, 2011; Sanhueza, 2015). Over three months in 2017, with a team of five local university students, we administered the survey to men in the 'ordinary' areas of 17 facilities (10 old and 7 new), excluding people in solitary confinement, medical areas, maximum security, or facilities for day release or elderly people; our final sample was 1,240 respondents. We spent one to three days in each facility, visiting most areas but spending most of our time in collective areas (chapels, patios, classrooms). Also, I interviewed 39 currently and formerly incarcerated people and 91 other actors, such as prison staff, justice system officials, non-governmental organisation (NGO) staff, and journalists.

Background: The Dominican Prison Reform Process and the New Prison Management Model

The Dominican New Prison Management Model was the project of a few visionary leaders, Dominicans and Europeans, in the early 2000s (Paniagua Guerrero, 2015). They established a new correctional officer figure (*Agente de Vigilancia y Tratamiento Penitenciario* (VTP), or Penitentiary Treatment and Security Officer), first at a small scale and then in a formal Academy (*Escuela Nacional de Administracion Penitenciaria*, ENAP) that emphasises human rights and operational procedures. A key rule in recruiting VTPs is that anyone with police or military experience was not eligible. Over the years, the government renovated or built the 'new' prisons – called Centers for Correction and Rehabilitation (CCRs).

A crucial feature of the CCRs is that they prohibit overcrowding: once beds are full, the CCR refuses to admit more prisoners. Any 'overflow' people – which ends up being two out of three – are sent to traditional prisons, which are in military or police barracks. In 2019, there are 22 CCRs, out of 41 total prisons, which range from 90 to 1,500 bed spaces, and hold about 35% of the total incarcerated population (9,290 people out of 25,815 as of December 2018); old prisons range from 50 to 10,000 people in size. The current prison population is almost twice what it was when the reform launched, with over 60% of incarcerated people are in pretrial detention (DGP figures, 2018), despite a major judicial

---

[1] My research was funded by an independent Canadian grant, so I did not ask the prison authorities for any resources other than time.

reform in 2004 (Centro de Estudios de Justicia de las Americas (CEJA), 2018; Espinoza, 2016). Another central distinction is that CCRs generally provide basic amenities – beds, food, transportation – for free, whereas people traditional facilities have to pay or work for basic daily needs, apart from very meagre meals. This unofficial economy works through a prisoner-led committee, with 'delegates' holding responsibility for distributing resources, overseeing transactions, and negotiating with the formal institutional authorities.

Space and Boundaries

On first glance, the most striking contrast between 'old' and 'new' facilities is the buildings and physical space. All CCRs are painted an identical shade of pale yellow and blue, so incarcerated people call them *azulitos* ('little blue ones'). My first visits to these were on escorted tours, and while I was struck by the orderliness, friendliness, and array of activities, I assumed this was the 'tour day' version of things. On subsequent visits alone, there was usually less organisation, but the CCRs always feel remarkably calm. The reception areas have subtle cues to authority of a doctor's office or a school, to make one remain silent unless spoken to. Inspirational posters and phrases cover the walls, along with prominent signs displaying the UN Mandela Rules, the principles of the New Model, and the daily schedule. In my first visits, the spaciousness and knowing I could access a bathroom with a toilet felt like a relief. The open-air, well-tended gardens and sports areas seemed to be deliberately invoking a 'less harsh' prison environment (Hancock & Jewkes, 2011).

The traditional prisons are hidden from outsiders, usually in a low-slung concrete-block building, surrounded by barbed wire, in the back of a military barrack or police station. From a distance, one can hear shouting and see clothing hanging and electrical wires hanging out of the space between the cement wall and the tin roof – the signs and sounds of confined people spilling out from the walls. On visitor days, there are lines of people outside the main gate bringing food and other supplies. This is a striking illustration of the permeability between 'inside' and 'outside' in Global South prisons (Martin, Jefferson, & Bandyopadhyay, 2014), with the primary role of women in the unofficial, but open, exchange of goods and services (Fontes & O'Neill, 2019)

Inside the old prisons, incarcerated people hold the keys to the gates and doors. In these spaces, amid intense heat, noise, and darkness, people sit on stools or buckets and start casual conversations the way they would in a crowded marketplace. The interior space, in the daytime, has very few cell bars, closed doors, handcuffs, or uniforms. What feels different, and sometimes oppressive, is the sheer number of men moving through a constrained space.

Overcrowding is the defining feature of the traditional prisons. The largest traditional prison, La Victoria, a former fortress, held about 9,000 people in 2018, *malcontados* (poorly counted, as in the real number is unknown). It has numerous sectors, and both prisoners and officers charge entry fees for the more comfortable ones. The names evoke the physical conditions of each sector: the most expensive is called Alaska, for the prevalence of air conditioners, whereas the most dirty and crowded cell blocks are called Vietnam, Iraq, or Kosovo. At the entrance of Alaska, there is a police officer sitting relaxed at a desk, with a list of names and a ring of keys, usually chatting with prisoners and looking at YouTube videos on their cell phones. One immediately senses the geographic and economic borders of this sectorisation.

Despite the lack of metal doors, the cells in old prisons are extremely narrow, dark, and full of people at all times of day. Originally narrow cement-walled rooms, with little or no natural light, they are now divided into layers of makeshift 'bunks' along the walls, creating narrow hallways between. Mattresses and hammocks are piled at each end, to be spread in the hall floors at night. The 'bunk' sleeping spaces are called *goletas*, which look like stacked boxes, made of wood or plywood, about the length of a coffin and tall enough to sit up in. Along a wall, four or five *goletas* are stacked on top of one another, horizontally, with the side facing the hallway opening upwards, often with a padlock (used by the prisoner), with no window. Still, these are the most expensive place to sleep – people pay rental fees of at least US$20 per week or spend hundreds of dollars to purchase them. Walking through these hallways in the daytime, one sees the legs of people in the higher bunks dangling down, lit by a few lightbulbs, and hears radios, fans, TVs, cell phone videos, and shouting. The floors are remarkably clean – less fortunate prisoners seem to be mopping constantly – but the hallways smell mostly of wet clothing, kerosene, and a mix of cigarette and marijuana smoke. Again, these are the accessories and smells of a working-class Dominican apartment building, but one feels a sense of confinement due to the constrained space.

Numerous people described the *goletas* as 'sleeping in a box' – but with the benefit of privacy: one said, 'I close the door and it's dark but I'm alone'. Others made a point of showing me that they have TVs, cell phone chargers, mirrors, posters – evidence of some economic status and also of normal life. In surveys and interviews, the people who shared *goletas*, sleeping two or three men to a box, mentioned physical discomfort ('You know, sharing a bed with another man is not easy, another man's feet in your face, his snoring, not like women'). But they always said something like, 'At least I'm not a *rana*' – referring to the people who sleep on the bare, wet floors and are called 'frogs' (*ranas*). People almost never complained about the lack of light, but I often heard complaints about the lack of dry space to sleep. The more expensive *goleta* cell blocks had fewer *ranas* and more open floor space.

As researchers, entering these sleeping spaces, even briefly, feels like invading the private space of others: men half-dressed, partway through shaving or sleeping. When men realised that women were about to enter the space, they quickly and politely put on t-shirts, stubbed out their cigarettes, and greeted us. In one facility, the lead prisoner made everyone exit the cells before we could go inside, and I was surprised to see at least 40 people walk out from a space that seemed to contain only a dozen or so *goletas*. Standing in a narrow hallway, I could usually see the 'bathroom' at the end of the hallway – a shower or pipe pouring onto the floor, and sometimes a toilet or a hole in the floor around the corner.

The *patio* (open area) in old prisons is where most of daily life occurs, with rhythms indecipherable to a new arrival. From about 9 or 10 a.m. until about

4 p.m., when cell gates are unlocked, most people spend unstructured time in this space. The overwhelming feeling here is of a crowded *barrio* marketplace in any large Latin American city: small stalls, with people scurrying between these and loudly haggling over prices. Some people had cooking spaces, with hot plates connected to electric wires strung across the walls in tangles or small barbeques using charcoal. Along the edges, individual prisoners sell specific products: ice and cold drinks, chips and snacks, used cell phone parts, sunglasses. Most men sit in small groups, often gathering around a dominos game or card games, or waiting to rent cell phone minutes. There is not much room to walk around, as the middle part of the patio is filled with mattresses drying in the sun and laundry hung from lines above. Here, the strict stratification-by-price of cellspace shifts into a more fluid circulation of most residents.

What is remarkable here is that within this constrained space, there is a significant degree of autonomy in people's actual use of this space, at least in the patio. In the words of Martin et al. (2014), this is an example of people 'cobbling together customary orders' – not necessarily a sign of disorder or 'poor' governance. As others have argued, when incarcerated people freely conduct 'normal' activities and consume food, music, clothes, and products brought in by families, this can be a form of resisting the control of the penitentiary regime (Rice, 2016) and dismantling the sensory difference between life inside and outside (McClanahan & South, 2020).

When I entered these areas, alone or with my students, people noticed and greeted me but often ignored us, assuming we were church volunteers. We often had to make an effort to gather people in a group and announce the purpose of our visit, inviting people to participate. This usually resulted in a first batch of people eager to talk. We typically retreated to the chapel area, set off to the side from the patio, for surveys and interviews. It felt like a physical relief to take a seat here, as the chapel was always very clean and quiet. A small group of men was constantly mopping the floor and rearranging plastic chairs. Later in the day and on subsequent days, we circulated in the patio area to have informal conversations with people less interested in our presence: those who were resting in corners, working at small shops, cutting hair, washing clothes, absorbed in gambling games. Often, they were reluctant to be interrupted, often saying very politely that they could not afford distraction from their work. The residents' relative lack of attention to outsiders – particularly women – reinforced to me the sense that people were comfortable in their self-established spaces and routines, without the assumed deference to visitors that happens in more regulated prisons.

On occasion, it was obvious that our presence did affect the regular activities of the patio. One Friday afternoon, a committee delegate asked us to depart before a certain time, as lunch was over and their 'other market' was set to begin. Seeing my blank face, he explained that this is the weekly 'other' market and made a gesture referring to marijuana. On visit days (during which we did not conduct research), according to what I heard, delegates create separated areas in the patio: one area for children to play with their families and another area where men can set up small, makeshift tents to host their girlfriends or sex workers. In some prisons, people told me they hesitated to bring their children to visit, since they would see this 'inappropriate' activity only a few metres away. One person expressed appreciation that the delegates organised stand-alone 'kids' days' where family visits could occupy the whole patio, as he could 'have a picnic with my kids' – alluding to a sense of normalcy.

In the new CCR facilities, prisoners have more space but less say in how they use it. The standard staff teams – security, treatment, legal support, and administration, as well as a medical area – have separate offices, where four or five staff crowded around a couple desks. Outside, the 'modules' (dormitory areas) are usually spaced apart, with basketball courts and gardens in the central area, and kitchens and classrooms off to one side. Because of the warm climate, there are many open areas without roofs. This gives most of the areas more sunlight and wind, which made spending days in these facilities much more comfortable for me. When I remarked on this, even mentioning the contrast to old facilities, most people shrugged and said that what is better in CCRs is reliable electricity and water supply, not sunlight or breeze. One exception was the minimum-security facility for elderly men, who reside in small cabins spread across a large field. These men told me they felt safer and more relaxed here, as the cabins were 'like a house with a porch where you can sit and watch the world go by', in the words of one. Again, this more open-format design deliberately echoes architectural designs meant to promote 'rehabilitation' through space, colour, and some presence of nature (Moran, Jewkes, & Turner, 2016).

Another area that feels distinctly unlike a prison is the children's visiting area, which is, according to one officer, always outside the reception area so that children do not have to go through bars. This is a large, open room painted with children's movie characters and filled with small furniture and toys. Once or twice a month on Sundays, children visit their incarcerated fathers, for two-hour blocks. In my survey, among the most common responses to a question about the advantages of CCRs compared to old prisons was that people feel comfortable having their children visit. They described the space as safe, pleasant, appropriate. On other days, the room sits empty and no one uses it for other activities. 'It makes us sad to be there without our children', said one man when I asked about this. Notably, when prison administrators brought outside visitors on tours (which I witnessed several times), they always emphasised the children's playroom as an example of space and design oriented towards 'relationships' and 'rehabilitation'. The children's room is perhaps the only area of the prison where descriptions from prisoners and prison staff were mostly aligned about the purpose and the feel of the space.

The sleeping modules are separated by a gate with bars, and within each module, there is a common area with plastic chairs and a landline phone attached to the wall. On the walls of these areas, there were often inspirational or religious posters specifically about resilience and moral change – a contrast to traditional prisons, where posters were usually Hollywood movie or quasi-pornographic images, along with quite a few standard Catholic church posters. I was disconcerted by the uniformity of these phrases across facilities, especially after hearing people's grievances about harsh discipline by staff. The incarcerated men told me they were bothered by these posters, but they were indignant about restrictions on personal decorations (photos of family) in their bunk bed area. (All the bunk walls looked bare; people kept such mementos in their lockers or otherwise hidden.)

Along a hallway off of the common room, there are four to eight cells, each containing bunk beds for six to 18 people, as well as a toilet, sink, and lockers. On the door of each module, there is a sheet with the names of the people who live there and their behavioural status (indicated traffic-light style by a red, yellow, or green sticker). The fact that sleeping areas are identical and free is striking compared to traditional facilities; prisoners commented frequently that they were relieved to no longer burden their families with costs. Prison officials described the sleeping areas most commonly as 'clean', 'orderly', and 'dignified' and frequently implied that such spaces promote rehabilitation (Wener, 2012). However, a common complaint was that as of a few years ago, incarcerated people had to purchase their own mattresses (average cited price 300 pesos or US$6) and sheets for their beds, contrary to official policy. Furthermore, they criticised the way people were allocated to cell spaces. One told me,

> We come from the same neighborhoods, we know each other. We know who gets along or not. But the [administrative] officers make us share rooms with people we don't know.

In CCRs, the official rules reign and officers dismantle self-organised arrangements.

The CCR solitary confinement cells are a sharp contrast to the dormitories. When I visited these cells, the most striking trait is that they are small, dark, lacking basic amenities like mattresses, and they have a heavy metal door – despite their being called 'reflection space', which was painted in cursive over the door to the sector. To me, they combined the worst of both types of prisons: the material deprivation of the old model with the strict discipline of the new model. When I spoke to people in these cells, they were sullen or indignant about the physical deprivations, expressing none of the 'penitence' or 'reflection' that the CCR staff, following nineteenth-century American discourses, said was supposed to occur here (Rubin & Reiter, 2017).

The primary spatial differences in the two types of prisons are the actual amount of space, the beds and other amenities, and the sense of access to natural light and green spaces. The new CCRs do have some additional security features – such as guard towers, electric fences, and more elaborate entrance procedures – but they prioritise, in discourse and in design, the 'rehabilitative' elements of their design. This relies explicitly on the notion that it is important to mitigate the 'pains' of imprisonment related to sanitation, noise, and crowdedness, as tracked by scholars of prison architecture (Moran & Jewkes, 2015). Dominican officials and prisoners contrasted the spaciousness of CCRs to US prisons, which they almost always described as 'harsh' or 'cold'. Indeed, in CCRs, people wear regular clothing, circulate without escorts or line-ups, laugh, share snacks, shout, sing, even hug one another. No one wears handcuffs or shackles, except occasionally groups of men arriving from court. The solitary confinement cells are an obvious exception to this ambience. But more generally, there is a tension between the outward appearance of 'rehabilitative' design and the restrictions on basic amenities and people's ability to determine their own use of space inside the prison.

Visibility and Surveillance

Being inside a prison usually means being watched constantly, by staff, cameras, and other prisoners. In traditional Dominican prisons, there are no cameras and very few officers or guards inside the building. As a visitor, especially as a white woman, I felt highly visible due to the sheer volume of people packed into a small space, curious about us – with the difference of knowing that due to my gender and race, people would go to extra lengths to 'protect' me. When police or military officers or administrative staff walked through, I observed the incarcerated men moving to make room and let them pass, offering greetings, and sometimes following to ask for help on specific issues. Whenever an officer asked about a particular prisoner, someone would say 'oh, he's always in the chapel', or 'he's in the patio by the *colmado* [shop]'. This suggests that though the security staff are largely absent, the other prisoners have a high awareness of the movements of other people in their immediate sector.

In old facilities, as noted above, people have significant freedom of movement, but other forms of social control operate. Some of this is through individual favours with police guards. But mostly, the surveillance system works through the inmate self-governance committee (delegates). Inside the prison, sometimes they introduced themselves to me by name, but never with their committee role. Of the 10 or so head delegates (chiefs) I met, all were noticeably dressed in clean, more expensive-looking clothing, often with sunglasses and several cell phones. We observed several delegates walking with batons swinging and making sure people respected the line-up for lunch, and sometimes reprimanding men verbally. When I spoke with some of them individually, they described their duty as keeping people in order, often using metaphors of running a school or a government.

This form of surveillance manifests in sensory forms indirectly: people adjust their demeanour when they feel under observation. Some rearrange themselves to let the delegates pass by, or cast their eyes down and drop their voices, while others confidently greet the delegates or shake their hands. The incarcerated men spoke to me in whispers and notes about their sense of being watched by the delegates. They felt comfortable writing long notes on the survey paper but were hesitant about speaking one on one; they preferred speaking in pairs or groups. I noticed that when delegates walked by, some people I was speaking to would pause or drop their voices; others would greet the delegate warmly as though to demonstrate trust. People freely criticised the formal administration and the judicial system, but were more cautious in their critiques of the inmate committee system. For example: One said, 'There is a lot of corruption among the *alcaide* [prison director] and military officers', while another said, 'The discipline committee is composed of people with good capacity, to control discipline and hygiene'. Some commented that the delegates and the chief had too many undeserved privileges

Space, Surveillance, and Sound in Pre- and Post-Reform Prisons 133

and were partial towards their friends. 'They take care of their associates before the *infelices* [colloquial term for indigent prisoners]'.

Numerous scholars have written about elaborate rules developed by prisoners and how they monitor one another, in Latin America (Darke, 2018; Weegels, 2018) and in the Global North (Gundur, 2018; Maier & Ricciardelli, 2019; Skarbek, 2014). In Dominican prisons, the rationale for this self-organisation, according to both delegates and regular prisoners, is to ensure that everyone has some access to basic amenities (space, food, water, safety) and to reduce conflicts. The porosity of the prison to the outside world is extensive and bidirectional, with economic and social transactions between prisoners and families (Fontes & O'Neill, 2019; Jefferson & Martin, 2020). The role of the prisoner delegates in surveilling both prisoners and visitors has two effects: not only more orderliness and predictability for these interactions but also a lack of privacy for individual prisoners and visitors. Although this system is hardly democratic, incarcerated people seem to understand and accept its basic logic: the rules are clear and everyone benefits, albeit according to their assigned position in the hierarchy.

In the officer-run CCRs, surveillance is more obviously in the hands of officers. The facilities emphasise officer–prisoner interactions over cameras and metal detectors, evoking notions of dynamic security and managerial supervision (Hancock & Jewkes, 2011; Jefferson & Martin, 2020). There is a lot more casual conversation between VTP officers and prisoners than what is standard in a US facility, where technology is primary (Morin, 2013). Instead of cameras and metal detectors, VTP gate officers keep never-ending paper lists of names of people coming in and out of a given area and give regular pat-downs; prisoners wear prominent ID badges. Once inside a given area – for programmes or dormitory – the incarcerated men can sit wherever they want and move around freely.

But from what I observed, the VTP officers' surveillance focuses largely on compliance with a set of rules and behaviour norms – and the consequence often outweighs the infraction. For example, they monitored prisoners' behaviour during meals, where everyone must eat exactly the same portion size in relative silence. After one lunch that our team attended, we requested to speak with people being held in solitary confinement. The first person we found there had been at the lunch, and so I asked why he was now in solitary confinement. He told me it was because he had put a piece of chicken in his pocket, to 'save for later, because we don't often get chicken'. An awkward silence ensued, as we all knew that immediate solitary confinement is reserved only for violent infractions or drug-related contraband. The guard quickly said that the detention in solitary was just 'for a few hours'. Later, I saw the same man in the common area, and he told me they let him out only because we had asked about his situation. We heard over and over again about this pattern: breaking a small rule of order or appearance led to immediate solitary confinement detention, not the official process of a write-up and a lesser penalty (like losing sports time). What stayed with me from this incident was the capricious punishment by officers in response to a prisoner's choice that was clearly driven by the most basic sensory experience: hunger.

CCR surveillance also enforces body language. Incarcerated men are required to walk single file, hands clasped behind their backs, heads bowed forward.

Upon arrival, are required to shave their heads and facial hair regularly – purportedly for health reasons. Many complained mainly about the fact that the facility charges 75 pesos (US$1.50) for a haircut. Two black men, one Dominican and one Haitian, in two different facilities told me that when they were admitted, they had dreadlocks. Both felt a sense of indignity and resentment at being forced to cut these off. One said, 'It's a cultural thing for me'.

In contrast, those who join religious groups that promote similarly 'humble' body language – particularly evangelical sects or a charismatic form of Catholicism called *Hermandad Emaus* – benefit from extra privileges. These also prohibit swearing, homosexuality, and loud music. Several prisoners told me they joined the 'religious cell' groups not due to religious practice, but rather to gain some relief from VTP monitoring and punishment.

As an outsider in Dominican prisons, the degree of social interaction and the absence of camera surveillance often felt refreshing. The social surveillance in both types of prisons still has a sensory manifestation. In the crowdedness of the old prisons, fellow prisoners constantly watch one another, adjust their positions and voices, and leverage their community ties and reputations to participate in the economy of basic commodities – all beneath the only-somewhat-visible monitoring of the delegates. In the new prisons, the surveillance is more open, but unidirectional, with VTP officers overseeing prisoners' daily routines and enforcing conservative behaviour norms. Although this arguably provides more privacy than cameras at every corner, the disjuncture between the officers' claims of 'humane' and 'rehabilitative' practices and the strictness of their surveillance and punishments is stark. One interpretation of this is that in the Dominican CCRs, there was what some scholars describe as 'role conflict' – as occurs in Northern prisons that claim to be 'empowering', but in practice are controlling (Shammas, 2014). This lack of alignment can be jolting, generating cynicism and frustration among prisoners.

Sounds and Noise

Dominican prisons are very loud, constantly. But the noise is not typical noise of North American prisons, like bars and doors clanging, announcements over the intercom, guards yelling, or the sounds of advanced technologies (Hemsworth, 2015). Traditional prisons are louder than CCRs, mainly because more people are packed into a smaller and more enclosed space, but the sources of sound are similar. The noise comes mostly from groups playing music, listening to the radio, domino games, cooking food, shouting encouragement at basketball matches, and holding phone calls or WhatsApp video visits. In other words, these are the general daily noises of a Dominican street block on a weekend, minus the women and children. Even in CCRs, officers often shouted in friendly tones to one another, rarely using their assigned walkie-talkies. In the vocational workshops, participants played the radio at top volume. More than once, I saw everyone – prisoners and officers – perk up when a popular song came on, and everyone would dance for a minute or two. Sometimes they teased me – 'don't be so serious!' – for not joining in as readily. These kinds of relaxed moments would be, to me, very anomalous in a US facility. The fact that both prisoners and staff actively choose to generate these sounds of 'normal' (non-prison) life points to a degree of social freedom, as authorities do not seek to control them – an important distinction from Global North settings where such sounds are often interpreted as a form of resistance to authority (Rice, 2016).

The most constant and dominant sound in Dominican prisons is the sound of church. Scholars in the Global North have noted the conspicuous absence of the weekly auditory routines of Sundays as part of the blurring experience of confinement (Kutzler, 2014). In the Dominican setting, church events are near daily, so provide normalcy but not a way to mark time. Although the country is predominantly Catholic, evangelical Christianity is rapidly growing (Thornton, 2016).[2] Inside prisons, church services are one of the only activities that happen every day, as they do not need staff time or equipment. Prison staff frequently told me with pride that they respect freedom of religion in prisons and then would say something like, 'It doesn't matter if you're Catholic, Mormon, Jehovah's, Pentecostal – everything is fine' – but they never mentioned a non-Christian religion or atheism. All meals and events open with a lengthy prayer, usually led by a prisoner.

Evangelical groups run long *cultos* (worship services) in which participants sing along to chants or call-and-response songs. Intermittently, preachers speak in a frenetic tone, revving up a group's energy, and playing songs or other sermons off their phones or cassettes. Occasionally, I observed an evangelical 'pastor' walking through sectors, carrying a portable microphone and speaker, preaching as he went. The rhythm of these meetings is almost hypnotic: dozens of men shouting and murmuring in synchronised rhythms, often kneeling and bowing together. Although I found these songs grating, I could understand the appeal of a collective chant that carries one's mind to another place. Catholic church services were more formal, led by local women volunteers or nuns (rarely a priest), at specified times; usually someone brought out a guitar for hymns.

Beneath the music and rhythm, there are consistent tropes and narratives of redemption. A typical message focuses on 'finding the devil within', repenting, and surrendering to Jesus – but very repetitive, with lyrics such as

> When you fight that demon, that demon in you, that tricky demon,
> you will struggle, you will try again and again and again, because
> he is Lucifer and he does not give up!

Often, these messages quite directly said that alcohol, drugs, adultery, homosexuality, and profane language were signs of the devil's presence among us. Sometimes, in interviews, certain prisoners would roll their eyes when the sounds

---

[2] In my surveys, 42% of respondents identified as Evangelical and 40% as Catholic, while only 16% of respondents said they are non-religious, 2.3% said they follow an 'other religion' (this includes sects such as Mormons and Jehovah's Witnesses), and 0.7% said they were Muslim.

became louder and make dismissive comments about 'the evangelicals', but most ignored them or said they liked them. Scholars have noted that these kinds of redemption messages resonate with people trying to survive a prison sentence or struggling with an addiction (Kerley, Bartkowski, Matthews, & Emond, 2010).

The prevalence of these *culto* songs made the official 'programs' or *charlas* ('chats') in both types of prisons more striking, as they have very similar messages, without the music or collective physical experience of chanting. These were often one-time presentations by 'professionals' – from the prison authorities, other government ministries, or local NGOs or foundations – to a group of dozens of prisoners, usually about building self-discipline – in the guise of 'vocational skills' or 'conflict resolution' or 'anger management' or other familiar behaviour-change buzzwords. The speaker would often shout rhetorical questions or phrases – messages along the lines of,

> When you are frustrated with things going badly in the day, which path will you take? The dark path of rage or the light path of doing the right thing? You will feel free and strong! Let us look at the example of ...

While not explicitly religious, the underlying concepts of individual salvation through repentance are the same – with no place for social or structural causes of problems. But prisoners usually seemed bored in these events. This suggests that the sensory experience – the music, movement, shouting – of the religious events (which have a similar thematic content) is what draws people in.

Music is an important source of relief and pleasure in difficult settings and is often constrained in prisons (Edri & Bensimon, 2018; Herrity, 2019). While I heard other popular Caribbean music, like bachata and reggaeton, regularly in Dominican prisons, religious music was far more prevalent. I asked a few times about this, and the men told me that religious music is uncontroversial and that the officers never restrict it. In the traditional prisons, people played a more typical mix of music, but it sounded more cacophonous because many people were using their individual cell phone speakers. Almost always, religious music was still the loudest and most common.

I did not miss the metallic and technological control sounds of US facilities, but the religious sounds and their paternalistic messages often felt inescapable. Some scholars argue that sounds generated by incarcerated people is a sign of agency by the prisoners (Rice, 2016) and that it is important to understand the 'prison cacophony' in terms of how prisoners themselves interpret and participate in the sounds (Kutzler, 2014). In the Dominican setting, based on what people told me, playing music – including church music – is a way that prisoners try to make suffering more tolerable and to make daily life more similar to their home lives. What is interesting is that the managerial strategies try to convey very similar 'redemption' messages (about individual behavioural change) and could leverage the popularity of religious music. But they seem to entirely miss the central appeal of this experience: the rhythm, melody, and collective vocalisation – perhaps regardless of the content.

Discussion and Conclusion

To an outside researcher more accustomed to North American facilities, the sensory experience of Dominican prisons is dramatically different and more relaxed. 'Regular' social interactions and sounds largely replace the 'typical' sense of being inside a prison – close control by officers, clanging noises, constant cameras. While the new prisons (CCRs) give an initial feeling of the benevolent orderliness of a boarding school, they also hold a mix of raucous noise and strict officer monitoring of prisoner behaviour. The old prisons are viscerally overcrowded and often uncomfortably dank and hard to navigate, but they also feel somehow less constrained. Yet, these are only the superficial sensory experiences.

The design of the Dominican CCRs is based on European concepts of normality in the physical design of prisons (Moran et al., 2016) and on a major role for corrections officers with formal roles and a significant social work orientation (Pinales Matos, 2014). Welcoming colours, rooms for children's visits, encouraging posters, gardens, and sports areas, are meant to spark positive individual behaviour change. Some call this 'therapeutic landscapes' (Williams, 2019); Dominican CCR staff often used similar terms, referring to vocational workshops as 'occupational therapy' and gardening or outdoor work as 'spiritual therapy'. However, scholars of prison design note that even in the most pleasant facilities, incarcerated people still experience pain and deprivation – especially when the social experience does not match the purported principles of the facility (Jewkes, Moran, & Turner, 2019; Shammas, 2014).

When one looks beyond the physical conditions – focussing on the less-visible dimensions of carceral dynamics (Schept, 2014) – the extent of monitoring of minor aspects of people's behaviour in CCRs becomes evident, dissonant with the ever-optimistic slogans on the walls. That the CCR buildings are filled with green gardens, libraries, and music makes it seem less overtly carceral at first. Incarcerated men consistently expressed, though, that the staff surveillance felt arbitrary and intense. The constant sound of religious music and preaching, while different than 'typical' prison noises, feels oppressive to me, but less so to the men who live there. But the fact that men in CCRs feel obliged to hide food and use collective singing as a means of mental escape suggests that they are still experiencing suffering, not rehabilitation, in confinement. In many ways, the rehabilitative trappings of the facilities are mostly a visual veneer over a still-harsh surveillance system that enforces subjugation and individual remorse – not meaningful internal change towards social reintegration.

What is most striking in the traditional prisons is that people talk about appreciating their relative autonomy in daily routines, combined with the *barrio*-like atmosphere of small sales carts, music, games, visits, sex, and drugs – and church, of course. Even the material deprivation and inequality in the physical conditions can seem 'normal' to them, as they put it, because these also exist in the impoverished communities they come from. The surveillance – and order – generated through the prisoners' committee creates some predictability, but it also employs severe punishments.

The contrasts between the initial sensory experience of CCRs versus old prisons reinforces the official story about the differences between them: deprivation versus amenities, chaos versus order. Overall, both kinds of facilities are far more permeable to 'regular' Dominican social life than North American prisons are – and regular life includes poverty and violence, sometimes. Prisoners' accounts of life in old and new prisons suggest that material conditions do matter, and that music and movement are just as important as bed space and toilets. But, ultimately, people's perceptions of how 'humane' their incarceration is seem to hinge mostly on the degree of autonomy they feel they have in the details of their daily lives.

Acknowledgement

This research was supported by the Pierre Elliott Trudeau Foundation and the Social Sciences and Humanities Research Council of Canada.

References

Bergman, M. (2018). *More money, more crime: Prosperity and rising crime in Latin America.* Oxford: Oxford University Press.

Carranza, E. (2012). Situación penitenciaria en América Latina y el Caribe ¿Qué hacer? *Anuario de Derechos Humanos, 8,* 31–66.

Centro de Estudios de Justicia de las Americas (CEJA). (2018). *La Justicia Penal Adversarial en América Latina. Hacia la Gestión del conflicto y la fortaleza de la ley.* CEJA. Retrieved from http://biblioteca.cejamericas.org/bitstream/handle/2015/5621/PUBLICACION_LAJUSTICIAPENLADVERSARIALENAM%c3%89RICALATINA_26122018_ok.pdf?sequence=17&isAllowed=y

Dardel, J. D., & Söderström, O. (2018). New punitiveness on the move: How the US prison model and penal policy arrived in Colombia. *Journal of Latin American Studies, 50*(4), 833–860.

Darke, S. (2018). *Conviviality and survival: Co-producing Brazilian prison order.* Basingstoke: Palgrave Macmillan.

Edri, O., & Bensimon, M. (2018). The role of music among prisoners and prison staff: A qualitative research study. *European Journal of Criminology, 16*(6), 633–651.

Espinoza, O. (2016). *Sistema Penitenciario en Republica Dominicana: Revision Normativa e Institucional. Dominican prison system: Review of laws and institutions.* Unpublished Report. Universidad de Chile.

Fonseca, D. S. (2018). Expansion, standardization, and densification of the criminal justice apparatus: Recent developments in Brazil. *Punishment & Society, 20*(3), 329–350.

Fontes, A. W., & O'Neill, K. L. (2019). La Visita: Prisons and survival in Guatemala. *Journal of Latin American Studies, 51*(1), 85–107.

Gundur, R. V. (2018). The changing social organization of prison protection markets: When prisoners choose to organize horizontally rather than vertically. *Trends in Organized Crime,* 1–19. https://doi.org/10.1007/s12117-018-9332-0

Hancock, P., & Jewkes, Y. (2011). Architectures of incarceration: The spatial pains of imprisonment. *Punishment & Society, 13*(5), 611–629.

Hemsworth, K. (2015). Carceral acoustemologies: Historical geographies of sound in a Canadian prison. In K. M. Morin & D. Moran (Eds.), *Historical geographies of prisons: Unlocking the usable carceral past.* London: Routledge.

Herrity, K. (2019). *Rhythms and routines: Sounding order and survival in a local men's prison using aural ethnography*. Unpublished Ph.D. thesis, University of Leicester.

Jefferson, A. M., & Martin, T. M. (2020). Connecting and disconnection: Exploring prisoners' relations with the outside world in Myanmar. *The Cambridge Journal of Anthropology, 38*(1), 105–122.

Jewkes, Y., Moran, D., & Turner, J. (2019). Just add water: Prisons, therapeutic landscapes and healthy blue space. *Criminology & Criminal Justice*, 1–18. https://doi.org/10.1177/1748895819828800

Kerley, K. R., Bartkowski, J. P., Matthews, T. L., & Emond, T. L. (2010). From the sanctuary to the slammer: Exploring the narratives of evangelical prison ministry workers. *Sociological Spectrum, 30*(5), 504–525.

Kutzler, E. A. (2014). Captive audiences: Sound, silence, and listening in civil war prisons. *Journal of Social History, 48*(2), 239–263.

Liebling, A., assisted by Arnold, H. (2004). *Prisons and their moral performance: A study of values, quality, and prison life*. Oxford: Oxford University Press.

Liebling, A., Hulley, S., & Crewe, B. (2011). Conceptualising and measuring the quality of prison life. In D. Gadd, S. Karstedt, & S. F. Messner (Eds.), *The Sage handbook of criminological research methods* (pp. 358–372). London: Sage Publishing.

Maier, K. H., & Ricciardelli, R. (2019). The prisoner's dilemma: How male prisoners experience and respond to penal threat while incarcerated. *Punishment & Society, 21*(2), 231–250.

Martin, T. M., Jefferson, A. M., & Bandyopadhyay, M. (2014). Sensing prison climates: Governance, survival, and transition. *Focaal, 68*, 3–17.

McClanahan, B., & South, N. (2020). 'All knowledge begins with the senses': Towards a sensory criminology. *British Journal of Criminology, 60*(1), 3–23.

Moran, D., & Jewkes, Y. (2015). Linking the carceral and the punitive state: A review of research on prison architecture, design, technology and the lived experience of carceral space. *Annales de Geographie, 702–703*(2), 163–184.

Moran, D., Jewkes, Y., & Turner, J. (2016). Prison design and carceral space. In Y. Jewkes, B. Crewe, & J. Bennett (Eds.), *Handbook on prisons* (2nd ed.). Abingdon: Routledge.

Morin, K. M. (2013). 'Security here is not safe': Violence, punishment, and space in the contemporary US penitentiary. *Environment and Planning D: Society and Space, 31*(3), 381–399.

Paniagua Guerrero, Y. E. (2015). *Variables de Impacto de Gestion de la Reforma Penitenciaria en la Republica Dominicana y su Influencia en America Latina y el Caribe, 2003–2013.* [*Variables of impact in the management of the prison reform in the Dominican Republic and its influence in Latin America and the Caribbean, 2003–2013*]. Unpublished Master's Thesis, Penitentiary Administration, Universidad Autónoma de Santo Domingo.

Pinales Matos, B. (2014) *Análisis de la selección y formación por competencias como eje transversal del nuevo modelo de gestión penitenciaria – Período 2013–2014.* [*Analysis of the selection and training by competencies as a cross-cutting axis of the new prison management model, 2013–2014*]. Unpublished master's thesis, Economic and Social Sciences FCES 0039, Universidad Autónoma de Santo Domingo.

Rice, T. (2016). Sounds inside: Prison, prisoners and acoustical agency. *Sound Studies, 2*(1), 6–20.

Rubin, A. T., & Reiter, K. (2017). Continuity in the face of penal innovation: Revisiting the history of American solitary confinement. *Law & Social Inquiry, 43*(4), 1604–1632.

Sanhueza, G. E. (2015). Diseño e implementación de la Primera Encuesta de Percepción de Calidad de Vida Penitenciaria en Chile: Propuestas y desafíos para el sistema penitenciario. *Economía y Política, 2*(1), 5–32.

Schept, J. (2014). (Un)seeing like a prison: Counter-visual ethnography of the carceral state. *Theoretical Criminology*, *18*(2), 198–223.

Shammas, V. L. (2014). The pains of freedom: Assessing the ambiguity of Scandinavian penal exceptionalism on Norway's Prison Island. *Punishment & Society*, *16*(1), 104–123.

Skarbek, D. (2014). *The social order of the underworld*. Oxford: Oxford University Press.

Thornton, B. J. (2016). *Negotiating respect: Pentecostalism, masculinity, and the politics of spiritual authority in the Dominican Republic*. Gainesville, FL: University Press of Florida.

Weegels, J. (2018). *Performing prison power, agency and co-governance in Nicaraguan prisons*. Unpublished Ph.D. thesis, University of Amsterdam, Amsterdam.

Wener, R. (2012). *The environmental psychology of prisons and jails: Creating humane spaces in secure settings*. Cambridge: Cambridge University Press.

Williams, A. M. (2019). Therapeutic landscapes. In *International encyclopedia of geography: People, the Earth, environment and technology*. https://doi.org/10.1002/9781118786352.wbieg0138.pub2

Part III

Subverting the Senses

Chapter 9

Sensing and Unease in Immigration Confinement: An Abolitionist's Perspective

Victoria Canning

Lost in the Field

There is fieldwork, and then there is being lost in a field. On the afternoon of an April day in 2017, these ordinarily different experiences – for a criminologist at least – collided. On my way to meet the Governor of one of Denmark's two closed immigration detention centres, I had taken the two-hour train, bus and walking journey to *Ellebæk* centre in North Zealand, and a number of wrong turns. Rather than the fortress-like welcome of grey gates that I had anticipated, I was stood next to a thicket of bushes, listening to the sounds of gunfire. I squinted to be sure I was clear in what I was seeing as an army tank passed in the distance. It was. I was most definitely not in the right place.

Under any other circumstances, this scene might be the opening of a poor comic effort at 'Carry On Criminology'. As reality would have it, there was no comedy in this image. The scene unfolding came the day after I had witnessed the forced removal of a woman and her children from an asylum centre[1] to a deportation centre. Having visited Faiza almost daily for three weeks, including in a mental health institution where she had been sectioned after a suicide attempt, I had arrived for our breakfast of chapatti and eggs. Instead, the room was packed with black bin bags and neighbours from the small block in various states of distress. Faiza and her two children had been given 24 hours' notice that they would

---

[1]People seeking asylum are expected to live in asylum centres, or *asylcenters*, while their claim is under review. This centre was approximately 1.5–2 hours from Copenhagen, and thus around three hours from the deportation Faiza was sent to. They are often in rural and difficult to reach areas of Denmark, a strategy which increased after the surge in applications in 2015.

be leaving the open asylum centre and moved to await deportation at *Sjælsmark*. Rather than challenge the centre staff – the Danish Red Cross – Faiza wanted to fight her case through lawyers once she reached *Sjælsmark*, the place I was now unknowingly standing near surrounded by military practice.

That morning before remains one of the lowest days of my activist research life. In facilitating Faiza's wishes, rather than do what I think should be done and resist movement, I helped her finish packing and looked after her children with her upset neighbours whilst she worked on bureaucracy. To echo Bhatia, I was positioned 'on the edge of academic boundaries and made me feel like a bystander who observes the victims of injustice, but keeps walking without immediate intervention' (2014, p. 167). This was not a regular political stance for me.

The hammer blow came when the leader of the removal operation, a senior centre manager for the Danish Red Cross, put his hand on my shoulder. The only white person witnessing, he reassured me he understood 'that things like this can be difficult to watch'. Whilst Faiza's children were rebuffed for crying, the white witness was comforted by the embodied inflictor of the children's anguish. The feelings seeped well into the next day where I was feeling metaphorically and literally lost in the field.

Sandholm, Sjælsmark and Ellebæk: A Triangle of Variable Confinements

Denmark is a country of contradictions. It is often lauded for freedom and human rights, consistently sitting in the top 10 of the CATO Institute's Human Freedom Index (see CATO, 2018). It is a country which also imposed the 'Jewellery Law' in 2016 to confiscate any valuables over the value of 10,000 kroner, or 1,300 euros from people seeking asylum (Eule, Borelli, Lindberg, & Wyss, 2018).

'Enhanced motivation techniques' refer to a schema of mechanisms to reduce migrant desires to stay in Denmark and thus motivate people to leave. They have been employed in Denmark since 1997 – a way of facilitating coercive self-deportations by encouraging reductions in autonomy and welfare allowances (Eule et al., 2018; Suárez-Krabbe, Lindberg, & Arce, 2018). However, a much harsher policy – and more similar to the UK's 'Hostile Environment' – was later promoted by the former Danish Minister for Immigration, Integration and Housing, Inger Støjberg, who promised to make life 'intolerable' for people on 'tolerated stay[2]'. Also, people who have been accepted as refugees are affected, as a director at a Danish support facility for survivors of torture told me,

> The new policies that have come into place for refugees that have achieved asylum are really tough, they've never been more tough than they are right now and we're seeing levels of poverty that we have never experienced before. I mean this is really devastating.

---

[2]This is when people cannot be removed to a country of origin because they are stateless or are not acknowledged by their state as a citizen. It can also include people who refuse to leave Denmark.

The policies to which he refers were known as *50 Stramninger*, literally 'tightening' or *The 50 Restrictions* (as of April 2019, increased to 114 restrictions).

Denmark is relatively unique in its geographical approach to housing, and controlling, people seeking asylum. It is in the area of North Zealand where I had been lost that most people seeking asylum have to stay in Center Sandholm, a former military barracks, for weeks or months[3] when they first lodge an application for refugee status. Although officially free to come and go with minor checks at the gate, Mahira, a survivor of domestic abuse and false imprisonment, reflected,

> You don't have money and you cannot go out if you don't have money so how do you pay for the bus, for the train? So you cannot go out, you can walk ... but you cannot go out. You can get a ticket, a bus ticket, a bus pass, only if you have an appointment with your doctor.

Mahira's observations struck a parallel of my own when I first visited Sandholm in 2013 (see Canning, 2013). In comparison to closed centres, the aesthetics didn't seem overtly problematic. Spending a day shadowing a psychologist shifted my perspective. The more I walked, the more obvious it became that the (mostly Black and Brown) people using public space were biding time, waiting but not necessarily knowing what for. In a personal sense, this was my first experience of feeling like a spectator in a human zoo, a white bystander wandering with irrelevance between buildings to be shown by other white people how a centre that contains migrant populations can function.

As well as Sandholm and the immigration detention centre[4] Ellebæk (to which we will return later), this triangle of variable forms of confinement includes Sjælsmark, a deportation centre which is also technically open, but which sets curfews and – as I will address below – other violations of autonomy and freedom. All three centres are situated close to military barracks, a point I had forgotten when lost and wondering in the Danish fields that they are isolated in. Indeed, as a psychologist working in one of the centres told me in 2013,

> Sometimes you have military rehearsals around Sandholm. So they stand practising how to throw a grenade like 100 metres away, and all the people in Sandholm are just like, back in the war. People with PTSD ... it's completely absurd.

Her concerns mirrored my own when listening to gunfire from the field in April. Having grown up in Northern Ireland during the 1980s and 1990s, the sound of shots was a nightly presence on the news and, on a number of occasions later on, sounds from a paramilitary affiliated area next to where I lived.

---

[3]Interviews I undertook with staff members working there raised concerns that some were staying for periods of months.
[4]This is referred to as an 'Alien's centre' in Denmark.

I was never in danger, but it is a sound I still deplore. The thought of having been subjected to sustained conflict where death or injury is an imminent possibility, and then secondarily subjected to the sounds of conflict in a 'safe country', seems devoid of sensory recognition or potential for traumatisation. This is a serious trauma risk – people held in confinement can experience sensory trauma from sounds and smells, focussing, for example, on door slamming or keys if held in detention[5] (see Canning et al., 2017; Herrity, 2019). As the psychologist above highlights, it serves to reason that similar risks are run for people detained in this particular triangle of confinement – of arrival, deportation and detention centres. From a criminological perspective, this is in and of itself an extra form of aural penalty and inflicts upon those confined an extra sense of militarisation and indeed conflict. From a zemiological perspective, it is the further *avoidable* infliction of psychological harm on survivors of conflict and persecution, to whom such sensory politics have engrained histories, and thus conflict specific emotional reactions (see Canning, 2019d). Since the area has long been steeped in military history – indeed, both Sandholm and Sjælsmark are former barracks – this is not necessarily a deliberate aural spectacle (Herrity, 2019). Rather it is the outcome of a process of invisibilising the lives, needs and histories of specific migrant groups. It is the product of keeping people at the peripheries of Danish society, and thus a spatial and political lack of consciousness to the lived realities of people who have fled conflict elsewhere.

In any case, people generally spend three to four weeks at Sandholm before they are transferred to an asylum centre, centres dotted around the Danish countryside which house people awaiting the outcome of their claim to refugee status. At the height of the European refugee reception crisis in 2015, Denmark opened multiple new centres. Many of these closed as the number of applications for asylum dropped, with only around nine centres in operation (not including departure or deportation centres) most of which are situated in rural, isolated areas in Jylland.

The Asylum for People Seeking Asylum

Prior to its closure, I spent one month visiting and meeting with women in an asylum centre in rural South West Zealand, where I had met Faiza and where the removal scene above unfolded. The centre was two hours west of Copenhagen by train, with limited support or services specific to asylum or migration in the centre or the town where it was situated. In any case, like Sandholm, the lack of funds people had meant that few were able to exercise much autonomy over meals, although collaborative cooking was a key way to maintain friendships, healthy eating and collegiality.

---

[5] In 2011, in an interview with a psychologist, I was told of a client who had collapsed at the smell of a butchers' shop Manchester having been previously subjected to rape and torture in prison – an insight into the potential for sensory retraumatisation of survivors of abuse in confinement and elsewhere.

There is a peculiar history to this asylum centre with which one is confronted immediately on arrival. Set in peaceful grounds on the outskirts of a rural town, an almost semi-circular congregation of three-storey buildings, the sign above the door welcomed those staying there,

DIANALUND NERVESANATORIUM
DANMARKS FØRSTE FOLKESANATORIUM
FOR NERVØSE
AABNET 1928

This was 'Denmark's first people's sanatorium for the nervous'. Since remembered as 'an oasis for epileptics and sensitive types' (Børgesen, n.d.), the building itself spoke of psychology and psychiatry. Sanitised and separated from the rest of the town, rooms stood in a parallel line, with little evidence of life other than shoes tidily lined up outside, as is custom in Muslim tradition. The long, sanitised corridors were painted bright white, dotted signs to the now non defunct psychologist area on the second floor. It was an historical architectural asylum for people seeking asylum.

In the section I visited and stayed, dedicated to women survivors of abuse, trafficking and violence, the historic contingencies of the psychologised madness of women (Ussher, 2011) were not lost on me. Here I gathered oral histories with women who had experienced violence that ranged from multiple-perpetrator rape, forced prostitution and being burned by men with cigarettes (Canning, 2019a). Yet none of the women I spoke with had had sustained psychological support and were instead experiencing further significant social and emotional harms based on their feelings of isolation and fear of deportation. More importantly, this set of ironic circumstances was not lost on those living there. Jasmine, a trans woman and survivor of significant and multiple abuses joked, 'we're all crazy now. We're all in the asylum now'.

This sense of 'craziness' and spatial isolation also impacted on relationships between women, both positively and negatively. When Faiza was facing deportation, it was women who sat holding her hand on her bed, helping her pack and building solidarity. As they condemned her would-be deporters, they were also facing their own fears of deportation. One woman from Afghanistan pointed out that it may be Faiza today, but it could be anyone else tomorrow. As Jasmine echoed, 'this is not just Faiza – this is all women!'

The other side of this isolating process was also a kind of self-confinement (Jefferson & Gaborit, 2015) and inherent to the continuum of confinement across the variable centres. Some women I spent time with felt they did not want to build friendships because they did not know who they could trust and did not want their business shared amongst the people they lived with, without knowing how long for. And why make friends today when one of you could be deported tomorrow? The result was often spending hours at a time in small rooms. Antonia and her then two-year-old toddler shared a small room – one bed, curtains permanently closed for privacy as 'I don't have friends. I don't say hi to them, they don't say hi to me. I go to my home, they go their home. Because I don't want to have contact with them'. The room in which we sat was no more than 12 foot by 8 foot, with four suitcases leaning precariously on one side. Like many women I met in asylum centres, Antonia chose to stay in her room most for significant periods of time.

In this sense, some aspects felt reminiscent of Charlotte Perkins Gilman's *The Yellow Wallpaper*,[6] an ode to the containment and control of women in the nineteenth century. The heroine, medicalised and confined, eventually chooses confinement over freedom,

> For outside you have to creep smoothly on the ground, and everything is green instead of yellow. But here I can creep smoothly on the floor, and my shoulder just fits in that long smooch around the wall, so I can find my way (Perkins Gilman, 1892, p. 30).

So many women had spent so long in centres, moved from one to another, that breaking the routine of waiting was a complicated feat. The fresh Nordic air and promise of spring – this 'oasis' in the beautiful Danish countryside – very much felt like it belonged to the outside of the centre. Instead, inside many women waited for news, for asylum decisions and for time to creep past.

Extending this, people are technically able to leave asylum centres, but childcare and lack of money reduce the real-life opportunities for this, making Antonia feel that 'they just got you like prisoners in the camp'. Boredom and isolation are common, as she reflected, 'It's so boring … You eat, you sleep, did you come to Europe to come and eat and sleep? Nothing!' Instead, as Antonia suggested, a sense of disorientation can set in,

> Asylum makes people crazy, when you sick in asylum, it's not what you expect you get when you are asylum, sister … In asylum you will not know your whereabouts, where you are going to.

The sensory encapsulation of past loss, compounded by now feeling lost, was a stark reminder that foresight of and power over the future is sometimes a luxury withheld from people whose everyday realities are built on bordered precarity.

When we first met, Antonia had been living in asylum camps awaiting the outcome of her application. She felt that, 'I'm tired of living … by next month, on the 2nd I will complete three years in the camp'. When I last visited a departure centre in August 2018, I asked women where she was. She was living with her child in another centre at the other side of Denmark, bringing their time in camps to almost five years. Unlike most prison sentences, people often stay in asylum centres for indeterminate periods of time. They watch their time disappear. Some

---

[6]Thanks to Lynne Copson for highlighting these comparisons at a time when I could not make sense of what are actually completely rational reactions to existential confinement for women seeking asylum.

children I met had spent all their lives in such centres being moved from asylum centre to deportation centres.[7]

Although I will expand on sensory exposure in closed detention centres later, it is the formally open asylum, departure and deportation centres which are most conflictual in memory. The harms of closed detention are known and well documented, and they are finally part of the criminological imagination (see Bosworth, 2014). We know they exist. Asylum centres, on the other hand, felt like hidden extensions of existential confinement. An asylum for people seeking asylum.

'Just Like a Prison House'

Alongside asylum centres, Denmark has created an additional layer of administrative confinement which aims to facilitate increased deportations: the *udrejsecenter*, a formal term meaning departure, or *udvisningscentre* as known to 'residents', meaning deportation centre. Orchestrated to 'motivate people to leave' (Red Cross staff member), the two centres (*Kærshovedgård* and *Sjælsmark*) are also spatially isolated, with harsh, securitised architecture. Ironically, and unintentionally, my first visit was the day after Faiza had been moved. I had a long-scheduled meeting with the governor, and felt the political conflict of researcher and activist, of academic and human. This was a position I had never been in before. Historically, my research has centred on the lived experiences of people seeking asylum, and access to those who hold powerful positions in the machinery of border controls was secondary to my objectives.

Unlike Sandholm or Dianalund asylum centre, Sjælsmark is more deliberate in its overbearing architecture. Also technically open and a former military barracks, it is guarded by hundreds of metres of wire and curfew begins at 10 p.m. Visiting requires a pass and identification, and visitors are not usually allowed access to the cafeteria, although I was granted access on one day. The living blocks are curiously literally iterative of concentration camps, reflective of its military history. This is not a flippant remark, but an observation reiterated by both people living in the centre (referred to as 'the camp') and people working there. As one LGBIQ asylum support worker reflected, 'I'm always there when the weather is bad at this centre, but it really reminds me of a concentration camp'.[8] The coupling of weather with sensory oppression itself exposes a point I have discussed elsewhere. In Southern Sweden, men from Iraq, Afghanistan and Iran, amongst other

---

[7]One afternoon at the asylum centre, women rushed around to collect gifts and fruit for a woman returning from hospital with her newborn baby. Through the smiles and well wishes, all I could silently wonder was how a government could let a baby and its mother enter this isolated, temporally insecure limbo.

[8]Linguistically from the original German, it is also useful to separate concentration (*Konzentrationslager*) from extermination (Vernichtungslager) since the former was effectively an organised space to contain the unwanted other, those who were 'not German' or 'not German enough'.

countries, told me how the coldness of asylum centres – some placed as far North as the Arctic circle – had kept them from being able to take part in any activities that related to outdoor cultures of communal living (see Canning, 2019c). In Northern England, women told me that they avoided leaving their houses after dark for fear of increased Islamophobic abuses at night. For some women, this meant night began at 3.30 p.m., stemming some of our fundraising activities and limiting campaign meetings to daytime on many occasions (see Canning, 2017). Once more we are reminded of the powerful implications of not sensing the obvious: that spatial isolation, racism, xenophobia or Islamophobia can limit the freedoms of people who are not afforded many of the social freedoms of whiteness or permanency. Whilst this support worker would leave *Sjælsmark* at the end of each day, those held in any of the three centres are left to contend with cold and darkness once Nordic winter comes.

In any case, activity space is limited at the deportation centre and, as one immigration support worker stated, 'at *Sjælsmark* we're discussing whether you should be allowed to do anything because it's supposed to be motivating, motivating people to depart'. Another pointed out that 'The key is cut off people's access to networks, to anything that may make them want to stay'. Existential confinement is built into the politics of the centre: by cutting off the means to have autonomy, it bores and exhausts people into leaving. Faiza equated this a limitation on existence, in that,

> It's just like a prison house, where you can't live according to your own choice, but yes you have a life like you eat, we have some food, some milk and yes we have some also doctors who can check out we are able to live.

The outcomes for some are thus the reduction of existence to a confinement which is not inherent to bricks and mortar or locks and keys, but instead manipulate the decisions people make in the everyday which facilitate either self-confinement within centres (Canning, 2019a, 2019c).

According to Pemberton (2015), autonomy harms 'result from situations where people experience "fundamental disablement" in relation to their attempts to achieve self-actualisation' (p. 29) as well as role-deprivation, or 'the absence of available opportunities to engage in productive activities' (Pemberton, 2015). Although difficult to quantify, autonomy harms are central to the overall degradation of people seeking asylum in Britain, reducing the potential for people to make decisions not only about their own futures – of which they are uncertain whilst the claim to asylum is being processed – but in their current and everyday lives. This form of autonomy harm[9] is also built into the architecture. The blocks of brown-red building are presented in rows and surrounded by wire fencing. Even between the nursery and the living areas is a wire corridor segregating

---

[9]For full discussions on autonomy harm, relational harm and spatial harm, see Canning (2017, 2019a, 2019b, 2019d).

concrete from grass. There is a sense that this is to stop people using space: where the grass might be used for football or picnics, it is kept in the shadow of a wire wall that acts as a visual reminder that this institution may be open but still confines. As the coordinator of a national support service for refugees in Denmark summarised in the context of deportation centres: 'They [deportation centres] are designed to make life as intolerable as possible, to persuade people to go back'. This is 'enhanced motivation techniques' in practice.

It is thus here that the significance of temporal and spatial harms become evident. Rather than neutral by-products, banality, infantilisation and the reduction of autonomy are manifestly deliberate: tools to orchestrate social othering, exclusion and removal (see also Khosravi, 2009; van Houtum & van Naerssen, 2002). This is often at high costs to the individual affected, often incurring emotional, psychological and relational harms.

Formalised Confinement: Immigration Detention in *Ellebæk*

Returning back to the field in April, I was eventually able to find my way to Ellebæk, one of two closed immigration detention centres. Although Denmark does not officially release statistics for the number of people held in detention, it currently has the capacity to detain around 400 people. It is highly securitised and has been administratively operated by Prisons and Probation *(Kriminalforsorgen)* since 1989. No mobile phones are permitted, including by staff or researchers since, as the governor told me, 'according to Danish practice in places where you deprive people of their liberty, mobile phones are a threat to security because of the risk of escapes, to plan escapes'. The architecture is itself restrictive, with small cell-like conditions for people to sleep in, although television and some games are available otherwise.

As the role of *Kriminalforsorgen* is to operate the centres rather than take any involvement in immigration issues, there is a clearer sense of prison regulation in *Ellebæk*. Staff are uniformed, and the interior and exterior of the building is guarded and locked. On entering, and having my phone and laptop removed, the securitisation of the space was palpable. Having remarked on this, I was told I would know the difference if it was a prison, since guards here are allowed to walk small groups of people through the centre. Ironic, I thought, that freedom is reduced to how many guards it takes to move detained people around areas of confinement.

Under successive Aliens Acts (see Eule et al., 2018, Whyte, 2011), Denmark sanctions the use of solitary confinement in immigration detention for up to 28 days for people seen to be problematic or non-compliant with the centre regimes. Although I knew this before entering, these are small, bare rooms with barred windows which, on first entering, I had assumed to be disused parts of the building. Ornamented with disintegrating decor, the walls were strewn with writings from people previously imprisoned there, including a pencilled picture of a mosque and a prayer. The religious serenity of this image contrasted writing I had seen in a corridor earlier, a simple political message: 'fuck your racism'.

As I was shown around the various living sections – again, a wall of whiteness shuffling through mostly Black people – I was struck by the vision of a heavily pregnant woman leaning against a wall, waiting for the phone. In the UK, a country now notorious for indefinite detention and acts of degradation (Girma, Radice, Tsangarides, & Walter, 2014), pregnant women are to be detained only in exceptional circumstances and for no longer than 72 hours (Home Office, 2016). As with the human freedom index discussed earlier, the international image of Denmark as a mecca for both child and women's rights seemed quashed by this one picture. Separately, detention and pregnancy can be significantly stressful. Holding a pregnant woman in confinement seems a degradation unfitting of the international reputation of Denmark as a beacon of rights.

Working on the Inside

Interviewing people in powerful positions is complex, and by no means easy. Before interviewing the governor, we sat with a cup of coffee. As I sat on my chair, coffee in hand, various conversations ensued through which feeling at all comfortable became difficult (see also Jefferson, 2011). The first was the presentation of a box. Covered in flags, it had been painted by a woman detained. Her name on the side read 'Malaika'. This name I recall without needing field notes: Malaika is also the name of a Swahili song which the choir of the migrant rights co-operative I have long worked with sings. It is a song we reflected on in our collective book by Migrant Artists Mutual Aid, 'Strategies for Survival, Recipes for Resistance' and one that we have sang together for more than half a decade. This box, I was told, would be given to the new Director of Prisons as a way to 'to give them a face, that they're not just inmate number 118'. The words 'them' and the idea that anyone should or would ever be a number collided with the intent to humanise this space and the people in it. Meanwhile, who Malaika is or where she might be – deported, detained or released – is separated from the box, itself a tribute to the historical powers of the representation of flags.

Pleased to have a criminologist from the UK, I was then shown the small shelf of books, the standout being 'Understanding Prison Staff' by UK-based criminologists Jamie Bennett, Ben Crewe and Azrini Wahidin (2008). As with interviews I undertook in immigration detention in Sweden (see Canning, 2019c), there is a clear conflation here between expectations of working in prison, and those working in immigration detention. Although based on the (il)logic of confinement, these are not the same entities, and they do not have the same objectives or outcomes (see Bosworth, 2014; Bosworth & Turnbull, 2015). Nonetheless, this opened a conversation on work, at first on the feeling of working in confinement as a staff member but then also with regard to work by people detained.

Ironically, of the three forms of centre outlined in this chapter, it is in formal immigration detention that access to work is easiest for detainees. There are restrictions on working in Denmark whilst seeking asylum. Although in some cases the right to work may be granted after six months under specific conditions,[10] it can

---

[10] These conditions include co-operating with the immigration authorities seeking to process your application for asylum if it is still being processed and/or assisting with the deportation process if you have received a final rejection of your application for asylum or has withdrawn the application (Nyidanmark, n.d.).

be difficult to gain access to the job market. In *Ellebæk*, detained people can apply to work a regular 37-hour week in a large warehouse in one of the wings. For around two euros per hour, as the governor disclosed, people can undertake 'simple work'.

Much has been written about detainee work within prisons (Bennett et al., 2008), but less so in immigration detention. In their analysis of work in immigration detention in the UK, Bales and Mayblin (2018) point to the inequalities in wages. But more over, and crucial to conditions in Ellebæk, is that the opposite of working is mostly doing nothing, and this is how work in detention becomes justified. Under the conditions of work in detention, the reality is a 'state-sanctioned exploitative, coercive and unfree labour amongst a hyper-precarious group of the population' (Bales & Mayblin, 2018, p. 191).

This moved us further into discussion on work in immigration detention, and more political ironies ensued. What did people work at in confinement here? What constituted 'simple work', itself an assumption that people who are detained migrants are inherently unskilled or incapable of complexity? The answers were, to me, astonishing. The first related to penis enlargements,

> one time we had simple work for a company making penis enlargements <chuckles> so they were actually putting together these ... So they would put two or three parts together and then put it in a large box, two or three ... it's very, very simple work because you have to be able to explain it to people from all over the world with all different kind of language backgrounds.

The justification for 'simple work' becomes associated with management and facilitation of multiple nationalities. Since there are people from all over the world, the 'logic' is thus situated in managing complex identities, multiple languages and varied skill sets, therefore gleaning over the inherent internationalised inequalities in borders which would lead people to be confined on the basis of such hierarchies in the first place. The set-up is devoid of recognition of the potential for degradation of people who are religious or who come from backgrounds where sex or sexuality is taboo. It is, after all, just 'simple work'.

On later reflection of the conversation, I thought of the gendered dynamics of how this conversation unfolded. Would the same governor have opened discussion on penis enlargements in the same way had I not been his junior and a woman? Having previously worked in the monitoring of sexual health and pornography websites as a graduate, there is little that can phase me in this context but that might not have been the case for someone else in my situation. Indeed, whilst I was reflecting on power dynamics in the centre, gendered and age dynamics slipped my recognition until long after.[11]

---

[11] In fact, this recognition only surfaced two years later while discussing it with Andrew Jefferson, who I thank for listening to my experiences throughout that time.

It was, however, the next conversation that most reflects the ironies engrained between work for illegalised or deportable migrants in and outside of immigration detention and where the nexus between state and corporate begins to strengthen. As the interviewee went on to reflect,

> We have a workshop with the different kind of jobs coming in; we get a lot of jobs from imports of Italian mineral water, San Pellegrino. We get thousands of bottles of Pellegrino then the inmates here will put a sticker on each of these saying that if you put this into a return machine you will get one Danish krone, because we have this refund system in Denmark. This mark here means that if you put this into a refund machine you will get one-and-a-half krone back. So that's why you don't see … well, you don't see a lot of bottles lying around in nature in Denmark because they are actually worth money.

The 'inmates', again a term most associated with prisons, place a sticker on bottles. Outside of the centre, those bottles are swapped for small amounts of cash. Whilst my focus at the time was the clear issue of state-corporate exploitation of confined migrants, the political irony of it all came to me later. Sitting at the bottom of Nørrebrogade with friends who work on the rights of migrants in Copenhagen, I watched as mostly white bodies sat in the sun drinking beer and soft drinks, all marked with pant stickers. Between the bins weaved Black bodies, picking up the pant. The production line was circular: the pant sticker being placed by confined migrant bodies held on the inside and exchanged by Black bodies confined by poverty on the outside.

Conclusion: Abolishing Illusions

> This is the basic aim of the Kyriarchal[12] System of the prison: 'Returning the refugee prisoners to the land from which they came' (Boochani, 2018, p. 165).

Exactly two years from being lost in the field, in April 2019, Behrouz Boochani joined a group of activist academics[13] in our panel to support the UK launch of his book *No Friend but the Mountains* (2018). Streaming in by video link from Manus Island, where he had already been detained for six years in his

---

[12]Kyriarchy is a term coined by feminist scholar Elisabeth Schüssler Fiorenza (1992) and central to the work of Behrouz Boochani (2018). It refers to social connections between domination, oppression and submission, which Boochani relates directly to his time held in confinement on Manus Island Prison.

[13]The panel was held at the British Sociological Association and was organised by Ala Sirriyeh and included Hannah Lewis, Omid Tofighian (who translated Behrouz's book from Farsi to English) and me.

offshored exile en route to sanctuary in Australia, Boochani highlighted the horrors of life stuck on an island prison. As with his book, he outlined the violence of Australia's deadly border regimes. Queues for toilets, a lack of medical care and constant hunger perforate the sanity of the prison camp.

As we discussed on that April afternoon, at surface level, there is little correlation between such spaces of incarceration and those I reflect on in Denmark. With the exception of *Ellebæk*, the other centres discussed in this chapter do not even formally constitute a form of detention. People were in theory free to come and go. In reality, however, they were far away from the next city and hardly had the financial means to get there. People had to report to the authorities in the detention and deportation centres on a regular basis. Sjælsmark is surrounded by fences, which gives a constant feeling of confinement for the families held there. Children go to school on the territory and their way to school is fenced in. At the time I was there they did not offer many activities, and the constant feeling of uncertainty about the future amongst people living there made it nearly impossible to develop a sense of community. People were allowed to play with a football, but they were not to make teams or tournaments to play against each other. The fracturing of certain futures was and remains built into the physical and political architecture of such a space.

With this said, there is certainly no way that these environments harbour much in the way of comparison to Manus Island. Conditions are not malarial, and the sun does not bake detainees throughout the heat of the day. However, what we must do is scrape this surface to expose the kyriarchy of both existential forms of confinement and formal immigration detention. I have often been told that things could be 'much worse' than they are in Northern European countries. I have been asked if I have heard of Moria on Lesvos, or Dadaab in Kenya. I am assured that these are much worse conditions, and of that physical fact there is little doubt.

However, it is time that immigration detention and other such forms of confinement stop being confronted as a race to the bottom. The control and regulation of migrant bodies inside and outside of detention is part of the same politised kyriarchal continuum that Boochani so powerfully demonstrates. It is one based on whiteness, colonialism and othering. Places like this are designed to make people's stay intolerable and, in the end, freedom is often exposed an illusion. The only ethical, anti-racist way forward is situated in their abolition.

Acknowledgements

Many thanks to Faiza, Mahira, Antonia, Jasmine, Asma and Nour. Thanks to all practitioners for their insight, to colleagues at the Danish Institute Against Torture and to Andrew M. Jefferson for insight and discussion. Thanks also to Andrew Douglas and Lotte Bælum Mortensen and Alice Minor. This research is funded by the Economic and Social Research Council, grant number ES/NO16718/1.

References

Bales, K., & Mayblin, L. (2018). Unfree labour in immigration detention: Exploitation and coercion of a captive immigrant workforce. *Economy and Society*, *27*(2), 191–213.

Bennett, J., Crewe, J., & Wahidin, A. (2008). *Understanding prison staff*. Oxon: Routledge.

Bhatia, M. (2014). Researching 'bogus' asylum seekers, 'illegal' migrants and 'crimmigrants'. In K. Lumsden & A. Winter (Eds.), *Reflexivity in criminological research: Experiences with the powerful and the powerless* (pp. 162–178). Basingstoke: Palgrave Macmillan.

Boochani, B. (2018). *No friend but the mountains: The true story of an illegally imprisoned refugee*. London: Picador.

Bosworth, M. (2014). *Inside immigration detention*. Oxford: Oxford University Press.

Bosworth, M., & Turnbull, S. (2015). Immigration detention and criminalization. In S. Pickering & J. Ham (Eds.), *The Routledge handbook of crime and migration studies*. Oxon: Routledge.

Børgesen, I. M. (n.d.). The Filadelfia Colony and Dianalund Sanatorium, Kulturav. Retrieved from http://www.kulturarv.dk/1001fortaellinger/en_GB/the-filadelfia-colony-and-dianalund-sanatorium. Accessed on September 24, 2019.

Canning, V., Caur, J., Gilley, A., Kebemba, E., Rafique, A. & Verson, J. (2017). *Migrant Artists Mutual Aid: Strategies for Survival, Recipes for Resistance*. London: Calverts Publishing.

Canning, V. (2013). Illusions of freedom: The paradox of border confinement. Oxford border criminologies. Retrieved from https://www.law.ox.ac.uk/research-subject-groups/centre-criminology/centreborder-criminologies/blog/2013/10/illusions-freedom. Accessed on September 24, 2019.

Canning, V. (2017). *Gendered harm and structural violence in the British asylum system*. Oxon: Routledge.

Canning, V. (2019a). *Reimagining refugee rights: Addressing asylum harms in Britain, Denmark and Sweden*. Bristol: Migration and Mobilities. Retrieved from http://www.statewatch.org/news/2019/mar/uk-dk-se-reimagining-refugee-rights-asylum-harms-3-19.pdf

Canning, V. (2019b). Degradation by design: Women seeking asylum in Northern Europe. *Race & Class*, *61*, 46–64.

Canning, V. (2019c). Keeping up with the Kladdkaka: Kindness and coercion in Swedish immigration detention. *European Journal of Criminology*. Retrieved from https://journals.sagepub.com/doi/abs/10.1177/1477370818820627. Accessed on August 7, 2019.

Canning, V. (2019d). Zemiology at the border. In A. Barton & H. Davies (Eds.), *Ignorance, power and harm* (pp. 183–203). Basingstoke: Palgrave Macmillan.

Eule, T. G., Borelli, L. M., Lindberg, A., & Wyss, A. (2018). *Migrants before the law: Contested migration control in Europe*. Switzerland: Palgrave Macmillan.

Girma, M., Radice, S., Tsangarides, N., & Walter, N. (2014). *Detained: Women asylum seekers locked up in the UK*. London: Women for Refugee Women.

Herrity, K. Z. (2019). *Rhythms and routines: Sounding order in a local men's prison through aural ethnography*. Unpublished Ph.D. thesis, University of Leicester, Leicester.

Home Office. (2016). New time limit planned for pregnant women in detention. Retrieved from https://www.gov.uk/government/news/new-time-limit-planned-for-pregnant-women-in-detention. Accessed on September 13, 2019.

Jefferson, A. M. (2011). Comparisons at work: Exporting 'exceptional norms'. In T. Ugelvik & J. Dullum (Eds.), *Nordic prison practice and policy, exceptional or not? Exploring penal exceptionalism in the Nordic context* (pp. 100–117). Oxon: Routledge.

Jefferson, A. M., & Gaborit, L. S. (2015). *Human rights in prisons: Comparing institutional encounters in Kosovo, Sierra Leone and the Philippines*. Basingstoke: Palgrave Macmillan.
Khosravi, S. (2009). Sweden: Detention and deportation of asylum seekers. *Race & Class, 50*(4), 38–56.
Nyidanmark. (n.d.). Conditions asylum seekers must meet in order to work. Retrieved from https://www.nyidanmark.dk/en-GB/Words%20and%20Concepts%20Front%20Page/US/Housing/Conditions_for_occupation_of_an_asylum_seeker. Accessed on September 12, 2019.
Perkins Gilman, C. (1892). *The yellow wallpaper*. Sweden: Wisehouse Classics.
Pemberton, S. (2015). *Harmful Societies: Understanding Social Harm*. Bristol: Policy Press.
Schüssler Fiorenza. (1992). *But she said: Feminist practices of biblical interpretation*. Boston, MA: Beacon Press Books.
Suárez-Krabbe, J., Lindberg, A., & Arce, J. (2018). *Stop killing us slowly: A research report on the motivation enhancement measures and criminalisation of rejected asylum seekers in Denmark*. Roskilde: Roskilde University.
Ussher, J. M. (2011). *The madness of women: Myth and experience*. Oxon: Routledge.
van Houtum, H., & van Naerssen, T. (2002). Bordering, ordering and othering. *Tijdschrift voor Economische en Sociale Geografie, 93*(2), 125–136.
Vásquez, I. & Porcnik, T. (2018). The Human Freedoms Index 2018. https://www.cato.org/sites/cato.org/files/human-freedom-index-files/human-freedom-index-2018-revised.pdf, CATO Institute, last accessed 26th October 2020.
Whyte, Z. (2011). Enter the myopticon: Uncertain surveillance in the Danish asylum system. *Anthropology Today, 27*(3), 18–21.

Chapter 10

Rumbling Stomachs and Silent Crying: Mapping and Reflecting Emotion in the Sensory Landscape of the Courthouse

Lisa Flower

> Walking into the courthouse using the main entrance for the first time, I notice there is a document torn into shreds on the ground. It is ripped into pieces and is spread out over several of the courthouse steps. It seems to me to be representative of emotions in the courtroom – only their trace should remain. The violent act of ripping up the document – the emotional content of leading up to the act is gone, yet visible in the remaining evidence. Soon to be cleared away and forgotten. (Field note)

The sensory landscape of the Swedish courtroom is subdued. It is a scene of silent sobbing and subtle sentiments. Visible displays of outrage may be glimpsed on the steps of the courthouse as the opening excerpt from my field note indicates; however, once inside the courtroom, emotional expressions tend to be more muted. As a courthouse ethnographer, one becomes accustomed to the subtle weeping of plaintiffs and the louder crying of defendants. One picks up the occasional smell of alcohol emanating from the public gallery which frequently consists of the defendants' and plaintiffs' friends and family. One also becomes attuned to the smell of sweat wafting through the throng of the waiting room in highly publicised cases where everyone is jostling to enter the courtroom. The rustling of a tissue, gripped hard in the hand of a plaintiff's mother can, at times, be the only sound that is heard in the courtroom. This, in turn, makes the work of a courtroom ethnographer a sensory smörgåsbord.

Yet despite this bounty of sensory empirical material – a treasure trove of jewels, contributing to a richer and deeper understanding of courthouse interactions and performances, I can confess that until now, I have only given nominal attention to how these sensorial encounters impact on my understanding and experience of criminal trials, as well as those of courthouse-goers and legal professionals. Or perhaps, more accurately, I have not given each of the senses equal attention. This comes as a rude awakening for me. After all, ethnography is about using the senses to make sense of things (Atkinson, Delamont, & Housley, 2008, p. 179). Thus, in writing this chapter, I have been forced to come face to face with my own blind spot.

It comes therefore as a small comfort to discover that I am not alone in having such a flaw. For instance, Emeritus Professor in Social Anthropology, Terence Marchand (2015) notes that, in his work on the senses and place-making, he discovered that the participants' emotional expressions and displays 'formed merely a backdrop to what they did and said' thus leading Marchand to attempt to 'redress the balance of "emotion"' in his earlier writings (p. 67). It seems that, as a researcher of emotions or a researcher of the senses, one risks falling into a trap of either not sensing emotions or not emoting senses.

Similar to Marchand's quest to re-dress the absence of emotions in his previous work, in this chapter, I revisit my field notes written from ethnographic fieldwork conducted of over 50 criminal trials at four district courts in Sweden in order to map the sensorial experiences that construct the emotional landscape of court spaces, and I highlight the sensory textures of my own research experience (see Åkerström, Jacobsson, & Wästerfors, 2006, for a discussion on reanalysing empirical material). The ethnographer, Professor Sarah Pink (2015), writes that the senses should be attended to throughout the research process (p. 7), therefore I consider the ensuing reanalysis to be another step in my research process. In this way, I hope to make sense of the emotional landscape of court spaces by reflecting on my sensory experiences in this process (Hervik, 1994; Rudie, 1994).

My focus is thus on how this scene is formed and shaped, not only by emotions but also by the senses. Indeed, it is by lifting culturally significant sensory phenomena that the emotional landscape is understood and constructed (cf. Atkinson et al., 2008). I will begin by mapping the landscape of the courthouse by describing my sensory experiences, in particular the contrasts between inside and outside the courtroom. I will then go on to reflect upon the sensory experiences of my own emotions that have arisen in the field. However, before embarking on this, I would like to address the emotion ethnographer's blind spot more directly.

Coming to One's Senses as a Courthouse Ethnographer

The research field of emotion and law, which my work fits into, has focussed – amongst other things – on presenting legal professionals as emotional beings who are expected to reflect upon and regulate their emotions to ensure that they are appropriate to the situation and their role within (Hochschild, 1983). This is a process aimed at upholding the illusionary dichotomy between law and emotion – we want to believe that the law is exercised *sine ire et studio* – without anger and passion (Bandes, 1999; Bergman Blix & Wettergren, 2018; Flower, 2019; Maroney, 2006, 2011; Weber, 1921/1978). This process attempts to silence the emotions of legal professionals thereby rendering emotions invisible and shaping legal professionals' emotional performances into muted displays of subtlety (Flower, 2019).

Indeed, as may be apparent from the opening paragraph of this article – the most immediate way in which the emotional landscape of the courthouse is tangible is by observing the non-legal actors present. The reader may note that upon reading and picturing these scenes, he or she inscribes an emotional content to them. Perhaps one of sadness. What is important here is that this emotional interpretation is based on the sensory description presented. It is the sight and sound of sobbing, the smell of bodies and the like, that leads the reader to understand the courthouse as an emotional sphere.

The sensory thus leads to the emotional. Indeed, this is apparent in the definition of emotion – the labelling of emotions is linked to the context as well as the display and recognition of expressive gestures (Thoits, 1985).

However, when we attempt to construct a valid knowledge of the courthouse, specific sensorial aspects are often neglected in law and emotion research (Hastrup & Hervik, 1994, pp. 1–2). We fail to include the full range of our 'ethnographic sensorium' (Atkinson et al., 2008, p. 180). When the senses are mentioned, the sight and the sound of the courthouse prevail, to the detriment of the remaining three – the smells, tastes and tactile feel of entering a courthouse, of taking part in a criminal trial and so on. Indeed, much of the previous research on courthouses has focussed on language (for instance, Conley & O'Barr, 1990) which is perhaps not surprising given the principle of orality – that all evidence to be considered must be orally presented in Swedish courts (see Bens, 2018, for more discussion).

A reason for this could be that we assign different values to our senses which in turn influences how we conceive of the world (Classen, 1993, p. 3). The legal sphere and, indeed, many areas of sociological research triumph the visual and the audio. We may note the décor of the courtroom but not lift the lumpiness of a waiting room bench which adds to an already heightened feeling of discomfort for those taking part in a trial, particularly for the first time. We might note the quietness of the gallery but not present the taste of vending machine coffee – a bitterness that is the source of small talk, shared experience and feelings of togetherness. A taste that may conjure up memories of other bureaucratic settings (see Pink, 2015, pp. 107–110; Seremetakis, 1994). Such sensory reflections are rarely dwelled upon or explored more deeply, rather they are seen more as a way of setting the scene on which the drama is played (Goffman, 1959). Instead we need to consider them as 'foreground phenomena, rather than things in the background' (Atkinson et al., 2008, p. 180). We need to bring them into ethnographic focus.

In the next section, I will take the reader on a virtual tour of the courthouse in order to present the sensory landscape – a landscape which both constructs and reconstructs the courthouse as a ceremonial place where justice is exercised impartially and neutrally – where emotions are associated not with legal professionals but with lay participants. I have previously written about this landscape in terms of an emotional regime (Flower, 2019; Reddy, 2001) – an overarching framework of rules guiding our emotions and interactions. I would now like to revisit how I came to this understanding by focussing on the sensorial experiences of an emotional regime, which I will now consider in terms of an emotional landscape.

Mapping the Emotional Landscape of the Courthouse

I have previously shown that the courthouse can be divided into emotional spaces, each with its own rules regarding emotional expression and ways of interacting (Flower, 2019; cf. Marchand, 2015, for a presentation on the contrast of pilgrims' emotional displays related to the space they are in). I will now show the sensory contrasts. By focussing on such contrasts, it is possible to construct these emotional places in the landscapes (see also Walenta, 2020).

The Courthouse Building

The initial sensory impression one receives of the courthouse is the sight of its exterior. In Sweden, there is a vast range of styles of courthouse, stretching from Malmö's District Court built in the middle of the fifteenth century, to Stockholm's Vasa-style courthouse constructed in 1915, to the 1960 dull brick monstrosity of Eksjö, to Lund's copper-laden architecture-award-winning building completed in 2018. I find that standing before the older, stately buildings and seeing their grandeur can be slightly imposing yet also comforting – justice has been sought here for many centuries. I feel a sense of tradition, but with a hint of stuffiness. In contrast, several of the courthouses in Sweden scream 'bureaucracy' with boring brick exteriors. They stand in stark contrast to the newer buildings, with their shiny glass walls and quirky angles, which convey that the justice system is modern and contemporary.

Even though these styles of courthouse may differ, they have all tend to have signs on their front denoting that the building is a district court, for instance, *Stockholms Tingsrätt* (Stockholm's District Court) or perhaps just *Tingsrätten* (District Court). Similarly, many courthouses bear a coat of arms – either the traditional coat of arms for all Swedish courts which depicts the scales of justice balanced on a sword or a combination of this together with the district's coat of arms – for instance, Malmö has a griffin head underneath the sword-balancing scales of justice. Each coat of arms is topped with a bejewelled crown adorned with a version of the Swedish flag and a crucifix.

These signs and images, together with the styles of building can be seen as an attempt to bring forth an expectation that justice will be done in a Weberian bureaucratic manner *sine ire et studio* – without anger and passion, or in other words, rationally and without emotion (Weber, 1921/1978). They are a first step towards constructing the emotional landscape of the courthouse. In short, a district court usually looks like a place where official business will be impartially conducted. However, these buildings may also symbolise a cynicism in the criminal justice system for others or a distrust that justice will be executed, stemming from previous encounters or interactions with the system and which shape one's feelings towards it (Collins, 2004). Such feelings may then be triggered by seeing the symbol of the courthouse.

Feeling and Sensing Security

The first sight after entering is commonly at least one security guard who asks for one's pockets to be emptied and one's bag to be placed on the conveyor belt of the security scanner. The uniform the guards wear echoes the garb of police officers – with handcuffs and baton (but without the police officer's service weapon). Any weapon, or indeed anything remotely weapon-like, is not permitted in the courthouse and is thus confiscated and returned on leaving the courthouse (I have had such deadly objects as a bicycle helmet and a bottle of wine confiscated and returned upon departure). Coats should also be removed. One then walks through a metal detector, collects one's bag (minus lethal weapon) and continues into the courthouse and its waiting areas. The sensation of removing one's coat and placing one's bag on the conveyor belt brings strong associations and muscle memory from the security process airport departure gates. It signals the gravity of a courthouse and can produce feelings of nervousness, perhaps even irritation. The nerves arise from the irrational worry that one has forgotten about the deadly weapon at the bottom of one's computer bag. The irritation stems from the delay in going about one's business. This may be compounded by the sight of a prosecutor or defence lawyer being waved through the scanners by the guards.

The sight of the scanner, the guards, their weapons, the metal detector – all of these construct the courthouse as a space that could be dangerous and violent. It thus awakes feelings of fear. It is also a space where we – the non-legal actors – are not treated in the same way as legal professionals. We see that they are key players – ones who can be trusted to not bring in weapons. People whose routine visits to court provides them with a sense of belonging. The rest of us are outsiders – treated with respect and courtesy but nevertheless a source of suspicion. I will now continue my exploration of the courtroom by comparing the spaces inside and outside the courtroom in the next section.

Contrasting the Atmospheres Inside and Outside the Courtroom

In sociology, we look for deviations in order to reveal the everyday rules of interaction because, as the interactionist and ethnographer Phil Strong (1988) writes, '[h]ow does the fish get to notice that it is surrounded by water (since it is all the time)? Only when it is hooked out on to dry land' (p. 236). This is often achieved by using contrasts, therefore, in order to continue mapping the courthouse's emotional landscape, I will now focus on juxtaposing the sensory experiences inside the courtroom with those spaces outside the courtroom. I have already touched upon the foyer, but I will now also include other zones such as corridors and waiting areas.

Noises

One of the most noticeable, yet diffuse ways in which these areas differ is in terms of atmosphere – 'the "air" or tone of a social environment' (Wästerfors, 2018, p. 320). This tone is not detached from the social environment, that is, from things, people and their constellations, rather it emerges from encounters and interactions between people and their surroundings (see also Böhme, 1993, p. 122; Pink & Leder Mackley, 2016, p. 176). There is thus a strong sensory element to atmospheres, just as there is simultaneously an intrinsic collective emotional component being produced and reproduced, which cannot be reduced to the individuals and their bodies they emerge from (Anderson, 2009, p. 80; Collins, 2004).

One sensorial aspect that contributes to the construction of an emotional landscape's atmosphere is what we hear – both sounds and noise. As I sit here writing this in a library, I am listening to the *sound* of music in my headphones in order to drown out the *noise* of nearby students discussing Tinder. Noise, as Professor of Media and Communications, David Hendy writes, is thus unwanted, irritating and distracting (see Hendy, 2014; Parker, 2011, pp. 964–965, for a discussion on other aspects of 'acoustic jurisprudence'). Upon entering the courthouses – one is usually surrounded by sporadic background noise however it tends to remain at a muted level. This may consist of security guards chatting to each other or visitors, or the quiet murmurings between defence lawyer and client. Whispering is the norm with louder levels permitted next to the vending machines. Conversation in an otherwise normal tone of voice is unusual. There is no music being played or radio in the background. Occasionally, laughter may be heard – between legal colleagues, for instance, however even this tends to be hushed (I will return to laughter shortly). This near-silence is striking – symbolising the formality and gravity of events unfolding within the walls of the courthouse (see Atkinson et al., 2008, pp. 196–200). It contrasts not only with the sounds of traffic, shouting, birds, the wind, whatever it may be that may be heard outside the courthouse. It is a silence that grows even more deafening after one has entered a courtroom and proceedings are underway marking the ceremonial quality of trials. The silence of a criminal trial is the silence of a funeral. It is a sacred silence. The all-consuming, heart-wrenching quietness of a plaintiff who is trying to find the words to describe how she felt when she realised her children could see as her husband slammed her against the floor is one of the loudest silences ever heard. The sacredness of these silences should not be broken by whispering to one's neighbour in the gallery for instance. Even shifting in one's chair is avoided. To do any of these things would be a sign of disrespect, just as at a funeral. This is a shared understanding by all those watching that an intrusion of noise would be 'a major moral pollution' (Atkinson et al., 2008, p. 199).

The transition from the near-silence of the waiting room to the total silence that can be heard in the courtroom is marked by an announcement over the courthouse's speakers: 'The court is now in session for the main hearing in the case between the prosecutor and Anders Larsson'. Upon this announcement, it is now permitted to enter the courtroom. In trials with a large number of members of the public and journalists present, a hush falls over the gathering in the final seconds before the announcement is made, in preparation for the formality ahead. This transition and preparation for shift in landscapes is shown in the following extract which is taken from my field notes whilst waiting to go in to a murder trial that has been highly publicised beforehand and which has therefore attracted an unusual amount of attention (I am usually one of a small handful of people in the public gallery at trials):

> There are around 30–40 people standing near the entrance to the courtroom. I was one of the first to arrive and I am standing

opposite the door. People are chatting with each other in normal tones of voice. Next to me are three reporters who are talking about various cases they have covered and what they think will happen during the day's proceedings. The trial is due to begin at 9am and at 8:59am the chatting dies out and there is quiet in the waiting room. People stand a little stiffer, many facing towards the door. It is eerily quiet, everyone waiting for the announcement over the loudspeaker that the trial is going to begin and that we are permitted in to the courtroom. When the announcement is made at 9am, the little light on the wall by the courtroom's door switches from red to green showing that proceedings are underway. People being to push each other slightly to get through the door and I feel like I have to push back in order to enter. Although I was one of the first to arrive, I end up in the midst of the crowd of people jostling to get in. (Field note)

As I stood amongst reporters, relatives, friends and other members of the general public, there was a distinct shift in mood with the atmosphere becoming heavier as the hands of the clock ticked closer towards the doors. Indeed, this was the only sound heard. The atmosphere changed from one befitting a waiting room, to one befitting a courtroom, despite the same room consisting of the same things, people and their constellations (cf. Bens, 2018). How did I observe this? From bodies, laughter and rumbling stomachs amongst other things, as I will now explain.

Atmospheres and Bodies

The sociologist, Professor David Wästerfors (2018), writes about feeling the expectation to sit up straight when he conducted fieldwork in a classroom, in contrast to the expectation to sit in a more relaxed manner when his fieldwork took him to a nursing ward. I felt a similar expectation when sitting in the courtroom, in contrast to sitting in the waiting room and I became alert to how my body can convey the 'wrong' message (Goffman, 1959). For instance, in my field notes of an attempted murder trial I write,

> I suddenly realise that I am very aware of not leaning forwards too much, particularly when the footage of the attack is being shown. I do not want the family members to misconstrue it as morbid fascination or that I am watching the trial as a form of entertainment. (Field note)

As a researcher we can therefore trace our feelings regarding what is expected of us – our bodies, our actions, how we should position ourselves, where we should look and so on, in order to reveal the atmosphere. In this way, an atmosphere may be wordless and elusive, but it can also be tangible and visible.

As already noted, the noise levels subsided in the waiting room becoming quieter as the chatting died out. Bodies changed orientation – switching from being positioned towards those one had been interacting with to being positioned towards the door of the courtroom. Bodies also became less relaxed – those who had been resting on windowsills or sitting on sofas stood up. Backbones straightened, necks stiffened. Bodies became even more tightly packed as the throng crowded to enter through the narrow doorway. Even though there is jostling to enter the courtroom, there is still a civilised control at hand – this is not the wild elbow-pushing of a Christmas sale, but more of a nudging to enter, stemming from a fear of not securing a seat. In such a legal sphere where order and rules abound, this relative disorder is jarring.

We can furthermore see that the straightening of one's back is synecdochal – it stands for the formality of the courtroom which will soon be entered (Hammersely & Atkinson, 1983/2007). It stands for the respect that should be shown to the official ritual of a criminal trial. It is also a posture seen in the courtroom. The courtroom is a place for straight backs, with hands in laps, movements controlled and measured for all – particularly legal professionals but also for those watching and the non-legal participants. The only deviant player to be seen is the defendant who may slouch, wave his or arms around or place their head on the desk. The following excerpt is taken from my field notes of an assault trial and depicts the difference in courtroom postures between legal professionals and defendants.

> The defence lawyer has sat still throughout the presentation of facts, only moving to remove her glasses and replace them at one point or shifting slightly in her chair. When the witness is being questioned by the prosecutor the defence lawyer frowns slightly or raises her eyebrows occasionally. When the witness claims that her friend (the plaintiff) told her that she was being abused by the defendant the defence lawyers says quietly yet forcibly, 'what?' and looks at the judge, rocking forwards and backwards in her chair slightly. (Field note)

We see in this excerpt that a protest, the Swedish 'objection!' is accomplished by the defence lawyer with a small frown, a slight rocking back and forth in her chair and a hushed comment. She embodies the control and restraint of law, conveying protest in subtle ways (Flower, 2019). This contrasts in the following excerpt from a theft trial where the defendant vehemently denies the crime. We join proceedings as the defendant is being questioned by the prosecutor.

> The defendant waves his arms around, leaning forwards and backwards in his chair. His movements are large, body suddenly leaning towards the judge before just as suddenly rocketing back in his chair again. His voice is loud, far louder than the prosecutor who is asking questions, and even louder than the judge who is forced to interrupt him to ask for clarifications. The defendant then puts

his head on the desk in front of him and states that he cannot answer the question of whether he has taken the clothing he is accused of stealing. He starts to cry. He makes no noise but tears start to fall and he wipes them away, sniffing loudly a couple of times. His defence lawyer does not look at him and remains sitting upright in his chair, leafing through the papers on the desk in front of him. (Field note)

The defendant's whole body is involved in his protest – unconstrained by the rules of interaction in the same way that the defence lawyer's is in the previous example (Goffman, 1959). The defendant's protest takes up more space and is less controlled in his body movements. He embodies anger and outrage. However, it is important to note that the defence lawyer also embodies anger, but it is anger appropriate to the Swedish courtroom – a controlled and civilised anger (Flower, 2016, 2019). This is also reflected in their voices – the defence lawyer's is controlled, a protest made quietly yet forcibly. The defendant's, in contrast, is loud and raw. It is in this contrast that we see the different unwritten rules in play for legal professionals and non-legal actors, and it is in this contrast that we also see the emotional playing field. For instance, towards the end of the second excerpt, the defendant begins to cry but is not comforted by his lawyer – there is no calming hand on the arm, no holding of hands. Touching is avoided and is indeed something that I rarely observed between defence lawyer and defendant in the courtroom. This contrasts with the waiting areas and corridors where there may be more physicality – a clap on the shoulder for instance. We see therefore that there are boundaries outlining how roles may be accomplished relating to space (see also Crouch, 2001). These boundaries shape how we may sound, how we may touch each other and how we may move around. They shape not only what is emotionally appropriate but also what is sensorially appropriate (Flower, 2019). This is particularly evident, not only when it comes to touching but also regarding laughing.

The Sound of Laughter, Crying and Rumbling Stomachs

Throughout my fieldwork, I have only heard laughter on a handful of occasions; however, I have seen silent laughter more often. Audible laughter tends to come from the gallery – it is unusual for legal professionals in Sweden to laugh loudly during a trial. There might be a polite chuckle at a convivial joke that has been made, for instance, during one criminal trial I observed, the defence lawyer joked that the prosecutor looked better than he did. This was met with a polite ripple of chuckling. It is more common that audible laughter stems from the gallery. This laughter is usually a scornful or incredulous laugh in response to a defendant's claims – a short outburst of disbelief. Finally, I have also observed inaudible laughter between defence lawyer and defendant, a brief, soundless mirth. This is by no means an exhaustive presentation of laughter; however, it helps towards our understanding of the emotional landscape of the courtroom.

The sensory experience of laughter is similar to that of crying. Tears may be cried – tears of sorrow, regret, shame or hatred; however, the tears in Swedish courtrooms tend to remain composed – sobbing is either noiseless or muffled. Noses are wiped or blown discretely. This contrasts to crying in waiting areas which may be louder and less contained. The following excerpt highlights contrasts in crying and is from my field notes of a murder trial of a mother and her baby. We join proceedings as a family member is entering the courtroom and then begins to describe the impact the murders have had on the rest of the family:

> She walks into the courtroom with her head up, dressed head-to-toe in black – even black hairclips. She holds a glass of water and is having difficulty swallowing (like she might be sick any second). She describes the victim as her 'absolute best friend' and tells the court that her mother's physical and mental health have deteriorated rapidly because of the knowledge that 'we are going to live our whole lives' without the victim. She begins to cry silently, wiping tears away discretely and wiping her nose with a tissue. Several people in the gallery start to cry, also quietly, unobtrusively. The witness takes a deep breath and continues.
>
> After she has given evidence, the defendant (who has been listening in an adjoining room as the witness did not want him to be present in court when she was there) returns to the courtroom. He blows his nose loudly. (Field note)

This may seem like a trifling incident – the defendant blowing his nose – however, the noise of it is jarring. It is a deviant noise, one rarely heard from within the courtroom although the reader may remember from the excerpt with the crying defendant, that he also sniffs loudly. Such sniffing breaks the ceremonial silence and borders on the morally offensive (Atkinson et al., 2008) – perhaps particularly because it stems from the defendant. The defendant thus falls into the category of one who should not make a noise, in contrast to the plaintiff – the victim of the crime – who has a wider and louder soundspace for manoeuvre (cf. Rose, Nadler, & Clark, 2006).

Another everyday noise that risks breaking the fragility of such sacred moments is the loud rumbling of a hungry stomach. This is indeed a noise in accordance with Hendy's (2014, p. xi) definition: 'a sound that someone somewhere doesn't want to be heard'. The following excerpt is taken from an attempted murder trial at around mid-morning.

> I feel hungry during proceedings and attempt to stifle my stomach rumbling. I hear other stomachs rumbling in the gallery. It feels disrespectful to think about food during the trial and even eating during the break feels wrong. This is a murder trial, not a day out. (Field note)

Rumbling Stomachs and Silent Crying 169

There is an expectation that bodily needs, such as hunger, and bodily noises, such as sniffing, should be dampened or controlled in the courtroom. It is perhaps a stretch of the analytical imagination to suggest that the muting of these needs reflects the law's strive for justice to be executed impersonally, combined with a demonstration of the court's power to silence even our bodily noises; however, it is less of a stretch to understand the courtroom as a quiet space, in comparison to the relatively less restrained waiting areas (cf. Hendy, 2014, for a discussion on noise, power, control and anxiety). The courtroom is a space where only the voices of those involved in the trial should be heard. It is a space that curtails the body and its bodily needs (cf. Crouch, 2001). In the next section, I move on to a short reflection of my sensory experiences and their emotional counterparts.

Reflecting on My Own Emotional and Sensory Experiences

My starting point in this section is that my emotions are always present – even when conducting fieldwork as a qualitative researcher. However, the researcher's emotions are often seen as an impediment to good science and our senses are often undervalued. In this section, I attempt to bring together these two aspects: emotions and senses to reflect upon my work and my role as a researcher.

Shame and Intimacy

I begin this section by using the following extract from my field notes from an assault trial – where the defendant is accused of multiple assaults on his partner – to explore the various emotional hurdles I have faced as a researcher, as well as the ways in which reflecting on my sensory experiences can lead to me making sense of the situation. This was one of the first trials I observed as part of my doctoral dissertation on the emotion work of defence lawyers, and my discomfort is immediately evident:

> I feel like a peeping Tom, like I don't belong here. Is it right that such highly personal and private events should be open to the general public? It must be hard enough for all involved without having an audience. The plaintiff has to sit in the same room as the man who abused her during the course of two years. She has to listen to her friends and family witness her behaviour, how she pushed them away, how she didn't listen to their advice. There must be feelings of shame present in the plaintiff, how does an audience affect these feelings? How must it feel to sit opposite the man who did this to her and see how ashamed he is? To see someone you have loved attempting to hide in plain view of everyone? I discover that, immediately, I have taken the side of the plaintiff. I believe that the accused is guilty – an innocent man wouldn't sit slumped in his chair, trying to hide his face behind a hat and his hood surely? I try not to look at the plaintiff too much. I don't want her to think that I am judging her or that I am there for some kind of

> entertainment. This is also true of the defendant. I try not to look
> at him either, instead focusing on the defence lawyer. (Field note)

Here there are a number of emotions that have arisen that I reflect upon in the moment and after the trial. I feel 'vicarious shame' (Welten, Zeelenberg, & Breugelmans, 2012) – even though I am not the plaintiff or defendant sitting in a courtroom full of strangers who are privy to my most intimate secrets, I place myself in the plaintiff's shoes and experience the threat to self that a criminal trial may constitute. I feel her shame of being negatively evaluated by others for not living up to societal expectations (Scheff, 2000) – for instance, for not leaving an abusive relationship. Throughout this trial, the plaintiff takes up less and less space, her body drawing into itself, arms crossed over her body, attempting to escape from events unfolding before her. I feel even the shame of the defendant whose violence is described in detail – his body slumped and his avoidance of eye contact shaping my perception of him. Although there is no 'dock' for the defendant to sit in in Sweden, rather defendants sit next to their defence lawyer, they are nevertheless on public display, taking place in their own degradation ceremony (Goffman, 1961; McKay, 2015)

I also feel my own embarrassment and discomfort – my face feels red and warm, my palms sweaty – stemming from the notion that my presence may be exacerbating others' feelings of shame. Should I be there? I know that I am allowed to be there – in Sweden, the law states that the majority of criminal trials are open to the general public – only trials involving defendants who are under 21 years and trials for sexual offences are held behind closed doors. I am therefore legally permitted to observe. However, ethically and morally I feel as though I am in murkier waters. I still feel like an intruder, a voyeur. In the following excerpt from the same trial as the previous excerpt, I attempt to convey my impartiality to the plaintiff – that I am not a threat. I attempt to present myself as a professional researcher, not a hack journalist or someone there for entertainment. I do this by using eye contact and by touching the plaintiff's phone gently. Just as the plaintiff and defendant are exposed to the evaluation of others, I too feel that I am being judged in their eyes.

> There are very few seats left after the break as there is a class of school children (maybe 16 years old) who have come to watch a trial as part of their studies. They choose this one. I feel territorial and defensive. This is my trial. I want to protect the witness too. I can see that this is tough for her and I want to help her through it.
>
> I have to sit on the last chair available which has a mobile phone lying on it, charging. The screen is totally smashed. Totally. Yet it is still charging. I have to move the mobile onto the floor in order to sit down and as I do so, the plaintiff looks over, realising that her phone is where I am about to sit. I move the phone to the floor with exaggerated care. I point to the floor and smile. I want to convey to her that I am on her side. That she is safe. The phone is a metaphor – still charging despite the cracks. (Field note)

By touching the mobile phone with exaggerated care, I attempt to convey to the plaintiff that I am not a threat – that my presence should not alarm her. I find that I am intentionally conveying or – 'giving off' (Goffman, 1959, p. 2) information. Yet at the same time, I endeavour to hide my sympathy for her along with my antipathy for the defendant. I become overtly aware of my facial expressions and gestures. For instance, I do not nod my head in agreement with her version of events, nor do I shake my head or draw my lips back into a sneer when hearing the defendant's claims of innocence. I become very aware that I am sending information about myself in the way that I hold my facial features, the clothes that I am wearing, how I am sitting – am I leaning forwards or am I slouched backwards? All of this information is, in turn, being read by the others in the courtroom who then categorise me. Am I journalist? Am I a relative? Am I a random member of the public? Goffman (1959, pp. 203–230) describes this process of presenting ourselves and reading others as 'impression management' – a way of intentionally conveying certain information about ourselves to a certain audience. In this case, I am attempting to show the plaintiff that I am not a threat, that I am not there for entertainment – that I am there in a professional capacity. I attempt to send a small amount of intimacy to her using my body and eyes.

The sociologist Georg Simmel (1997, p. 111) writes that eye contact is the 'most direct and purest interaction that exists' between individuals – a unique connection or relationship that is immediately broken when one looks away. Without eye contact, interactions between individuals would be changed immeasurably. Intimacy, enmity, empathy or disdain are shown with eye contact. This contrasts with merely observing someone – stripped of direct eye contact. For the observing researcher, eye contact may be inadvertently made, opening a line of communication between the observer and the observed as 'the eye reveals to the other the soul that he or she seeks to reveal' (Simmel, 1997, p. 112). In the previous example, I made eye contact with the plaintiff and used it to communicate to her. However, on many other occasions, I have avoided or broken eye contact with defendants and plaintiffs, in order to avoid opening a connection and in order to avoid inadvertently sending revealing my emotions.

Another emotion that has arisen in me during fieldwork and which required management is fear.

Fear and Foolishness

I have only felt fear on two occasions, one of which entailed observing a trial where there was a risk that I would recognise the murderer from my local area. The second was when I was observing a trial for a defendant accused of possessing and supplying drugs. In this second case, the defendant entered the courtroom wearing a leather jacket with the logo of a notorious motorcycle gang on the back. The sight of this was unnerving for me, compounded by the fact that there were also four members of the same motorcycle gang sitting in the front row of the gallery, all of whom smiled and waved at the defendant as he entered the courtroom. All of this made me somewhat uncomfortable in openly writing notes. I attempted to pluck up the courage to take out my notebook from my bag but to no avail. I noticed that two of the supporters were watching me during the trial – they turned their heads to look at me, whilst a third seemed to be watching me out of the corner of his eye. The following excerpt is from my field notes capturing this.

> In the break, I go and sit around the corner to avoid the supporters so that I can scribble down what I have observed. I look up just in time to see one of the men coming towards me and I quickly hide my notebook and feel slightly ridiculous. He walks straight past me. (Field note)

In this situation, my feelings of fear stemming from the sight of the motorcycle gang jackets and emblazoned heads culminates in feelings of foolishness. However, the basis of this fear may also be traced back to my initial sensory impression when faced with the security monitoring at the courthouse entrance – one of possible danger and violence. These feelings of fear culminate in a feeling of foolishness. I am embarrassed to find myself writing my field notes in hiding, an embarrassment stemming from my fear of confrontation and conflict which, in turn, heightens my feelings of embarrassment thus leading to a spiral of fear/shame (cf. Retzinger, 1987).

Closing Words

My aim in this chapter has been to open up my ethnographic gaze to include all of the senses in order to show that the emotional landscape of the courtroom is a rich sensory experience (Pink, 2015, p. xiii). The culmination of this serves to reproduce the courthouse as a sacred place, where the display of emotions is formed by spaces and one's role within. It is not only the conspicuous sensory impressions like a sobbing mother that construct these spaces but also those inconspicuous ones such as the rumbling of a stomach or the whispered chatting of the waiting room.

I have also shown that ethnographic fieldwork taking place in strictly unemotional and neutral spheres such as courthouses may nevertheless place emotional and sensory demands on the researcher. These demands entail not only ensuring that one is highly attuned to the subtle atmospheres and emotions at large but also that one is able to reflect on how one is impacted by these sensations.

As may be seen, it is often the absence of sensorial impressions that impacts one as a researcher. The role of the researcher is thus to make these indistinct impressions distinct – to capture the noise of silence. To seize the scent of stress. To tease out the taste of monotony. To trap the feel of furniture. The emotional landscape of the courthouse can be mapped out by paying attention of these sensing experiences that are shaped by the law's overarching emotional regime aimed at triumphing the absence of emotional involvement in judicial processes. The impartiality of law: *sine ira et studio* is conveyed not only through the subtlety of legal professionals' emotional performances but also through pastel colours and innocuous art, through silent crying and rumbling stomachs.

References

Åkerström, M., Jacobsson, K., & Wästerfors, D. (2006). Reanalysis of previously collected material. In C. Seale, D. Silverman, J. F. Gubrium, & G. Gobo (Eds.), *Qualitative research practice: Concise paperback edition* (pp. 314–327). London: Sage.
Anderson, B. (2009). Affective atmospheres. *Emotion, Space and Society*, *2*(1), 77–81.
Atkinson, P., Delamont, S., & Housley, W. (2008). *Contours of culture: Complex ethnography and the ethnography of complexity*. Walnut Creek, CA: AltaMira Press.
Bandes, S. (Ed.). (1999). *The passions of law*. New York, NY: New York University Press.
Bens, J. (2018). The courtroom as an affective arrangement: Analysing atmospheres in courtroom ethnography. *The Journal of Legal Pluralism and Unofficial Law*, *50*(3), 336–355. doi:10.1080/07329113.2018.1550313
Bergman Blix, S., & Wettergren, Å. (2018). *Professional emotions in court*. Abingdon: Routledge.
Böhme, G. (1993). Atmosphere as the fundamental concept of a new aesthetics. *Thesis Eleven*, *36*(1), 113–126.
Classen, C. (1993). *Inca cosmology and the human body*. Salt Lake City, UT: University of Utah Press.
Collins, R. (2004). *Interaction ritual chains*. Princeton, NJ: Princeton University Press.
Conley, J. M., & O'Barr, W. M. (1990). *Rules versus relationships: The ethnography of legal discourse*. Chicago, IL: The University of Chicago Press.
Crouch, D. (2001). Spatialities and the feeling of doing. *Social & Cultural Geography*, *2*(1), 61–75. doi:10.1080/14649360020028276
Flower, L. (2016). Doing loyalty: Defense lawyers' subtle dramas in the courtroom. *Journal of Contemporary Ethnography*. doi:10.1177/0891241616646826
Flower, L. (2019). *Interactional justice: The role of emotions in the performance of loyalty*. Abingdon: Routledge.
Goffman, E. (1959). *The presentation of self in everyday life*. Harmondsworth: Penguin Books Ltd.
Goffman, E. (1961). *Asylums: Essays on the social situation of mental patients and other inmates*. Harmondsworth: Penguin.
Hammersely, M., & Atkinson, P. (1983/2007). *Ethnography. Principles in practice*. London: Routledge.
Hastrup, K., & Hervik, P. (1994). Introduction. In K. Hastrup & P. Hervik (Eds.), *Social experience and anthropological knowledge* (pp. 1–12). London: Routledge.
Hendy, D. (2014). *Noise: A human history of sound and listening*. New York, NY: Ecco.
Hervik, P. (1994). Shared reasoning in the field: Reflexivity beyond the author. In K. Hastrup & P. Hervik (Eds.), *Social experience and anthropological knowledge* (pp. 78–100). London: Routledge.
Hochschild, A. R. (1983). *The managed heart: The commercialization of human feeling* (2nd ed.). Berkeley, CA: University of California Press.
Marchand, T. H. J. (2015). Place-making in the "Holy of Holies": The Church of the Holy Sepulcher, Jerusalem. In M. Bull & J. P. Mitchell (Eds.), *Ritual, performance and the senses* (pp. 63–84). London: Bloomsbury Academic.
Maroney, T. A. (2006). Law and emotion: A proposed taxonomy of an emerging field. *Law and Human Behavior*, *30*(2), 119–142.
Maroney, T. A. (2011). The persistent cultural script of judicial dispassion. *California Law Review*, *99*, 629–681.
McKay, C. (2015). Video links from prison: Court "appearance" within carceral space. *Law, Culture and the Humanities*, *14*(2), 242–262. doi:10.1177/1743872115608350
Parker, J. (2011). The soundscape of justice. *Griffith Law Review*, *20*(4), 962–993. doi:10.1080/10383441.2011.10854727
Pink, S. (2015). *Doing sensory ethnography* (2nd ed.). London: Sage.

Pink, S., & Leder Mackley, K. (2016). Moving, making and atmosphere: Routines of home as sites for mundane improvisation. *Mobilities, 11*(2), 171–187.

Reddy, W. M. (2001). *The navigation of feeling: A framework for the history of emotions*. Cambridge: Cambridge University Press.

Retzinger, S. M. (1987). Resentment and laughter: Video studies of the shame-rage spiral. In L. Helen (Ed.), *The role of shame in symptom formation* (pp. 151–181). Hillsdale, NJ: Lawrence Erlbaum Associates, Inc.

Rose, M. R., Nadler, J., & Clark, J. (2006). Appropriately upset? Emotion norms and perceptions of crime victims. *Law and Human Behavior, 30*(1), 203–219.

Rudie, I. (1994). Making sense of new experience. In K. Hastrup & P. Hervik (Eds.), *Social experience and anthropological knowledge* (pp. 28–44). London: Routledge.

Scheff, T. J. (2000). Shame and the social bond: A sociological theory. *Sociological Theory, 18*(1), 84–99.

Seremetakis, C. N. (1994). The memory of the senses: Historical perception, commensal exchange, and modernity. In L. Taylor (Ed.), *Visualizing theory: Selected essays from V.A.R., 1990–1994* (pp. 214–229). New York, NY: Routledge.

Simmel, G. (1997). Culture of interaction: Sociology of the senses. In D. Frisby & M. Featherstone (Eds.), *Simmel on culture: Selected writings* (pp. 109–135). London: Sage.

Strong, P. M. (1988). Minor courtesies and macro structures. In P. Drew & A. Wooton (Eds.), *Erving Goffman: Exploring the interaction order* (pp. 228–249). Cambridge: Polity.

Thoits, P. A. (1985). Self-labelling processes in mental illness: The role of emotional deviance. *American Journal of Sociology, 91*(2), 221–249.

Walenta, J. (2020). Courtroom ethnography: Researching the intersection of law, space, and everyday practices. *The Professional Geographer, 72*(1), 131–138. doi:10.1080/00330124.2019.1622427

Weber, M. (1921/1978). *Economy and society: An outline of interpretive sociology*. Berkeley, CA: University of California Press.

Welten, S., C. M., Zeelenberg, M., & Breugelmans, S., M. (2012). Vicarious shame. *Cognition and Emotion, 26*(5), 836–846.

Wästerfors, D. (2018). Observations. In U. Flick (Ed.), *The SAGE handbook of qualitative data collection* (pp. 314–326). Los Angeles, CA: Sage Publications Ltd.

Part IV

Sensory Reflections

Chapter 11

Sensory Reflections on a Japanese Prison

Yvonne Jewkes and Alison Young

Introduction

In this chapter, we provide a sensorially attuned narrative located within a Japanese corrections facility. Kyoto Prison provides a fitting case study for a contribution on sensory penalities because it enables us not only to bring to the fore 'unconventional' (i.e. sensory, atmospheric, visceral) ways of understanding spaces of punishment and coercive control through introspective reflections that are usually kept hidden in academic publications, but it allows us to do so in an 'unconventional' penal environment that is itself largely hidden within Western criminology. Some of the practices at Kyoto Prison appeared to us strange, idiosyncratic and unusually punitive when compared to prisons in the UK and Australia, for example. Our aim, however, is not to measure Kyoto Prison's regime according to Western notions of 'what works' or 'what works best'. Comparative interpretations across very different criminal justice systems can result in the entrenching or reconfiguration of hierarchies. Nelken (2009) has pointed to the existence of 'two opposing dangers' when researchers 'compare and contrast our ways of responding to crime with those practised elsewhere' (p. 291). The first is ethnocentrism: 'assuming that what we do, our way of thinking about and responding to crime, is universally shared or, at least, that it would be right for everyone else' (Nelken, 2009, p. 291). The other is relativism:

> the view that we will never really be able to grasp what others are doing and that we can have no basis for evaluating whether what they do is right. (p. 292)

Seeking to avoid these dualisms, our aim is to unjudgementally draw out the many aesthetic and atmospheric similarities that Kyoto Prison shares with other prisons, while highlighting other aspects of its regime, operation and daily life that are quite distinct from those found elsewhere. Following Nelken's exhortation, we acknowledge that 'criminal justice practices gain their sense from the setting that shapes them and the conditions with which they have to deal', while, as outsiders to the prison's local setting, we will simultaneously 'evaluate [them] according to cosmopolitan and not only local criteria' (Nelken, 2009, p. 292).

That we were outsiders was obvious when we visited Kyoto Prison. We were there as part of a group of British and Australian criminology academics and students: there are multiple lines of difference contained within that description. Although we were accompanied by two Japanese academics, we are not Japanese speakers, and we are not Japanese. We are not criminal justice practitioners and specifically not professionals working in the arena of corrections. Our group included both men and women, but in writing this chapter, we are cognisant that we do so as two women whose experiences of this all-male prison are generated partly by our gendered positionality within it. And, as is often the case for academics researching a carceral setting, we visited it in privileged conditions, the most significant being that we were able to leave at the end of the afternoon. The restrictions placed on foreign visitors in Japanese prisons make understanding the phenomenology of their architecture and space more challenging than in most custodial settings. Nonetheless, if we attune to what we can see, hear, feel and smell within a prison, we may develop a fuller and more nuanced understanding of both a particular carceral apparatus and the fundamental properties and meanings inherent in *all* experiences of enforced confinement. Mindful, then, that all prisons are essentially statements of societal failure and that the aesthetics and atmospheres of coercive confinement are to some extent universal, this chapter demonstrates that even the most unfamiliar criminal justice settings can, and should, be engaged with by outsiders (Nelken, 2009; Young, 2019).

There is always something especially compelling about the accounts of prison scholars who turn anthropological attention to custodial facilities in jurisdictions that most of us do not know well – especially if they are written as 'affective encounters'. These authors will mostly be deeply immersed, doing rigorous and prolonged ethnographic research. We can make no such claim, and we are acutely aware of our limitations in this respect. We cannot contend that our account of Kyoto Prison is 'thick description' or 'deep inquiry' (Geertz, 1973). We were 'prison tourists'[1] and are well aware of the justifiable criticism that has been directed at others who have written and published based on what can only be regarded as very shallow engagement in the field.

---

[1] The afternoon spent at Kyoto prison in September 2019 was the first visit by Yvonne Jewkes and the second by Alison Young, who had been to the facility two years earlier (discussed in Young, 2019). The visits were part of an intensive master's study programme organised by the University of Melbourne and included a group of 11 criminology students. The group was accompanied by two Japanese academic colleagues, one of whom acted as translator.

Yet, so absent are Japanese prisons from Western criminological scholarship[2] that we hope that what follows may be regarded not only as adding to the emergent subfield of sensory criminology but also as contributing to knowledge and understanding within sociological prison studies of a neglected penal context. Drawing on our observations of Kyoto Prison, subsequently written up field notes, our visceral responses to our time there, and on extant criminological scholarship on Japanese criminal justice, we provide this comparatively interpretive, sensorially attuned essay as a contribution to three nascent bodies of work: (i) on the sensory dimensions of criminological inquiry (Millie, 2019; McClanahan & South, 2019), to which this volume is an important addition; (ii) on the emotional texture of prison scholarship (Jewkes, 2012); and (iii) on architecture and the senses (Pallasmaa, 1996; Zumthor, 2006).

Imprisonment in Japan: Contextualising Kyoto Prison

Like so much about the country, Japanese criminal justice is replete with contrasts and contradictions. There are 62 prisons in Japan, and the total number of people held in them is 51,805, down from 80,684 in 2007. Of those, 8.5% are female; 5.5% are foreign nationals. With a very low, and decreasing, prisoner population – 41 per 100,000 of the general population, compared to 140 and 172 per 100,000 for the UK and Australia, respectively (Walmsley, 2018), Japan's imprisonment rate is similar to that of Iceland and is substantially lower than the Nordic countries that are frequently held up as models of exceptionally low incarceration levels. Consequently, many Japanese custodial facilities run under capacity; the estate as a whole was operating at 62.6% at the end of 2016, and Kyoto Prison has a capacity of 1,477, with a current population (in August 2019) of 1,100. As we will further describe below, this gave parts of Kyoto Prison an eerie feeling of near emptiness. In the accommodation units, one corridor's cells were being used as 'display cells', including renderings of lived experience, despite these spaces having clearly lain unoccupied for some time. The 'absence-yet-presence' of life here was disconcerting and is a theme to which we will return.

Despite its unusually low prisoner population, Japan can hardly be regarded as 'soft' on crime. Its conviction rate is 99.9%, and its reconviction rate is 60%. The juxtaposition of strong impression management in the prison with unusual candour about the high level of recidivism and returns to custody can be partially explained by the fact that causes of reoffending are pushed squarely back to the offender, their family and their immediate community. Recidivism and reimprisonment are presented less as a result of a failure of the prison regime and more as a consequence of poor choices made or limited options available after release. Japan also still retains the death penalty ('judicial hanging'[3]), which can be car-

---

[2] Some examples of Western or Anglophone scholarship *about* Japanese prisons includes Johnson and Hasegawa (1987), Johnson (1990), Lane (2005), Lawson (2015) and Young (2019).
[3] There is a significant public mandate for capital punishment (80.3%): see Jiang, Pilot, and Saito (2010).

ried out by any prison officer in the eight prisons with an execution chamber. The most common offences for which prisoners in Kyoto have been sentenced are drug offences (40.9%) and theft (26.8%). The average age of prisoners is 51 years, and 23.7% are aged 60+. The median term of imprisonment is three years and three months, but the average number of returns to prison is five. One third of inmates are on at least their sixth sentence. The most rapidly rising prisoner population is the elderly: 19.0% are aged 60 or over. In part, this reflects the rising numbers of the general elderly population in Japan (25%, as compared with 14.7% of the Australian population, and 18% of the UK population).[4]

Seen through the lens of Western punishment, the experience of life at Kyoto Prison seemed intense and harsh to many of us in the visiting group. In the jargon of penal ethnography, it felt 'deep' (i.e. highly securitised and psychologically invasive, with all the connotations of being buried deep below the surface of freedom; Crewe, 2011) and 'heavy' (overbearing, insistently forceful; Crewe, 2011). One of the most obvious manifestations of the depth and weight of Japanese incarceration is that rigorous regulation and control extend into numerous aspects of everyday life. A major example relates to prison work. Almost every prisoner is serving a sentence of 'imprisonment with labour' with the only exemptions being for ill-health, physical or mental disability or infirmity arising from extreme old age.

Manual work takes up most of the day. Prisoners rise at 6.45, have roll call, breakfast in their cells at 7 a.m. and must then move to the workshops, or 'factories', where they change into work clothes, are subject to a body search and do warm-up exercises.[5] The working day runs from 8 a.m. to 5 p.m. during which prisoners work in silence. The only regular interruptions to the day are lunch, taken from 12 p.m. till 12.40 p.m. in an adjacent room, and a 10-minute break at 2.30 p.m. Sometimes, prisoners will be allowed to leave work to receive visitors or use the communal baths (they are permitted to bathe twice a week in winter and three times a week in summer). After another roll call at 5 p.m., they eat supper, followed by three hours free time when they can read, watch TV or write letters. Lights out is at 9 p.m.

Activity and movement within Kyoto Prison are not only subject to strict temporal control: their spatial and sensual manifestations are similarly limited. In *The Eyes of the Skin: Architecture and the Senses* (1996), Juhani Pallasmaa argues that the way spaces feel, their sound and smell and the materials used in their construction have equivalent importance in the experience of an environment, and should be given equal weight to the visual appearance of a space. His analysis is essentially utopian; he describes how 'life-enhancing' architecture must address all the senses simultaneously and strengthen our sense of self (p. 12). As with many carceral institutions, it is hard to imagine that Kyoto Prison could be said to 'entice and emancipate' perceptions, thoughts and experiences in the manner

---

[4]On crime by the elderly in Japan see Lewis (2016) and Enoki and Katahiri (2014).
[5]Communal warm-up exercises are a feature of many Japanese workplaces, from construction sites to retail premises.

recommended by Pallasmaa. In the remainder of this chapter, we will recount the ways in which the prison felt, smelled, sounded and appeared to us.

Approaching Kyoto Prison

Kyoto Prison has stood on its current site since 1927 but underwent extensive renovation between 1986 and 2001. Architecturally, like many relatively recently built custodial facilities around the world, the prison presents an attractive enough façade to visitors, with a low-rise, modern reception building fronted by a curved area of tarmac, which envelopes a grassed lawn. With its clean lines and deeply sloping green roof, framed by mature trees, an expansive blue sky and dramatic hills behind it, the architectural style of the administration building looks not unlike modern corrections centres in Victoria, Australia, for example, Ravenhall, or the newer prisons in Scotland, such as HMP Low Moss. Our visit took place in September 2019. There was an atmosphere of barely subdued nervousness among the group, mixed with some relief that we had arrived in time for our appointment, given that we had stayed on the metro a few stops past the station where we were supposed to get off. On arrival, we assembled in the prison's car park, next to the shop selling goods made by prisoners. As is usual for Japanese prisons, Kyoto Prison is surrounded by apartment blocks occupied by prison staff and their families: the walkways and balconies of these three- and four-storey buildings directly look into the outer prison grounds. For prison staff, then, home and work are effectively co-located.

As would all official visitors (as opposed to family members visiting prisoners), we went first to the administration block, where we were greeted by one of the Prison Directors who was our host for the afternoon. With us at all times was a group of six uniformed guards, two of whom were English speaking. The Director provided us with booklets in English and Japanese about the prison, along with a separate booklet about 'penal institutions in Japan'. Using a PowerPoint presentation filled with pie charts and graphs, he spoke about inmate demographics, educative and training programmes and the prison's daily routine.

Thus briefed, our tour could begin, but not before we received a succinct but very firm set of instructions: 'You are strictly prohibited from exchanging words and articles with inmates'. In addition, we were to take nothing with us into the prison: no phones, no notebooks, no pens, while within the secure area we must at all times move in two parallel crocodile lines, and on no account must we speak to or make eye contact with any of the inmates. The firmness with which these instructions were delivered was slightly intimidating; in other contexts, it might have felt infantilising. But we had anticipated that order in Japanese prisons is unyielding, and we felt fortunate to be their guests. Moreover, while such restrictions would generally be regarded as highly constraining and limiting to proper engagement, they had the unexpected benefit of making us fully alert to the sensory qualities – the sounds, smells and feel – of the buildings and spaces as we moved through them. In short, our awareness that there was limited time in the institution and that our conduct was seriously circumscribed arguably made us more attuned to its atmospheres. Criminologists McClanahan and South (2019, n.p.) comment, 'Atmospheric characteristics of spaces, places, and settings are grasped before any conscious observation of details is made'. Similarly, architect Peter Zumthor (2006, p. 13) notes that we 'perceive atmosphere through our emotional sensibility – a form of perception that works incredibly quickly'. He adds, 'Not every situation grants us time … [but] something inside us tells us an enormous amount straight away'. Without the time available to the ethnographer who spends lengthy periods in a location, and with hardly any opportunity for even the smallest interaction with prisoners, the physical, sensual and embodied essences of the spaces became foregrounded, eliciting a response that was spontaneous and elementary (Zumthor, 2006).[6]

Senses of Imprisonment: Entering the Secure Spaces of Kyoto Prison

While our presence within the corporate corridors and meetings rooms of the administration block was subject to monitoring and control, a change in spatial and affective atmospheres became apparent as soon as the group moved into the secure space of the prison proper. Outside the administration building, koi carp swam in a pond, an incongruous decorative feature, flanked by two small trees and two large sculpted stones. It decorates a transitional space between corporate administration and closed-off punishment. Because it is some way off to one side, visitors can see the pond but not look into it. Guards might glimpse the carp if they walk past, but with no seats to encourage contemplation or relaxation the pond is an embellishment with no function other than for officials to be able to say that such a pond exists. It felt to us poignant and very nearly pointless.

Our time inside the secure spaces of the prison started with our passage through doubled security doors, enclosing a tiny gatehouse that could only accommodate our group in stages. Once in the secure area, the Director invited us to admire the perimeter wall, which was not particularly high but was topped with wire which would sound an alarm if touched. Our impression was immediately of an austere environment that brought together industrial and institutional aesthetics with mostly 'hard' elements that included bars, barriers, screens, mesh, concrete and razor wire. Unsurprisingly, the soundscape was similarly 'harsh' and 'metallic' – a jangling, banging, echoing cacophony that felt as jarring and non-natural here as it does in all other custodial environments.

Prisoners and prison guards were immediately visible. The guards were dressed in dark blue military-style uniforms with epaulettes and braiding on pale blue shirt pockets and stiffly formal navy blue caps. With a reputation for being well-versed in martial arts, they were an ostentatious and somewhat intimidating presence.[7] Prisoners, meanwhile, wear uniforms made of dense cotton, clearly designed to last for many years. Unlike the drab colours commonly associated with prison

---

[6]The sense of intensified atmospheric awareness within the prison was also noted by Young (2019) on her prior visit in 2017.
[7]We saw two female guards during our visit, who were petite, smiling and silent.

attire in Western jurisdictions (dark green in Australia, navy blue or grey in the UK) the uniforms in Kyoto are a pale green. They consist of baggy trousers or shorts, jackets (sometimes a white T-shirt worn underneath or instead) and soft, foldable caps with a small peak. Whenever we approached, guards made prisoners stop, stand in formation and shout 'their' numbers; a move that was explained to us as both a distraction technique (so that they would not engage with us – and almost certainly so that we would not try to interact in any way with them) and a security measure arising from the prison's low staff-to-prisoner ratio. That the relationship of guard to inmate is deeply hierarchical and authoritarian cannot only be seen in the relative textures of clothing, whereby the guards' uniforms are pressed, shiny and starched in contrast to the inmates' sturdy twill clothing and soft caps, but can be heard in the repetitive and obedient chanting and shouting. Immediately, then, we witnessed highly symbolic visual and audible evocations of the power/status hierarchy that echoed other carceral contexts from UK Borstals to the chain gangs of the deep American south to the concentration camps of Nazi Germany. In the prison factories, inmates must call the guards 'Daddy' or 'Boss'.[8]

Just as striking as the disparity between the clothing and behaviour of prisoners and guards is the way in which Kyoto's décor conforms to the institutional palette and format of many custodial institutions around the world. Cream and dark green are the predominant colours; the corridors in the house-blocks have the addition of dark grey ceilings with artificial strip lighting affixed, which have the effect of lowering the ceiling height. Corridors are reasonably wide, but the colour palette and strip lighting enforce a sense of monotony and airlessness reminiscent of Gresham Sykes' (1958) famous depiction of New Jersey State prison in the 1950s:

> When we examine the physical structure of the prison the most striking feature is, perhaps, its drabness ... a Kafka-like atmosphere compounded of naked electric lights, echoing corridors, walls encrusted with the paint of decades, and the stale air of rooms shut up too long. (pp. 7–8)

In an article recounting her earlier visit to Kyoto Prison, Young (2019) surmises that:

> A visitor looking into the cell through its small corridor window would be able to discern very little about any individual within it;

---

[8] Although initially shocking to us, there are ways in which this makes sense in Japanese criminal justice. First, community police officers have been described by the National Police Agency (2005) as 'someone who is gentle but strong, like a big brother', referencing not Orwell's all-seeing surveillance but rather adverting to an idealised older sibling figure within the family unit. Following on from this, it should be noted that in Japan, the family is a hierarchical structure, and in the criminal justice system, it is seen as a crucial locus for social control.

instead, personality dissolves into the group of bundled mattresses and belongings, with none of even the 'small manipulations' or 'micro-spatial arrangements' that register individual identity within cells in some British prisons. (pp. 776)

Each of the cellular spaces at Kyoto not only provides the quarters for six men to sleep cheek-by-jowl but also squeezed into the space is a large flat-screen television set. We enquired of our Japanese colleagues why the TV sets were disproportionately large (disproportionate, i.e., to the size of the cell). We could only imagine how the visual and noise exposure would 'fill up' this tiny, enclosed space and how ontologically damaging it might be for any non-acquiescing occupants to be exposed, unwillingly, to such overwhelming stimuli. But perhaps that is a parochial interpretation. Our Japanese colleagues' non-plussed response was 'everyone has a large TV in Japan'. The only other furniture in cells is a bank of lockers along one wall in which prisoners must stash all their belongings; a form of volumetric control of personal items that mirrors similar restrictions in other jurisdictions – except that in Japan each locker is little more than the size of a large shoe box. The natural light in the cells would be insufficient to read or carry out intricate tasks and, given what we later would hear about the rationing of air conditioning in the administration block, we thought it likely that electricity for lighting in the prisoners' accommodation would be similarly restricted: the light switch is on the outside of the cell and is controlled by guards.

As in the workshops and during meals, when in cells, prisoners are expected to conduct themselves in silence and can only converse during association hours or in scheduled exercise periods. The odd juxtaposition of prisoners' silence and the rather ostentatious sonic presence of the guards is one of the most intense features of the Japanese carceral atmosphere because it so explicitly underlines the differential power balance. At night, however, the silence is total. Along the linoleum-covered floor of the wings there runs a strip of dark green baize about a foot from the cell doors. Its purpose is to provide a quiet walkway for the guards to patrol after lights out, the felt carpet muffling the squeaking sound generated by the officers' heavy rubber-soled boots. A tacit acknowledgement of the unwelcome intrusion that 'official' noise as a technique of punishment brings to bear on suppliant subjects, the practical reason for this sound-dampening strategy may well have been bound up with the non-punitive control techniques employed in these factory-prisons (Melossi & Pavarini, 1981). A productive labour force requires a good night's sleep.

(a) Absence-and-Presence as Spatial Control

There are some green spaces within the prison, thanks to a few trees and low-level plantings. Curiously, however, and unlike custodial landscapes in Britain and Australia, these plants made little visual and no olfactory impression. They were simply there, scattered in spaces beside pathways and screened corridors. One substantial area of green space is a sports field where we stopped to watch a group of prisoners at exercise, playing baseball. What was plain was the joy that team sports can bring, of mirth and banter as the players shouted and whooped when someone hit a home run. But the sounds of people engaged in sport were in sharp contrast to most areas of the prison, which were silent. This is not unusual in prisons in Japan; as a 1995 report by Human Rights Watch (HRW) observes:

> For an outside observer familiar with different prison systems throughout the world, perhaps the most striking feature of Japanese prisons is silence: both literal and the one caused by the seal of official secrecy surrounding them. (n.p.)

Breaking the silence – and in doing so, symbolically reinforcing their power and status over their prisoner subordinates – in every part of the prison that we visited were the sounds of guards bellowing commands at the top of their lungs, to each other and to groups of inmates, and the enforced responses that the prisoners must comply with, as previously described by Young (2019):

> Prisoners move between the workshops and accommodation blocks in groups: they must march in time, chanting as they go, matching their bodies' movements to a choreography devised by the prison authorities. 'One, two! Left ... left! One, two, three, four!', chant the guard. 'One, two! Left ... left! One, two, three four!' echo the prisoners, as they march along the pathways, taking steps of a prescribed size and with arms swinging to a prescribed angle. (p. 776)

According to HRW (1995), the first two weeks in prison are largely spent practising the march, after which prisoners may be punished for imperfect execution of the prescribed steps. Their report describes a visit to Fuchu Prison, observing a group of prisoners being marched to the baths:

> It was an eerie sight: a column of several dozen men with their heads shaven, in grey, drab uniforms, marching to the accompaniment of a repetitive shouting. They goose-stepped, swinging their arms to the height of the shoulder and chanted 'one-two, one-two'. According to our interviews, in other prisons the step and the chant may be different, but the idea of the military-like marching is widespread in male prisons.

As previously noted (and very much in the manner envisaged by Melossi & Pavarini, 1981), the Japanese criminal justice system couples disciplinary training with capitalist production and Japanese prisons are run as factories – when ex-prisoners return to the community, the 'imprisonment with labour' sentence is transmuted in common expression to 'I've been to work in prison'. In Kyoto Prison, there are 15 factory units, each manufacturing different goods, and prisoners are allocated to dormitories close to the factory they work in. This partly is used as a logistical means of segregating prisoners whom the prison wants to keep apart (co-accused offenders and members of *yakuza* gangs). Factories are large and contain as many as a hundred or so prisoners standing or sitting at individual workbenches arranged in strict rows.

Although no conversation between prisoners is permitted, the factory is not silent. Guards issue occasional instructions to prisoners, and there are many sounds associated with work – confectionary boxes being assembled, sewing machines clattering, a hissing steam iron pressing newly manufactured overalls. It is a busy space and all these sounds seemed amplified within it. Nonetheless, the space is markedly less noisy than might have been expected, and the relative dearth of human voices (meaning that there were no audible sounds associated with the emotions one might usually expect to witness in a workplace, such as humour or friction) was felt by some of our group to be oppressive. However, relative silence or deep quiet is common in many parts of Japanese life and society, evidenced by signs at temples instructing tourists to be silent, in the rules prohibiting mobile phone use on trains and buses, and in workplaces: as Hayes (1981/1983) observes in an article for the *Harvard Business Review* about why Japanese manufacturing industries are so productive and efficient, factories across this country tend to be 'exceptionally quiet and orderly, regardless of the type of industry' (n.p.).

What *does* mark a prison factory as different from one on the outside is the set of rules accompanying unscheduled breaks. If a prisoner has to leave the workshop, to use the bathroom, for example, he must move in a prescribed and rather ridiculous manner, with an awkward, half-jumping gait that must be executed silently, yet inevitably disrupts the rhythm-scape and calm equilibrium of the workspace. The extra physical effort and energy required by the caricatured movement is regarded as an effective securitising strategy. The general uniformity of movement within the prison means that any deviation from the norm stands out and makes it easy for the guards to see if someone is not exiting and re-entering the workspace efficiently and compliantly. The bizarre gait also distinguishes a solo prisoner from prison staff: any guards scrutinising the walkways or corridors would be able to identify an individual half-hopping in the prescribed way as a prisoner. Furthermore, the exaggerated, stylised movement has the added benefits of ensuring prisoners become fatigued (and therefore more docile) while at the same time humiliating them: an effective disincentive to taking unscheduled breaks from work.

Many of our party felt most uncomfortable when trooping in our parallel lines through these workspaces, as if we were trespassing, interrupting, gawping. Having been explicitly told not to have any interaction with the prisoners, many kept our heads bowed, our feelings of embarrassment emanating from the desire not to contribute to an impression of prisons as 'human zoos'. Similarly, most prisoners kept their eyes firmly fixed on the task they were engaged in. However, among both groups, curiosity got the better of some individuals and brief, barely conspicuous, eye contact was made. Those of us from the university group who locked gazes with factory workers in the prison hoped it was human connection and empathy that was communicated, not voyeuristic curiosity.

In other areas of the prison, too, shared glances between prisoners – and, indeed, between prisoners and staff – are viewed as potential means of coercion or corruption, especially, we were told, by *yakuza* members. In order to reduce the possibility of such interaction, screens have been erected in the middle of each walkway, obscuring the upper half of bodies from view. Inside the accommodation blocks, windows are similarly obfuscating. Each cell has an interior window, so that officers can see in from the corridor, and a second window located on the far wall which does not look out onto any exterior aspect. According to prison staff, being able to see out is considered risky, so flat metal screens have been affixed to the outer wall with a gap of approximately eight inches between the wall and the window, creating just enough open space to act as a constant reminder of the removal of the view. As Young (2019) notes, in Japanese culture, absence is regarded as being as significant as presence, and the empty, view-less space provides a perverse reminder that, despite the window, the inmate has no exterior visual space.

(b) Atmospheres and Air

As discussed above, the constraints imposed on our visits to Kyoto Prison (short duration and circumscribed activities) resulted in an intensification of our awareness of the prison's *atmospherics*. 'Atmospheres', Anderson (2009) writes, 'are the shared ground from which subjective states and their attendant feelings and emotions emerge' (p. 78). Although intrinsically connected to the materiality of any environment, atmospheres draw heavily from more diffuse elements such as the relative temperature, smell or humidity of a space. As Adey (2013) writes: 'air is more than just air but constitutive of the material affective relations that animate the experience of the city in a way which we might say is *atmospheric*' (p. 293; see also Adey, 2010). In carceral settings, the air can be part of the punitive nature of the institution.

Pallasmaa says that the most persistent memory of any space is often its smell. During the authors' debrief after the Kyoto Prison visit, three odours were, and remain, uppermost in our memories. The first is the aroma of the communal bathhouse, where 60 prisoners at a time bathe. The smell was soapy, but actually smelled like cheap washing powder (an odour often encountered in prisons in the UK too, though in laundries and on wings, rather than in areas dedicated to ablutions). We were hurried past the baths, which had flimsy cotton or bamboo screens at each end to shield their occupants from the eyes of visitors, though they did an inadequate job: when we passed by, one man leaned out of the doorway, entirely naked except for a strategically placed loofah! It appeared to be knowing and performative, and the sounds from within the bathhouse were of banter and laughter.

The second smell we recall was the musty aroma of the cells. Because the facility was under-occupied, the Director showing us around the prison was able to give us access to an empty house-block (we thought it unlikely that we would have been shown accommodation were it not for the fact that some of it had been taken out of use). Many of the cell doors were open, yet still there was a distinct odour of staleness: futon mattresses become slightly damp in the summer humidity, and old, worn *tatami* mats, whose straw no longer had its fresh, grassy fragrance, and a stale residue of bodies, feet and institution.

In these unoccupied cells, which were clearly used as 'show' cells for visitors, at the end of each *tatami* mat, a futon was neatly folded into a small rectangle. One cell contained a surprise. Four futons had been unrolled and in one of them was a life-size human dummy, illustrating what the cell would look like with one person sleeping in it. The irony of this tableau was not simply that the remaining three beds were unoccupied, it was that it was being used to generate a paradoxical (and false) impression of spacious accommodation. The other cells that we glimpsed had six *tatami* mats in them, laid so they were touching each other and filling the entire floor space. Why some of the realities of prison life were being obfuscated in this way is a matter of conjecture, but our Japanese colleague confirmed that prison accommodation comprises six men per cell. There was also a partially enclosed toilet (which was in a cabinet, the top half of which was glazed, so that officers could see prisoners in it through an open cell door) and a small stove at which prisoners cook and eat their evening meal in silence.

The smell of prisons is often powerful, yet frequently overlooked in prison research. Once asked what is missing from media portrayals of prisons, Benjamin Zephaniah, the poet and playwright, who has served time in prison, answered:

> I was in a prison called Winson Green in Birmingham where we did nothing. We were banged up 23 hours a day. We were just let out to walk around a yard ... And one thing I always think is missing is the smell of the place – when you're in a room which was built for 1 or 2 people and you've got 4 or 6 people in there ... We used to slop out so we used to have chamber pots, for want of a better word, and you've got the smell of 4 or 6 people's urine, the smell of masturbation, in one little room. I mean you can never capture that ... ('Start the Week', Radio 4, 22 December 2003)

In the occupied cells of Kyoto Prison, the musty scent of stale *tatami* and mouldering futon mattresses will combine with the other smells generated by close cohabitation in situations of physical stress and confinement. When filled with six men who must sleep, eat, excrete and pass three hours each evening 'relaxing' in close proximity to each other, such spaces will generate numerous difficult olfactory intensities.

The third aroma that stayed with us from our visit was the smell of sweating bodies in humid air. After our time within the secure space of the prison, we spent approximately two hours in the administration block's meeting room. It was a late summer afternoon, and the room became somewhat oppressive: the door was closed and blinds on the window were down. Outside, the temperature was around 80°C, with 85% humidity. There were 18 people in the room, and it rapidly became hot and stuffy. We were informed later that the administration block had an air conditioning system, but it was not turned on due to budgetary constraints: the prison director was conserving electricity and funds.

Temperature is physical and psychological (Zumthor, 2006); it is in what we see, feel and touch. In that meeting room, the warmth was reminiscent of the comment made by a prisoner in Halden Prison in Norway who described his living quarters as 'warm' because of the number of bodies in enclosed spaces:

> so, not that good warm, like you have on the beach, but when you are in a room that is too crowded or on the subway or the bus, where it's a bit too warm, you understand? (Jewkes, 2020)

While the famously high-spec prisoner accommodation at Halden could not be more different from that at Kyoto Prison, the recognisability of the feeling of proximate clammy bodies and the odour of sweat found in institutions where one cannot simply open a window or a door for fresh air illustrates that carceral atmospheres share numerous atmospheric characteristics, one of which is the way that the air itself can become punitive.

HRW (1995) notes that Japanese prison cells tend to be very stuffy during the summer and very cold in winter (only on the northern island of Hokkaido do prison cells have heating). During the cold winters, when it often snows in Kyoto, some inmates, especially the elderly, die from pneumonia; in the hot, humid summers, death from heatstroke can occur. Despite this, we were informed that it was not seen as the prison's responsibility to take care of inmates if they developed 'weather-related' health problems. The prison manages weather-related deaths as it does other cases of mortality within its populations: there is a small building within the prison walls in which the corpses of prisoners can be refrigerated before being transported for funeral services.

Weaponising weather is not unknown in Western penal cultures either. Just one month before our visit to Kyoto, news stories emerged about the now notorious Don Dale Youth Detention Centre in Australia's Northern Territory, which, in 2016, was exposed for state-administered torture, becoming the subject of a Royal Commission. Writing for Australian Human Rights organisation Right Now, Maynard (2019) notes that the testimonies of the young people held in detention at Don Dale underline that not all violence is visible. She draws particular attention to the 'spectre of the weather … [t]he force of oppressive heat, humidity and poor ventilation' (n.p.) and explains the affective dimensions of extreme weather:

> These testimonies … reveal how Australia's carceral system weaponises more-than-human forces, like the weather … The weather is not an 'out there' phenomenon, but intersects with, and co-produces, material worlds. As Neimanis and Hamilton (2017) assert, cultivating an attunement to 'how our own bodies, and bodies of others, experience weather' necessitates attending to how meteorological and atmospheric forces are managed 'architecturally, technologically, professionally and socially'. Weathers collide with, spread around, and travel through carceral infrastructures. This process is not an apolitical or neutral one.

Just as at Don Dale, Kyoto Prison thus manifests institutional indifference to the readily available environmental abatements that could be implemented to manage extremes of temperature, allowing instead the flourishing of atmospheres that may cause injury or at least accumulating stress and misery. Air, then, with its constituent smells, gusts, thickness and droplets of liquid, may be the agent of slow violence on behalf of the institution that declines to improve it, refusing to see its atmospherics as a harm that should not be inflicted on the individuals who live within it.

Concluding Thoughts: Sensing Kyoto Prison

Our aim in this chapter has been to describe a carceral context that is unusually difficult to access, especially for Western visitors and therefore unknown to most prison researchers. Our impressions of Kyoto Prison were both fleeting and tangible. We were struck by the visible and audible absence of the prisoners in most parts of the prison that we were permitted to enter, but equally aware of their presence, even when it was not 'physical'. The stage-set cell with its misleading number of mats and futons and single 'body' in repose was clearly an attempt to showcase the prison accommodation as something it is not; yet it had the opposite effect for, even with only four beds in use, the space appeared crowded. Visual and cultural geographies tell us that absences are not simply 'things missing'; they are what was there and now is not any longer, or what should be there and yet is not (Adami, 2015). Absence-and-presence is evoked through a range of social, spatial and sensory practices which, in the case of the Japanese prison's atmosphere, reinforces an impression of human sequestration, withdrawal, reduction, diminishment and silencing. The human form has been shrunk to marching legs; the view from cell windows reduced to a gap of eight inches; the view from windows that do look out onto an external vista have been shuttered with blinds; the appearance of inmates is as 'uniform', in every sense, as it is possible to impose on other human beings – even prisoners' haircuts must be selected from three approved styles: crewcut, short-back-and-sides or short Mohican. Inmate behaviour is similarly de-individualised for most of the time. In many ways, the regime felt rigid and controlled to an almost perverse degree. Yet what seemed bleak and dystopian about it from a Western perspective was, even from that Western perspective, not uniformly experienced, either within different parts of the facility or by different members of our party. When we discussed the visit later with the students, some said that it hadn't been as bad as they thought it would be, others said they had no expectations prior to the visit, one said she felt traumatised by what she saw.

Had we been able to interview prisoners at Kyoto, we might anticipate finding similar experiences to those expressed during research in prisons in other jurisdictions. Even at facilities at the other end of the penal spectrum, such as Halden Prison in Norway, grievances include poor ventilation and temperature control ('when it's hot, it's boiling hot inside, and when it's cold it's often very cold'); 'bad smells' in parts of the prison due to poor air circulation; the 'sterility' of the interior design ('I like colours on buildings ... I think the grey is depressing'); the 'soft' (and sometimes parental) power exercised by prison staff; and the fact that prisoners' movement is highly restricted (Jewkes, 2020). While these examples may seem relatively trivial to the outsider, Sykes (1958, p. 68) reminds us that, in conditions of confinement, 'normal' material goods and services may take on a heightened significance with 'subtle symbolic overtones', which few of us in the 'free' community are able to fully appreciate. Moreover, like any prison, Kyoto must be viewed within the social and cultural context within which it sits. Culture is semiotic, and we must not overlook that it is context that makes behaviour and artefacts meaningful. From a perspective attuned both to Japanese social, cultural and economic norms and to the broader picture of Japanese criminal justice policy, the practices we witnessed during our visit to Kyoto Prison arguably seem more comprehensible and less challenging than they would if we were guided by ethnocentric Western norms and experiences.

The prison's emphasis on silence and on routinised behaviour, for example, makes cultural sense when one considers that eating in silence and following a rigorous daily routine are central aspects of Shinto and Buddhist religions. Domestic life tends to be quiet, 'contained' and respectful of others' privacy in a country whose citizens mostly live in very close proximity to one another and in houses constructed from organic materials like timber, bamboo, bark, straw and paper. Blinds over windows shuttering out any view are common, both in the domestic setting and in bars or restaurants: at home, the aim is to emphasise privacy; in the 'floating world' of entertainment premises, the aim is to generate a sense of separation from the demands of home and work. Airing and central heating are relatively rare throughout Japan and are often not used even when installed, part of the country's post-Fukushima awareness of the ways electricity use can be linked to environmental disaster.

Even when we shift from attempting to understand the Japanese prison within its own cultural setting, and perform a directly comparative assessment of its regime, there are aspects of it that should at least raise questions about taken-for-granted norms and practices within a Western institution. While the notion of imprisonment with labour sounds oppressive and might thus be easy to criticise, we wonder whether the provision of a regularised schedule of activities is not preferable to the chaotic or precarious uncertainties that might have been experienced by some inmates prior to their arrival in prison. It also seems possible to us that days filled with activity might have some value, unlike the days in some Western institutions, where 'boredom sits in the walls' (Bengtsson, 2012, p. 526). We do not mean to imply that incarceration with labour is intrinsically 'better' than without: far from it. The prison's relative lack of meaningful educational programmes means that low-level labour of varying kinds is the only real activity on offer for inmates, and we recognise that menial work can have demeaning and dehumanising effects on inmates. But even low-level labour is viewed with some pride in Japan. Work is also seen as a crucial aspect of the social or psychical purification rituals embedded in the Shinto tradition that still structures many Japanese systems of thought. After release, when prisoners say 'I've been to work at Kyoto Prison', it is not merely a translation of legal discourse, it is also a statement of affirmation that the past has been expiated through that labour.

To end, it is our contention that if, as researchers, we can combine the insights generated by a sensorily activated criminological analysis with those of a culturally sensitive but critical interpretation of the Japanese prison, we might arrive at an account that encompasses both the social origins, meanings and objectives of its penal practices and the intricate details of its atmospheric and affective dimensions. Such a combination, it seems to us, offers the greatest opportunity to capture the dense 'texture or intensity' of carceral spaces (McClanahan & South, 2019, n.p.).

References

Adami, E. (2015). In the presence of absence. *Mnemoscape* issue 2. Retrieved from https://www.mnemoscape.org/in-the-presence-of-absence. Accessed on November 8, 2019.
Adey, P. (2010). *Aerial life: Spaces, mobilities, affects.* Oxford: Wiley-Blackwell.
Adey, P. (2013). Air/atmospheres of the megacity. *Theory, Culture and Society, 30*(7–8), 91–308.
Anderson, B. (2009). Affective atmospheres. *Emotion, Space and Society, 2,* 77–81.
Bengtsson, T. T. (2012). Boredom and action: Experiences from youth confinement. *Journal of Contemporary Ethnography, 41*(5), 526–553.
Crewe, B. (2011). Depth, weight, tightness: Revisiting the pains of imprisonment. *Punishment & Society, 13*(5), 509–529.
Enoki, H., & Katahiri, K. (2014). Statistical relationship between elderly crime and the social welfare system in Japan: Preventative welfare approach for the deterrence of elderly crime. *Niigata Journal of Health and Welfare, 14*(1), 48–57.
Geertz, C. (1973). *The interpretation of cultures: Selected essays of Clifford Geertz.* New York, NY: Basic Books.
Hayes, R. H. (1981/1983). Reflections on Japanese factory management. *Harvard Business School Background Note,* 681–684.
Human Rights Watch. (1995). Prison conditions in Japan, 1 March 1995. Retrieved from https://www.refworld.org/docid/3ae6a7ee4.html. Accessed on October 7, 2019.
Jewkes, Y. (2012). Autoethnography and emotion as intellectual resources: Doing prison research differently. *Qualitative Inquiry, 18*(1), 63–75.
Jewkes, Y. (2020). 'An iron fist in a silk glove': The pains of Halden prison. In B. Crewe, A. Goldsmith, & M. Halsey (Eds.), *Power and authority in the modern prison: Revisiting the society of captives.* Oxford: Clarendon Press.
Jiang, S., Pilot, R., & Saito, T. (2010) Why do Japanese support the death penalty? *International Criminal Justice Review, 20*(3), 302–316.
Johnson, E. H. (1990). Yakuza (criminal gangs) in Japan: Characteristics and management in prison. *Journal of Criminal Justice, 6*(3), 113–126.
Johnson, E. H., & Hasegawa, H. (1987). Prison administration in contemporary Japan. *Journal of Criminal Justice, 15*(1), 65–74.
Lane, C. (2005). On death row in Japan. *Policy Review, 132,* 69–76.
Lawson, C. (2015). Reforming Japanese corrections: Catalysts and conundrums. In L. Wolff, L. Nottage, & K. Anderson (Eds.), *Who rules Japan? Popular participation in the Japanese legal process.* Cheltenham: Edward Elgar.
Lewis, L. (2016). Japan's elderly turn to a life of crime to ease cost of living. *Financial Times,* March 27, 2016. Retrieved from https://www.ft.com/content/fbd435a6-f3d7-11e5-803c-d27c7117d132, Accessed on November 8, 2019.
Maynard, S. (2019). Weaponised weathers: Heat, Don Dale, and 'everything-ist' prison abolition. Retrieved from http://rightnow.org.au/opinion-3/weaponised-weathers-

heat-don-dale-everything-ist-prison-abolition/. Published August 13, 2019. Accessed on November 2019.

McClanahan, B., & South, N. (2019). 'All knowledge begins with the senses': Towards a sensory criminology. *British Journal of Criminology*, *60*(1), 3–23. https://doi.org/10.1093/bjc/azz052

Melossi, D. and Pavarini, M. (1981). *The Prison and the Factory: Origins of the Penitentiary System*. London: Macmillan.

Millie, A. (2019). Crimes of the senses: Yarn bombing and aesthetic criminology. *British Journal of Criminology*, *59*(6), 1269–1287.

National Police Agency. (2005). *Japanese community police and police box system*. Tokyo: National Police Agency.

Nelken, D. (2009). Comparative criminal justice: Beyond ethnocentrism and relativism. *European Journal of Criminology*, *6*(4), 291–311.

Pallasmaa, J. (1996). *The eyes of the skin: Architecture and the senses*. Chichester: Wiley.

Sykes, G. (1958). The Society of Captives: *A study of a maximum security prison*. Princeton, NJ: Princeton Univeristy Press.

Walmsley, R. (2018). World Prison Population List 12th edition, ICPR. Available at https://www.prisonstudies.org/sites/default/files/resources/downloads/wppl_12.pdf

Young, A. (2019). Atmospheres of Japanese criminal justice. *British Journal of Criminology*, *59*(4), 765–779.

Zumthor, P. (2006). *Atmospheres*. Basel: Birkhauser.

Chapter 12

The Everything Else

Amy B. Smoyer

In 2010, I began to move in and out of prison spaces as a social worker and social science researcher. My social work practice and pedagogy includes facilitating a support group for HIV-positive women, teaching college classes for incarcerated people, and organising re-entry services. My programme of research seeks to build understanding about women's lived experience of incarceration and the impact of this experience on health and psychosocial outcomes. I have conducted individual interviews, focus groups, and observation in correctional settings. The data I collect, analyse, and publish are narrative texts: words recorded, transcribed, and explored. Here I share a little bit of everything else.

An Accidental Ethnographer

As an undergraduate in New York City during the late 1980s, I majored in Women's Studies and volunteered as a peer health advocate in the University Health Center. Our role as advocates was to meet with women before their gynaecological appointments in order to explain the procedures, especially the vaginal exam, and answer patients' questions about sexually transmitted infections or birth control. My plan was to pursue my interest in women's health as a nurse practitioner or midwife. However, after spending time in the clinic and reviewing the nursing curriculum, I realised that I didn't actually want to spend my days taking pap smears and inserting intrauterine devices (IUDs); what I wanted to do was *talk to women* about their bodies, their lives, and their healthcare choices.

Meanwhile, as I was sitting in gender theory classes, volunteering as a health advocate, and thinking about my future, in the neighbourhoods surrounding my university's campus, HIV/AIDS was taking centre stage. This was the era of ACT UP. AIDS activists were marching in the streets, staging public 'die-ins', and demanding to be seen, heard, and included. One of my professors, a lesbian who wore a black leather motorcycle jacket with a pink triangle pin, told us everything about what was happening in the meetings she attended downtown. Her entire persona, from her fiery diatribes to her messenger bag and Dr Martens boots, now seems clichéd but at the time she was very unique and daring and brave. I realised that this social movement – the fight to end AIDS – was the real-world manifestation of the ideas about gender, sexuality, social justice, and health that had been stirring in my imagination. I joined the movement and spent the next 10 years as a community organiser working to prevent transmission and support people living with HIV through affordable housing, educational outreach, needle exchange, and local planning processes. In all of this work, it was always about the story. What are the stories we tell ourselves and others about sexuality, drug use, safety, fear, and family? How can we get people with power to care about our stories? How do we survive when our stories are dismissed?

There were a lot of things that went on that decade and when the dust settled, I found myself relocated to a new city with two small children and no job. My son was only six months old, and I stayed at home with him, breastfeeding, taking my school-age daughter where she needed to go, and trying to get enough sleep. When there were snow days and bank holidays, all the working parents of my daughter's friends would bring their children to our apartment to play. After a few months of this, her best friend's father asked me, 'What do you do? Do you have a career outside the home?' When I told him I was a social worker, fighting to end transmission of HIV and support people living with the virus, his face lit up: 'So am I!' What serendipity! The two little daughters-of-HIV-activists in Mrs Bannister's class had somehow found each other, from the very first day of school, and facilitated an awesome connection.

My new friend went on to clarify that he was a professor of Public Health with a programme of research related to needle exchange and the health of people who inject drugs. He asked if I would be interested in working on HIV-related research projects at the university. My first reaction was no. Research? Who wanted to be locked inside an Ivory Tower with an Excel spreadsheet? I wanted to be organising with community! But my new friend was persistent and arranged for me to meet one of his colleagues who was building a team for a new National Institutes of Health (NIH)-funded project. The researcher told me her goal was to examine the impact of mass incarceration and drug policy on HIV transmission and access to health care among African Americans. She needed someone to help her by attending meetings, building collaboration with community partners, recruiting people who had been to prison and were willing to talk about their drug use and sexual behaviour, gather these stories, and analyse and organise the data into a narrative that could be shared with policy-makers, community members, and academics. I recognised these community organising, interviewing, and storytelling tasks as activities that were a part of my social work practice. While I had a lot to learn about research methodology, the core skills that this work required were already a part of my wheelhouse. I began working with her part-time and then full time. Later, I went back to school in order to earn the PhD I would need to become an independent researcher. Upon graduation, I completed a two-year postdoctoral fellowship and began working as a professor at a regional state university.

Data collection for that very first NIH-funded study which launched my research career took place primarily in the community with formerly incarcerated people. However, the study had a longitudinal design and when participants were incarcerated, I would follow up with them in prison to learn about the circumstances that brought them back to jail and keep them engaged in the project. The first vignette that I will share here, *Hair*, comes from one of my first jail visits with a study participant. My notes from that meeting about the circumstances of his arrest and his major concerns at the time could not fully capture what I had seen, heard, and experienced in this interaction. There was no place on the Progress Report to record *The Everything Else* – the noise, the smell, the lights, the chipped paint, the staff's glances, the stiff air, his unkempt hair. It was these sensory encounters that sparked my curiosity and fury about our country's correctional system. Most of the stories I heard from incarcerated people were not surprising to me. I was familiar with community and family trauma, addiction, mental health issues, and poverty. What shocked and surprised me was the carceral place. My own class and race privileges had shielded me from these sights, sounds, and smells. My desire to explore, understand, and reveal the complexities of these places continues to fuel my research. Still, the data I disseminate are primarily based on participants' spoken words. Therefore, this opportunity to share my sensory perceptions, recorded in informal field notes, personal journal writings, and indelibly etched into the hippocampus (#blasleyford), is welcome.

Ten Stories

I. Hair

What I remember most about this small room, the legal room for 'professional' visits, was his hair. The room was so small that even as we sat on opposite sides of the table we were still close. The bright florescent light exposed everything. I had to remind myself not to be afraid. The correctional officer (CO) stood just outside the door, peering. The young man's hair is what I remember: messy, unkept, and filled with small things. Pieces of cotton and dust rested on his scalp. His short curly hair, unable to cover them. He had a lot to say about what had happened, how he had gotten caught up again, swept back into this place, what had gone on since we last spoke, in the community, when his hair was combed and clean.

II. Sour Spicy Sweet

When you walk in, on the way to the library, the school, the medical unit, you pass the kitchen. The automatic doors swish open as your weight sinks into the ground. The ceiling of this hallway is very high with a glass peak at the top that lets the sun shine in. Still, even in such a huge space, as the doors swish open, the smell envelopes you. It is not the smell of your family's kitchen. It is not the smell of the doughnut shop where you used to work. It is not the smell of your college cafeteria. It is a not rotten, but not clean smell. It is a smell like nothing you know or have experienced elsewhere and yet it is familiar. One thousand women living in tiny rooms eating potato chips and sweets from plastic bags because they did something after lots of other people did nothing. It smells a bit like old water mixed with tabasco sauce that has turned sour and yet is also, somehow, sweet.

III. Just Visiting

>Old angry lady.
>Pepper spray spit mask response.
>Watch. Remain silent.

I was late again that day, a combination of traffic and delays at the gate. I was late again that day, so she had been sitting in a chair waiting for group to start, when she spoke and looked in a way that she should not have spoken or looked and a threat was perceived and contained in the form of pepper spray to the face and restraints to the body. I was late again that day, and when I got there she was lying face down on the floor for just a moment and then they carried her away. I was late again that day, and still the pepper spray was so strong in the air of that corridor that it stung my eyes and burned down deep into my lungs. I was late again that day, but there was no movement until the code could clear and so the group could not start. I was late again that day, so I left the corridor to wait in an adjacent room until the air could clear.

IV. Thick

I only went to this prison one time and so I am not exactly sure where I was taken but I ended up in a small triangular room with glass walls on two sides. I sat with my back facing the one wall of concrete blocks and when he came in he sat across from me with his back to the two glass walls and so it felt like I was the only one who could see his face. The room was sealed, soundproof. We couldn't hear what happened in the hallway, could they hear us? I imagine this is what astronauts in a space capsule feel like, squeezed into this narrow space, surrounded by glass. As we sat in silence, the incarcerated man who had volunteered to be in this study, a stranger I had just met, tried to decide what he wanted to tell me and how to express it. He knew why I was there and knew that I knew one thing about him that he had never told anyone. We sat in this thick silence for many minutes. I looked out the glass window at nothing passing by. I looked at his face. I watched my fingers sitting on my lap. We sat there together, waiting for the capsule to lift off.

V. Clink

With every step, the keys hit against her hip, right below the belt. There must be at least a dozen keys on the ring. As we walk towards the unit, this is the sound that rings out. A tiny little smash to the side. Cling. Clank. One key for the door after the automatic gate. One key for the meeting room. We listen together to the clink. Walking in time. Cling. Clank. Footsteps. Breath. 'Looks like the weather will be nice this weekend'. Cling. Clank. Two women at work.

VI. Commute

Before I got this new car, I had the old one that was covered in dog hair, sand, and bits of food from 15 years of transporting everyone of all ages. It was grimy, but it had really good cup holders that fit my big water bottle. The new one is much fancier. An AUX cord to connect me to my phone. Seats that move back and forth with ease, heated for the winter. Cool air, effective defrost, smooth windshield wipers. And so the drive back and forth to the prison, which is located at the farthest edge, has become more pleasant. I can listen to my podcasts or talk to my sister. When I use the blinker to indicate a lane change, a small yellow light will flash if there is an approaching car so I won't make a move that I regret. An hour there, an hour back, not every week but most weeks. Probably about 100 hours every year driving from here to there. On the way home, there is usually less podcast and phone chatter as my mind works very hard to sort everything that was just seen, heard, smelled, touched, and felt into the little baskets in my brain. Luckily, the new car practically drives itself.

VII. Mother

Inside the rooms where we meet, the temperature is always the same. It's a climate controlled space. Hard to know from inside what month it is, what time of day. But walking across the yard to reach that space, you know what day it is. You know because the rules don't allow you to wear a coat with lots of pockets or a hood and she won't let you forget her power. Bright blue blinding sun sky or clouds puffy, flat, streaked orange and black. Air that enters hot and muggy all summer long and then turns cold and crisp. The quiet anticipation of incoming snow. A wind that pushes so hard against you that you have to bow your head. Big pounding rain drops, soft drizzle, thick fog.

You will want to move as quickly as possible into the building which offers protection from the elements. Your power and privilege allow you to seek shelter in this dangerous space. But you will notice, as you hustle along, that many of the women walk slowly, their faces turned up to the sky. They take their time, embracing the chance to feel her against their faces, smell her ocean, hear her whisper in their ears. One participant told me, 'The best part of breakfast is the walk to the cafeteria'. No outdoor recreation time, 24-hour lockdown at least once a week, tinted windows that do not open, manufactured air and light. Slow down on the walkway and share in their fleeting joy.

VIII. Pink

Except for the black tattooed heart ring on her left hand, all 10 of her fingers are pink and puffy. They are wide like a man's hand, with pronounced knuckles. Her skin is thin, stretched out to hold everything inside. I am on purpose trying not to stare at her hands, but I do notice them. She moves them around in front of her body as she tells her story of recovery and explains how everything will be better this time. Her hands interrupt this confidence, centring the addiction and reminding me of previous chapters.

I wonder what the inside of her hands might look like. I imagine her long finger bones suspended in a pool of liquid, like protagonists in a science fiction film. Will the trapped fluid ever be released? Could her fingers return to how they were before? Before he did what he promised not to do, before the solutions to all her problems were found in a small baggie, before the three children were removed, before the virus was transmitted, before the item that had been on the shelf was discovered in her purse and she was brought back to this place to rest.

IX. Tint

The front door is a revolving door. Easy in. Easy out. This door leads into a lobby with wooden benches and a large portrait of the warden for whom the facility is named. To the right, there is a locked door that leads to administrative offices. Just to the left of this door is a machine that can be used to deposit cash into commissary and phone accounts. In case they want to call you. Or eat. Or buy flip flops. To the left, are the two bathrooms with doors that shut but do not entirely close or lock. Stay alert while you pee quickly.

Upon entering the lobby, most visitors will walk straight ahead to the glass booth with a door, a round hole, for speaking, and a small opening for sharing documents. There are one or two staff members inside this booth. If the staff can find your name on their list, you will be buzzed in by a third staff person who sits just beyond the booth in a room you cannot see. Once in the booth, you will wait for the door of the booth to shut behind you. Once the booth is secure, the third staff person who sits just beyond the booth in a room you cannot see will buzz you into the next room. This is a small square room, with four doors: visiting room, warden's office, prison, back to the booth. Wait there. When the sliding door closes behind you, the third staff person who sits just beyond the booth in a room you cannot see will open one of these four doors for you.

After many years, in the middle of the summer, a tint went up on the glass booth. Now, as you come through the revolving door towards the glass booth, none of the staff inside are visible. Not the staff in the booth and certainly not the staff who sit just beyond in the booth you cannot see. The tint is golden and shimmers in the light. Like Dorothy approaching Oz, you speak through the round hole not knowing who sits on the other side. When the voice asks for things, you put them through the small opening. Even as you approach the tinted glass, it reveals nothing. Only the tips of fingers at the small opening suggest a person on the other side. When you look at the booth, eyes straight ahead with the hope of somehow making eye contact, the person who you see staring back at you from inside the prison is your own reflection.

X. Detection

When the Department of Correction's Research Committee reviewed the protocol, it was clear the priority was to protect the institution, not the human subjects. Two questions: How much staff and other institutional resources will be required for the research project? Will the data reveal anything that could damage us? For both questions, the responses are clean, scientific, and convincing. The focus groups will take place during regular business hours at a time and place that is convenient for the institution. We will start after morning count and everyone will be back in place by the midday count. Our goal is to illuminate, not expose. Findings will inform operations. Results will be shared with the committee before going to press. Our goal is your goal: increase the safety and security of the institution. Wouldn't you like to know what they really think?

In the community, with our students, around the dinner table, the purpose is described differently. We talk about resistance, abolition, empowerment, and coalitions. We read *Blood in the Water* and plan trips to Attica. We like and share and post. We are biased. We have a point of view. We fight to convince.

On the day of the focus groups, after storing all our things in the locker, we stand ready to pass through the metal detector. After all the background checks and committee hearings, here is one last chance to detect danger. We run though the possibilities: belts, loose change, metal rods in shoes. We look like their moms and their wives. White, middle-class, women with soft bellies and practical hair. Will the machine detect danger? That we are actually there with the intention of shutting. It. Down. Or is this threat that we strive to produce actually so small and insignificant, buried deep in the chapter of a forgotten book or minor journal, that no alarms will sound?

A Reflection

In novels and motion pictures, we bear witness to amazing stories and are encouraged to imagine what happens to the characters afterwards as they continue to mature and make choices in our imaginations, long after the official story has ended. While the lives of characters and places in these carceral stories may also continue to evolve in our imaginations, these people are actually living real lives beyond our sight. How convenient is it for us, the researchers, to feel the sting of the pepper spray, the cold of the windowless room, the gaze of the hostile staff, and then turn away into the sunshine and shade of our own existence. As deeply as we may be touched by the sensory moment, it is fleeting and the young man with the messy hair, the woman with the pink fingers, the COs, and the astronauts all move beyond our observation back to their cells (or offices) and eventually into the homes of their family and friends who feed them, clean them, love them, sacrifice for them, cry with them, hold them up, and let them go.

These stories reflect an intimacy of shared breath and footsteps that does not last. We kidnap these moments and bury them deep inside our own minds. Further, we have often never obtained the permission of either the individuals or the institutions to experience these things and record them and share them. Research ethics specifically prohibit us from collecting data from 'human subjects' without their permission. The staff behind the tinted glass, the women who work in the kitchen, the person on the outdoor walkway, were never consented. They have not given permission for us to notice them and share the conditions of their lives or fancy what they are thinking. However, it is impossible for us to share our own lived experience without these details. Which begs the question, to whom do these smells and sights and sounds belong?

I believe that the fact that these are real people and places that exist in the world, and sensory consent is not obtained, explains why these types of perceptions are not usually shared. As I write, edit, and review each story, I ask myself, 'What would she say if I read this story to her?' and 'How will the warden react when he reads this?' What is the price of sharing these visceral details? What is the price of keeping them hidden? Like the sour spicy smell wafting from the kitchen, this is all not rotten yet not clean either. Not wrong or right, an in-between space which is unattractive to scholars who benefit from positioning themselves as experts who know something to be true. And so there are costs but none as great as continuing the charade of objectivity which denies the humanity of the scholar. We do hear and smell and see and feel. Our eyes water when pepper spray or vulnerability is hurled at us. We feel the rain on our faces, the hesitation in their voices, the thickness of place. We hope so much to reveal the humanity of the characters in our stories and the idea that we can do this without revealing our own humanity is ludicrous. Why would we position our own selves to be above the laws of nature?

And so with these sensory perceptions, we move forward with an intention to build a more authentic representation of our shared humanity:

> The modern university – in its knowledge generation, research, and social and material sciences and with its 'experts' and its privileging of particular forms of knowledge over others (e.g. written over oral, history over memory, rationalism over wisdom) – has played a key role in the spreading of the colonial empire ... The decolonization of the academy requires, at minimum, an interrogation of not only the disciplinary fields and their borders, but also the everyday commonsense practices of the institution itself.
> (Sensoy & DiAngelo, 2017, p. 561)

Qualitative work and research about prison already exists in the margins of most modern universities. This is not work that generates million-dollar research grants or national headlines. This positionality offers the freedom to lean away from the centre, pay attention to all our senses, and generate new ways of building knowledge and researcher identities to promote social justice. *The Everything Else* is not the scraps that fall to the ground after the hearty data are consumed. *The Everything Else* is the thickest cut that bleeds when you chew it, gets stuck in your throat, turns over in your stomach, and gives you a taste of what is actually being served.

Reference

Sensoy, Ö., & DiAngelo, R. (2017). 'We are all for diversity, but ...': How faculty hiring committees reproduce whiteness and practical suggestions for how they can change. *Harvard Educational Review, 87*(4), 557–580.

Chapter 13

Ethiopian Notes

Ian O'Donnell

This chapter describes the assault on the senses that characterised a series of visits to a prison in southern Ethiopia. Foregrounding facets of the research experience that are seldom given the benefit of sustained academic attention it addresses themes of going, seeing, hearing, smelling, tasting, touching, being, reflecting and comparing. It attempts to redirect the criminological gaze to sites where it seldom rests and to augment it with sounds, smells and other sensations. While in no way downplaying the difficulties associated with properly comprehending a prisoner society from which the observer is separated by a wide cultural gulf and a high language barrier, it shows nonetheless that sensory experiences can add heft and nuance to any analysis of penality.

Prison researchers usually report impressions based on what they have observed – other sensory inputs, if acknowledged, are discounted as of secondary importance – and their observations are largely made in the Global North. These twin trends result in scholarship that can be insufficiently ambitious intellectually and limited geographically. Imprisonment is universal and for those subjected to it the visual is but one layer in a multisensorial – and highly mutable – experience. The monotony of the cellular prison where inmates wear a uniform, eat food that is selected, prepared and served to them and follow a rigid timetable is worlds away from the conviviality of a congregate environment where prisoners provide their own clothes, cook their own meals and devise their own daily routines. The tools we have devised to understand the one are of limited value when it comes to interrogating the other and may need to be re-engineered or even replaced. Their utility will depend on their capacity to adapt to changing circumstances and to deal with the kinds of sensory data that fieldworkers may view as by-products of their craft which, if noted, are seldom elevated to (let alone celebrated on) the printed page.

If we are to understand how imprisonment truly feels, it is essential to take seriously the ways it is seen, heard, smelled, tasted and touched. This involves both a process of revisionism and the opening up of new sites of inquiry. This chapter is a hesitant attempt at the latter, an exhortation to twist the kaleidoscope

---

Sensory Penalities: Exploring the Senses in Spaces of Punishment and Social Control, 203–216
Copyright © 2021 Ian O'Donnell. Published under exclusive licence by Emerald Publishing Limited
All rights of reproduction in any form reserved
doi:10.1108/978-1-83909-726-320210014

of penality in the expectation that exciting new patterns will be revealed for us to interpret. Embracing the unconventional nature of the collection in which it appears the chapter has no truck with secondary sources, relying exclusively on primary data generated by the author's eyes, ears, nose, mouth and skin with a view to providing a thick description of a previously unexamined carceral world.

Going

In 2016, Paddy Moran, a missionary priest, invited me to accompany him to a prison in the Southern Nations, Nationalities and Peoples' Regional State of Ethiopia, where he had been working for many years. The brief was fairly loose. I was to make a visit, see what struck me and prepare a short report in conclusion. These were unusually unspecific instructions (but none the less welcome for that) for one who is used to being trammelled by the bureaucratic demands of grant-making bodies. I updated my travel insurance, arranged for the necessary vaccinations and set off.

Prior to departure, I gathered information about the size of the prison, the makeup of its population, the number of guards, the timetable and dietary, its mission statement and stated values. This was an attempt to sketch an outline picture which could be added to during my visit, to fix a set of arrangements that was foreign to me in a context that was familiar by discovering what I could about policy, administration and operations. This exercise was, at best, a partial success.

I learned, for example, that there were 14 dormitories and had a count of how many people each one accommodated, but I had no sense of how cramped or hot they would feel or how their inhabitants organised their lives. I knew that, with the exception of one dormitory set aside for recidivists and another for those on remand, allocation was by gender and sentence length with no account taken of crime, age or ethnicity but had no sense of whether this integration policy was a cause of dissatisfaction and tension. Did it heighten the risk of interpersonal violence? Did it stifle the emergence of dominant groupings?

I learned that there was an art project but had no idea what to expect in terms of what the prisoners painted, or why, or where. Did they take commissions? Did they have a gallery? Was it financially lucrative? Where did they get their materials?

I learned that the prison food consisted of *shai* (tea) and bread (a 200-g loaf) for breakfast, followed by a 400-g helping of *injera* for lunch and dinner. But I did not know what *injera* was. What did it look/taste/smell/feel like?

I had no idea what degree of access would be permitted. Would I be allowed to meet with prisoners? Would I need to be escorted by a member of staff? Would I be safe? How would the prisoners respond to my presence? What were relations like between staff and inmates? Would I have to exercise caution associating with the former for fear of alienating the latter? Were there particular inmates who were held in high (or low) regard and would I be vicariously valorised (or tainted) if I paid attention to them? How should I greet those I met; would they have preconceptions about Irish professors that might colour our interactions?

I had visited prisons in Europe, the United States and Australia but never in Africa, and it was difficult to prepare in advance by reading – a particular disadvantage for a bibliophile – as the pertinent literature was virtually non-existent. In short, I had no sense of potential pitfalls or pratfalls. For someone who had been studying prisons for almost 30 years, this was a reminder of early days in the field when uncertainty reigned.

Seeing

The prison that I visited (for a week in 2016 and for a few days in each of the two following years) resembled a small and bustling village with a population of around 2,000 men and 100 women. It was located in a large town, a short drive from the main thoroughfare with its traffic honking and braking, drivers shouting and waving, livestock wandering, in a weirdly crash-free synchrony. There was a steep and potholed hill up to the prison where progress was slow and pedestrians waved and greeted Fr Moran and myself as we progressed – swervingly – towards the prison gate in a battered jeep.

The immediate vicinity was busy with traders touting for business, the ubiquitous three-wheeled, blue-liveried, *bajaj* taxis whizzing around collecting and delivering passengers, sometimes perilously overloaded, children walking to school and playing. A metal sign had been erected just inside the gate upon which one of the prisoners had painted an almost life-size representation of a member of staff in camouflage-style uniform. The sign requested visitors to stop and cooperate with any security checks. The figure in the painting offered a respectful salute, suggesting an ethos of cooperation rather than coercion. Not being able to read the official language, Amharic, was a challenge that I had neither the time nor the talent to overcome. It was impossible for me to make sense of the written word, its mystery adding to its elegance in this stranger's eyes.

To my delight, access was entirely unproblematic. Fr Moran had done all of the hard work in advance in terms of gaining trust with the prison administration. Guided by Nelson Mandela's observation that, 'If you talk to a man in a language he understands, that goes to his head. If you talk to him in his language, that goes to his heart', he had made a considerable effort to master Amharic. By dint of unwavering commitment to the prisoners, he had won their ungrudging respect. Several of his initiatives had led to significant material improvements in their lives (e.g. ventilation in the dormitories, a medical clinic, classrooms, beds and mattresses, a roof for the weavers to work under, a dining area). He was held in high esteem not just for this work but also for his presence, good humour, generosity of spirit and determination to see the best in everyone.

Entering the prison for the first time I was struck by the vibrant colours, the lack of uniformity in dress and the sartorial range. Some prisoners wore threadbare, mismatched items, while others were impeccably groomed. My guide and interpreter – who was the prisoners' elected chairman during my first two visits – wore a fresh outfit every day, neatly laundered and pressed. I was hot and bothered and somewhat dishevelled. He was cool and collected.

The prison provided life's basics: food, shelter, schooling and health care. Prisoners were responsible for their own clothing, toiletries and any extras that they desired to ease the burdens of confinement. Many had families to support, and as a result, every available space within the compound was occupied by someone attempting to generate an income. The biggest source of employment was weaving cotton yarn to produce *netela* (scarves) and *gabi* (blankets), the occupation of around 1,000 prisoners. Another 300 made fishing nets, 100 embroidered, 150 crocheted and 30 carved wood. Several wove *mesob* (decorative baskets).

The sheer amount of activity was impressive. Weavers and carvers were busy in their sheds; fishing net makers worked wherever they could make room (including in the dormitories until an agreed cut-off time of 10 p.m.); barbers trimmed and clipped in their shops; cooks boiled, baked and fried at their fires; messengers ran hither and tither; work parties assembled to walk to the prison farm – under armed escort – where they planted, weeded and harvested; visitors queued to gain admission, always bringing news and sometimes laden with supplies; traders manned stalls in the visiting area. Twice every week, the Commercial Bank of Ethiopia called to the prison so that prisoners could lodge or withdraw cash. Some of the more entrepreneurial among them managed to acquire significant wealth and had greater earning capacity than the guards, while others remained impoverished and dependent upon the charity of their peers.

The prison had a team of volunteer dispute handlers who wore purple hats to indicate their status. They helped to ensure that the days unfolded in an orderly, frictionless fashion, according to the dictates of a written code of conduct that the prisoners' chairman had drafted. (The chairman of the prisoners and his team were designated their own office, with computers and printer, indicating the essential role they played in the organisation of daily life.) The code was the product of a long process of negotiation. It had been circulated for discussion in small groups, redrafted, debated in plenary session and agreed upon by the prisoners and the prison administration. It was a guide to the kind of behaviour that would ease the burdens of captivity, addressing matters such as assault, theft and intimidation; gambling and playing games; political agitation; attempting to escape; being disrespectful to staff, visitors or other prisoners; borrowing money; using electricity; personal hygiene; education and training. Breaches of the code resulted in a series of responses ranging from verbal warnings and counselling, to physical exercise drills and unwelcome cleaning duties, to loss of work or transfer to a less comfortable sleeping space.

Staff were outnumbered by around eighty to one. They rarely ventured inside the compound other than to unlock and count the prisoners in the morning and to recount them and lock the dormitory doors each evening. As they were few in number, they were fully engaged keeping the perimeter secure; searching visitors; escorting prisoners to and from court; and overseeing the busy circulating area between the prison gate and the entrance to the compound which was traversed by prisoners going to school and workshops, by family members, teachers and others entering and exiting, as well as by vehicular traffic. Some of the staff carried firearms, and it was understood that they would shoot in the event that a prisoner attempted to flee. Relations with staff were generally cordial and, insofar as I could establish, the prison's commander was seen as decent, fair and progressive.

Another striking visual experience was the purpose-built art studio, located beside the classrooms and frequented by a cohort of talented painters whose work was characterised by spontaneity, colour and the human drama. (The oils and canvasses that they used were sourced in Addis Ababa or brought from Ireland by Fr Moran and his various guests, who took full advantage of their baggage allowances.) There were opportunity costs associated with these endeavours as every day spent painting was a day when money could not be earned working as a weaver, fishing net maker or service provider of one kind or another. While the painters benefitted from the occasional commission, their activity was inspired by more than the potential profit associated with sporadic sales.

When asked what I made of one particular painting displayed on an easel in the studio, I opined that a grid-like pattern in the background was suggestive of prison bars. The artist was surprised at this observation given his desire to conjure the meshing of male and female qualities that he felt defined humanity. He allowed that prison bars were an alternative interpretation although this was a concession to the biases of a Western observer whose understanding of penality was rooted in the cellular prison and who saw as representational what was intended as abstract.

The women's compound, which was separate and self-contained but located within the same secure perimeter, was very different. It was marked by a lack of constructive activity, particularly for the children (who could remain with their mothers until they reached 13 years of age). The available space was limited, especially the communal ground outside the dormitories, and the inmates were less content than their male counterparts. There were lots of small fires where food was prepared for the children; the overall impression was of a smoky and claustrophobic environment. Women attended the same school as the men, but there was no formal contact. They seemed bored and underemployed. Just as in other countries where female prisoners are in a small minority, they occupied a peripheral place in a system designed for men.

One of the women I met had become pregnant when on bail and gave birth to a son who accompanied her into prison when he was one month old. She named him Biruk, which means 'Blessed', because she felt so fortunate to have him with her. The children had access to a Kindergarten in the mornings but otherwise lacked the kind of intellectual nourishment required for adequate cognitive development. At least they were not denied the opportunity for maternal care and affection and this, no doubt, went some way towards compensating them for the tight parameters within which they spent their formative years. The potential failure to thrive must be weighed against the bleak prospects of growing up outside the prison in the absence of a mother, a challenge faced by any siblings who remained at liberty.

It must be acknowledged that even intact families struggled to subsist outside the prison. Having visited some local dwellings I was struck by the many practical difficulties encountered in terms of sanitation, education, nutrition, health care, shelter and crowding. Ethiopia's population has grown rapidly – from around

40 million in the mid-1980s to over 100 million today – and this places the developing infrastructure under great pressure. There is no doubt that for those on the margins, prison life offers a measure of security and stability.

Hearing

The prison soundscape was characterised by a high level of ambient noise. Looms clacked. Radios and televisions muttered. Announcements were made over the public address system. Men played pool, carambola and table football, while onlookers applauded their efforts. Others walked and talked. At night-time, there was enforced silence for the television news. One of the dormitory leaders clapped his hands at 8 p.m., and there was quiet for half an hour so that the main stories could be followed without interruption. It was an offence against the prisoners' code to speak at this time.

There was a high level of participation in organised religion and worship was noisy. The Orthodox and Protestant churches were packed during weekly services (around 800 in the former and 1,000 in the latter). There was also a mosque for the dozen or so Muslim prisoners and prayer spaces for a handful of Jehovah's Witnesses and members of the Apostolic Church. The town within which the prison was located had many churches whose leaders' enthusiasm for prayer knew few bounds. They took advantage of powerful amplification systems to declare their piety, day and night, and with particular abandon during religious festivals. The prisoners in their dormitories were not the only ones whose repose was disturbed as a result; some of my field notes were made at 5:30 a.m. when I had given up on the prospect of any sleep on account of the determination of the local preachers to spread the Word (regardless of the willingness of those in the vicinity to receive it).

This competitive praying was a form of religious acoustic warfare that was engaged in continuously with no obvious winner. It was a strident declaration of a position, taken without consideration for those who could not avoid hearing it, even if they would prefer a night of unbroken sleep.

Adding layers to the sensory experience were the sounds of words spoken in Amharic and in local languages and dialects all of which were new to my ears. Sometimes a question I posed in English was translated into Amharic, rerouted into another language, answered, retranslated and relayed back to me. After a while, despite the aural confusion, I could appreciate the rhythm of the conversation (if not the content) and the sentiment being expressed. This was especially true of the long and mellifluous formal greetings that people exchanged, the ritual questions and answers, the enquiries after each other's health, the thanks given to their God, that were integral to the courtesy of everyday interactions.

The level of noise was particularly marked in the women's quarters where things were more cramped, there was less to do and the children – like children everywhere – were insistent in their demands for attention. During one visit (accompanied, as always, by a female member of staff), a sick child wailed incessantly and piercingly in one of the dormitories. He could not be soothed and his distress could not be ignored. A hospital visit was hoped for but, until it took place, the only respite for the other residents was when he slept, fitfully and on his own terms.

This added to the overall level of discomfort for all concerned especially at night when the dormitories were locked and relief could not be sought by moving outside and attempting to remain out of earshot or to dilute the intensity of the child's cries with the cacophony of everyday life. Many of the women were mothers themselves and their collective inability to relieve a child's suffering must have weighed heavily; a parental imperative was fatally compromised, providing a powerful reminder that the deprivation of liberty – regardless of any material improvements that may accompany it – erodes agency. This is a ripple effect of imprisonment that can threaten to submerge.

The children made their presence felt in other ways; less upsetting but nonetheless poignant. They were keen to connect and to hold hands and to have an audience; any *ferengi* (foreigners) were a welcome distraction.

Smelling and Tasting

There were olfactory and gustatory sensations too; the former less intense than I expected and the latter more so.

Given the press of numbers, the heat, and the lack of running water in the dormitories, I had expected the air to be pungent at best, fetid at worst. But they were less malodourous places than I anticipated. This was explained by a strong emphasis on hygiene and personal grooming in the prisoners' code. Prisoners were required to clean their sleeping, eating and working places every day. Hair was to be cut neatly. Buckets were provided in a corner of the dormitory to meet the overnight demand for toilet facilities. They were carried away in the morning, sluiced out and returned; this was a punishment duty or a poorly paid job towards the cost of which all residents contributed a nominal monthly amount (they also pooled their resources to cover the price of the satellite television subscription). These precautions were vital to prevent the spread of disease in a place with too many people and too little plumbing.

Ventilation had recently been added. This comprised a metal grille between the top of the wall and the roof; a simple but effective method of allowing air to circulate without jeopardising security. Smoking was only permitted in specified locations and never in the dormitories. Similarly there was a designated area for washing clothes; this was adjacent to the shower block.

Dormitory doors were left open all day. Mattresses were taken off the ground and rolled up after unlock, bags of possessions were packed and stored and the floors were thoroughly swept. Anyone entering a dormitory left their footwear at the door and from time to time small groups would gather inside to play board games or to talk. There was a high degree of organisation and the available space was used to its maximum potential. Everything was in its place and one or two members of each dormitory were employed by the others to oversee things during the day. If something went missing on their watch, they were expected to replace it.

Mealtimes were sociable occasions. Prisoners queued to collect their ration of *injera* which, as I soon learned, is a spongy, sour-tasting bread made from teff. It is used as a base for other foods which are served on top of it and picked up with it, thereby obviating the need for cutlery. I found it to be delicious and can easily appreciate how it is sorely missed by Ethiopian emigrants. (There was a saturating smell of burning wood in the prison kitchen where the *injera* was prepared and even today the notebook that I carried retains a smoky bouquet.)

Sometimes men collected food for their *mequres* (dining companions), standing in line as the freshly prepared portions were doled out, while the rest of the group found a suitable place to gather in the dining hall. If they desired variety and could afford to do so, they patronised one of the prison's cafés. Having eaten there, I can attest that the sweet potatoes were particularly appetising and that the smell of meat being fried with spices and herbs was an aromatic connection with life outside. I was seen as an elder – it is a young population after all! – and when we ate together I was called upon to say a blessing before we broke bread. Despite much time in many prisons, this was the first occasion I had ever sat down on equal terms with a group of prisoners to share a proper meal. I have tasted food in other institutions, but it is often served by prisoners and eaten with staff or sampled on a walk through the prison kitchen. (I passed on the offer of a portion of goat, being a little uncertain as to its age and provenance and whether it had been adequately handled and refrigerated and suspecting that my constitution might be ill-equipped to deal with the likely consequences of its ingestion.)

Other interesting taste sensations were the bananas I was offered during my visit to the prison farm (my choice was insufficiently ripe as a bemused observer soon informed me) and the sugar cane that was cut for me on the walk back (I struggled to chew the stalk but enjoyed releasing its sweetness and spitting out the fibrous remains). My companions were surprised that what was mundane to them was exotic to me, and amused when I told them that the bananas I ate at home and the coffee I drank had been transported from thousands of miles away, perhaps even from Ethiopia.

Before travelling to the prison each morning, my breakfast consisted of local produce, often a plate of scrambled eggs with onions and peppers accompanied by crumbly white bread spread with honey. In the evenings dinner was fried fish (Nile perch) or vegetables with *injera*, invariably a pleasant culinary experience.

To remain hydrated, I sipped regularly from the bottle of water that was my constant companion. This was supplemented by many small cups of sweetened *shai*, and *buna* (coffee) stirred with a small bunch of *Tena Adam*, a fragrant herb used to add flavour. Both were drunk in one of the prison's cafés, or in the art studio, or ordered from a bench or slab of rock if one could be found somewhere shady.

To my palate the fruit was especially tasty and I remember enjoying mango brought into the prison by local girls to sell to prisoners and their visitors, for which I was handsomely and cheekily overcharged. I knew by this stage not to eat in the absence of company so made sure to buy enough to share. On a previous occasion when I sat down during a quiet moment for a quick lunch, my interpreter and guide immediately ordered a meal for himself to spare me embarrassment.

In Ethiopia, eating alone is a faux pas while in many prisons in the developed world solitary dining is the (antisocial) norm.

Touching and Being

The prison was a tactile place. During periods of leisure, it was not uncommon for men to hold hands or to drape an arm over a friend; I was used to a greater degree of social distance. Salutations had a physical as well as a verbal component. The shaking of hands (right) was accompanied by the pressing of shoulders (right again) and embracing, once a relationship had been established. I was not around long enough, nor known well enough, nor sufficiently acquainted with even some key phrases to become involved in the intricacies of greetings; a handshake and an awkward hug seemed acceptable; although over time to maintain the greeting at this level would have appeared rude.

The press of people was considerable during the day but even more so at night when the dormitory doors were locked. Bunk beds were arranged around the room's perimeter. Each prisoner had a narrow foam mattress and anyone without a bed rolled their mattress out on the floor. If a newcomer had to be accommodated everyone squeezed more closely together, compressing the mattresses as required. Space was at a premium, and the prisoners slept shoulder to shoulder, some spending several years on the ground until a combination of availability and seniority won them a bed. Not all beds were equal. Most coveted was a corner position (meaning only one neighbour), on the upper tier (close to ventilation), near a light source and with a good view of the television screen. This was a long way from the unpleasantness of an uneven patch of floor near the urine buckets.

The fact that dormitory allocation was by sentence length rather than offence type, age or ethnic group did not appear to be a cause of aggravation, perhaps because the freedom of association allowed during daylight hours meant that those who shared a language, political view or tribal affiliation could work and socialise together without impediment.

Despite their best efforts to maintain a high standard of hygiene, bed bugs were a problem. Even when treated with the requisite chemicals, larvae that had been laid in cracks in the wooden bed frames could not be entirely eliminated. The nocturnal excursions of these aggressive mites added to the discomfort as they nibbled their way across the tightly packed bodies.

Other unusual touch sensations included the regular application of hand sanitiser to my skin; a slimy, if necessary, precaution. This product also came in useful when I cut my head on the corrugated iron roof of a weaving shed when standing up after concluding an interview. (I was glad then of my many vaccinations.) Mosquito bites were another small reminder that I was far from home as were the dirty, torn, barely decipherable banknotes that I peeled from a roll in my pocket to pay for various consumables.

There was great interest in my desire to meet people from every area of the prison (rather than confining myself to the observations offered by enthusiastic volunteers); to take measurements (e.g. of the floor area of various dormitories); to study the code of conduct drawn up by the prisoners (which I arranged to have copied and translated); to understand, as best I could given the constraints of time, the nature of relationships among prisoners and between them and staff; to identify words that prisoners used that would not have been in common parlance outside; to explore their ideas about prison reform and their post-release plans. This desire to learn more was reciprocated and on two occasions the prisoners' chairman gave me a questionnaire to complete. He was particularly concerned about sentence lengths in other jurisdictions, the aims of imprisonment and early release procedures.

When I sat in the coffee shop, the other patrons (staff and sometimes prisoners) made an effort to smile and nod and greet me with '*selam*'. I certainly felt that my introduction to the prison (via Paddy Moran), the support of its commander and the constant companionship and assistance of its chairman – who was held in high regard – exercised a powerfully beneficial cumulative effect. Few fieldworkers can have benefitted from a gate swung so widely open. I never once felt unsafe or unwelcome despite spending most of my time far out of sight of any member of staff.

While three visits hardly provides enough exposure to allow full attunement to a strange environment, I felt that a succession of long days spent in the company of an experienced guide, together with the comparative understanding brought from work in other jurisdictions, and enough time between trips to ponder and formulate new questions, helped me to come to terms with the tempo and sequencing of prison life.

I was struck by the harmonious nature of the prisoners' existence despite the obvious material deprivations. This is not to say that things were always peaceful. Over the two years that I was in touch with developments, one prisoner died after a dormitory fight, one escaped (then broke back in to burgle the safe in another prisoner's shop), and there was a major disturbance that resulted in two fatalities. But these were deviations from the norm. Ordinarily, the atmosphere was characterised by a level of (engaged and remunerated) productivity that is sorely absent from many prisons I have visited. And there was an air, in so far as this can be ascertained, of solidarity. The integrated nature of the dormitories, and the crowding, and the limited resources, did not appear to generate conflict. The high degree of compliance with the prisoners' own code was no doubt a factor in keeping relationships right.

Prisoners who were seen to associate with *ferengi* were assumed to benefit financially from the relationship, even if they did not, and this exposed them to pressure from those who wished to see some redistribution of wealth. I witnessed this on my final day in the prison when it was necessary to move out of sight of staff so that I could pay the artists from whom I had commissioned work.

The heat and humidity were bearable but whenever I sat down with my interpreter to speak to prisoners in a dormitory a crowd soon gathered, sitting, standing and crouching around us. They were curious, never menacing; always keen to listen to the discussion and to offer their own observations. There was little in the way of natural light and when the group in attendance grew large the atmosphere could be somewhat stifling. I was an object of some curiosity in a place where Irish professors were seldom, if ever, encountered.

There were some challenges for my kinaesthetic sense. Sitting on impossibly small stools conducting interviews was not conducive to comfort for a gangly researcher with a notebook on his knee. I needed to watch my step walking on the compound's uneven mud paths; they were dry during my visits which made them less hazardous than they would otherwise have been. A sense of always being in a racial minority was a novelty for me – I was told that I was the first white man to visit the prison farm – but this difference was not denigrated.

I had a sense of being out of place linguistically, culturally, geographically and also temporally. The Ethiopian calendar differs from the Gregorian calendar with which Westerners are familiar. It has 13 months (12 of 30 days and one of 5 (or 6 in a leap year)) and is 7 years, 9 months and 10 days behind the Gregorian calendar. The year begins with the celebration of *enkutatash* on 11 September (or a day later in leap years). This generated some confusion when making sense of dates on documents.

My connection with the prison continued between visits. The prisoners' chairman sent me video clips, poetry and two paintings (one of which hangs in my study). He wrote to me after my second visit, when he learned that I would be making a third, asking if he could have my suit so that when released – an event he hoped was imminent – he could walk out of the prison with dignity. He must have had a notion about what hung in my wardrobe in Ireland as I had always worn casual attire in the prison. He explained he did not want to buy a new suit (something that would have been easy for him to afford) but that he would prefer to have mine for his release day and his wedding soon afterwards. That my suit was too big and would require tailoring to bring it down to size and that the cloth was too heavy for the Ethiopian climate were not pertinent considerations. I had two dark suits at the time of his request. Now I have one.

The purpose of my third, and final, visit was to thank the prisoners and prison commander and to present them with copies of photographs I had made. I had arranged for large high-quality copies to be printed on plastic boards so that they would not perish as a result of dampness, intense sunlight or repeated handling. The distribution of these pictures was very positively received and I was touched to be presented in return with a hat that combined the Irish tricolour with the local colours of red, orange and black, a thoughtful (if somewhat disharmonious) combination.

Reflecting

My visits to the Southern Nations, Nationalities and Peoples' Regional State of Ethiopia – which resulted from happenstance rather than in the context of a formal research project – challenged me to rethink what I understand by imprisonment and left several lasting impressions.

First, how connected the world is. When I asked one prisoner how he had spent the previous evening he told me that he had enjoyed watching Arsenal's 3-2 victory over Manchester City in a pre-season match. That the prisoners followed English premiership football live on satellite television in their dormitories was all the more discombobulating given that where I was staying, electricity and broadband were intermittent.

Second, how modest aspirations, successfully realised, are often enough. This, I think, is captured by the prison commander's observation that: 'A good day is when no prisoner is hurt, the day is peaceful, and no prisoner goes hungry or thirsty'. Even in prosperous countries, where penological aims are sometimes laudably ambitious, it would be an acceptable outcome if imprisonment had a null effect.

Third, how leadership is important. The prisoners' chairman saw his purpose as facilitating a shift from charismatic to rational-legal authority. His signal achievement was the adoption by the prison community of the code he had pioneered and its stabilising effect on interpersonal relations. In his words: 'Before we had a code, the leader's strength mattered. Now there is a system, personalities matter less. It is more civilized'.

Fourth, how dignity and good humour can be found in abundance in places where they are not expected. Prisoners everywhere strive to master the art of living.

Fifth, how the most marginalised members of a society can embrace wider social goals. During one of my visits, a large painting of the Grand Ethiopian Renaissance Dam (under construction since 2011 and scheduled for completion in 2022) adorned the prison entrance. The prisoners, together with their patriotic peers outside, had offered financial support to this massive infrastructural project. Also they raised the money to buy a vehicle for the prison, at considerable expense, and were proud of this contribution to the betterment of the institution that deprived them of their liberty. A white pickup truck emblazoned with the prison's logo was their gift to their captors. It is difficult to imagine prisoners in the Global North taking such fund-raising tasks seriously.

Sixth, how important it is for scholars to broaden their gaze in the interests of theoretical elaboration as well as knowledge accumulation. We need to be prepared to revisit received understandings as we become aware of developments elsewhere. If accepted frameworks prove unfit for purpose they must be reconstituted or jettisoned.

Comparing

Not long before going to Ethiopia I visited a supermax prison in the United States. It is difficult to imagine a wider sensory gulf than that existing between the sterility and stimulus-poor environment of the supermax and the vibrancy and all-out assault on the senses that was the Ethiopian prison compound. The latter is akin to a village where everything is spatially compressed. The former has no parallel outside. The latter is communal and characterised by bustle and the urgency of self-sufficiency (the implications for an inmate's family of the lack of an income-generating system are profound so it is imperative that he makes money both to ease his own life and to support any dependants). The former is solitary and characterised by torpor and the lethargy of dependence. The latter is porous; the former is largely impermeable. In the latter, some prisoners have greater spending power than they would have outside as well as access to a wide range of goods and services. In the former, cash is of no value and purchasing is restricted to the limited range of items stocked in the prison commissary.

The idea that a prisoner in supermax might meander around the institution getting a haircut, buying new shoes and then deciding which café to patronise for lunch before playing a game of billiards seems fanciful in the extreme. Similarly that he might spend the day labouring to fulfil a contract (at market rates of pay), or that he might go to the bank to lodge or withdraw cash, before receiving a full-contact visit from family members or friends. That he could do all of this in the absence of any direct supervision by a member of prison staff adds to the contrast.

In each type of institution, inmates struggle to find meaning when denied their liberty. But in supermax, the struggle has more of a Sisyphean quality; the prisoners are denied autonomy to a marked degree, the rulebook is comprehensive and resistance is futile; change comes grindingly slow. Prisoners are not allowed to express their individuality in how they dress or choose to spend their time. Some alter their bodies with tattoos or display the scars of self-harm or combat. Rage simmers. Relations with staff are all too often toxic. (On a bathetic note, I was reminded while chomping on a mango with a prisoner in Ethiopia that his opposite number in a US supermax was not allowed to have fruit with pips for fear that they might be weaponised.)

Prisoners in both environments are separated from their families, and this is a common pain. So too, both are denied easy egress. Otherwise the solidarity and openness of the Ethiopian situation seem to make it more bearable. After repeated visits I did not have the impression of a place where cruelty was deeply embedded whereas a few hours in supermax gave a diametrically opposite sense. Speaking to a man whose manacles were left in place when he was placed in a visiting box with a thick glass screen separating us and preventing any possibility of contact, and seeing the tiny individual exercise yards and prisoners being escorted to them in full body restraints, it was difficult to draw any conclusion other than that security and control had become ends in themselves.

Institutionalisation is no doubt a factor in both contexts, but it may take a different shape. The transition back to community living would be less abrupt for the Ethiopian prisoner, although if ties had been destroyed, they would have to be rebuilt, and in some situations, their crime would make a return home impossible. The Ethiopian prisoner would be terrified by the lack of company that characterises cellular confinement, even in a low-security environment. Some of his US counterparts might find the enforced interaction to be an insuperable challenge.

Life expectancy is much lower in Ethiopia than in the United States, but prisoners will be released at the end of their sentences, or earlier, if certain conditions are met. They can hope for a pardon and work towards this end. They are not serving life without parole or determinate sentences that are so long as to be mathematically unsurvivable. Some Ethiopian prisoners are incarcerated for political reasons and benefit from periodic amnesties. Others are innocent (but miscarriages of justice are not unique to criminal justice systems in developing countries). This is very different to the long, lonely, sometimes indefinite, isolation endured by the prisoner in supermax whose incarceration complies with the rule of law but for whom hope barely glimmers.

A final difference is that I was never searched in Ethiopia. My body was not touched or scanned or photographed in the interests of security. The contents of my case were not examined. I was permitted to carry a camera and audio-recorder. This was quite a sensory change for one used to walking through a metal detector (having first placed his bag on a conveyor belt to be x-rayed); having a wand waved over his body, however lackadaisically, should the alarm sound; and, occasionally, being frisked. I did not have to produce identification or to wear a visitor pass. The fact that there were no white prisoners doubtless explains the lack of any perceived need for a visitor pass (prisoners' visitors were given a sash to wear which they surrendered on departure) but the less obtrusive searching differed qualitatively from my experience elsewhere.

Disciplinary conventions understate the importance of sensory aspects of the research process. But there is fertile ground to be cultivated here and it is hoped that tastes, sights, sounds and smells will loom larger in future studies and that they will jostle for position with traditional sources of data. Imprisonment is about pain and this is experienced in a multisensorial way thought dietary changes, forced interaction with strangers, inescapable sounds and smells and a severely limited visual field. Variations along these dimensions add texture to the experience of captivity and depth to understandings of how penality is embodied. In addition to incorporating these new reference points, it is hoped that the criminological imagination will wander further and probe deeper. Such movement cannot fail to lend perspective to our collective endeavours.

Chapter 14

The Street as an Affective Atmosphere

Alistair Fraser

The concept of 'the street' has a long and distinguished pedigree in criminology. A site of danger and protection, crime and culture, art and politics, the street represents some of the most vital components of the criminological imagination. Too often, however, the street has operated as inert backdrop – an incidental mise-en-scene to the main action of streetlife. Criminologies of the street tend to spotlight characters, encounters, action. By contrast, this chapter will attempt to pause and take stock of the aspects of streetlife that often remain unseen: the intersections of bodies, buildings and atmospheres that create an affective dynamic; the invisible yet tangible sensescape that imperceptibly shapes action and interaction. This approach draws on the concept of 'affective atmosphere' that has become increasingly influential in the humanities and social sciences (B. Anderson, 2009, 2014; B. Anderson & Ash, 2015).

This chapter will involve a series of episodes reconstructed from fieldwork experiences to form autoethnographic vignettes, following by conceptual discussions that speak to wider themes of affect, street culture and habitus. The probing of these sensory components of social life is intended to interrogate the unconscious, or *infra*conscious, ways in which non-visual and sensory registers of everyday experience form affective landscapes in public space. In so doing, I will engage with the notion of the 'carceral city' (Foucault, 1977), suggesting a continuum of sensory penality between prison and street (Wacquant, 2001). In certain circumstances, experiences of urban enclosure can be conceived as 'a mobile and embodied carcerality' (Moran, Turner, & Schliehe, 2017, p. 670) that might dialogue with the study of 'sensory penality' in institutional settings such as the prison. I suggest that studies of street culture would do well to tune into the sensory landscapes and atmospheric dynamics of the street; in short to move the backstage frontstage.

****

Two or three evenings a week, JP and I walk the streets of Langview. In biting cold and lashing rain, dark Friday nights and warm summer evenings, we walk.

Tracing and retracing our steps round the length and breadth of the area. We are youth outreach workers, performing search and rescue for lost souls on the street. It is hard work, repetitive and at times tedious. We look forward to a tea break like a holiday in the sun.

From above, the streets of Langview look uniform. Buildings are arranged in neat rows; gridded blocks of identical housing that suggest a common purpose. The outer perimeter is sketched by a free arc of railway and several open roads. From the street, though, the sense of movement is replaced by a feeling of enclosure. Points of entry and exit are carefully monitored. Foot traffic is shepherded towards flyovers and bridges, with CCTV cameras standing like sentinels against the night sky. Roads and railways feel more like closed borders than open corridors.

Tonight we walk out to find that winter has arrived and there is ice coating the pavement. Hoodies overlaid with thick winter jackets we walk slowly, carefully. Propping each other up, we head along the main street then up to the old flats, blowing our hands and bantering past fast-food outlets, newsagents, tanning shops and fancy cafes. The buildings are a mishmash of different ages, styles and condition. Social housing stands cheek by jowl with polished blocks of modern flats. There's not many out tonight, lone smokers grimacing outside pubs, but there's a lightness to the street. People walking gingerly, slipping, looking up to see if anyone noticed; catching their eye and having a giggle.

The outer edges of Langview can be walked in under an hour but the shift is three hours long. We take our time. Some buildings are in a state of total dereliction: windows broken, front locks damaged, storage cupboards open. Covered in graffiti, inside and out. I recognise a few spray-painted names and tags that appear on railings, police notices and the path itself. The bridge to neighbouring Hillside is coated in a chequerboard of graffiti, tit-for-tat tags coded like hieroglyphics on an ancient tomb. The letters L, Y and T written on top of each other into a palimpsest: LYT, Langview Young Team, the territorial gang associated with the area. The tiny, stylised initials written in the spaces between the letters belonging to the Langview Boys and their mates. On the ground, the legend 'You Are Now Entering Fleetland' is thickly painted, with a crude arrow. Despite the invisible barrier, the dark and calm are the same on both sides. There's a delicious waft on the wind, hot chips on a cold night. Despite myself, I feel a lurch of discomfort as we walk over the bridge into the neighbouring area, cars whistling beneath our feet.

Like two soldiers stuck in a lonely outpost, JP and I swap stories, share jokes, wind each other up. JP talks fast and loose, his words beaming out like searchlights. He radiates honesty, the kind of person who has the urge to share your innermost thoughts with. But more often than not you don't get a chance because we've turned a corner and he's off again, words unfurling like a great flag that you can't help but admire.

Tonight he tells me the story of the Easterhouse estate, in the east end. Battlelines were drawn early in the estate's history, as families were rehoused to populate the factories that sprang up. They were sold a bright new vision of progress but found themselves deserted on the edge of town, with only fields for company.

When communities were transplanted to this new estate, town planners hoped for a fresh start but territorial instincts kicked in fast. Without shops, jobs or facilities, young people made their own entertainment on the streets, forming into groups, playing football and fighting. Borders were formed in breaks between housing schemes, sorting young people into this or that faction, with gangs taking their names from the street or neighbourhood. They had persisted to this day. I ask JP how and he gestured to the area around us. 'It's deprivation. When you don't have much you'll fight for anythin. It's the law of the jungle'.

The Langview area, I learn, is one where loss and bereavement are part of rhythm and thrum of daily life. I read the statistics about deprivation and loss of industry but it's the small moments that hit home. The young father who committed suicide after being unable to find work. The survivors of domestic violence who fled to a refuge. The Range Rover with tinted windows that stops outside the youth project, the driver peeling 20-pound notes off and passing them to his 12-year-old boy. The Christmas 'wish tree', where kids would attach messages of hope. 'I wish for a new home'. 'I wish my mum and dad would get back together'. 'I wish my dad would be good'

We walk through quiet, empty streets, both lost in our thoughts. There is no noise. Fresh snowfall carpets the streets, and street noise is temporarily muted. A streetlamp casts a spotlight, and we walk into its cold glare.

****

For Simmel, the development of the city street represented a qualitative shift in the nature of social interaction. As compared with the Gemeinschaft of the rural village, the sheer breadth and rapidity of urban life fostered a layer of indifference to one's surroundings, a 'protective organ' from the hyper-stimuli of everyday life. Simmel famously termed this attitude the *blase*, an 'indifference toward the distinctions between things ... homogenous, flat and grey' (1948/2002, p. 14). The experience of urban living created both sensory overload and emotional alienation. Thus, for Simmel, a 'person does not end with the limits of his physical body ... but embraces ... the totality of meaningful effects which emanates from him temporally and spatially' (Simmel, quoted in Amin & Thrift, 2017, p. 20). By contrast, the urbanist Jane Jacobs (1961) viewed the street as a space for unfettered cultural expression, contrasting the vision of modernist planners with a view of social life 'from below'. For Jacobs (1961) 'streets and their sidewalks, the main public places of a city, are its most vital organs' (p. 29) – an open-textured space of human connection and sociability that contrasts with commercialised or domestic space (de Certeau, 1984). In different ways, both suggest an account of streetlife that goes beyond an inert backdrop for human interaction. Be it as an overwhelmingly affective landscape or as a space of implicit warmth and community, both hint at a form of agency that goes beyond the binary between human and environment.

Ethnographic contributions to the study of street culture have probed the interaction between people and place in depth and detail (Bourgois, 1995; Duneier, 1999; Hubbard & Lyon, 2018). E. Anderson's (1999) influential account of the 'code of the street', for example, specifies a 'partly specified but partly emergent' (p. 99) matrix of informal rules, character traits, social cues and self-presentations that are codified, but in a way that evades easy depiction or description. In E. Anderson's depiction of Germantown Avenue in inner city Philadelphia, we see a continuum of street-based interaction that mirrors shifts in the urban landscape. As shopfronts change, the emotional landscape is transformed from 'a pleasant ambience ... an air of civility' (E. Anderson, 1999, p. 16) to 'staging areas' in which social mixing and disambiguation occurs, to areas in which the code of the street prevails. The shift is invisible yet strangely tangible: youths on street corners, buildings with exterior bars and riot gates, boarded up windows and a handful of rundown discount shops and off-licences; here, 'people watch their backs' (E. Anderson, 1999, p. 21).

The atmosphere of the street in these areas – and Langview was one – is a keenly felt sensation. When walking with JP, I felt my walk change, my accent grow stronger, my gaze stray into the middle-distance. Like a magnetic field, the atmosphere of the street has a 'pull' or 'charge' that all who enter its orbit must position themselves in relation to. As a range of scholars of the street has documented – be they students of place-hacking (Garrett, 2014), graffiti (Halsey & Young, 2006), urban exploring (Kindynis, 2016) or political protest (Fraser & Matthews, 2019) – the streets can be electrified in moments of crime or violence in a way that is collective, sensory and embodied. Indeed, as urban scholars Amin and Thrift (2017) have reflected, the code of the street is not simply human interaction, but the *more-than-human* syntax that exists between bodies, cars, roads, buildings, senses and beyond. While the street has often formed a backdrop for criminological ethnography, seldom has the street itself been taken seriously as an agent itself. Though this may at first glance appear counter-intuitive, theory in the fields of humanities, legal studies and human geography suggests that this is not as outlandish as we might think. Though elusive, the shared experience of being moved by a positive atmosphere – at a gig, protest or sporting event – is a familiar one. Just as common is the experience of an atmosphere gone bad; a party, a conversation or experience that suddenly curdles. The concepts of 'affect' and 'atmosphere', following separate but linked trajectories, create a vocabulary through which these intangible-yet-tangible experiences can be approximated.

The notion of affect denotes the 'sensuous geographies' of shared bodies and space through which emotional resonances are constituted (Clough, 2007, p. 2). Affect emerges from bodies in space, and exerts discernible effects on individuals, but in a non-linear and elusive ways. Affect is, therefore, a register of experience that persists 'beneath, alongside or generally *other than* conscious knowing' (Seigworth & Gregg, 2010, p. 1). To be affected by an event or place is to be 'moved' in a way that we often struggle to explain. 'Affect' is often distinguished from 'emotion' in that 'affect' refers to non-representational forces working through non-narrative forms, while 'emotion' refers to feelings that can be more easily articulated (Anderson, 2008, p. 12). An emotion is more clearly tied to a subjective experience that can be more or less easily defined, whereas affect refers to elusive feelings at the outer limit of our semantic range. Through affect we are drawn into the 'combinatorial force field' (Amin & Thrift, 2017, p. 16) of human and non-human elements within the street, where 'agency [is] very much a hybrid of mind, body, machine and matter' (Franklin, 2017, p. 19).

The concept of 'atmosphere', emergent in the fields of philosophy and cultural geography, represents 'bubbles' of shared feeling that are anchored to particular spatio-temporal moments. These can operate at a societal level or locally, as in Williams (1985) discussion of 'structures of feeling'. Like affects, atmospheres are 'a class of experience that occur before and alongside the formation of subjectivity, across human and non-human materialities and in-between subject/object distinctions' (B. Anderson, 2009, p. 78). Such atmospheres can be felt materially as they 'press' and 'envelop' (B. Anderson, 2009, p. 78) but always evade precise description – influencing but exceeding felt emotional responses. As Böhme (1993) notes, an atmosphere is a 'spatially extended quality of feeling' (p. 118) filling a given space 'like a haze' (p. 114).

Affective atmospheres, therefore, can be thought of as inchoate forms of affect that are created by shared bodies in space. As Sara Ahmed (2004) has argued, shared feelings and emotions are precisely what gives rise to a sense of a collective or community, with the intensification of feeling capable of transforming the limits of a collective into an object, giving distinctions between inside and outside a material and affective sense (Ahmed, 2004, p. 9). An affective atmosphere, then, is produced by a moment that reaches out beyond subjects and 'touches' others, connecting self, other and space in a shared experience. However, this 'sharing' of affect must not be understood as a peaceful communalism, a relation of subjects in perfect harmony. An affective atmosphere, in a street or elsewhere, is a fractured, temporary and evanescent alliance of bodies in space, produced by and producing mobile and shifting subjectivities.

****

JP laughs a lot, but it's clear there are strains beneath the surface. Growing up in the scheme, he tells me, violence was a constant presence – a knot you could feel in the air and in your body. Pick a side and stick to it no matter what, like you would in a football team. Heads or tails, doesn't matter – as long as you choose. Because you are talking about two sides of the same coin. A tacit agreement had been struck. A line drawn in the sand. You earn a reputation and some local celebrity but it's a double-edged sword. Before long you can't leave your postage stamp of turf.

We turn left and cut through the park. Dogshit and broken glass mingle with a light layer of snowfall, but there are tracks to follow. Lit by streetlamps, we spot a group and watch as they sidle over to a pitch of black ice. They can't see us. They study it for a moment, hesitant and then – wham – they go wild. Sliding, shoving, tackling each other. One second they are bored, the next the air is thick with mischief. Their shouts blend into a gleeful chant that hangs for a moment before disappearing like smoke on the wind.

We quietly retreat, turning the corner to a kid's play-park, vandalised and usually empty. Two boys and one girl, around 14, sit on the swings. They are dressed in tracksuits and beanies, scarfs pulled up above their necks. They look freezing. I think I recognise one and step forward, rubbing my hands together,

222 *Alistair Fraser*

a big grin on my chops like a labrador. 'Awrite troops how are yous doin. Freezing night eh?'

No response.

I look round at JP, who gives a small shake of his head. When I turn back, one of the boys is standing on the swing, hurtling back and forth with rhythmic kicks. I hesitate. The other two are watching him now. He kicks the swing hard and jumps backward, eyeing the chain with a glare as it wraps around the bar.

I'm about to say more but before I do JP is holding my elbow and steering me up the path back the main street. He says nothing until we are out of earshot, his silence speaking volumes. 'They didny want to speak to us', he says. 'You have to give people space'.

I start to explain but JP starts off on a story of a former outreach worker he'd known, who saw it as his mission to 'engage' the most challenging young people. On the street, the rules are different. It's one of the few spaces that young people have that's theirs, and it needs to be respected.

Conversation turns, by degrees, to the ways that young people were policed. JP tells me, with a wide grin, about a police dispersal order that had been imposed the previous year. The police had been inundated with calls, but it later transpired that many were made about a series of snowball fights that youth workers had participated in. It became a running joke between outreach staff workers, and the police, that there were no young people around – 'you seen any young people tonight?' 'No. If we see any we'll give you a call'. This lasted for three months.

This was borne out on our shifts. Young people often complained about police stopping them for no reason. One told us, that the police had sent him back to his street, telling him 'just because you live in a shitehole doesn't mean you can turn this place into one'. They told us they felt like they couldn't even leave their own street.

****

Concluding a discussion of the 'great carceral continuum' (Foucault, 1977, p. 299) that extends from the prison gate to schools, factories, workhouses and beyond, Foucault offers a brief sketch of what he terms the 'carceral city'. Building on previous formulations of carcerality as a 'net' or 'network' (Foucault, 1977, pp. 299–300), the 'carceral city' refers to a coextensive web of disciplinary technologies through which citizens are shaped and surveilled. For Foucault, the disciplinary technologies developed in the prison – involving strict regulation of time, space and human interaction – were also writ large in the urban fabric. More recently, Mike Davis (1990/2006) updated readings of the 'carceral city' for the age of surveillance – tracking the progress of Los Angeles from a bright vision of futuristic urbanism into a dystopic 'carceral city' composed of police surveillance, security services and defensive domestic architecture (p. 256). In Glasgow, these processes became amplified during the planning of the Commonwealth Games. For Paton, Mooney and McKee (2012), efforts at street-cleansing and dispersal presented a view that 'working-class lives are … problematic, anti-modern and out of step with the revitalised and aspirational world of the new Glasgow, the new Scotland and the new UK' (p. 1486).

On the face of it, the street is a space where young people can have some degree of autonomy on their own terms (Leonard, 2006, p. 232). For young people, locked in a liminal 'waiting room' between childhood and adulthood (Miller, 2005), the streets become imbued with meaning and potential. It is an open-ended space, set apart from the norms and conventions of either home or school, where imagination and fantasy merge into what Soja (1996) terms 'thirdspace': 'a simultaneously real and imagined, actual and virtual locus of structured individual and collective experiences and agency' (p. 11). Thirdspace is a mid-point between the lived experience of place – for example, that of everyday life in a housing estate – and the 'imagined', perceived, meaning of space (Soja, 1996, p. 10). It is notable in this context that Thrasher (1927/1936, p. 193), in his study of street gangs in Chicago, describes the process through which unappealing spaces are magically transformed into exciting areas for play. He includes in this the gang names that create a 'magical' transformation from humdrum lives to 'Bandits', 'Blood Kings'; or 'Fleet', 'Monks', 'Thugs' and so on. As Childress (2004) argues:

> Teenagers occupy a different space than most of their adult counterparts: the meaning-laden space of use and belonging; the political space of appropriation; the temporally fluid space of arriving, claiming and departure. Kids make great use of their communities' leftovers – the negative space in the positively planned and owned world. (p. 204)

It is evident, however, that such efforts at spatial autonomy are gained in contest with efforts to control or regulate behaviour (Lefebvre, 1996). Drawing on de Certeau's distinction between the city 'from above' and 'from below', Hayward (2012) depicts the ways in which spatial strategies might interrupt or otherwise disrupt relations of spatial power in the city. In the context of limited space and resources, young people create 'microgeographies' and 'microcultures', gaining spatial autonomy from adults' control. The street in this sense operates as a 'parafunctional space' that is reimagined 'in terms of hidden micro-cultural practices, distinct spatial biographies, relationships (or non-relationships) with surrounding spaces/structures' (Hayward, 2012, p. 453). As Ferrell (1997) has argued, youth culture is frequently forged in the context of efforts at curtailment and surveillance – from skateboarding to street music, curfews to graffiti. Such practices nurture a sense of individual and group identity (Matthews, Limb, & Percy-Smith, 1998; Matthews, Limb, & Taylor, 2000) or personal space (Percy-Smith & Matthews, 2001), yet render street-visible youth subject to police surveillance and state control.

On streetwork in Langview, we witnessed all kinds of 'weird ideas' (Corrigan, 1979). Groups of young people smashed bottles, threw eggs at strangers, stole shopping trolleys, got into fights. They talked about going into shopping malls and noising up the security to get a chase; about tactics to sneak into football games and cinemas; about setting of fire hydrants and alarms. Their use of public space involved a perpetual repetition of group activities in the same public spaces – constantly searching for new excitements, dares and risks. Cohen (1973) refers to these diversions as 'character contests', determining 'who will have the honour and character to rise above the situation ... [in] the familiar settings of streets' (p. 53). In these circumstances, gang fights emerged as a means of puncturing the daily routine with a transgressive 'thrill' of violence or boundary-crossing (Katz, 1988). These activities, forged in close relation with the 'thirdspace' of Langview, created a loose yet noticeable atmosphere. Some thrived on it; others were fearful and carefully monitored their behaviour and movement (Garot, 2010).

The Langview Boys, who I got to know over the years, were avowedly in the former category.

****

I'm sitting with three of the Langview boys and the chat is about fighting. We're in a back room and there's a big map of the area spread out. There's Willie, small and wiry; Gary, tall and gangly; and Mark, short and stocky. The others aren't here, for reasons unknown. The boys are sticking pins in the map to show me where they live, where they hang out, where they feel safe, where they don't. The yellow 'home' and green 'safe' pins are clustered into a few streets, visual markers of belonging bunched tightly against the wide expanse of the map. The 'unsafe' red pins are more spread out, but their position is telling: boundaries with neighbouring areas.

I ask the boys, semi-innocently, if they had ever ventured across the border to Hillside. That bridge, pockmarked with graffiti, between safe and unsafe.

The atmosphere in the room shifts. There is an edge in the air. A quiet descends, ears prick up, rhythm slows. The classroom tenses like a Western saloon as a stranger swings in. The boys lean forward. They recount an episode from the year before, trying to get a name for themselves as local gang members, when they went over looking for a fight. They egged each other on, asking who could go the furthest, until they ran into the Hillside Fleet: men in their late teens and early twenties, carrying weapons. Out of their depth, they turned to run but found they'd lost their pal James. As Gary says,

> James ran doon the ramp, we looked around but couldnae find him, an that's when Ah thought 'they've caught James'. Then Ah shouted 'let's fucking go!'. Willie chips in, When we thought our pal got caught, that's when we all came round ... see when that adrenaline's kicking through you.

And I could. By this point, the boys were half-standing, talking over one another, reliving the moment in a jumbled sing-song of nostalgia and fear. The pins on the maps are forgotten and they are back in that fight or flight moment, when boyish dares tipped over into real danger. In that moment, I could feel the bond between the boys tighten like an invisible cord and suddenly understood something. It wasn't bravado but loyalty that brought them to the bridge. Loyalty and excitement.

The others on the bridge were Kev, the strong and charismatic leader; Daz, chief mischief-maker and shit-stirrer; and James, cheeky and chubby, the class clown. I can see the lot of them now, grinning back at me like the poster for trainspotting. They knew each other intimately, these boys; how to wind each other up and knock each other down; which buttons to press and which to avoid. They had known one another their whole lives – in and out of one another's houses, the local youth project, the school. They were everywhere I went. Their names were spray-painted on the back door of my building.

I found out later that several were listed in a police gang database and caught local murmurs of their involvement in fights. More than one had family members in prison for violent offences. They had a gang name, the LYT, that they graffitied everywhere, from walls to schoolbooks – they even added it to the end of their email addresses and told me I should too after I moved to the area. They had fights and admitted to carrying knives.

There was a timelessness to it that I hadn't expected. I was up on the branch with the boys, looking down and seeing history repeating itself. If I pressed rewind, I knew I'd see the 'big wans' get smaller and retreat to the tree. If I hit fast-forward, the Langview Boys would be out on the bridge and another group of 'wee wans' would take their place, jostling for position on the branch.

****

Of late, criminologists of the street have increasingly turned to the conceptual language of Pierre Bourdieu to interrogate the material and symbolic dimensions of urban streetlife (Fraser & Sandberg, 2020). In this work, the 'street' is conceived as a relational social space that is both structured and structuring, involving shared traits but also agentic decision-making, as distinct from the bureaucratic field of the State (Ilan, 2015; Sandberg & Fleetwood, 2016; Shammas & Sandberg, 2016). For Shammas and Sandberg (2016, p. 196), the street 'field' represents an agonistic space of social relations invested with transformative effects: a 'semi-autonomous domain of unified social action that obeys its own logics'. To study a field is therefore to study 'a social universe ... that is somewhat apart, endowed with its own laws, its own nomos, its own law of functioning, without being completely independent of the external laws' (Bourdieu, 2005, p. 33, cited in Shammas & Sandberg, 2016, p. 209). The 'street field' is constituted through symbolic hierarchies of respect established via street 'capital' and has effects such as the production of a distinct street 'habitus' (Fraser, 2013). A 'street' habitus is a form of *infra*conscious street sensibility, or street smarts, that is imprinted on the body – a schema of perception and response that is experienced as instinctive, flowing from an attuned response to material physical danger (Fraser, 2015).

For the Langview Boys, a 'street habitus' was forged through a deep-seated connection with the local area of Langview, formulated and embodied by a childhood spent in a small geographical area searching for excitement and ideas but constrained by a broader set of structural obstacles. Local places and spaces, bound up with individual and collective memory, become fused with self-identity, resulting in an intense place-attachment. As Wacquant (2007) notes, 'identification with one's place of residence can assume exacerbated forms that reflect the closure of one's lived universe' (p. 271). This form of habituation allows street-based youth to deal with unforeseen circumstances and through the generation of street capital (Sandberg & Pederson, 2011) develop local reputation and distinction. Similarly, for Taylor, Evans and Fraser (1996, p. 14), drawing on a study of local 'structures of feeling' amongst adults in Manchester and Sheffield, 'substance of locality' is defined by 'routinised relations, reproduced over time, because of the dependency of actors condemned to geographical immobility'. Street habitus is therefore a register of experience that stretches beyond the five senses, acting as a 'sixth sense' that emanates from hard-sprung sensorial experience.

Missing from current Bourdieusian approaches to street culture, then, is a sense of the street as a multisensory, 'thick', site of atmospheres and affects. There is a sense in which shared spatial and social experiences enter into our pre-conscious – in the form of habitus and accompanying schemas of perception and movement – in a way that is experiential and affective rather than an observable or articulable way. As Bourdieu argues, 'the factors which are most influential in the formation of the habitus are transmitted without passing through language' (Bourdieu, 1991, p. 51). As Wacquant (2014) has elaborated, the three components of habitus are *cognitive* (relating to classification and categorisation), *conative* (embodied, mobile and physical) and *affective* (emotional, sensorial and evocative). While cognitive and conative dimensions of street culture have taken centre stage, the affective background has seldom seen the spotlight. And yet, as Duff (2010), argues:

> Affects are, in this sense, not only indicative of the subjective mood of certain places; they also frame the array of activities and practices potentially enactable within that place. Affect ought here to be understood in two distinctive ways. Affect describes an array of feeling states characteristic of everyday life, with its constant shifts in mood and emotional resonance. (p. 884)

The concept has been put to work recently across a range of contexts. In politics, Stephens (2015) argues that the concept disrupts the view of decision-making as rational and linear but opens the way to understanding the ways in which points of intensity and heightened charge – in a room, in a historical moment or in a debate – might influence the outcome more than any individual. As he argues, 'the provocation of an atmosphere presents a different image of political space: diffuse and nebulous' (Stephens, 2015, p. 10). In criminology more broadly, Halsey and Young (2006) draw on the language of affect to delineate the ways in which graffiti can act as a conduit between writer and audience; connecting both through leaving of a visible imprint of communicative intensity (Campbell, 2013). More recently, Kindynis (2016) relays the affective atmospheres of urban exploring,

> an intoxicating cocktail of materiality, corporeality, atmosphere and affect; sweat, pigeon shit and concrete dust; the rushing lights of passing trains; echoes reverberating through subterranean tunnel networks; and the imminent threat of arrest, injury or death. (p. 5)

The language of affect has also been used to depict contemporary carceral landscapes (Turner & Peters, 2015), night-time economies (Shaw, 2014) and surveillance (Ellis, Tucker, & Harper, 2013).

The notion of the street as an affective atmosphere, in its insistence on viewing the street as a sensory, broadens and deepens the affective component of the 'street field'. We might conceive of the 'atmosphere' of the street as constituted not only by the people in the foreground but also by 'the arrangement of buildings and streetlights, the passing of cars and pedestrians, the stillness or motion of street-based groups, the sounds and smells, the threats and warnings' (Fraser & Matthews, 2019). Indeed, following B. Anderson (2014), we might view the atmospheric dynamics of the street to have a form of agency, 'albeit a curious, ambivalent, agency in which the very existence of an atmosphere may be revealed retrospectively by its effects' (pp. 156–157).

Conclusion

The language of affect and atmosphere, like shared experience, is partial, inchoate and fuzzy. Instead of traditional binaries between subject and object, or structure and agency, we are left with an amorphous yet diaphanous arrangement of human and non-human actors. Far from a weakness, the ambiguity of an atmosphere is part of its unique value; it seeks to approach a form of experience that so often falls through the cracks of more orthodox theorising. As recent criminological work has indicated, the sensory governance of urban security (Schuilenberg & Peters, 2018), olfactory landscapes of consumerism (Kindynis, 2019) and musical soundscapes of prisons (Herrity, 2018) suggest the need to engage with the experiential, affective and sensory dimensions of criminal justice. More than this, an attention to the atmospheres – in all their multisensory, tactile and textured complexity – creates a vocabulary through which to explore the commonalities of experiences between different forms of sensory punishment that extend, as Foucault (1977) suggests, from the prison to the 'carceral city' writ large.

References

Ahmed, S. (2004). Collective feelings: Or, the impressions left by others. *Theory, Culture & Society*, *21*(2), 25–42.
Amin, A., & Thrift, N. (2017). *Seeing like a city*. London: Polity.
Anderson, B. (2009). Affective atmospheres. *Emotion, Space and Society*, *2*(2), 77–81.
Anderson, B. (2014). *Encountering affect: Capacities, apparatuses, conditions*. Abingdon: Routledge.
Anderson, B., & Ash, J. (2015). Atmospheric methods. In P. Vannani (Ed.), *Non/representational methodologies: Re-envisioning research* (pp. 34–51). Abingdon: Routledge.
Anderson, E. (1999). *The code of the street: Decency, violence and the moral life of the inner city*. New York, NY: W.W. Norton & Co.
Böhme, G. (1993). Atmosphere as a fundamental concept of a new aesthetics. *Thesis Eleven*, *36*, 113–126.

Bourdieu, P. (1991). *Language and Symbolic Power*. Cambridge, MA: Harvard University Press.
Bourgois, P. (1995). *In search of respect: Selling crack in El Barrio*. Cambridge: Cambridge University Press.
Campbell, E. (2013). Transgression, affect, and performance: Choreographing a politics of urban space. *British Journal of Criminology, 53*(1), 18–40.
Childress, H. (2004). Teenagers, territory and the appropriate of space. *Childhood, 11*(2), 195–205.
Clough, P. (Ed.). (2007). *The affective turn: Theorising the social*. Durham, NC: Duke University Press.
Cohen, S. (1973). Property destruction: Meanings and motives. In C. Ward (Ed.), *Vandalism* (pp. 23–53). London: Architectural Press.
Corrigan, P. (1979). *Schooling the smash street kid*. London: Macmillan.
Davis, M. (1990/2006). *City of quartz. Excavating the future in Los Angeles*. London: Verso.
de Certeau, M. (1984). *The practice of everyday life*. Berkeley, CA: University of California Press.
Davis, M. (2006). *City of Quartz. Excavating the Future in Los Angeles*. London: Verso.
Duff, C. (2010). On the role of affect and practice in the production of place. *Environment and Planning D: Society and Space, 28*, 881–895.
Duneier, M. (1999). *Sidewalk*. New York, NY: Farrar, Straus and Giroux.
Ellis, D., Tucker, I., & Harper, D. (2013). The affectitve atmospheres of surveillance. *Theory & Psychology, 23*(6), 716–731.
Ferrell, J. (1997). Youth, crime, and cultural space. *Social Justice, 24*(4), 21–38.
Foucault, M. (1977). *Discipline and punish: The birth of the prison*. London: Allen Lane.
Franklin, A. (2017). The more-than-human city. *The Sociological Review, 65*(2), 202–217.
Fraser, A. (2013). Street habitus: Gangs, territorialism and social change in Glasgow. *Journal of Youth Studies, 16*(8), 970–985.
Fraser, A. (2015). *Urban legends: Gang identity in the post-industrial city*. Oxford: Oxford University Press.
Fraser, A., & Matthews, D. (2019). Towards a criminology of atmospheres: Law, affect and the codes of the street. *Criminology and Criminal Justice*. doi.org/10.1177/1748895819874853
Fraser, A., & Sandberg, S. (2020). Bourdieu on the Block: Punishment, Policing and the Street. Virtual Special Issue of *Criminology and Criminal Justice* Available at: https://journals.sagepub.com/page/crj/bourdieu-and-criminology.
Garot, R. (2010). *Who you claim: Performing gang identity in school and on the streets*. New York, NY: NYU Press.
Garrett, B. (2014). *Explore everything: Place-hacking the city*. London: Verso.
Halsey, M., & Young, A. (2006). Our desires are ungovernable: Writing graffiti in urban space. *Theoretical Criminology, 10*(3), 275–306.
Hayward, K. J. (2012). Five spaces of cultural criminology. *British Journal of Criminology, 52*(3), 441–462.
Herrity, K. (2018). Music and identity in prison: Music as a technology of the self. *Prison Service Journal, 239*, 40–47.
Hubbard, P., & Lyon, D. (2018). Introduction: Streetlife – The shifting sociologies of the street. *The Sociological Review, 66*(5), 937–951.
Ilan, J. (2015). *Understanding street culture: Poverty, crime, youth and cool*. Basingstoke: Palgrave.
Jacobs, J. (1961). *The death and life of great American cities*. London: Pimlico.
Katz, J. (1988). *Seductions of crime: Moral and sensual attractions in doing evil*. New York, NY: Basic Books.

Kindynis, T. (2016). Urban exploration: From subterranea to spectacle. *British Journal of Criminology, 57*(4), 982–1001.

Kindynis, T. (2019). Persuasion architectures: Consumer spaces, affective engineering and (criminal) agency. Theoretical Criminology. Online first: https://journals.sagepub.com/doi/abs/10.1177/1362480619894674

Lefebvre, H. (1996). *Writings on Cities*. Oxford: Blackwell.

Leonard, M. (2006). Teens and territory in contested spaces: Negotiating sectarian interfaces in Northern Ireland. *Children's Geographies, 4*(2), 225–238.

Matthews, H., Limb, M., & Percy-Smith, B. (1998). Changing worlds: The microgeographies of young teenagers. *Tijdschrift voor Economische en Sociale Geografie, 89*(2), 193–202.

Matthews, H., Limb, M., & Taylor, M. (2000). The 'street as thirdspace'. In S. Holloway & G. Valentine (Eds.), *Children's geographies: Playing, living, learning* (pp. 63–79). London: Routledge.

Miller, W. (2005). Adolescents on the edge: The sensual side of delinquency. In S. Lyng (Ed.), *Edgework: The sociology of risk-taking* (pp. 153–171). London: Routledge.

Moran, D., Turner, J., & Schliehe, A. (2017). Conceptualising the carceral in carceral geography. *Progress in Human Geography, 42*(5), 666–686.

Paton, K., Mooney, G., & McKee, K. (2012). Class, citizenship and regeneration. Glasgow and the commonwealth games 2014. *Antipode, 44*(4), 1470–1489.

Percy-Smith, B., & Matthews, H. (2001). Tyrannical spaces: Young people, bullying and urban neighbourhoods. *Local Environment, 6*(1), 49–63.

Sandberg, S., & Fleetwood, J. (2016). Street talk and Bourdieusian criminology: Bringing narrative to field theory. *Criminology and Criminal Justice, 17*(4), 365–381.

Sandberg, S., & Pederson, W. (2011). *Street capital: Black cannabis dealers in a white welfare state*. Bristol: Policy Press.

Schuilenberg, M., & Peeters, R. (2018). Smart cities and the architecture of security: pastoral power and the scripted design of public space. *City, Territory and Architecture, 5*(13).

Seigworth, G. J., & Gregg, M. (2010). An inventory of shimmers. In M. Gregg & G. J. Seigworth (Eds.), *The Affect theory reader* (pp. 1–25). Durham, NC: Duke University Press.

Shammas, V. L., & Sandberg, S. (2016). Habitus, capital and conflict: Bringing Bourdieusian field theory to criminology. *Criminology & Criminal Justice, 16*(2), 195–213.

Shaw, R. (2014). Beyond night-time economy: Affective atmospheres of the urban night. *Geoforum, 51*(1), 87–95.

Simmel, G. (1948/2002). The metropolis and mental life. In G. Bridge & S. Watson (Eds.), *The Blackwell city reader* (pp. 11–19). Oxford: Blackwell Publishing.

Soja, E. W. (1996). *Thirdspace: Journeys to Los Angeles and other real and imagined places*. Cambridge: Blackwell.

Stephens, A. C. (2015). Urban atmospheres: Feeling like a city? *International Political Sociology, 9*(1), 99–101.

Taylor, I., Evans, K., & Fraser, P. (1996). *A tale of two cities: Global change, local feeling and everyday life in the North of England: A study in Manchester and Sheffield*. New York, NY: Routledge.

Thrasher, F. (1927/1936). *The gang: A study of 1,313 gangs in Chicago* (2nd ed.). Chicago, IL: University of Chicago Press.

Turner, J., & Peters, K. (2015). Unlocking carceral atmospheres: Designing visual/material encounters at the prison museum. *Visual Communication, 14*(3), 309–330.

Wacquant, L. J. D. (2001). Deadly symbiosis: When ghetto and prison meet and mesh. *Punishment & Society, 3*(1), 95–133.

Wacquant, L. J. D. (2007). Territorial stigmatization in the age of advanced marginality. *Thesis Eleven*, *91*, 66–77.
Wacquant, L. J. D. (2014). Homines in extremis: What fighting scholars teach us about habitus. *Body & Society*, *20*(2), 3–17.
Williams, R. (1985). *Marxism and literature*. Oxford: Oxford University Press.

Afterword: Sensing Carceral Worlds

Eamonn Carrabine

Of all the 'turns' taken in the social sciences in the last few decades, which would include the 'cultural', 'linguistic' and 'visual', it is the 'sensory' that has the most potential to challenge deep-seated epistemological assumptions about how knowledge is produced and to pursue the implications that arise from this self-consciousness over the meaning of what it is to know. As the editors emphasise in their introduction, 'penality has an inherent sensory component', and the collection vividly demonstrates how the feel, sight, smell and sound of carceral space organises human experience in ways that are rarely considered in the criminological literature on imprisonment. It is no accident that each of the contributors are well versed in ethnographic methods, where sensory experience is an inevitable feature of the field encounter, and they have responded to the invitation to explore the senses in their own research with considerable flair and imagination. In this afterword, I want to take the opportunity to look back and reflect on what this collective endeavour has achieved and then to briefly look forward – speculating on some of the directions future work might take.

There is a rich tradition of ethnographic explorations of prison life, owing much to social anthropology and the study of indigenous cultures. Pauline Morris and Terrence Morris (1963, p. 8) memorably compared their 'research office' in Pentonville prison to that of 'the anthropologist's hut on the village street, in the centre of public activity', noting that aside 'from conversation, interviews, and the analysis of records', they also 'constantly observed the sights, sounds (and smells) of the prison'. Likewise, Gresham Sykes (1958, p. 8) sought to convey the 'Kafka-like atmosphere' of a maximum security prison, as Yvonne Jewkes and Alison Young remind us here, through a striking description of 'naked electric lights, echoing corridors, walls encrusted with the paint of decades, and the stale air of rooms shut up too long'. Other contributors have revisited Goffman's (1961) classic study of *Asylums* to ask what it means for an institution to be 'total' (Jason Warr), the 'feeling' and 'knowing' of place (Carla Reeves) and 'emotion management' in the courthouse (Lisa Flower). Such work demonstrates what can be achieved when classic ethnographic studies (or earlier field notes) are reinterpreted, through a renewed attention to sensory experience, so that fresh understandings can be developed.

Sensory Penalities: Exploring the Senses in Spaces of Punishment and Social Control, 231–238
Copyright © 2021 Eamonn Carrabine. Published under exclusive licence by Emerald Publishing Limited
All rights of reproduction in any form reserved
doi:10.1108/978-1-83909-726-320210022

One important theme that emerges from the collection is that not all the senses are treated equally, a point that was recognised in the 'anthropology of the senses' in the 1980s and 1990s, when anthropologists began to seriously question the relationship between perception and culture. Chief among them were efforts to engage with 'postmodern' sensibility in ethnography, which had been especially pronounced in anthropology, where James Clifford (1986, p. 6) forcefully argued that ethnographic narratives themselves are constructed fictions that only ever tell part of story, as they are 'built on systematic, and contestable, exclusions'. To attempt to understand a society is to write a story about it, and this 'writing culture' debate prompted much discussion of the ethnographer's authenticity, reflexivity and voice, which opened up a greater attention to subjectivity and experimentation in ethnographic practice. Not only did ethnography become more visual, but also virtual (Hine, 2000), as well as gendered (Bell, Caplan, & Jahan Karim, 1993), multisited (Marcus, 1995), intimate (Kulick & Wilson, 1995) and embodied (Coffey, 1999), as Sarah Pink (2012, p. 115) noted in her own efforts to develop a 'multisensory' account of the Internet. This focus on the senses has involved an investigation of both the sensory experiences and classification systems of 'others' (Goody, 2002) as well as the 'ethnographer her or himself' (Pink, 2015, p. 8) to examine the sites of embodied knowing.

Despite many intellectual controversies over the years, anthropology continues to be a highly visualised practice, where metaphors like 'observing', 'seeing' and 'reading' still predominate and analogies between the camera as external observer and recorder are often drawn. Yet, the use of visual material in anthropology remains a contested issue. At the heart of the tension lies the contradiction that the 'anthropological tradition has been to look *into* culture and society', whereas photographs and films 'have been looked *at*' (Edwards, 1992, p. 14, emphasis in original). The complaint is often cast against the ocular-centric bias in Western culture more generally, where anyone interested in vision and how it works, is condemned of 'epistemological imperialism' (Howes, 2003, p. 240). Others have rebutted this position, seeing in it an 'anti-visualism' that reinforces the 'visual/auditory dichotomy that has pervaded anthropological thought on sensory experience' (Rice, 2005, p. 201). Instead, perception should be regarded as multisensory, in that the senses are not separated out at the point of perception, but culturally defined modalities, so that vision should be understood 'in terms of its interrelationship with other senses' (Pink, 2015, p. 12).

Many of the contributors directly address this challenge, enlarging our understanding of 'carceral acoustemologies' (Hemsworth, 2015; Russell & Carlton, 2020) in the process. A key theme explored in the collection is the relationship between space, surveillance and social control – whether this be through a nuanced comparison of pub and prison (Kate Herrity), the distinct sensory manifestations experienced in pre- and post-reform prisons (Jennifer Peirce), the raw encounters experienced in carceral settings (Amy Smoyer) or the creative use of songwriting and storytelling to shed fresh light on supervision, which is itself a largely invisible and inaudible form of punishment (Jo Collinson Scott and Fergus McNeill). Likewise, the experience of embodiment in the field is brought vividly to life in Ethiopia (Ian O'Donnell) and death in a prison infirmary (Daina Stanley), demonstrating a remarkable awareness of being in place and the rhythms of daily sociality. As such, a defining feature of the collection as a whole is a deep appreciation of 'emplacement' (Pink, 2008, p. 175), that is both how the ethnographer is actively involved in place-making activities and generates interpretations of how people encounter their surroundings through embodied and imaginative practices.

This book also reminds us that the senses have a social life. Georg Simmel is largely responsible for insisting that sociologists study sensory experience in his 1907 essay on the 'Sociology of the Senses'. This was later incorporated into the first chapter and opening statement of his major agenda-setting opus *Soziologie* (Frisby & Featherstone, 1997, p. 9) and constitutes one of his later attempts to justify his unique approach to the fleeting, seemingly mundane details of everyday life. The German philosopher was the first in sociology's classical tradition to establish a distinctive interactionist understanding of society (Smith, 2017). In the essay, Simmel briefly analysed the changing role of the senses in social interaction and cultural differentiation, spending most time on sight and sound, covering only briefly the sense of smell – but noting how body odour has been used to police racial and class divisions. The tactile sense received no attention all, and his order of treatment follows historical, Eurocentric explorations of the senses, with the greatest attention given to vision. Despite these limitations, the essay highlights the types of 'knowing' mediated by the senses and the dynamics of 'repulsion' and 'attraction' they command.

A number of contributors to this volume acknowledge Simmel's influence on their own approach. In addition to those authors already mentioned, attention is drawn to the place of secrecy in magnifying reality (Julienne Weegels) and Simmel's classic account of blasé reserve unique to modern metropolises (Alistair Fraser), which neatly exemplifies Simmel's understanding of society as an 'event' rather than a 'substance'. The work of Erving Goffman offers a clear example of Simmel's legacy on interactionist sociology, though it is said that he 'gave Simmel less credit for founding this field than he deserved' (Davis, 1997, p. 370). Nevertheless, it is evident that Goffman (1967, pp. 2–3) was advocating a 'sociology of occasions' through his studies of interaction rituals, where he stated that he was not so much interested in 'men and their moments. Rather moments and their men'.

Evidently, Goffman shared Simmel's view that interaction was an emergent product of the activities of individuals. In doing so, Goffman captures how perceptions of social worth regulate human conduct, emphasising that we all move between normal and troubled worlds, and each of us falls short some of the time, such that embarrassment (and the anxious expectation of it) haunts every social encounter. Much of his thinking sought to explain why our daily interactions do not descend into a horrific ordeal but follow certain paths that involve us in a dynamic 'mix of cynicism, ritual and trust' (Manning, 1992, p. 72). Those who experience stigma and mental illness struggle, for very different reasons, with sustaining the mundane predictability of everyday life and his writing from the beginning offers a nuanced understanding of the plight of 'faulty persons', describing in some detail those 'who bring difficulty to many of the interactions in which they participate' (Goffman, 1953, p. 260).

In their inspiring call for a 'sensory criminology', Bill McClanahan and Nigel South (2020, p. 3) herald Kant's insistence that 'all knowledge begins with the senses', but the philosopher then argued that while all our knowledge begins with experience, it does not follow that it all arises from experience. Simmel derived his conception of experience from studying Kant. The key difference is that

> Kant focussed on *experience of the natural world*, organized by the universal mental categories of the outside observer, whereas Simmel focussed on *experience of the social world*, organized by the local mental categories of the participants themselves. (Davis, 1997, p. 370, emphasis in original)

Here the distinction between form and content in the study of society is developed (see also Smith, 2017, pp. 10–11). It is a position that demands a fully sociological investigation of human experience. The way we see the world may well be visual, but 'this is not in isolation from other sensory cues and conditions' (McClanahan & South, 2020, p. 4) and demands that we pay attention to broader sensory, affective and emotive experiences (Millie, 2019).

One of the best examples of such an approach is Nadera Shalhoub-Kevorkian's (2017) analysis of the occupation of the senses. Her work focuses on sensory technologies that manage language, sight, sound, space and time to the point of death in the colony, in this case, occupied East Jerusalem. She demonstrates how

> [t]he colonial regime works to inculcate a sense of control among the colonizers, while instilling discipline and obedience among the colonized. Settler colonial aesthetic and sensory displays of power act as a mode of fascism that ultimately aims to render the colonized senseless. (Shalhoub-Kevorkian, 2017, p. 1296)

Here, as Shalhoub-Kevorkian powerfully demonstrates, 'an account of the senses – and the myriad daily assaults upon them – is necessary in order to rethink our relations to domination and control, theorizing and criminology' (Brown & Carrabine, 2019, p. 201). This challenge is to the fore across the collection but is especially evident in Victoria Canning's harrowing account of immigrant confinement in Denmark, while Bethany Schmidt and Andrew Jefferson reveal, in the Tunisian context, the complex sensorial dissonance rendered in prison.

In looking back at some of the themes informing the collection, it is clear that it amounts to a formidable argument in favour of a criminology of the senses and is generous enough to acknowledge the intellectual precedents for this new direction in the discipline. By highlighting the smell, taste, sound and feel of incarceration, the place of sight remains a curious absence in the text. The editors state they

> deliberately prohibited the use of visuals in the book, as an attempt to urge authors to find a 'language' and way of

communicating that effectually described and represented their work and encounters.

As I have explained above, this prohibition is understandable in light of long-standing disputes over the use of visual material in anthropology, but it is to be hoped that future work heeds the following words of caution:

> A principal claim of the anthropology of the senses, of course, is to have dethroned vision from the sovereign position it had allegedly held in the intellectual pantheon of the western world, and to highlight the contributions of other, non-visual sensory modalities, above all to the sensory formations of non-western peoples. It is, therefore, ironic that in 'rediscovering' these modalities – of hearing, touch, smell and so on – anthropologists of the senses ... have implemented exactly the same manoeuvre as have their intellectual bedfellows in the study of visual culture. To the worlds of images conjured up by the latter, they have simply added worlds of sounds, of feelings and of smells. (Ingold, 2011, p. 316)

Following Ingold's critique, others have proposed a 'rehabilitation of vision' not 'as an isolated given but within its interplay with the other senses' (Grasseni, 2007, cited in Pink, 2015, p. 12) and future work would be well advised to recognise 'the importance of the *totality* of the senses as the essential site of knowledge production' (McClanahan & South, 2020, p. 5, emphasis in original).

Much of the book is finely attuned to affective encounters and corporeal experience, aspiring to a 'sociology of flesh and blood' (Wacquant, 2015) and opens up a distinctive mode of social inquiry concentrating on lived experience. As such, the arguments here provide an important complement to 'ghost criminology', which is ultimately concerned with the politics of (dis)appearance. I suspect one reason why criminologists have begun to deploy spectral metaphors in their writing is that they provide provocative ways of drawing attention to issues of invisibility, marginality and exclusion, as well as the processes of forgetting, repressing and denial that feature in our subject matter. Although some will be sceptical of this focus, I have set out elsewhere the key resources that have proved to be extraordinarily fertile in this turn to spectral politics (Carrabine, 2020). Avery Gordon's (1997/2008) now classic text on *Ghostly Matters* was an emphatic call for a new sociology, which could reveal and learn from subjugated knowledge. As she put it, the

> ghost is not simply a dead or a missing person, but a social figure, and investigating it can lead to that dense site where history and subjectivity make social life. (Gordon, 1997/2008, p. 8)

One of the appeals of ghost criminology lies in its 'appreciation of the discontinuous, distorted and multiple temporalities' of social and cultural life

(Kindynis, 2019, pp. 39–40). Moreover, there is an effort to make visible that which is inherently diffuse, abandoned, forgotten, overlooked or deliberately concealed or hidden. Here attention can be drawn to the US Central Intelligence Agency's (CIA) 'ghost' prisons and the hidden geography of state secrets (Paglen, 2009) through to the money laundered in the 'dead' spaces of speculative real estate and the lifeless dwellings of the super-rich (Atkinson, 2019). We live in a world where power and wealth move ever farther out of sight and beyond the reach of law. In his account of the 'offshore' practices of the rich and super-rich, John Urry (2014) reveals how their geographical mobility is at the heart of mammoth inequalities, which are sustained by a vast system of secrecy that damages not only democracy but the very future of the planet. There is not one secret world, but many: the offshoring of manufacturing work, of waste, especially e-waste, of energy, of torture, of leisure and pleasure, of CO_2 emissions and of taxation.

Of course, prisons across the world are heavily invested in keeping their inner workings secret, but as Julienne Weegels argues in this volume, 'many of the secrets they seek to keep take on the form of *public secrets*' (emphasis in original). In Michael Taussig's (1999, p. 49) classic definition, a 'public secret' is that which is generally known but, for one reason or another, cannot easily be articulated, instituting a pervasive 'epistemic murk' whose core is an 'uncanny' dialectic of concealment and revelation. Likewise, Jewkes and Young (this volume) demonstrate how the air itself is an 'agent of slow violence' in their discussion of Kyoto prison in Japan. With respect to climate change more generally, Rob Nixon (2011) has drawn attention to the fundamental visual dynamics of material crises caused by the Anthropocene. The problem, as Nixon (2011, p. 10) writes in his account of the structural violence of resource extraction and toxic waste, is that there is a 'representational bias against slow violence' in favour of spectacular eruptions and sensation-driven events. It is often the case that many environmental hazards resulting from industrial processes are slow moving, long in the making and observable only using certain forms of sensory technology. Slow violence, because it is so readily ignored, exacerbates the vulnerability of ecosystems and of the poorest communities.

The radical claim is that we need to stretch our understanding of the destructive impacts of global warming and toxic ecologies to address the 'slow violence' occurring across the surface of the earth. Each of the chapters in this collection is engaged in challenging the boundaries of perception, striving for 'the evidence of things not seen' and they stretch 'toward the horizon of what cannot be seen with ordinary clarity yet' (Gordon, 1997/2008, p. 195). Future ethnographers of the 'carceral condition' (Fassin, 2017) have here in their hands a rich resource for making sense of the sensory turn and a compelling argument for why the senses should be taken seriously, revealing the complexities of personhood and the shadowy social forces that lie 'beyond standard perception, cognition and experience' (Fisher, 2017, p. 8). A desire to recover subjugated knowledge lies at the very heart of this book, and it is genuinely innovative, written with a verve to match its subject matter – it is a defining statement in the criminology of the senses.

References

Atkinson, R. (2019). Necrotecture: Lifeless dwellings and London's super-rich. *International Journal of Urban and Regional Research, 43*(1), 2–13.
Bell, D., Caplan, P., & Jahan Karim, W. (1993). *Gendered fields: Women, men and ethnography*. London: Routledge.
Brown, M., & Carrabine, E. (2019). The critical foundations of visual criminology: The state, crisis, and the sensory. *Critical Criminology, 27*, 191–205.
Carrabine, E. (2020). After the fact: Spectral evidence, cultural haunting and gothic sensibility. In M. Fiddler, T. Kindynis, & T. Linnemann (Eds.), *Ghost criminology*. New York, NY: New York University Press.
Clifford, J. (1986). On ethnographic allegory. In J. Clifford & G. Marcus (Eds.), *Writing culture: The poetics and politics of ethnography* (pp. 98–127). Berkeley, CA: University of California Press.
Coffey, A. (1999). *The ethnographic self: Fieldwork and the representation of identity*. London: Sage.
Davis, M. (1997). Georg Simmel and Erving Goffman: Legitimators of the sociological investigation of human experience. *Qualitative Sociology, 20*(3), 369–388.
Edwards, E. (1992). Introduction. In E. Edwards (Ed.), *Anthropology and photography: 1860–1920* (pp. 3–17). London: Royal Anthropological Institute.
Fassin, D. (2017). *Prison worlds: An ethnography of the carceral condition*. Cambridge: Polity Press.
Fisher, M. (2017). *The weird and the eerie*. London: Repeater.
Frisby, D., & Featherstone, M. (1997). Introduction to the texts. In D. Frisby & M. Featherstone (Eds.), *Simmel on culture* (pp. 1–28). London: Sage.
Goffman, E. (1953). *Communication conduct in an island community* [Unpublished doctoral dissertation]. Department of Sociology, University of Chicago.
Goffman, E. (1961). *Asylums*. Harmondsworth: Penguin.
Goffman, E. (1967). *Interaction ritual*. Harmondsworth: Penguin.
Goody, J. (2002). The anthropology of the senses and sensation. *La Ricerca Folklorica, 45*, 17–28.
Gordon, A. (1997/2008). *Ghostly matters: Haunting and the sociological imagination*. Minneapolis, MN: University of Minnesota Press.
Hemsworth, K. (2015). Carceral acoustemologies: Historical geographies of sound in a Canadian prison. In K. Morin & D. Moran (Eds.), *Historical geographies of prisons* (pp. 31–47). London: Routledge.
Hine, C. (2000). *Virtual ethnography*. London: Sage.
Howes, D. (2003). *Sensual relations: Engaging the senses in culture and social theory*. Ann Arbor, MI: University of Michigan Press.
Ingold, T. (2007). *Lines: A brief history*. London: Routledge.
Ingold, T. (2011). Worlds of sense and sensing the world: A response to Sarah Pink and David Howes. *Social Anthropology, 19*(3), 313–317.
Kindynis, T. (2019). Excavating ghosts: Urban exploration as graffiti archaeology. *Crime, Media, Culture, 15*(1), 25–45.
Kulick, D., & Wilson, M. (Eds.). (1995). *Taboo: Sex, identity and erotic subjectivity in anthropological fieldwork*. London: Routledge.
Manning, P. (1992). *Erving Goffman and modern sociology*. Cambridge: Polity Press.
Marcus, G. (1995). Ethnography in/of the world system: The emergence of multi-sited ethnography. *Annual Review of Anthropology, 24*, 95–117.
McClanahan, B., & South, N. (2020). All knowledge begins with the senses: Towards a sensory criminology. *British Journal of Criminology, 60*(1), 3–23.

Millie, A. (2019). Crimes of the senses: Yarn bombing and aesthetic criminology. *British Journal of Criminology*, 59(6), 1269–1287.
Morris, P., & Morris, T. (1963). *Pentonville: A sociological study of the English prison*. London: Routledge & Kegan Paul.
Nixon, R. (2011). *Slow violence and the environmentalism of the poor*. Cambridge, MA: Harvard University Press.
Paglen, T. (2009). *Blank spots on the map: The dark geography of the Pentagon's secret world*. London: Penguin.
Pink, S. (2008). An urban tour: The sensory sociality of ethnographic place-making. *Ethnography*, 9(2), 175–196.
Pink, S. (2012). Visual ethnography and the internet: Visuality, virtuality and the spatial turn. In S. Pink (Ed.), *Advances in Visual Methodology* (pp. 113–130). London: Sage.
Pink, S. (2015). *Doing sensory ethnography* (2nd ed.). London: Sage.
Rice, T. (2005). Getting a sense of listening: Placing the auditory culture reader. *Critique of Anthropology*, 25(2), 199–206.
Russell, E. K., & Carlton, B. (2020). Counter-carceral acoustemologies: Sound, permeability and feminist protest at the prison boundary. *Theoretical Criminology*, 24(2), 296–313.
Shalhoub-Kevorkian, N. (2017). The occupation of the senses: The prosthetic and aesthetic of state terror. *British Journal of Criminology*, 57, 1279–1300.
Smith, G. (2017). Georg Simmel: Interactionist before symbolic interactionism? In M. H. Jacobsen (Ed.), *The interactionist imagination: Studying meaning, situation and micro-social order*. Basingstoke: Palgrave.
Sykes, G. (1958). *The society of captives*. Princeton, NJ: Princeton University Press.
Taussig, M. (1999). *Defacement: Public secrecy and the labor of the negative*. Stanford, CA: Stanford University Press.
Urry, J. (2014). *Offshoring*. Cambridge: Polity Press.
Wacquant, L. (2015). For a sociology of flesh and blood. *Qualitative Sociology*, 38(1), 1–11.

Index

Note: Page numbers followed by "*n*" indicate notes.

Abolitionist's perspective, 143
    asylum for people seeking asylum, 146–149
    formalised confinement, 151–152
    triangle of variable confinements, 144–146
Absence-and-presence as spatial control, 184–187
Accidental ethnographer, 195–197
Acoustic jurisprudence, 164
Action, 7
Affect, 220
Affective habitus, 226
Affective solidarity, 36, 46
Agente de Vigilancia y Tratamiento Penitenciario (VTP), 126
Alaska, 127–128
Alien's centre, 145*n*4
Anthropology, xxi
Arab Spring, 76
Asylums, 231
    for people seeking asylum, 146–149
Atmospheres, 165–167, 220–221
    and air, 187–190
Attention, xix
Attunement, 8–9
    'everyday' attunement, 12–16
    in flesh and blood, 16–17
Audition (hearing), 24
Auditory knowledge, 6
Azulitos, 127

Bar, ordering attunement in, 8–10
Being, 211–213
Bodies, 165–167
Boundaries, 127–132
Bourdieusian approaches, 226

Calabozos, 98*n*15
Camp, 149
Captiception, 25–26
'Captive narratives' literature, 28
Carceral
    acoustemologies, 232
    city, 222
    world, 26
Centers for Correction and Rehabilitation (CCRs), 126, 131, 134, 137
Centro de Estudios de Justicia de las Americas (CEJA), 126
Church music, 136
City Police Jail (CPJ), 95–96, 101–102
City street, 219
Civil death, 29
Climate of prison society, 15
Code of street, 219–220
Cognition, 7
Cognitive habitus, 226
Communal warm-up exercises, 180*n*5
Comparing, 214–216
Conative habitus, 226
Concealment, 101
Correctional officer (CO), 197
Corridors, 112–113, 183
Courthouse building, 162
Courtroom, contrasting atmospheres inside and outside, 163
Creative methods, 35–36
Criminal justice system, 74
Criminological scholarship, xxix
Criminology, xxv
'Crisis of reason', xxi, 23
Critique of Black Reason (2017)
Cultos, 135–136

Cultural
    citizenship, 79
    criminology, xxviii

Decision-making, 226
Department of Corrections (DOC), 56
Deportations, 149
Deprivation of autonomy, 27–28
Depth in musical sense, 46–47
Disciplinary time (D-time), 57
Dominican prison reform process, 126–127
Dominican Republic, 125
    Dominican prison reform process, 126–127
    research methods, 126
    sounds and noise, 134–136
    space and boundaries, 127–132
    visibility and surveillance, 132–134
Don Dale Youth Detention Centre, 189
Draga, 84–85

Earwitnessing, xxix
Ecology of survival, 16
Ellebæk, 144–146, 153
    immigration detention in Ellebæk, 151–152
Embodied captivity, 26
Embodied hospitality, 54
Emotion in sensory landscape of Courthouse, 159
    atmospheres and bodies, 165–167
    emotional and sensory experiences, 169–171
    fear and foolishness, 171–172
    mapping, 162–163
    noises, 163–165
    senses as courthouse ethnographer, 160–161
    sound of laughter, crying and rumbling stomachs, 167–169
Emotional regime, 161
Emplacement, deep appreciation of, 233
Empty time, 57–59

Enhanced motivation techniques, 144
Epistemological intricacies, 24
Equilibrioception (balance, gravity), 24
Escuela Nacional de Administracion Penitenciaria (ENAP), 126
Ethiopian notes, 203
    comparing, 214–216
    going, 204–205
    hearing, 208–209
    reflecting, 213–214
    seeing, 205–208
    smelling and tasting, 209–211
    touching and being, 211–213
Ethnocentrism, 177
Ethnography, 160
    ethnographic study, xxvii
European Society of Criminology (2018), xxii
'Everyday' attunement, 12–16
Evocation, 24
    of memory, xxvii
Eye contact, 171
Eyes of the Skin: Architecture and the Senses, The (1996), 180

Familiarisation, 7
Fear, 171–172
Feeling, 72–73
    of doing, 75
    and sensing security, 162–163
Fire, 21, 30
Five Senses: A Philosophy of Mingled Bodies, The (2008), 21
Fixation on rationality, xxi
Food, 78–79
Foolishness, 171–172
Formalised confinement, 151–152

Generating empathy, 46
Ghost criminology, 235–236
'Ghosting', 12n3
Ghostly Matters, 235
Glitch, 49
Going, 204–205
Goletas, 128

Index   **241**

Great carceral continuum, 222
Green space, 184
Gustation (taste), 24

Haptic expressions, 71*n*1, 78
Hearing, 208–209
Hermandad Emaus, 134
Hermeneutical injustice, 35
HIV/AIDS, 195–196
HMP Midtown, sensemaking at, 10–12
Hostile Environment, 144
Human Rights Watch (HRW), 185, 189

I and *Thou* relationship, 60*n*11, 62*n*14
'Ideal' reform prison, 81
Imaginary Penalities, xxii
Immigration detention in Ellebæk, 151–152
Imprisonment for public protection prisoners (IPP prisoners), xix
Imprisonment in Japan, 179–181
Inhumane treatment, 83
'Instinct', xxv–xxvi
Institutional thoughtlessness, 30
Institutionalisation, 215
Intangible sensory experiences, 107–108
Interpersonal touch, 62*n*13
Intimacy, 169–171
Intrauterine devices (IUDs), 195
Iraq, 127–128

Japanese prison (*see also* Prison)
  approaching Kyoto Prison, 181–182
  imprisonment in Japan, 179–181
  senses of imprisonment, 182–190
  sensory reflections on, 177

Knowing, xxv
Knowledge-making, 91–92
Kosovo, 127–128
Kriminalforsorgen, 151
Kyoto Prison, 177–178
  approaching, 181–182
  contextualising, 179–181
  entering secure spaces of, 182–190
Kyriarchal system of prison, 154
Kyriarchy, 154*n*12

Language of affect, 227
Leaving hostel process, 120–121
Life Inside, A (2003), 28
Life Without Parole (1996), 28

Making Sense of the Sensory, xxix–xxx
Malcontados, 127
Mass supervision, 35
Master and his Emissary, The (McGilchrist), xvii–xviii
Measuring the Quality of Prison Life framework (MQPL framework), 126
Memory, xxvii, 7
Moving with my research collaborators, 91–92
Music, 57*n*8, 136

National Institutes of Health (NIH), 196
New penology, 80
'New Prison Management Model', 125–127
Nicaragua's prison
  punishment, 89
  system, 99
Nicknames, 53*n*1
Nociception (pain), 24
Noises, 6–7, 134–136, 163–165
Non-governmental organisations (NGOs), 75*n*4, 126
'Non-smoking' lounge, 111–112

Occupancy levels, 82
Ocular-centrism, 44
  ocular-centric nature of prison research, 26
Old penology, 80
Olfaction (smell), 24

Ontological intricacies, 24
Order, 3, 16
Ordering attunement in bar, 8–10
Organisational theory, 3
Overcrowding, 82, 127

Pain, 27
  of sensory deprivation in prison, 82
Patience, xix
Patio, 128
Penal power, 89–90
Penality, 25
Perception, 7
Personal Support Specialist (PSS), 59n10
Pervasive Punishment, 36–38, 43
Pervasive Punishment: Making Sense of Mass Supervision (McNeill), 35
Phenomenologies of perception, 21–22
Physical instructors (PI), 15n5
Physicality of hostel, 110–114
'Picturing Probation' project, 40
Places, 108
  production, 114–119
Pop music playing, 60–61
Popular music, 43
Positionality, xxvi
Post-Revolution Tunisia
  prison life in, 71, 73–75
  'seeing is believing, but feeling is truth', 71–73
  sensing prisons in transition, 75–81
  sensual pains of overpopulation, 81–85
Postcolonial feminist theories, 45
'Postmodern' sensibility in ethnography, 232
Power, 96–99
Power to Punish, The, xxiii
Practising politics, 4
Prison Service Instructions (PSI), 29
Prison Service Order (PSO), 29

Prison(s), 3–5, 26, 29–30, 90–91
  (*see also* Kyoto Prison)
  climates, 15
  congestion, 82
  empty time, 57–59
  infirmary yard, 53
  life, 27
  researchers, 203
  researching dying and end-of-life care in, 55–56
  transport vans, 83n10
  warm(ing) hands and hearts in prison 'death room', 59–63
Prisoners, 54, 61, 77
Privacy, 84
Probation approved premises
  exploring sensory criminal justice experience, 109
  importance of sensory analytical reflection, 107–108
  leaving hostel process, 120–121
  physicality of hostel, 110–114
  production of place, 114–119
Proprioception (bodily position), 24
Pseudonyms, 53n1
Pub, 3–5
  making sense of sensemaking in, 5–8
Public secrets, 90, 236

Rational knowing, 91
Re-creation of home, 78–79
Reflecting, 213–214
Reflection space, 131
Reflexive intricacies, 24
Reflexivity, xxvi, 23–24, 232
Regional Penitentiary System (SPR), 90n2, 94–96
Rehabilitation of vision, 235
Researcher emplacement, 108
Residents, 114
Revisionism, 203
Rhythmanalysis, 7
Rhythms of social life, 7

Sandholm, 144–146
Sandinista 'revolutionary state-building project', 100
Scientific idealism, xxi
Secrecy, 89–91, 96–99
Secrets, 99–103
Seeing, 205–208
'Seen and Heard' project, 43
Segregation cell, 57
Semantic satiation, 47
Sense(s), 12, 25
    as courthouse ethnographer, 160–161
    of imprisonment, 182–190
Sensemaking, xxiv–xxviii, 4, 7, 72
    in flesh and blood, 16–17
    at HMP Midtown, 10–12
    making sense of sensemaking in pub, 5–8
Sensing, xxiv–xxviii, 72–73
    carceral worlds, 231–236
    food, smell, and re-creation of home, 78–79
    prison secrets, 91–93
    prisons in transition, 75
    reform, arts, and sensing change, 79–81
Sensing the Field, xxx
Sensory analytical reflection, importance of, 107–108
Sensory anthropology, 23
Sensory criminal justice experience, exploring, 109
Sensory criminology, 234
Sensory experience(s), xxi, xxvii, 231
    of life, 125
    of social interactions, 114–119
    of space, 110–114
    of time in place, 120–121
Sensory knowledge, xv
Sensory Penalities, xxii–xxiv
Sensory penology, 55
Sensory perceptions, 202
Sensory reflections, 161
Sensory Reflections, xxxi

Sensory scholarship, 55
Sensory story about supervision (McNeill), 37–43
'Sensory turn' in criminology, xxviii
Sensual pains of overpopulation, 81–85
Sensuous geographies, 220
Shame, 169–171
Shared feelings and emotions, 221
Sjælsmark, 144–146, 150
Smell, 78–79
    of justice, 108
Smelling, 209–211
'Smoking' lounge, 111–112
Social competency, 8, 14
Social deprivation, 58n9
Social interactions, sensory experience of, 114–119
Social navigation, 92
Social organisation, 6
Society of Captives, The (1958), 27
'Sociology of the Senses', 233
Sound(s), xxiii, 6, 16, 134–136
    of laughter, crying and rumbling stomachs, 167–169
    in prison social life, 4–5
    of prisons, 57n8
    significance, 9
Sounding failure, 49–50
Sounding supervision (Scott), 43–50
Space, 127–132
'Speaking nearby', 45
Stockholms Tingsrätt, 162
Stories, 197–201
50 Stramninger, 145
Street, 217, 223, 227
    criminologists, 225
    field, 225, 227
    habitus, 225–226
    studies of street culture, 217, 219
Structures of feeling, 221, 226
Subverting the Senses, xxx–xxxi
'Supervisible' project, 40
Surveillance, 132–134
Suspension in musical sense, 49
'Swift and Certain Sanction', 50

Tactition (touch), 24
Tangible sensory experiences, 107–108
Tarmac, 181
Tasting, 209–211
Tatami mats, 188
Technocratic rationalisation, 80–81
Temporal sense, 4–5
Thermoception (heat/cold), 24
Thirdspace, 223
Tightness, 120
   in musical sense, 48–49
Time, xix
Touch, 71n1
Touching, 96, 211–213
'Tough on crime' policies, 54
Trappedness, 21, 25, 28

(Un)muting, 93–96
Unoccupied cells, 188

Variable confinements, triangle of, 144–146
Verstehen, 22
Vietnam, 127–128
Violence, 10n2, 89, 96–99
Visibility, 132–134
Vision (sight), 24
Visual criminologists, xxix
Visual sense, 22
Voice, 232
Volumetric control measures, 81

Weight in musical sense, 47–48
Western criminological scholarship, 179

Youth culture, 223

Zombie walk, 83

Printed and bound by CPI Group (UK) Ltd, Croydon, CR0 4YY
15/07/2024

14528454-0001